Belief and Bloodshed

Belief and Bloodshed

Religion and Violence across Time and Tradition

Edited by
James K. Wellman, Jr.

ROWMAN & LITTLEFIELD PUBLISHERS, INC.
Lanham • Boulder • New York • Toronto • Plymouth, UK

ROWMAN & LITTLEFIELD PUBLISHERS, INC.

Published in the United States of America
by Rowman & Littlefield Publishers, Inc.
A wholly owned subsidiary of The Rowman & Littlefield Publishing Group, Inc.
4501 Forbes Boulevard, Suite 200, Lanham, Maryland 20706
www.rowmanlittlefield.com

Estover Road, Plymouth PL6 7PY, United Kingdom

British Library Cataloguing in Publication Information Available

Library of Congress Cataloging-in-Publication Data

Belief and bloodshed : religion and violence across time and tradition / edited
  by James K. Wellman, Jr.
    p. cm.
  Includes bibliographical references and index.
  ISBN-13: 978-0-7425-5823-6 (cloth : alk. paper)
  ISBN-10: 0-7425-5823-1 (cloth : alk. paper)
  ISBN-13: 978-0-7425-5824-3 (pbk. : alk. paper)
  ISBN-10: 0-7425-5824-X (pbk. : alk. paper)
  1. Violence—Religious aspects. I. Wellman, James K.
BL65.V55B45 2007
201'.7—dc22

2006029147

Printed in the United States of America

∞™ The paper used in this publication meets the minimum requirements of
American National Standard for Information Sciences—Permanence of Paper
for Printed Library Materials, ANSI/NISO Z39.48-1992.

To my father, who gave me courage

Contents

Introduction: Religion and Violence: Past, Present, and Future   1
James K. Wellman, Jr.

Part I: The Ancient and Medieval World

1   Dismemberment, Creation, and Ritual: Images of
Divine Violence in the Ancient Near East   13
Scott B. Noegel

2   Making Memory: Ritual, Rhetoric, and
Violence in the Roman Triumph   29
Sarah Culpepper Stroup

3   Taming the Beast: Rabbinic Pacification of
Second-Century Jewish Nationalism   47
Michael S. Berger

4   Violent Yearnings for the Kingdom of God:
Münster's Militant Anabaptism   63
Charles A. McDaniel, Jr.

5   Imperial Christianity and Sacred War in Byzantium   81
Paul Stephenson

Part II: The Modern World

6   Founding an Empire of Sacrifice: Innocent Domination and
the Quaker Martyrs of Boston, 1659–1661   97
Jon Pahl

7   Holy Culture Wars: Patterns of Ethno-Religious Violence in
    Nineteenth- and Twentieth-Century China   115
    David G. Atwill

8   Femicide as Terrorism: The Case of Uzbekistan's
    Unveiling Murders   131
    Marianne Kamp

9   Monks, Guns, and Peace: Theravāda Buddhism and
    Political Violence   145
    Charles F. Keyes

10 Avoiding Mass Violence at Rajneeshpuram   165
    Marion S. Goldman

11 "Obliterating an Idol of the Modern Age": The New
    Iconoclasm from the Twin Buddhas to the Twin Towers   179
    Joel Black

12 Is War Normal for American Evangelical Religion?   195
    James K. Wellman, Jr.

13 On Political Theology, Imperial Ambitions, and Messianic
    Pretensions: Some Ancient and Modern Continuities   211
    Bruce Lincoln

References   227

Index   263

About the Contributors   269

Introduction

Religion and Violence: Past, Present, and Future

James K. Wellman, Jr.

Religion kills. Religion brings peace. This volume argues that the dynamics of religion and violence are not unique to a post-9/11 world. Religion, conflict, and violence have intersected throughout history and across religious traditions. This volume uses a chronological plan to show that religious violence has been occurring for all of recorded history. It is neither new nor should it be surprising. David Martin, the preeminent sociologist of religion, argues, "Religion and politics are isomorphic" (2005, 47). Just as politics binds by coercion, often legitimated by law, religion binds groups by persuasion, although not uncommonly by force—legitimated by tradition, narrative, and practice. Thus the two (religion and politics) are by nature entangled in one another, which means by necessity they mirror and react to the other. Religion functions as an identity-forming mechanism that constructs and mobilizes individuals and groups, both to violence as well as to peace. Religion, like politics, forms identities and thus the two cannot help but move in relation to one another, sometimes antagonistically and sometimes in tandem. Politics, power, coercion, and religion may be strange bedfellows but they are structurally linked. Thus to say that religion is either always innocent or always evil is misguided. This volume makes lucid the complex interactions between religion, violence, and politics across time and tradition.

The format of the book accentuates the theoretical point: the chronological layout shows the arc of violence and peace across historical periods and cultures. It moves from the ancient to the medieval and into the modern world, ending climactically with Bruce Lincoln's chapter comparing the texts of the ancient Persian empire of the Achaemenids to the words of President George W. Bush. Lincoln shows how discourse from each period invokes the dualism of good and evil; the calls for divine intervention and the promises of salvation are similar past and present. Rationalizations by religion for political power and violence are not new.

Moreover, the book is based on a series of case studies that are at once sensational in detail and provocative for theory. It inspires interest in both historical and contemporary examples of religion and violence—addressing topics that will intrigue students, as well as facilitate theoretical debate, aimed at experts in religious studies, social science, the humanities, and history. The volume makes no claims to be representative; we emphasize more often the events when religion became violent. Nonetheless, we do not claim that religion is always violent; simply that it has potential for peace and violence.

The volume begins with the ancient and medieval world. Scott Noegel's chapter exemplifies the way in which Mesopotamia and Egypt created a cosmic world to legitimate their dominion. Noegel details how violence of the most gruesome kind is lauded in texts and monuments, depicting the "other" as enemy and violence as the way to restore divine cosmic order. Sarah Stroup's analysis explains how the Roman triumphs (whereby the Romans paraded the booties of war) functioned as a civil and religious ritual process that served to reintegrate violence into the social order. Michael Berger examines how the Rabbis in second- and third-century Palestine transformed Judaism toward quietism to quell violence and decouple religion from political force. As Berger argues, this was the "taming of the beast" and the beginning of a period of pacifism within Judaism lasting for nearly two thousand years.

A remarkable instance of religious violence is investigated by McDaniel in his chapter on the Anabaptists, who are known for their pacifism. The early sixteenth-century uprising in Münster, Westphalia, was led by zealous Anabaptists seeking to precipitate the kingdom of God; they were eventually defeated by Roman Catholic forces. This example shows that the potential for violence is always a part of any religious symbolic system, no matter how much it proclaims nonviolence.

Paul Stephenson's chapter unfolds the clerical and imperial models of Orthodox Christianity in the middle ages. Stephenson reveals that the Orthodox (contrary to what is conventionally understood) did indeed validate forms of "sacred war," offering spiritual rewards for warriors if they died in battle.

Jon Pahl's chapter introduces the section on the modern period. He illumines how seventeenth-century American Puritan religious practices led to the "martyrdom" of four Quakers; using the theories of René Girard and David Carrasco, Pahl frames these deaths as the early practices of sacrifice in the American empire.

David Atwill's chapter investigates the little-known persecution of modern Chinese Muslims (2 percent of China's population). Atwill outlines how this violence has always been intermingled with ethnic, nationalist, and religious ideologies. Again providing an illustration that religion and the secular cannot be separated, Marianne Kamp's chapter investigates the 1920s killings of 2,500 Uzbek women by Uzbek men sanctioned by Muslim authorities. Traditionally the murders have been called "honor killings," in part because the women were unveiled at the behest of the Communist Party. Kamp makes the provocative argument that the killings were in fact forms of femicide. Charles Keyes uncovers the complex responses of Theravādin Buddhism in twentieth-century Southeast Asia, as Buddhists both instigated violence to defend a nationalist identity and created what is called "engaged Buddhism" as a way to seek peace in the modern world. Marion Goldman shows how Oregon authorities helped to avert religious and civil violence in their interaction with the new religious movement at Rajneeshpuram in central Oregon in the 1980s. Joel Black evaluates the relation between the religious iconoclasm that destroyed the Bamian Buddhas and the secular iconoclasm that smashed the Twin Towers. Black argues that terrorism against art prefigures violence against humans. My own chapter interrogates the moral logic of American evangelical Christian support for state-sponsored violence. Conflict is normal for religions, but is war against "enemies" similarly normal? Lincoln ends the volume by drawing connections between the ancient world and the present, underlining the central theoretical point that religion and violence have a long history.

THEORY OF RELIGION AND VIOLENCE

What is religion? The past 150 years are strewn with definitional dead-ends in the study of religion in Western academia, in part because religion is difficult to define precisely because it is structurally linked to politics and culture, and in part because there is no essence of religion that can finally be pinned down. It is noteworthy that none of the classic and well-known definitions in the field have put conflict and violence near the heart of religion. For Edward Tylor, religion is a false explanatory system (Tylor 1871 [1958]); for Durkheim, religion is the social nexus of the group (Durkheim 1915); for Clifford Geertz, religion is meaning (Geertz 1973); for Rodney Stark and Roger Finke, religion is the terms of exchange with the god or gods (Stark and Finke 2000); for Christian Smith, religion is a moral orientation to life (Smith 2003); for Ninian Smart, religion is an ever-evolving organism with multiple sociocultural dimensions (Smart 1969).[1]

While all of these strike me as important approximations of religion, something is missing. All either protect religion from its more destructive tendencies or at least neutralize the effects religion has had on culture and politics. Religion becomes compartmentalized as integration, meaning, personal resource, or moral worldview. This book argues that conflict and violence are not tangential to our understanding of religion, but need to be part and parcel of what it means to study religion as a force in culture and politics.

The working definition I have developed runs as follows: *Religion is a system of symbols, composed of beliefs and practices, developed in a communal setting, often institutionally legitimated, which negotiates and interacts with a power or force that is experienced as within and beyond the self and group; this power or force is most often referred to as god/spirit or gods/spirits. The symbolic and social boundaries of religion mobilize individual and group identity, and create conflict and, more rarely, violence within and between groups.*[2]

I admit the provisional nature of this definition. Definitions are heuristic devices that educate rather than settle proofs and end debate. I start with the discursive makeup of religion as a system of symbols that provide a narrative infrastructure whereby beliefs are constructed and practices evolve. Words and actions function reciprocally; the two cannot be differentiated. The study of the history of religions shows how religious beliefs and practices change over time, depending on the inflections of context, the political balances of power, and individual and group preferences. The communal aspects of the development of religions simply underscore that language by its nature is a social act; individuals function, think, and innovate within networks of language and practice that cannot be disentangled. The question of individual innovation is interesting but does not lessen the importance of recognizing the communal context. New religions always combine with the old in new ways, perhaps adding a new twist, although commensurability between religions is always present.[3]

Institutionalization of religions is a matter of developing social complexity and adding social layers, including networks of elites. The differentiation of functions demands institutional rules and roles, proliferating with time and the growth of populations. Institutionalization has occurred for all the world's major religious movements, out of both Asia and the West. Of course, institutionalization of religion is not a necessary component when one considers forms of indigenized religions, untouched by the wider pluralistic contexts of modern life.

Every definition of religion is challenged for being too broad (and at times too narrow) and must be distinguished from politics or sports. I argue that religion negotiates and interacts with a power or force that is experienced as within and beyond the self. I don't say a supernatural force, in part because of its bias toward Western religions, and in part because many find this force or power within the natural, or permeating multiple worlds. To distinguish it further from secular social life, this power or force is most often referred to as god(s) or spirit(s). Of course, there is the problem of no god or spirit in elite Buddhism, although it is also often said that within popular forms of Buddhism there are realms of deities. Nonetheless, the experience of awakening within Buddhism is a form of power that is beyond the self and group, and even overcomes the self and group.

Finally, and most controversially, religion creates symbolic and social boundaries that include and exclude. By definition, these boundaries create tensions that differentiate the self from other, one group from another. In this sense religion shares much with other group-forming cultural mechanisms—ethnic and national concerns exercise similar processes of identity formation. Religion, I would argue, is an enormously effective boundary-maker and -marker. These boundaries can and do create conflicts and tension both internally (ascetic or self-denying practices) and with others, whether with one's family, the tribe, the group, one's nation, or indeed other nations. Moreover, in all periods of history religions by definition must and do interact with political fields of power, and in the modern era with nation-states. Thus, they join or reject the actions of the political order and the power of the state. This volume then underlines the case that the relationship of religion and politics runs across cultures and religions, even across historical time periods, the ancient, medieval, and modern periods.

EXPLANATIONS OF RELIGIOUS VIOLENCE

I am suspicious of the notion that we can ever identify necessary and sufficient criteria that explain the cause of religious violence. I have argued that religion is not necessarily violent—or peaceful. I have not seen anyone who has developed foolproof conditions for predicting religious violence.[4] Seeking explanations of the cause of religious violence is important, but I consider the work provisional, providing degrees of plausibility rather than proof.

There are a handful of theoretical explanations for religious violence that have been put forward over the last century. Hector Avalos's *Fighting Words: The Origins of Religious Violence* (2005) does a comprehensive job of outlining the various psychological, sociological, sociobiological, and humanistic explanations for religious violence. There is no need in this introduction to duplicate his efforts. However, it is worth taking a critical look at Avalos's hypothesis regarding religious violence and in so doing examine the leading theorists of the day.

Avalos generally avoids most of the usual errors in the academic study of religion. He does not try to protect religion from critical analysis; he feels no obligation to be neutral toward religion, nor does he claim that authentic religion by definition is a good and peaceful power in the world. His explanation in fact combines the recent economic, sociobiological (biological theory on social phenomenon), and cultural explanations for religious violence and thus can be used as a lens to see the overall state of the field.

First, Avalos's hypothesis for religious violence:

1. Most violence is due to scarce resources, real or perceived. Whenever people perceive that there is not enough of something they value, conflict may ensue to maintain or acquire that resource. This can range from love in a family to oil on a global scale.
2. When religion causes violence, it often does so because it has *created new scarce resources*. (2005, 18)

Avalos follows the recent economic and sociobiological explanations in proposing that social reality is at its base a conflict over scarce resources. When resources are plenty and fair distribution occurs, tensions decrease; when either the resources are scarce or distribution is unfair, conflicts arise and violence ensues. For the sociobiologist Richard Dawkins, religion is a cultural maladaptation; in other words, rather than benefiting the survival of genes it leads to their extinction (Dawkins 1976). At one point in our history religion may have increased our rates of survival, but in the modern world religions seem to lead to our destruction. Avalos is sympathetic to this perspective but moves his explanation toward the economic model. Most fundamentally, humans are resource managers and the lack thereof produces conflict and frequently violence.

For Avalos religion becomes particularly problematic because religion has "created" a scarce resource. In other words the "goods" of religion, its resources, are manufactured. Whether the good is a miracle, eternal life, mystical experience, or healing or communion with force, power, or god, all of these resources are ephemeral, nonempirical, and thus nonexistent. What is clearly most troubling for Avalos is that religions not only create resources but make them scarce in order to control individuals and groups, which by definition creates conflict: *"If any acts of violence caused by actual scarcities are judged as immoral, then acts of violence caused by resources that are not actually scarce should be judged as even more immoral. . . . Any act of violence predicated on the acquisition or loss of nonexistent entity is always immoral and needless because bodily well-being or life is being traded for a nonexistent gain"* (29).

For Avalos religion, by definition, is trafficking in nonexistent resources. Religion is thus a morbid fantasy, to say the least, or at the most, a useless waste of time. Avalos is certainly no apologist for religion, as he himself asserts. Neither is he neutral. He claims that religions are "prone" to violence; some have a greater capacity for it than other cultural forms. Religions use various forms of manipulation of nonexistent goods to maneuver believers, including: (1) access to the divine will; (2) claims to sacred space; (3) group privileging; and finally (4) exclusivist soteriology (study in matters of salvation). In other words, religions use a kind of shell game that keeps people believing that god(s), spirit(s), and forces will show them how to live, give them a place of their own, set them apart as special, and promise them rewards that no one else can gain.

But is it a plausible explanation? Avalos makes a clear argument that scarcity in general tends to create tension and violence within and between humans. In agreement I have argued that religions create symbolic and social boundaries that engender individual and group identity and in doing so include and exclude. Religions' "extra reasons" are powerful markers of identity that shape behavior, promise rewards, and mobilize social action (Bruce 2003). These extra reasons correlate to Lincoln's shorthand theory of religion in this volume, that religions make "exceptional claims" that mark common demands with a divine self-evidence. So far, so good—but don't various cultural processes create boundaries that both include and exclude? That is, we know that race creates identity markers, but does it exist? Ethnobiologists say no, there is no empirical referent for race; we all come from a common gene pool. Race is a nonexistent human resource. This is simply to say religion is not unique in how it functions in the human enterprise. Indeed, other cultural processes, even though they have no empirical grounding, have made impact for good and for ill.

Like race, religion has no empirical referent for its goods. However, there is a difference. There is no way that we can disprove that religious "goods" per se don't exist. Gods, powers, or forces are said to be experienced by believers; human beings in all religions and cultures claim experiences of powers and forces that are at least said to transcend individual human and group consciousness. Thus, do we know that they are "nonexistent"? The answer is, we don't know. We can claim they are a human product, which I do, but we cannot know with certainly their final etiology—the origin of religions. This creates a problem for both the believer and the skeptic. As Rodney Stark has argued, the main problem for religion is "faith," precisely because the resources of religion have no empirical grounding. Religions cannot be disconfirmed. Belief is sustained by faith and trust in something that ultimately cannot be adjudicated empirically. But as Stark argues, this does not mean that the action of belief is irrational (Stark and Finke 2000). Indeed, one doesn't usually say that our belief in love (affective feelings and attachments toward another) is irrational. And yet there is no way to prove that love exists; we have a sense that it is real because of its consequences. One can argue that love is non-existent because it cannot be empirically verified. Few of us, however, would be willing to give up the experience of love because we cannot verify it empirically. Religion can make the same claim, as William James contended in *The Varieties of Religious Experience* (1994); something can be taken as "real" by its effects, and not to do so makes our empiricism narrow and sterile. James believed in a "radical empiricism." To be a true empiricist the full spectrum of human experience must be acknowledged; the feelings, intentions, relations, and thoughts to the world must be investigated (563). One can certainly dispute James's proposals that there are "plural worlds" and whether they are "higher or lower," but to place "religious" experience as outside of empirical analysis by definition is non-empirical.

I would argue Avalos contradicts his own criteria by forcing a nonempirical judgment on his hypothesis. Empirically he cannot prove that religion points to nonexistent goods. Thus, for him to start with this assumption (even implied) is problematic, not morally but scientifically. Many would be happy, including this author, to be able to empirically adjudicate the existence of these religious goods one way or the other, but in the meantime, building an argument based on false assumptions is problematic to say the least.

This book is differentiated from several other important analyses of religion and violence. One is René Girard's psychological analysis of violence as a "crisis of differentiation." What Girard means by this is that human beings through "mimetic desire" come to seek the same thing and this competition causes a crisis (Girard 1974). The crisis is "solved" by sacrifice. That is, groups scapegoat a victim in order to vent their rivalry and relieve the group of its tension. This lasts for a time, but a new scapegoat is inevitably needed. For Girard religions are instrumental in creating sacrificial rituals that "sanctify" the process and act to renew the social order. What Girard proposes is that—as he observed through his study of the world's great literature—the process is a human universal. Christianity both participates in the scapegoating process but also exposes it; for Girard, Christ is sacrificed as a scapegoat to lance social chaos, but Christ is innocent. Thus, the New Testament reveals the scapegoating process and reveals it as pernicious. For Girard, the New Testament's message is that sacrifice of victims for stabilizing the social order must end, since innocents die.

Girard's theory, while fascinating, is problematic, not least because it elevates Christianity as the myth that "solves" cultural and political violence. Moreover, it emphasizes a specific form of Christianity. Many Christians believe or at least act in ways that contradict Girard's main claims; for Christians who believe in the substitutionary theory of the atonement (that Jesus' blood pays the price for human sin), the violence of the crucifixion is essential for salvation. In this sense violence is redemptive. Thus, the death of Christ does not expose a false sacrifice but is the heart of divine redemption. For many Christians across the ages, the New Testament does not undercut the use of violence but informs their use of violence, as this volume illustrates.

Another important theorist in religious violence is Mark Juergensmeyer. His work on contemporary religious violence has been critical in bringing to the forefront the prevalence of violence across religious traditions. He claims that recent acts of religious violence are "forms of public performance rather than aspects of political strategy." Thus contemporary acts of religious violence are "symbolic statements" that empower "desperate communities" (2000, xi). To some extent this is difficult to argue against; Joel Black's chapter addresses these issues in his work on religious iconoclasm. But Juergensmeyer overlooks how religion and violence have been related across history; moreover, I think his separation of religion from the political field is artificial and theoretically not useful. As I have argued, religion and politics are structurally linked; symbolic and social boundaries are always related. No act is only symbolic but arises out of a complex latticework of cultural and political layers of persuasion, power, and force. Social and political forces are by definition entangled in our symbolic language. Thus to disconnect these layers creates abstractions.

Finally, Scott Appleby's work on fundamentalism and more recently on what he calls *strong religion* is an important resource for thinking on these issues (Appleby 2000; Almond et al. 2003). What I find problematic in Appleby's work, which is mirrored in other commentators on religion and violence, is that there is an implicit claim that religious violence is somehow new. Or, more importantly, that religious violence and particularly terrorism is a function of its reaction to the "secular state" or to modernity in general. Religions become strong and violent because of the rise of strong secular states with which they must negotiate. Appleby makes the important point that the state is religion's main competitor; where we differ is that modernity somehow creates a unique situation. The power of secularity in the modern state may be greater in degree, but the relation of religion and politics has not changed structurally. Similar relations occur across time and tradition. Again, the unique aspect of this study is that is tackles these issues across the ancient, medieval, and modern periods, showing continuity rather than difference.

Finally, we return to Avalos's assertion that religions are by nature prone to violence. This question hovers over this volume. It is a question that we must ask. The chapters in this volume exemplify the ways religions are involved in coercive and often violent actions. Even pacifist traditions, such as the Anabaptists, could and did become violent—although this was noteworthy because it was exceptional. Nonetheless, religion has the capacity for peace and war. So, is religion prone to violence? The question simply can't be answered definitively. Exceptions, whether toward violence or toward peace, undercut the rule; prearranged assumptions about religion simply don't wash. Early rabbinic Judaism, rather than creating conflict or violence, went in the opposite direction, moving Judaism toward pacifism. Forms of Sufism and Christianity have had similar roles as resources of nonviolence. Buddhism, for the most part, has practiced nonviolence. I would assert that the better argument is that religion does create social and symbolic boundaries, and that these often do lead to conflict, and more rarely, violence. The advantage of my perspective is that a causal relationship between religion and violence is not a predetermined conclusion; historical and cultural research should tackle problems without prearranged judgments or at least be open to alternative explanations, theories, and outcomes. This volume is an experiment in this kind of research.

NOTES

1. I have drawn on parts of my article published with Kyoko Tokuno for this introduction (Wellman and Tokuno 2004). Tokuno was also helpful in editing Charles Keyes's chapter, for which I am grateful.

2. By conflict I mean disagreement with others short of emotional or physical injury. Violence is thought of as relational and collective action that creates injury to others either emotionally or physically using words and/or actions.

3. This is disputed philosophically, but I agree with Donald Davidson's assertion that all human knowledge has a "natural history" and therefore there is no private knowledge per se; language always has a social causation, and thus religions are natural and public phenomena, and in the end knowable (Davidson 1999).

4. Robert Pape (2005) studied every suicide bomber from 1980 to 2003. He argues that the independent variable for suicide bombings is a felt or real sense of political occupation; the secondary variable is that the bomber's religion is different from his or her oppressor. I would argue he underestimates the power of religion to motivate these acts.

I

THE ANCIENT AND MEDIEVAL WORLD

1

Dismemberment, Creation, and Ritual: Images of Divine Violence in the Ancient Near East

Scott B. Noegel

The temples and palace reliefs of ancient Mesopotamia and Egypt abound in religious texts and depictions of sacred rituals and divine figures. This is what one expects to find on such monuments. Less expected, however, are numerous depictions of some of the most brutal mutilations known to human history. In Egypt, one can find temples "decorated" with piles of hands, heads, and even phalluses, or images of victims' bodies severed beneath chariot wheels. In Mesopotamia, one encounters similar cases of maiming and finds images of people being flayed alive, having their lower lip cut off, or being impaled on stakes and disemboweled.

In every case, these brutal acts were carried out in accordance with what was believed and/or claimed to be divine will. The gods commanded these Gadarene aggressions, and the atrocities that followed were justified in their names. These acts of ritualized brutality represent some of the earliest recorded holy wars.[1]

Besides their extreme violence, two things are shocking to the noninitiate about these images: their abundance and their decidedly religious context. Mangled bodies and severed limbs are juxtaposed seamlessly with religious iconography—portraits of rituals, priests, and gods. The violence of these images led nineteenth-century historians to characterize the Mesopotamians and Egyptians as primitive, warmongering peoples obsessed with battle[2] and to see them as providing "visual backdrops" for the "truth" of biblical stories.[3]

More recently, historians have offered more balanced portraits of these peoples by underscoring their numerous cultural achievements. They

Figure 1.1.   Label of Pharaoh Den smiting enemy. Abydos; ca. 2900 BCE; ivory;
H. 4.5 cm.; London, The British Museum, EA 55586. © The Trustees of the British
Museum

have stressed the importance of examining these monuments from the cultural views provided by the Mesopotamians and Egyptians themselves.[4]
While some have stressed the propagandistic nature of these images,[5] others have focused on the aesthetic,[6] magical,[7] and symbolic purposes of certain compositional elements.[8] Together these scholars have demonstrated
that whether historical or not, the holy wars depicted on the monuments
are constructed in accordance with aesthetic and cultural conventions. An
excellent demonstration of this is the portrait of pharaoh smiting his enemies with a mace, an image that constitutes a "type scene"[9] (e.g., Pharaoh
Den in fig. 1.1). Established already in the pre-dynastic era, this artistic
template was adopted by numerous pharaohs throughout Egypt's long
history from King Narmer,[10] the legendary founder of Pharaonic Egypt
(fig. 1.2), to the emperor Trajan. The use and re-use of this image by the
pharaohs reinforced pharaoh's role as conqueror of chaos.[11]

   The symbolic and propagandistic import of such images begs the question of whether other violent depictions of holy war may be communicating something more than just a historical event. It is in this light that the
theories of Bruce Lincoln and Mary Douglas are especially enlightening.

Figure 1.2.   Narmer Palette. Hierakonopo-
lis; ca. 3100 BCE; greywacke; H. 64 cm., W.
42 cm.; Cairo, Egyptian Museum, JE 32169
(CG 14716)

Lincoln argues that warfare constitutes a form of ritual sacrifice.[12] Whether or not one agrees with his use of the term *sacrifice,* the definition of which he admittedly broadens, the argument that warfare is a form of ritual seems to me to be beyond question.

Douglas argues that one of the main functions of ritual is to recognize, correct, and control society's anomalies, and in so doing, restore cosmological order.[13] Cosmological order is achieved, in part, by subjecting the individual, and thus also the human body, to forms of social control informed by cultural predispositions. Thus, controlling the body is also a way of controlling society at large. It is this perspective on warfare that I adopt in what follows: warfare as a ritual to restore cosmic order.

From this it follows that we might better understand the numerous images of divinely sanctioned violence by looking at them through the lens of ancient Near Eastern cosmological or "theological" systems. Doing so reveals a striking correlation between ancient Near Eastern depictions of divine violence and conceptions of divine order. And, because these conceptions of divine order were shaped by beliefs concerning the creation of the cosmos, these violent representations employ mythological and ritual idioms associated with creation.

A number of scholars in other fields have shown how cosmological and theological systems inform the ways violence against others can be enacted in the name of a religion.[14] The same can be said about ancient Mesopotamia and Egypt, where mass acts of violence were grounded in preconceived systems of order imagined in terms of cultural stereotypes that distinguished sharply between "us" and "them."[15] Egypt sometimes referred to the warriors of Libya (its enemy to the west) as women, children, and animals. They called the nomadic sheepherders of the desert unclean beasts. Sumerian scribes of southern Mesopotamia recall the raids of Gutians from the east by describing them as having the faces of monkeys. Captive enemies are sometimes described as walking on all fours. The enemy is invariably a stupid barbarian who is more animal than human.[16]

Mythmaking about the "other," especially when constructed in theological terms, was more than a rhetorical trope of hatred—it was a means for establishing order and social control.[17] To facilitate this control the leaders of the ancient Near East rallied support for their holy wars by conceptualizing their neighbors as barbarians or beasts. To justify aggression, the enemy was demonized. He was imagined as dwelling beyond the periphery of civilization, outside the world order—or in theological terms, beyond the border of all that is holy and good.[18]

DIVINELY SANCTIONED VIOLENCE IN MESOPOTAMIA

Geographic borders in Mesopotamia were conceptualized as cosmological borders.[19] The tablet shown in fig. 1.3 is one of the earliest maps on record. It shows Babylon seated at the center of the cosmos with canals running through it. The circle around the map depicts the great chaotic and primeval ocean believed to surround the world.[20] It is in the ring of the great unknown where mythological beasts are said to dwell. Sometimes the ocean is depicted as a serpentine beast representing the forces of chaos. Elsewhere, it is depicted as a lionlike creature with wings.

At the center of Babylon stood the palace and the king. The geographic placement of the palace was also understood in cosmological terms, the entire structure mirroring the divine world with the state god at its center.[21] The boundaries of Assyria were categorized as the four quarters of the world, in the center of which sat the king.[22] The palace stood by metonymy for the state and the cosmos.[23]

Guarding the threshold to the palace were gigantic *lamassu* figures. Part human, part eagle, part bull, they represented and embodied the liminal

Figure 1.3.   Babylonian Map of the World, Sippar, ca. 700-500 BCE; H. 12.2 cm., W. 8.2 cm.; British Museum, BM 92687. © The Trustees of the British Museum

area they were created to protect.[24] As a crossed species they were able to cross the boundaries that separated the ordered world of humans and gods. Other mythological creatures served similar apotropaic functions. They guarded the king from chaotic forces that continually threatened the cosmos.

Much effort was put into depicting the king as one who maintains the cosmic order. The image in fig. 1.4 depicts the Assyrian king Assurnasir-pal II (ca. 883–857 BCE) pollinating the female date palm with the male palm flower, an image that symbolized the wealth and abundance that the god Assur bestowed upon the Assyrian kingdom through his agent the king.[25] Since Assur was the god of the Assyrian nation, his connection to the sacred tree bore an implicit political meaning as well, one that under-scored Assyrian hegemony over the entire world. It fittingly stood behind the king's throne.

One way for the Mesopotamian king to maintain cosmic order was through ritual. Holy war, as I have noted, constitutes a form of ritual, but

Figure 1.4.   Assurnasirpal II (ca. 883–857 BCE) pollinating the date palm. Palace bas-relief from Kalhu (Nimrud). © **The Trustees of the British Museum**

there were others as well. One such ritual was the lion hunt, most thoroughly rendered on a series of reliefs from the palace of Assurbanipal (ca. 669–627 BCE) at Nineveh. The images of the hunt depict a great number of lions captured, caged, and let loose in a small fenced garden guarded by soldiers. Within the confines of the fence the king of beasts was stalked and ritually killed by Assurbanipal, the king of kings, with the help of professional hunters. Courtiers then carried the dead lions to the libation table where rituals were performed and wine was offered to Ishtar, the goddess of war. The rituals, like the lion hunt itself, connected the slaying of the lions with the military prowess of the king.[26] These images were not just descriptive; they served to accomplish ritually what they depicted— the king's position as ruler of the universe.[27] By using the "bow of Ishtar" to put down the body of the lion, an animal that prowled the periphery of Assyrian lands, the king ritually put down the threatening outer world of chaos and showed himself to be the symbolic shepherd of his people.[28] Violence was ritually woven into the fabric of the cosmos.

In fact, extreme violence was how the cosmos began in Mesopotamia.[29] The most salient witness to this is the account of creation, *Enuma Elish*, a text known in various forms in both Babylon (south) and Assyria (north). In the Babylonian version, the god Marduk (who is replaced in the Assyrian version by the god Assur)[30] creates the cosmos from the dismembered body of the goddess of the sea, Tiamat.[31]

The story relates how Marduk suffocated Tiamat with wind and then shot arrows into her stomach. He then flung her corpse down, an act that struck dread into her army. Described as a demonic horde, they fled in all directions. Marduk chased them down, smashed their weapons, and bound them by the arms with ropes to await later punishment. Having secured her army, Marduk then returned to Tiamat's corpse. He trampled it under his feet and smashed her skull with his mace. He sliced her veins and the north wind carried away her blood. When the older gods saw this, they tried to calm his rage by bringing him gifts, which apparently worked, at least for a short time. But later, Marduk returned to Tiamat's body and sliced it in half like a fish for drying. With one half of her body he made the heavens and with the other he established the underworld. Her head he threw on a pile. He stabbed her eyes, and out poured the Tigris and Euphrates. Marduk then proclaimed himself king of the gods and promptly established his throne over her once chaotic cadaver.[32]

Enuma Elish was recited aloud annually before the important peoples of Mesopotamia on the fourth day of the New Year's festival,[33] an event that celebrated the victory of Marduk over Tiamat.[34] The New Year's celebration marked the time of the royal lion hunt, as discussed above—an event also dedicated to the goddess Ishtar. The festival thus served to legitimate the king as ruler over the cosmos.[35] It also was a time for governors, officials, and other high-ranking officers to renew their oaths of loyalty to the king and state. The event aimed to legitimate the reigning monarch, the national god, and the capital city.[36]

Just as the gods kiss Marduk's feet in the creation story, the king's subjects kissed his feet during the New Year's festival.[37] The story of creation reminded everyone who heard it of the king's role as maintainer of the cosmos. Hence the king's epithet: "the perfect image" of Marduk or Assur.[38] Marduk and Assur's roles as slayers of chaos were naturally transferred to the king.[39]

It is this view of creation, of violently imposing order on chaos, that is reflected in the numerous images adorning the Assyrian palace. The king's enemies, themselves embodying the chaotic elements on Assyria's geographic periphery, are dismembered, disemboweled, and humiliated like Tiamat. They are not just killed in battle; they are ritually taken apart in a way that mirrors Marduk's victory over chaos. In essence, the macabre images of beheading, dismemberment, and maiming reenact the very methods by which order was originally imposed in the cosmos.

Even when battles are recounted in texts the king is described in terms that connect him with the gods.[40] He draws near to battle with a divine aura of splendor surrounding him, an aura that puts everyone who sees him to flight. Two gods march at his sides bearing his shields and weapons, and his own weapons are likened to a cosmic flood.[41] Sometimes the king is given the epithet "destructive weapon of the gods."[42] One chronicle informs us that King Assurbanipal made four of his captured enemy kings

Figure 1.5.   **Assurbanipal (ca. 669–627 BCE) on his divan in the royal garden. Palace relief from Nineveh. © The Trustees of the British Museum**

draw his chariot through the streets, reminiscent of the four winds that drew Marduk's chariot.[43]

With this background in mind, it is interesting to consider the image in figure 1.5, which was placed in the palace amid some of the goriest battle scenes. In fact, to the left of this scene the head of the Elamite king Te-Umman hangs in a tree by a mouth ring (see detail of figure 1.5). The scene depicts King Assurbanipal reclining on a royal bed in the royal gar-

Detail of Figure 1.5.   **Head of Elamite king Te-Umman in tree**

den. He is being fanned by courtiers while listening to the strumming of dulcimers and tending to his royal appetite for hors d'oeuvres and wine. Seated on the royal chair beside him is his wife, Libbali-sharrat.

On one level this scene depicts a confident and relaxed king, a symbol of order in a chaotic world. On another level, however, the scene evokes associations with Assur and Ishtar. This is suggested first by the location of the scene: a zoological and botanical garden. Such gardens were attached to palaces and temples and were intended to re-create divine paradise on earth. They naturally evoked the ceremonial and ideological aspects of kingship that identified the king as hunter and gardener of the gods.[44]

Moreover, since the king was the "perfect image" of Assur, it is difficult to avoid connecting the king's wife with the goddess Ishtar. It is noteworthy that one important ritual in the Neo-Assyrian period involved a royal bed placed in a temple garden on which the god Marduk and the goddess Ishtar were believed to make love, thus ushering in from paradise the fertility of spring.[45] One historical account informs us that the sacred bed was plundered in a raid by King Assurbanipal and appropriated for the worship of Assur. Libbali-sharrat's chair is adorned at its base with a lion, the very totem of the goddess Ishtar.[46] The idyllic garden pose thus communicated two interconnected messages: the royal couple as harbingers of fertility, and the king as the font of order. The contrasting images of divinely sanctioned atrocities that surround the garden scene thus underscore the notion that in Mesopotamia political order *is* cosmic order.[47]

All battles are cosmic battles.[48] All wars re-enact the first primeval moment when order was violently imposed on chaos. The ferocity with which war is depicted, if not also carried out, replicates the cosmological beliefs upon which Assyrian religion was founded. In line with Michel Foucault, we might say that these scenes of violence enscript cosmologically significant messages upon peoples' bodies in such a forceful fashion that the messages destroy them.[49]

DIVINELY SANCTIONED VIOLENCE IN EGYPT

Cosmology similarly informs depictions of holy wars in ancient Egypt. Nevertheless, since Egyptian and Mesopotamian cosmologies differ, the ways in which these wars are depicted and described also differ.

The Nesitanebtashru papyrus in figure 1.6 depicts the cosmos as the Egyptians saw it. It shows the sky goddess Nut, held up over the earth god Geb, by the god of air Shu. Assisting in the lower left-hand corner is the god of magic Heka. The area around, and therefore beyond, the cosmic

Scott B. Noegel

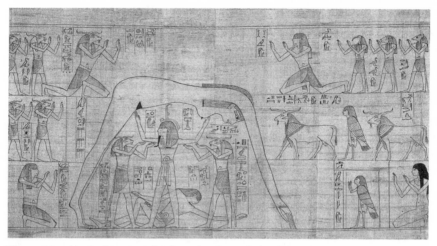

Figure 1.6.   Book of Nesitanebtashru, daughter of Pinudjem I, high priest of Amun and king of Upper Egypt, ca. 1065–1045 BCE. Papyrus. © The Trustees of the British Museum

structure is described: "The upper side of the sky exists in uniform darkness, the limits of which . . . are unknown, these having been set in the waters, in lifelessness. There is no light . . . no brightness there."

Much like the realm beyond the borders of Babylonian geographic knowledge, the outer world of the Egyptian universe was unknown, watery, and chaotic.[50]

Order was achieved in the cosmos by way of the sun god Re and his circular journey through the heavens by day and the underworld by night. This journey was sometimes visualized as a trip through the body of the sky goddess Nut. Nut would devour the sun every night and give birth to him every morning. More often, however, the journey was depicted as a nautical one, with the sun god Re aboard his solar boat.[51]

Since Egyptians believed the pharaoh to be an embodiment of the sun god in the form of Horus, even his final tomb replicated the cosmos. Stars adorned the ceilings, and the floor, usually made of basalt, represented the fertile earth.[52] Upon death, the pharaoh, in the form of Horus, would board the solar boat and begin his journey through the heavens.[53]

The sun god's watery journey was peaceful except for one moment during the night when the serpent of chaos, Apep, threatened to attack him. Assisting Re on his journey, however, were the temple priests whose incantations and rituals paralyzed Apep, allowing Re to repel him and return safely as the sunrise. According to these texts Apep is repelled "in his time" (*m ꜣt.f*), that is, according to a divinely ordained and cyclical schedule.[54] Just as it happened during the original creation, so also does it occur every night. The incantations identify the rebel Apep as Re's enemy and describe his destruction as an act of repelling and crushing.[55]

Chaos, or *isfet*, was also embodied by the god Seth. In a famous mythological text, Re battles Seth for possession of divine kingship in the form of Horus. Seth loses the battle and is similarly repulsed and crushed "in his time" *(m ꜣt.f)*. This text provides an etiology for how Re became king at the beginning of creation.

Since the pharaoh was the embodiment of the sun god, he was described as re-enacting these powerful cosmic moments in the historical sphere. Thus, just as Re repelled Apep, the pharaoh is said to repel *isfet* from his borders by appearing as the god Atum himself, the form that Re takes at sunset.[56] Elsewhere Pharaoh is depicted as the divine presence in the form of a sphinx trampling all foreign lands.[57]

After driving out *isfet*, "order" *(ma`at)* was firmly put in place and the land is said to be as it was "at the first time,"[58] that is, as at the beginning of creation. It is this cosmological system that is reflected in the wrestling and boxing matches that took place during sacred festivals in which the primeval battle between Horus and Seth was ritually re-enacted. It is also within this cosmological system that we must view Egyptian depictions of divinely inspired violence.

As did Mesopotamians, Egyptians also conceptualized their geographic borders in cosmological terms,[59] with their temple as the cosmic center.[60] Since Re set in the west, the area west of the Nile was associated with the dead, and so it became a location for countless royal burials. The lands to the north and south of Egypt were associated with *isfet*. For this reason, the Egyptians identified the forces of chaos with its enemies bordering its three vulnerable sides: Libyans to the west, Nubians to the south, and Asiatics to the north.

The image of Egypt smiting its major enemies (e.g., figs. 1.1–1.2) became a "type" image symbolizing pharaoh's Re-like victory over chaos. It was a victory in accordance with primeval and cyclical time. It was an image that invoked the victory of order over chaos, and thus, reminded viewers of the divine battles of Re against Apep and Seth. In essence, each successive king maintained *ma`at* by repelling *isfet*. Each successive king participated as the sun god incarnate in the cyclical nature of the cosmos. For this reason, foreign campaigns are described as "setting the fear of Horus" into the land, and as bringing light to a people living in darkness.

In addition to resorting to holy wars, the pharaoh also maintained *ma`at* in the cosmos by way of other rituals.[61] One such ritual performed by the priests is known as "execration." It involves inscribing the names of enemy peoples and their potential acts of rebellion on small red pots or on human figurines. These figurines were then ritually destroyed. They could be buried, smashed, stabbed, pierced with nails and knives, boiled in urine, or otherwise destroyed. Some were made of wax and melted in fire. Often they were buried in abandoned cemeteries for added insult.

Another ritual employed to quell chaos was the hippopotamus hunt— a violent ritual reminiscent of the Assyrian lion hunt.[62] The hippopotamus was, and is today, the most dangerous animal in Africa. Hunting one down and killing it was a fitting symbol for crushing *isfet*. As such, this ritual re-enacted the cosmic defeat of Seth at the hands of Re.

It is highly unlikely that any of the brutal hunts or gruesome ritual wars depicted on these monuments ever happened exactly as presented, but that is not the point of such images. They are idealized portraits of how kings established order over humans and nature and cultivated a correct relationship with the divine. They project royal history through a cosmological lens and recount contemporary events in ancient idioms associated with creation.[63] The mutilated bodies that "decorate" the temples and palaces of the ancient Near East reflect not just the terrors of ancient holy wars, but also the distinctive cosmological beliefs with which they were justified.

NOTES

I thank Gay Robbins and David Frankfurter for their helpful comments on previous drafts of this essay.

1. I define *holy war* as an organized act of hostile force by one people against another that is given divine justification and sanction.

2. See, e.g., the comment of Erman (1971, 526–27). There are exceptions to this portrait, e.g., Wilkinson (1994 [1836], 405–406). For a survey of early attitudes toward the Assyrians see Porter (2003, 81–84). Some, e.g., Bersani and Dutoit (1985, 3), still consider them to be an "intensely nationalistic, imperialistic, and violent people." Dalley (1995, 413–22) corrects this portrait.

3. E.g., Layard (1853, 631–32).

4. For "emic" approaches to Mesopotamian art see Winter (1997, 359–81) and Bahrani (2003). For an emic approach to Egyptian cultural memory see Assmann (2002).

5. See, e.g., Russell (1998, 655–715), and Reade (1999, 33). In the Neo-Assyrian period one finds such inscriptions for Assurnasirpal II, Sargon II, and Sennacherib (translations appear in Albenda 1998, 29). On the propagandistic use of administrative cylinder seals and their relation to palace reliefs see Winter (2000, 51–87). On integrating cosmology into the study of Assyrian ideology see Liverani (1979, 297–317). On a rethinking (read: neutralization) of the word *propaganda* in the Neo-Assyrian period, see Tadmor (1997, 325–38). Porter (2003, 81–97) argues that the palace reliefs of Assurnasirpal II offered a balanced image of intimidation and benevolence.

6. Hrouda (1965, 274–97); Winter (1995, 2569–80).

7. On the "magical" purposes of Assyrian art see Reade (1999, 27 and 38; 2005, 9); Porter (2000, 216); Barnett (1970, 31–32).

8. Bahrani (2003).

9. On literary and artistic *topoi* in such scenes see Westenholz (2000, 99–125).

10. The Narmer palette was an apotropaic item. See O'Connor (2002, 5–25).

11. See Hall (1986). The borrowing of "type scenes" is especially pronounced in battle accounts where at least five different pharaohs are depicted as killing a Libyan king before the eyes of his wife and two sons. In each case the wife is named Khutyotes and the two boys are Usa and Uni. Noted by Schulman (1995, 293). For a discussion of Egyptian monumental art as suggesting continuity of rule see Jansen-Winkeln (2000, 1–20). On the stereotypical nature of Assyrian art see Bersani and Dutoit (1985, 7).

12. Lincoln (1991, 203–5). As with other rituals, warfare elevates the social status of the individual, in this case, the king among his peers in other lands.

13. Douglas (1966) and (1970).

14. See the works of Stacey (1998, 11–28), Kieval (1994–1995, 52–72), Frankfurter (2004, 511–33), and Strickland (2003).

15. See Liverani (1979, 301).

16. On this aspect of Mesopotamian ideology see Mazzoleni (1975).

17. As such it was also a means of helping warriors transcend the shock of killing other "men" by dehumanizing them.

18. For the development of this concept in Mesopotamia see Pongrazt-Leisten (2001, 195–231). Making one's enemy a monster is a common characteristic of wartime ideology; Lincoln (1991, 141–45).

19. Horowitz (1998).

20. On the cosmological conception of Assyria's geographic borders see Villard (1999, 73–81).

21. Cosmological and ideological conceptions inform the layout of Babylon's streets and its monuments; Mieroop (2003, 257–75).

22. Note the related Assyrian expression "king of the world" (*šar kiššati*) and its dual meaning as "king of hostility"; Garelli (1979, 319–28).

23. The palace was a metonym for the state with the king as its symbolic center; Winter (1983, 15–31; 1993, 27–55).

24. These liminal figures have many protective aspects; Kolbe (1981), Madhloom (1970, 94–117), and Wiggermann (1992, 2002). On the cross-gender of these figures see Dalley (2002, 117–21).

25. Porter (1993, 129–39); Lambert (2002, 321–35). Parpola (1993, 161–208) interprets the tree as representing both the king and the totality of gods encompassed in the form of the state god, Assur. Others challenge this view: Cooper (2000, 430–44), Porter (2003, xii–xiii, 21–29), and Lambert (2002).

26. The image of the lion was invoked in bloody ritual dances following battles. The throne room of the Assyrian king Assurnasirpal II depicts the ritual dancing of two men garbed in lion costumes and two others waving the heads of their enemies. See Collon (2004, 96–102, especially 101).

27. The composition and motifs employed in creating these reliefs contrast the military superiority of the king and the helplessness and submissiveness of his enemies; Albenda (1998, 12–13, 26); Watanabe (1998, 439–50).

28. The establishment of order suggested by the lion hunt scenes is conveyed by way of their compositional structure, which "gives a sense of balance and harmony"; Albenda (1998, 22). On the "bow of Ishtar" see Reade (2005, 23).

29. See Dalley (2002, 119) with regard to the dismemberment of primordial gods as a means of creating new life in a pre-sexual world. The analogy she draws is to a plant that one can separate from its stock and make to sprout new roots.

30. For the role that Marduk played in the Neo-Assyrian period see Porter (1997, 253–60).

31. Convenient translation found in Foster (1997, 398–99).

32. Tiamat's re-purposed limbs and the placement of her bow in the heavens should be examined in the light of what Frankfurter has called "negative relics," i.e., trophies of war that transform "the body of the vanquished into a clarified and assimilable form of subordination" (2004, 526).

33. The connection between Assur and Marduk was encouraged during and after the reign of Sennacherib (ca. 704–681 BCE); Black and Green (1992, 38); Porter (1997, 253–60). For the rising importance of Marduk in the Neo-Assyrian period see Sommerfeld (1982, 193–95).

34. Lambert (1963, 189–90).

35. See E. Weissert (1997, 339–58). On the New Year's festival as a cultic drama see Jacobsen (1975, 65–97).

36. On this aspect of the Babylonian festival see Bidmead (2002). A discussion of the relationship between the festival and the creation epic appears on pp. 63–70. On the festival in Assyria see Driel (1969, 162–67).

37. Kissing the feet as an expression of loyalty also appears in Neo-Assyrian letters addressed to the king.

38. See Parpola (1993, xvii). On this title in the context of Assyrian conceptions of "image" see Bahrani (2003, 143).

39. Cf., an ancient description of a relief that no longer survives that depicted the Assyrian king Sennacherib assisting the gods in their battle against chaos (Reade 1979, 332). On Sennacherib's throne room see Russell (1998).

40. On the connection of solar mythology with the king in early Mesopotamia see Polonsky (1999, 89–103).

41. Marduk also is referred to as "the flood." See Oshima (2003, 109–11). The likening of the god and king to a flood and other "weapons" substantiates the observation of Lincoln (1991, 145) that "the warrior must dehumanize himself before he can become an instrument of slaughter."

42. E.g., the "Standard Inscription" of Assurnasirpal; Grayson (1991, 276).

43. See Tadmor (1999, 55–62, especially, 60).

44. On the sexual, ideological, and ceremonious aspects of royal and divine gardens see Andre (1947–1952, 485–94); Oppenheim (1965, 328–33); Fauth (1979, 1–5); Wiseman (1983, 135–44; 1984, 37–43); Deller (1987, 229–38); Glassner (1991, 9–17); and Novák (2002, 443–60). On Ishtar's dehumanization of the "lion-like" Teumman see Reade (2005, 21).

45. For the purpose of this bed see Porter (2002, 523–35).

46. The animal in question may be a hyena; Kilmer (1999, 53–61).

47. The equating of cosmic and political order appears in an oracle from the god Assur to king Esarhaddon: "I will put Assyria in order, I will put the kin[gdom of] heaven in order" (Parpola 1997, 18).

48. Liverani (1979, 307) remarks: "The imperialistic expansion of the central kingdom is therefore the prevailing of cosmos over the surrounding chaos, it is an enterprise that brings order and civilization."

49. Foucault (1977).

50. See Brunner (1954–1955, 141–45); Hornung (1956, 28–32).

51. On differing depictions of the journey that a deceased pharaoh takes see Goebs (2003, 238–53).

52. Allen (1994, 5–28).

53. Hornung (1990, 155–56).

54. For solar and "Osirian" temporal aspects of Egyptian funerary belief see Assmann (1975, 35–48).

55. See Morenz (1960, 77).

56. For the present use of the primordial past in Egypt see Assmann (2002). Compare Assmann's discussion of the demonization of Seth and his association with foreigners (389–408).

57. It is depicted on the throne arm of Thutmosis IV (Robins 1997, 136).

58. Morenz 1960, 168.

59. On cosmological conceptions of Egypt's geographic borders see Galán (1999, 21–28).

60. See, e.g., Finnestad (1985, 8–64).

61. On rituals for the goddess *ma`at* ("Order"), see Teeter (1997).

62. Pharaohs also undertook the ritual hunt of wild bulls in the marshlands, a land similarly associated with chaos and creation.

63. One could cite many analogies. For discussions on the construction of such *vitae parallelae* see Smith (1978, 240–64) and Smith (1990).

2

Making Memory:
Ritual, Rhetoric, and Violence
in the Roman Triumph

Sarah Culpepper Stroup

THE RETURN TRIUMPHANT

The eternal city is in an uproar. The triumphant general, flush with recent victory, prepares to enter Rome for the first time since he has left the field of battle. The day is marked by Saturnalian inversions of the norm: the temples of the city stand bedecked, with doors thrown wide open; trays of food and vessels of wine are offered for the pleasure of any passerby; temporary bleachers have been constructed along the triumphal route and the paths along which the celebrants process are defined not by brick and marble but rather by teeming crowds of spectators.[1]

The whole of the first day is reserved for the massive display of captured artworks from exotic lands. Statues, paintings, and colossal figures are borne along in some two hundred and fifty chariots, each beginning its journey from a mustering point in the Campus Martius and entering the city in the area of the *Forum Holitorium*, or vegetable market, at the point of the "Triumphal Gate," or *porta triumphalis*.[2] As the chariots make their way through the streets of the city, their "real time" spectacle of appropriation is augmented by the display of vividly painted placards depicting decisive moments in the recent battle. The wealth of conquered nations is brought before the eyes of the people, and the very struggle for victory is made pictorially and literally manifest for the assembled crowd.

At dawn of the second day, it is the military wealth of the fallen enemy that is paraded before the people. In a display of defeated military might, the arms of the newly vanquished glitter brightly in the sun and crash noisily over the din of an urban audience carried along on waves of pride

29

and awe. The end of the day specifies the end point of Roman dominion: coinage, silver vessels, and drinking horns beyond number are carried aloft to the Capitoline in an endless river of exotic treasure.

On the third day and final day of return, the triumphant general prepares to cross the *pomerium*—the sacred boundary that separates interior from exterior, city from country, and domestic from martial—and penetrate the city proper.[3] But first come the trumpeters, who sound not an upbeat marching song but rather a fearsome call to battle. After these parade great numbers of oxen destined for sacrifice: with gilded horns and heads decorated with fillets and garlands, they are a strange admixture of nature and artifice. A second display of foreign wealth—this time gold coinage and jewelry—is followed by the empty chariot of the conquered general; the royal children, teachers, and nurses are led before the eyes of the people as Rome is introduced to her newest slave population. The foreign general or king comes next, and after him a flood of golden wreaths, symbolizing again the irresistible victory of Rome.[4] Finally, the *triumphator* himself enters the city on the *currus triumphalis*, a high, two-wheeled chariot drawn by four white horses. He holds in his right hand a laurel-branch, and in his left an ivory scepter. His face is painted red, and he is clothed in richly embroidered scarlet raiment: the man is a thing of terror, more like a king or divinity than a Roman citizen or soldier. Behind the *triumphator* in his chariot stands a public slave, who holds above the *triumphator's* head a heavy gold wreath and who whispers in his ear, *Respice post te; hominem te esse memento*—"Look around you, and remember that you are a mortal."[5]

As the sun begins to set, the solemn group winds its way through the densely packed Roman Forum and comes to a rest at the base of the Capitoline. Here the chief captives of war are led off to be executed, while the *triumphator* readies himself to ascend the hill and, in a Romulan pantomime many centuries old, to perform the symbolic return of Rome's military power to the house of the only god who could properly contain it.

WHEN VIOLENCE BECOMES RELIGION

The Roman *triumphus*, or triumph—a citywide religious celebration culminating in the grand victory parade of a returning general and his army—was a cultural phenomenon of unsurpassed magnitude and impact for a period of over one thousand years. As a phenomenon that spoke as seductively to the Rome of the Kings as to that of the Emperors, the triumph was an act of power and display both hauntingly ephemeral and aggressively eternal. Although the event was typically confined to a single day (occasionally extending over two or three), the visual and literary rhetoric of the triumph has left indelible impressions, not only on the language and cultural formations of the people who celebrated it, but also on the physical and architectural structure of the urban space in which it was enacted.

Modern scholars have long recognized the profound political, cultural, and architectural impact of the triumph.[6] And yet in spite of the pervasive echoes of the phenomenon throughout our literary and visual sources— from Livy to Plutarch;[7] from monumental arch to finely wrought silver cup—the triumph itself, and in particular the way in which it contained acts of external military violence within the form of civic and religious ritual, remains at the borders of our understanding of Roman culture. As much as it has been located as an integral element in the continual creation of Roman identity, the triumph holds this location as an ineffably odd expression of the Roman fascination with the ritualized display of military conquest.

There is a wealth of evidence for the ritual of the triumph, from expansive historiographical accounts of individual triumphs,[8] to the use of triumphal imagery in the works of the orators and poets,[9] to the large-scale triumphal arches of Titus, Septimius Severus, Constantine, and Trajan.[10] And yet for as much evidence as we have for the triumph, and for as much as we can trace the impression of the rite on the civic and religious mind of the city, the overarching thrust of the ritual has remained just out of our ken. We know it was big. We know it was popular. We know it was important. But we just don't know exactly what it *was*.

Or to restate: we know that it *seemed to be* many things all at once. This chapter addresses a function of the triumph that has not generally been discussed in the past, but one that does much to argue for its immense popularity and impressive duration: that of a religious transformation of violence from "fact" to "memory." Within this transformation, the triumph mediates between an original act of violence (the battle) and the later religious ritual (the triumphal parade) in which it was contained— and remade—for public consumption (in the triumphal arches and literature that commemorate the parade). For as much as military victory—and military power—is the focus (or at least, prerequisite) of the triumph, it is the triumph—the socially palatable and religiously sanctioned "memory" of socially fraught martial violence—that becomes the primary focal point of subsequent commemoration.

I argue that the triumphal parade functions as a religious transformation of violence—as opposed to an act of "ritualized violence." Whereas an act of "ritualized violence" (ritualized corporal punishment, e.g.) would have the ritual itself consist of an act of violence, the religious *transformation* of violence replaces, for the public imagination, an original act of violence (a military victory) with a religious ritual (a public parade and its concomitant literary and artistic representations) designed precisely to represent it. Thus the triumphal parades of Republican and Imperial Rome transform an act of overwhelming physical violence (the original battle) into an "act" of nonviolent public display (the triumphal retelling of this battle) precisely by melding military with religious might.[11] In its revision of socially fraught martial power into socially palatable religious rite (and "right"), the triumph both forged a religiously sanctioned memory of victory for a people who had not directly witnessed it and created a Rome that could be simultaneously the greatest military force in the world and the eternal, if heavily idealized, City of Peace. In its religious transformation of violence, as I argue, the triumph satisfied the need for a Roman power—and a Roman memory—that could be divinely insulated from itself.

But first a word on this particular brand of religious and martial violence. In the Rome of the Republic, as much as that of the emperors, military victory was a zero-sum game that centered in large part on the control and increase of the phenomenon of military *imperium*.[12] *Imperium*, often introduced to the student as a kind of "ultimate power to command" but what I propose for the purposes of this study as *"the potential of irresistible violence,"* functioned as the predominant means through which both military command and subsequent military victory were achieved. It is thus *imperium*, and its movement (more specifically, its ritual reintegration), I identify as the focal point for a discussion of violence and the triumph. In its capacity as "potential violence," I suggest, *imperium* was subject to entropy if not periodically activated. Power is only powerful, violence only effective, as long as you keep sight of its potential unleashing. And because the marks of Roman military *imperium* within the city could not even be displayed (much less enacted) under normal circumstances, it was an inherent characteristic of military *imperium* that it must leave the city in order to be actualized in and increased by a martial victory of sufficient magnitude. But as much as the violence of *imperium* needed to escape the boundaries of the city in order to be refreshed by a new victory, once such a victory had been achieved it required a ritualized return to the city and a re-transformation of enacted violence into its prior state as "potential" violence (cf. Livy 45.39.10–11). Thus the dynamic force of *imperium* is alternately *centrifugal*—in that it needs to leave the city in order to be fully realized—and *centripetal*—in that it must return to the city of its origin in order that the city itself might feed off the increase in power and further pad the coffers of public (and so, religious and political) memory.[13] And, as I argue, it is in this need for *return*, this necessary reintegration of violence in the name (and form) of religious ritual, that we have the triumph itself.

THE "RITUAL TRIUMPH": ORIGIN AND FORM

All archaeological and historical evidence suggests with some certainty that the Roman triumph in its earliest form was adopted from an Etruscan ceremony of similar construction and meaning.[14] Now, within the context of Roman ritualized display, the "ritual triumph" appears not unrelated to Roman funereal and ludic *pompae* ("parades"), but it has been widely recognized that the magnitude of this particular procession is without par. Critics have suggested variously that the "primary" purposes of the triumphal procession included (1) the purification of the troops, (2) the justification of the campaign to the Senate and Roman people, (3) the dedication of this campaign to the gods, and—or—(4) a general celebration of Roman victory.[15] Versnel has argued convincingly that there is little in the triumph itself that can argue for purification as a major "purpose" of this ritual, and that if the purpose of the triumph is primarily one of the justification of might, there is no evidence in what we know of Roman cultural practice to suggest that the triumph would be an expected form of such justification.

If the ritual itself entered Rome via Etruscan social and linguistic influence (and whatever other origins the mythologies might offer this seems certain), both Plutarch (*Romulus* 16) and Livy (Book I) seem to locate the seeds of the practical phenomenon in Romulus's dedication of the *spolia opima*—"choice spoils"[16]—following the Roman victory over Acron, king of the Caeninenses. Livy describes this somber Romulan proto-triumph[17] as follows:

> Thence he led his army back in victory, and Romulus, a man no less outstanding in his deeds than eager to display them, arranged the spoils of the slaughtered enemy leader on an apparatus fashioned just for the purpose and carrying it himself he climbed the Capitoline. (Livy 1.10.4)

We must consider three aspects of both the victory over Acron and the first ritual presentation of spoils that served to mark this victory. First, there is the intersection of autochthony and empire. The Caeninensian attack on Rome is represented in the sources as a direct response to the Roman abduction of Sabine, Caeninensian, Crustuminian, and Antemnatian women. In other words, both the attack and the subsequent dedication of Acron's arms are tied not only to Rome's mythological (and deeply religious) foundations but also to that precise moment when the alien male colonizers use violent means to establish autochthonous links with the land via the fertility of the native female inhabitants. Second, there is the role of martial violence as an innate force in the growth of the city. Plutarch indicates in his account that before dedicating the *spolia opima*,

Romulus offered asylum and citizenship at Rome for all of the inhabitants of the conquered Caenina;[18] Livy relates that the final outcome of the battle was the ultimate assimilation of Sabines, Crustuminians, and Antemnatians (and, of course, their wealth) into the developing Roman population. Thus, in the victory over the Caeninenses and the subsequent Roman colonization of Italy, we are given an image of the symbolic and literal augmentation of the city by means of its military force.[19] Finally, there is the use of the triumph as a means of establishing a link between religion and violence. The first dedication of the *spolia opima* both marks the founding moment of the temple of Jupiter Feretrius[20] on the Capitoline hill and sets aside the Capitoline precinct as both the aboriginal source of all military victory and the divinely mandated endpoint for all the wealth of conquered nations.[21] In sum, and whatever the actual ethnic source of the celebration, the historiographers of the late Republic and early Empire located in this Romulan proto-triumph not only the foundation and early colonization of the *urbs* as distinct from the surrounding areas, but also the creation of the first temple in Rome and the identification of *Iupiter ipse*—and the house in which he abides—as the "Alpha and Omega" of all Roman military force.[22]

The "ritual triumph" was an exceedingly popular phenomenon—in all senses of the word. From the mythical foundation of the *urbs* through the time of Vespasian (69–79 CE), Rome celebrated over 360 triumphs. In the early years, triumphal celebrations were relatively infrequent and unadorned. Both the frequency and complexity of these displays increased during the period of the middle and late Republic—probably under the influence of the Hellenistic kings—and in the years between 220 and 70 BCE the city witnessed triumphal celebrations approximately once every year and a half.[23]

The right to triumph was restricted, at least nominally, to individuals who had held the office of dictator, consul, or praetor. The general was required to be situated in office during both the victory and the triumph itself; the battle had to have been fought under official auspices and within the province and with the soldiers of the general seeking triumph. At least five thousand enemy soldiers must have been slain, with Roman losses comparatively small (no triumphs for pyrrhic victories); the war needed to be a legitimate one against public foes; the victory needed to include a genuine extension of the dominion of the state; and the peace attained had to be stable enough for all soldiers to be pulled out of the campaign and returned to Rome.

In practice, of course, almost all of these restrictions were at various times either challenged or ignored. Pompey the Great triumphed before having held top offices (81 BCE); Cnaius Manlius Vulso triumphed in a war outside of his province and over which he had no order of authority

(187 BCE); and Constantine triumphed following his defeat of his co-emperor (and brother-in-law) Maxentius (314 CE).

But these are precisely the exceptions through which we might attempt to reconstruct the "rules"; and by way of focusing on the role of *imperium* in the right to seek triumph we can note that this right was reserved for individuals who held both the title *imperator* ("supreme general") and the full powers of *imperium militiae domique* (martial and domestic *imperium*). In the Empire both title and power were in constant possession of the emperor; but in the Republic, this rank could be achieved before the battle by virtue of a formal election in the *comitia centuriata*[24] and the passing of a *lex curiata de imperio*,[25] or—in the case of a battle fought originally outside of the traditional "restrictions" of triumph-worthy campaigns—immediately following a victory by means of an *appellatio imperatoria*[26] ("*imperator*-naming") held in the field of battle. Indeed, in later years the *appellatio* became a standard milestone on the road to triumph even in the case of magistrates who had been formally elected in the *comitia*. In any case, however, nominally excluded from the possibility of triumph were magistrates who had resigned their office, persons who did not hold the highest command during a battle, a magistrate who had handed over his command and his troops before returning to Rome, and the *vir privatus*—"private citizen"—who might be given extra-urban *imperium* but who did not possess the full range of *imperium* in which the martial power might be distinguished from the civic.

If all requirements for the triumph were judged to have been met in a deliberation held outside the boundaries of the *pomerium*, the Senate would proclaim the victorious general worthy of the triumphal rite, declare a formal holiday for the city, and allocate public funds to defray the expenses of both the general's triumphant return and the festivities associated with it.[27]

THE RHETORICAL TRIUMPH: A TALE OF RETURNING VICTORY

Descriptions of the triumph occur throughout our ancient sources and are unbound by literary genre or political climate. Whether it is Livy's relatively unadorned account of the sixth-century triumphs of the Etruscan kings,[28] Plutarch's more expansive display of the triumph of Aemilius Paulus,[29] or Ovid's subtly suggestive exilic daydream of a Roman triumph (that would never come to be),[30] the triumphal procession was always the stuff of which good stories were made.

Let us turn, then, to a brief look at a particularly compelling description of the triumphal transformation of violence into religion, that of Josephus's account of the victorious return of Vespasian, Titus, and Domitian, following the sack of Jerusalem and destruction of the Temple in 70 CE.[31]

Josephus's strangely cinematic description walks the line between inti-
macy and detachment: as much as he may style himself the objective observer, it was only by the grace of imperial favor that the author was
saved from being one of the captives on parade.[32] But at the same time it
underlines the singular ability of the triumph to "make memory" in its
representation of the original victory for a public that had not witnessed
it firsthand:

> But nothing in the procession was as astonishing as the structure of the mov-
> ing pictorial scenes . . . for many of [them] were covered over in tapestries in-
> terwoven with gold, and every one of them had a framework of gold and
> ivory. The war was shown by many different representations [*mimêmatôn*],
> divided by battles, allowing an exceedingly vivid view of the episodes. Here
> you could see a prosperous countryside devastated; there entire regiments of
> the enemy slaughtered, here a group in flight; there a group led in captivity;
> walls of amazing size destroyed by war machines, stout fortresses overcome,
> cities with fully-manned defenses completely seized and an army pouring
> within the defensive walls, every area soaked in gore, the hands of those in-
> capable of resisting stretched forth in supplication, temples set afire, houses
> crashing down upon their owners' heads, and, after utter desolation and
> dark sorrow, rivers flowing not over cultivated land—offering no drink to
> man or beast—but across a country yet in flames on every side. For to such
> sufferings did the Jews hand themselves over when they plunged into war;
> and the art [*technê*] and great workmanship of these scenes now portrayed
> the events to those who had not witnessed them, as though they were hap-
> pening before their eyes. (Josephus, *Bel. Iud.* 7.139)

The world of battle depicted by Josephus is one in which all natural order has gone awry—armies flow like blood, and rivers have leapt their
banks and clash with fires yet raging[33]—but as Josephus brings to a close
both the triumphal procession of Titus and Vespasian and his own vi-
brantly violent account of it, he makes pointed reference to both the in-
terconnection of ritual and violence and the peculiarly transformative nature of the phenomenon:

> For the city of Rome celebrated this day as a festival [*heôrtazen*] of victory
> [*epinikion*] in the war against its enemies [*polemiôn strateias*], as the end of its
> internal strife [*emphuliôn kakôn*], and as the beginning of its hopes for happi-
> ness [*eudaimonias elpidôn*]. (Josephus, *Bel. Iud.* 7. 157)

Thus the triumph—this strange spectacle of reintegration and appropriation, in which the decidedly Roman and the irrefutably foreign are
morphed into one grotesque whole—combines, as if by default, religious
ritual (*heôrtazen*) with war (*strateias*) even as it transforms internal strife
into expectations of better times ahead. But how does it do this?

In the account of Josephus we see in the *triumphator* not so much a victorious general before his troops as a highly theatrical—and certainly artificial—caricature of extraordinary power and might. But whatever the *triumphator* represents by his costume and conduct—whether he is pantomiming the early kings of Rome or Jupiter himself—it is clear that he is at a far remove from anything that is normally present in the city of Rome. For just as the moment of triumph transforms military violence in religious ritual, so too does it transform the victorious commander, if momentarily, from his normal identification as either general or Roman citizen and into his temporary role as what we have come to call the *triumphator*. By assuming the dress and aspect of an ultimately superior "Other," the *triumphator* functions as a kind of divinely mandated human receptacle for the divinely mandated martial force of Rome: he becomes *imperium* incarnate. And thus in his ritualized return of *imperium* to the point of its origin, and in his physical movement from the field of battle to the temple on return, he enacts an official shift from the "civil miseries" of war to Rome's hopes for "better times ahead" and—at least symbolically—a return of peace.

In all instances of the "rhetorical triumph," whether this triumph is to be understood as historical (so Josephus's account) or as fictitious (so Ovid's account of a "fake" triumph in *Tristia* IV.2), it is the strikingly visual nature of the phenomenon that is emphasized. Even in relatively brief accounts of historical triumphs—those of Cicero and Suetonius, for example—it is inevitably the visual power of the triumphal display (an event is often described as a *spectaculum*) that is emphasized in the language of the description.[34]

In the lengthier accounts of Josephus, Plutarch, and Ovid, however, the visual elements of the procession are not merely emphasized; they take control of the description entire. The event is cast not only in terms of "what happened" on the level of corporate memory but also in terms of "what could be seen" by the individual observer and, subsequently, reader, who would himself form a personal memory of the event based on the literary account of it. The exceedingly visual quality of the "ritual triumph," then, bleeds over into the vicarious sensibility of the "rhetorical triumph"—an account ideally, but not necessarily, predicated upon the former.

In a sense, then, the triumph is the ultimate in interactive entertainment. And yet, not only does the display of the triumph make its mark on the literature that records and commemorates it, so too does the distinctly centripetal force of the ritual itself. For as I suggested in the introduction of this chapter, one of the most important aspects of *imperium*—and so of the triumph that serves to manage its movement—is precisely its centripetition. And so, although the simple use of the verb *triumphare* ("to triumph") in the finite is somewhat preferred by Livy, the formula *triumphans redire* ("to return, triumphing"; a formula used by Livy as well as Cicero and Seneca), in which the verb "to triumph" is placed in the present participle and the verb "to return" in the (more emphatic) finite, is rather more telling.[35]

Indeed although the noun *triumphus* appears abundantly in literary descriptions of (and more often, brief references to) the triumphal phenomenon, the denominative *triumphare* is used most frequently in relatively unadorned accounts of the event: it functions as something of a shorthand for victory, but not for the triumphal phenomenon itself. In contrast to this, the combination of the verbs *triumphare* and *redire*—a combination that underlines precisely the inward-bound circuit of the *triumphator* and his *imperium*—tends to be the choice of authors writing more elaborate accounts of the phenomenon (as true as it is that our Roman sources are sparse). In *"triumphans redire"* we have expressed both the spectacular characteristics of any one triumphal display in particular, and the centripetal impulse of the cultural phenomenon as a whole.

The centripetal force of returning *imperium* seems to draw everything into its current: not only the physical property and material wealth of conquered nations, but the people themselves, their slaves and their children, their names and their towns and their histories. If Rome's *imperium* was able to overrun the boundaries of nations and peoples on its outward-bound journey, then it seems to do the same upon its return to the city. Thus Suetonius's account of the (questionably earned) triumph of Claudius (cited in note 34, above) includes the detail that the event brought a temporary return not only for the governors of the provinces but also for a number of political exiles.[36]

Based upon our written accounts of the political and performative details of the triumph, then, we can say that just as the ritual itself enabled the Roman people to envision and welcome home a victory the original of which they did not witness, the literary accounts of this ritual both mimic this "visualization" of foreign victory and underline the notion of the triumph as a phenomenon marking the return of military might and the transformation of that might into religious ritual (Josephus's *heôrtazen*) and renewed civic strength. In the poetic fantasy of Ovid, mentioned only briefly above, the centripetal pull of the triumph is imagined to apply not only to the return of the victor and his violence, but also to a return for the exiled poet. In the historically minded account of Josephus (so too those of Cicero, Suetonius, and Livy), by contrast, the spectacular reintegration of the *imperator* serves as an undeniable validation of the legitimate use of force and, as a consequence, the divine mandate of Rome's victory. Indeed, one of the most compelling aspects of the triumph's translation of military violence into religious ritual is precisely that the latter is framed in such a way as to give unimpeachable authority to the former. The literary commemoration of this act only further fixes this authority in the mind of the reading audience. For just as the "ritual triumph," in its precise conflation of victory and its return, transforms violence into religion, the "rhetorical triumph," in its deliberate focus on the spectacular and reintegrative functions of the event, transforms religious ritual into a public memory waiting to be "viewed"—that is, *read*—again and again and again.

THE ARTISTIC TRIUMPH: VICTORY, SET IN STONE

The freestanding triumphal arch seems always to have found favor with the city as a lasting memory of the triumph. Ostensibly an elaborate statue-base—typically topped by a large-scale bronze depicting the *triumphator* in his chariot[37]—the triumphal *qua* architectural element arch perfectly embodies the transformative, reintegrative, and atemporal characteristics of the phenomenon of which it is the material representation. In its peculiar function as "gate-without-a-wall," the earliest triumphal arches of which we have record are those of Stertinius of 196 BCE (Livy 33.27.4); it is likely, however, that such structures began to adorn the city even in earlier periods. To be sure, archaeological evidence and literary testimonia would indicate a large number of triumphal arches at Rome,[38] and in the Imperial period the city would have been awash in these monumental representations of past victories.

The arch of Titus,[39] which will serve as our case study, was erected in honor of Vespasian and Titus's siege of Jerusalem (70 CE) and in specific commemoration of the triumph of celebrating this siege (71 CE). Although vowed after their return from battle, it was not finished or dedicated until 81/82, shortly after Titus's death (and so after the writing of Josephus's account, completed in its Greek version between 75 and 79). A relatively simple single-fornix arch[40] situated on the *summa sacra via*, the high point of the "Sacred Way," the exterior frieze (running just below the attic) presents a detailed panorama of the original triumphal procession.[41] In small scale but deep relief, the viewer is carried in a circuit around the arch by representations of civic and military individuals, animals decorated for sacrifice, returning soldiers, and even a recumbent River Jordan carried into Rome—a fitting pantomime of the appropriation of foreign lands and peoples—on the backs of three men.

But the most powerful aspect of the arch, and the means by which it most famously transforms ephemeral ritual into lasting monument, comes not from its exterior ornamentation but rather from that of the reliefs of its inner jambs, each of which freeze in time key moments in the victor's original, triumphant return to the city. The southern relief represents what we might imagine as one of the earliest points in the original triumph: spoils from the temple—the table of shewbread, the seven-branched menorah, the silver trumpets (as well as explanatory placards that would have presented painted details)—are carried aloft by the returning soldiers as they prepare to enter a highly ornate *porta triumphalis*, itself represented, in rather imperfect perspective, at the extreme right margin of the relief. In its somewhat awkward depiction of the *porta triumphalis*, an "arch-within-an-arch," the arch of Titus not only memorializes the moment of reentry into its own physical structure; it provides the viewer with an unimpeachable etiology for its presence.

As she moves through the arch, the viewer's steps mimic those of the Roman soldiers' on the relief: she re-enacts the sack of Jerusalem and the return to Rome even as she moves through the arch reading this sack for (let us imagine) the first time. But because this relief focuses precisely on the spoils taken from the conquered city, it makes explicit that the sack of Jerusalem and the appropriation of its goods is the first stage in the final return of *imperium* to Rome. The viewer of the arch starts, in a sense, as a viewer "of (and nearly "in") Jerusalem": for, surrounded by the wealth of the second Temple in this moment before it enters the city, she is made to imagine the original battle no less than the observers of the original parade.

But the viewer who begins in Jerusalem ends in Rome. For if the southern relief is distinctly eastern in nature and representative of the starting point of the triumph, the northern relief, by contrast, is decidedly Roman and allusive to its end. Titus is shown standing in the triumphal chariot, surrounded by a seminude personification of the Roman people and a togate personification of the Senate; a winged Victory holds a laurel crown over his head, while the personification of Roma calmly leads his horses to their destination. A relief in the crown of the coffered vault shows the apotheosis of Titus, his bust born to heaven on the back of the eagle of Jupiter. Thus, whereas the southern relief features the exotic objects of an eastern culture only lately seized by Rome's *imperium*, the northern frieze places the whole of Rome's *imperium* in the body of the returning *triumphator*. We need no placards or explanatory titles for what we see.

The narrative direction of both reliefs runs from east to west. Indeed, these reliefs only "make sense" if viewed in this direction, the ancient (and modern) viewer of the arch is encouraged—even compelled—to enter from the east, "read" the reliefs to her left (south) and right (north), and then exit the arch to the west, facing not only the forum but the endpoint of the original "Romulan" parade, the Capitoline itself. In the process of viewing this arch as it should properly be viewed, the viewer is made to relive and reenergize the original event of which it is a commemoration.

CONCLUSIONS

I began this chapter by noting that the triumph has long been located as an integral element in the continual creation of Roman identity. I located it as the primary tool via which *imperium* was returned to the city, and argued that as such it came to function as a tripartite epinicion of power and religion, the visualization and reintegration of military might and divine sanction. As a phenomenon that transforms martial violence into religious ritual, and religious ritual into public memory, the triumph provides a good check against our assumption that the Romans—or any culture with which we are not intimately involved—are "just like us." Indeed, in large part the triumph can helpfully remind us of just how alien this alien culture really was.

But now I wonder: how alien an experience *is* the triumph—when all is said and done? Is the transformation of ("dangerous") military force into ("safe") religious ritual so strange a concept to a modern thinker? Is it really that foreign to the experiences of a relatively young nation seeking ever to validate its foreign conquests—and the blood and money spent in achieving them—in the name of an irresistible divinity?

I want to suggest, of course, that it is not. As other chapters in this collection make clear, the connection between violence, power, and religion is not only anything but modern—it is anything but ancient. For as temporally, culturally, and psychically distanced as we are from the triumphal parades of ancient Rome, the corporate desire to witness one's power and to return that power to its source—with, of course, divine sanction—seems, far from alien, a most uncomfortably *human* characteristic.

The triumphant general in his ticker tape parade hardly sports the regalia of a god or a king, but he will more than serve as a recognizable, if rapidly evanescing, modern example. In the image of the high-ranking commander in full costume of war, borne through the streets of a city that has for this day been transformed into a stage of corporate victory—in this image once emblazoned on the front pages of newspapers, now stored mainly in microfiche archives and our collective imagination—we have something not altogether different from the triumphal procession of Titus and his father—and the triumphal arch that commemorated it.

But the very fact of these representations, the fact that we have the reliefs of the arch of Titus as well as the photographic record of ticker tape parades, brings me back to why I consider the triumph a culturally pervasive transformation of might into rite rather than a self-contained military parade or dedication to the gods. For both the Roman triumph and the American ticker tape parade represent not only the civic reassimilation of a definitively noncivic victory, but also the ultimate separation of that victory from the man who achieved it: a transformation of the violence that brought victory into a memory—either religious or civic—that could both outlast that victory and provide a kind of religious capital through which future victories might be gained.

If victory is fleeting, so too are the celebrations of victory if they are not recorded for posterity in a sustainable form. We know that the triumph was well attended and abundantly depicted in both literature and art. But these literary and visual representations do not merely record the victory—they create it. Put it this way: What if you held a triumph and no one came? What if no one erected an arch in your honor, no one described the great panoply of your return to Rome in historical treatises or poems of praise? The "ritual triumph" enacts a fleeting visualization of victory and a reintegration of power. But without the "rhetorical" and "artistic triumphs" that eternalize and reenergize this visualization, would the military power that prompted the triumph have been properly returned to its source, made safe for the city in the form of religious ritual? Would the triumph have been achieved in the first place? Without a record of the triumph, in other words, and without the ultimate transformation of violence into religion—and religion into memory—who is to say that the war has ever been won?

NOTES

1. The description of the triumphal procession with which this chapter begins has been loosely adapted from Plutarch's detailed account of the triumph of Aemilius Paulus in 167 BCE. For the complete description, cf. Plut. *Aem. Paul.* 32.1–35.4. On the physical "reshaping" of the city, see esp. Favro (1994), to which cf. Josephus's description at *Bel. Iud.* 7.122; for the triumphal route (esp. with respect to the Flavian triumph) see Makin (1921).

2. The identification of the *porta triumphalis* remains contested. On the possible location(s) or identification of the *porta triumphalis*, see Coarelli (1968); Lyngby (1963); Platner-Ashby (1926, 418–19); and Versnel (1970, 132–63 [with bibliography]; 152; 394–96). For a discussion of the triumphal route, including the location of the *porta triumphalis*, see Citarella (1980) and Favro (1994); for the suggestion that the *porta triumphalis* was a gate in daily use, see Richardson 1992, 301.

3. Although it has become standard to refer to the triumphant general as *triumphator*—and this chapter follows suit—the term itself is purely postclassical, and does not appear in authors writing of the triumphs considered in these pages. Traditionally, the *triumphator* does not cross the *pomerium* before the day of the triumph; in practice, and especially in the Imperial period, it is difficult to determine to what degree this prohibition was upheld (cf. Versnel 1970, 191, and Mommsen 1887, cited there; cf. also Phillips 1974a).

4. In the case of Josephus's description of the triumph of Vespasian, Titus, and Domitian, the "expected" position of the conquered foreign leader is occupied instead by the Torah scroll taken from the Temple. Plutarch's account, which is rich

in the language of the tragic stage, may in fact suggest that Paulus's decision to display the children of Perseus was a less than stellar idea.

5. Or alternatively, "consider the future, and remember . . ." (I would argue for the temporal sense of the preposition over the spatial). This phrase, although uniformly—and perhaps wrongly—adopted as a "standard" part of the triumphal procession, appears in none of our ancient sources, but is to be attributed (with suspicion) to the early Christian writer Tertullian (*Apol.* 33).

6. Versnel (1970) remains the starting point for any investigation into the historical and religious elements of the triumph; Beard's forthcoming study promises to add new considerations to the established scholarly lines. On the history and development of the triumph, see also Develin (1978), Künzl (1988), Payne (1962), and Warren (1970); on the triumph as spectacle, see especially Brilliant (1999) and, for the late antique triumph, MacCormack (1981).

7. It is a matter of no small import that save Livy's lengthy and rather theorizing discussion of Paulus's contested triumph in Book 45, there is a dearth of extended descriptions of the triumph in Latin authors.

8. I include in this category not only the lengthier narratives of, e.g., Suetonius, Livy, Plutarch, Josephus, and Gellius, but also the fleeting references to the triumph and triumphal paraphernalia as made by, e.g., Servius *Serv. ad Verg. Ecl.* 10.27 (on the *triumphator's* possession of the *insignia* of Jupiter) and Pliny, *NH* 33.111 (on the use of red face coloring by the *triumphator*).

9. The speeches of Cicero and the poems of Ovid (*Trist., Ars Am., Ex Pont.*) both contain considerable triumphal imagery and adapt the language of the triumph as descriptive of the personal victories involved in oratory, politics, love, and the production of poetry. On Ovid's use of triumphal imagery, see Hardie 2002a and 2002b.

10. Cf. Triumphal imagery on private sarcophagi as well as the so-called Tiberius cup (Louvre; BJ 2367). For an overview of artistic representations of the triumph, see Ryberg (1955, 141–62); on the distinctly "Roman" arch, see especially Wallace-Hadrill (1990).

11. For the role of the triumph in Roman army religion, see Helgeland 1978.

12. The concept of *imperium* in its many forms is an exceedingly complex one; for a summary of the problem with respect to the triumph, see Versnel (1970, 313–19 [with bibliography]). On *imperium* as a form of mana see Wagenvoort (1941); for consideration of the triumph as a "dynamistic" phenomenon involving the movement of *imperium*, see Versnel (1970, 378–84).

13. This "necessary circularity" of *imperium* is made most explicit in the lengthy speech of Marcus Servilius (Livy 45. 37–39), which might in some ways count as the historian's programmatic theorizing on the overarching meaning of the ritual.

14. On this see Versnel (1970), chapter 1 (esp. 48–55) and Warren (1970). Diodorus Siculus, writing in the first century BCE, associates the triumph with the god Dionysus (one of whose epithets was "Thriambos"), and thus with the east, for this god "was the first of those . . . to lead a triumph from the field of battle into his homeland" (Diodorus 4.5).

15. See Ryberg (1955) for a discussion of the chronological shift of focus—from the *triumphator's* sacrifice to Jupiter to his fulfillment of vows—in the visual representations of the triumph.

16. On this term, Plutarch (*Rom.* 16.7), following Varro (*Antiq. Rom.* 2.34), suggests that *opima* comes from either *opes*, "wealth," or *opus*, "deed." The right to display and dedicate the *spolia opima* was allowed to only three military commanders: Romulus, for his defeat of Acron; Cornelius Cossus, for his defeat of Tolumnius (437 BCE); and Claudius Marcellus, for his defeat of Britomarchus (222 BCE). Cf. also Dionysius of Halicarnassus, 2.34.1. The dedication of the *spolia opima* is without a doubt an altogether different rite than that of the triumph proper, but the structure and apparent meaning of the rite make for unavoidable comparison.

17. On the dedication of the *spolia opima* as an historically received "proto-triumph," cf. Plutarch (*Rom.* 16.6), as well as the account of Dionysius of Halicarnassus, 2.34.3.

18. Although Plutarch's representation of Romulus early in these sections is less than favorable, he later notes, "[Romulus] in no way wronged those captured, but ordered them to tear down their dwellings and follow him to Rome, promising them that there they would become citizens (*politai*) equal to the rest" (*Rom.* 16.4).

19. As Plutarch explains it, "This, then, more than anything else, gave increase to Rome: that it always united and incorporated with itself the peoples whom it had overpowered" (*Rom.* 16.5).

20. Plutarch (*Rom.* 16.6) indicates that the trophy set up by Romulus on the Capitoline was designated a dedication to Jupiter Feretrius, "for the Romans say that 'to smite' is '*ferire*'; for Romulus had pledged 'to smite' his opponent and to overthrow him."

21. So Habinek (2002, 49) notes that the triumph is at its heart a "celebration of the resources of the world moving into Rome." Josephus's description (discussed below) is similarly suggestive of this reading of the triumph as an act of the "collecting" of culture, cf. Josephus, *Bell. Iud.* 7.132–33.

22. The linguistic origin of the triumph presents further difficulties of interpretation but leads us again to an Etruscan prototype. It appears that the Latin *triumphus* and the cry "*triumpe!*" share some relation to the Greek words *thriambos* and *thriambe*. Linguistic evidence argues that the words themselves came into Latin not through the Greek, but through Etruscan. In any case, a few things seem likely. First, that the appellativa *thriambos*—the original meaning of which was probably something like "Dionysiac song"—is a back-formation from the ecstatic cry, *thriambe*. Second, that a non-Greek parent word connected with Dionysus-worship was adopted into Greek as *thriambe* and, independently, into Etruscan in a similar form. And finally, that the words *triumpe* and *triumphus* came into Latin through the Etruscan and at a time approximately contemporaneous with the earliest Roman celebrations of the ritual. On this see further Versnel 1970, chapter 1.

23. Richardson (1975).

24. The *comitia centuriata* was a timocratic assembly charged especially with the enactment of laws, the election of senior magistrates, and the declaring of war and peace.

25. Curial law on the assumption of *imperium*. On this, see Versnel (1970, 320 and following).

26. Versnel 1970, 343. Not everyone who held the title *imperator* had it before he went to war. The *appellatio imperatoria* allowed that an individual could be publicly recognized as imperator after a victory in war. In this case, the pronunciation of the title *imperator* was able to bestow *imperium* following a victory in much the same way as the *lex curiata de imperio* worked to bestow *imperium* prior to a victory.

27. Generals denied the right to a traditional triumph (the end point of which was the Capitoline) would occasionally self-finance a "private" triumph, the end point of which was Monte Alba (on which cf. Brennan 1996 and Miller 2000, 409).

28. E.g., Livy 2.7.4, 2.16.6, etc. The first time the verb *triumphare* appears (in present participle form), it is of the victory of Tarquinius Superbus, the first Etruscan king of Rome, in Book 1.

29. Plutarch, *Aemilius Paulus*, 34–36.

30. Ovid, *Tristia* IV.ii; on the description of the triumph in this poem, see Hardie 2002b, Beard 2004, and, in partial response to Beard, Stroup 2004.

31. Josephus's first version was composed in his native Aramaic; what we have now is a Greek "translation," prepared by Josephus, for Greek speakers in the east.

32. So Beard (2003, 551): "But for the grace of Titus, Josephus himself would have been on display, re-enacting his own capture."

33. On the religious imagery of this passage, cf. Paul (1993, 65–66); on Jeremiah and Polybius as likely models for Josephus, cf. Cohen (1982).

34. Cicero, *Verr.* II.v.77; *Lege Manilia*, 8; *In Pisonem*, 92; and Suetonius, *vita Dom.*, 13. Of particular interest to this study is Suet., *vita Claud.*, 17: "and [Claudius] allowed not only the governors of the provinces to come to the city in order *to witness the spectacle, but indeed some of the exiles as well.*"

35. On Livy's use of the verb, see Phillips (1974b).

36. Similar evidence for the magnetic pull of the triumphal spectacle can be found in Ovid's *Tristia* IV.2, noted above. Ovid's description of Tiberius's triumph over the Germans is rich in the language of vision and spectacle. But whereas most instances of the "rhetorical triumph" are predicated upon *the prior celebration* of a "ritual triumph," Ovid challenges the accepted order of events and writes of a "ritual triumph" that has not yet occurred, and for a military victory that has not yet been (nor would be) achieved.

37. Such was certainly the case for the arch of Titus as attested by iconography from coins of the period.

38. For an overview of arches in Rome—triumphal (the usual purpose) and otherwise—see Nash (1968, 79–135 [with fine plates]), Platner-Ashby (1926, 33–47), and Richardson (1992, 22–31 [all three with bibliography]). On the arch of Titus in particular, see Nash (1968, 133–35), Platner-Ashby (1926, 45–47), and Richardson (1992, 30).

39. Not to be confused with the (no longer extant) triple fornix arch of Titus (also called the arch of Vespasian and Titus) in the Circus Maximus, similarly erected toward (or at) the end of Titus's life (80 or 81), similarly by the Senate, and similarly in commemoration of the sack of Jerusalem.

40. Made of Pentelic marble with travertine foundations, the arch measures 13.5 m. high, 15.4 m. wide, and 4.75 m. deep.

41. The inclusion of the original triumphal parade on the arch that commemo-rates it is not unusual. The arch of Septimius Severus (203 CE), also located in the forum, contains such scenes over its side arches; the arch of Trajan in Benevento (114 CE) includes both a running frieze of the triumph and individual relief pan-els depicting specific moments of return.

3

Taming the Beast: Rabbinic Pacification of Second-Century Jewish Nationalism

Michael S. Berger

When religion is invoked to support and encourage violence, scholars naturally turn their attention to similar historical precedents in order to identify patterns and trends of this sort of social or cultural process. But it is equally important for scholars to seek historical moments when religion was actually used to quell violence, to calm tempers and reverse patterns of brutal or inciteful behavior. One such case is the second and third centuries CE, when the Rabbis of Palestine took a significant interpretive turn and developed or stressed an understanding of Judaism that eschewed violence as a path to achieving political or religious goals.

This was no small achievement; both the Hebrew Bible and the messianic literature of the late Second Temple period offer readers many justifications for violence, from divine commandments to annihilate certain peoples to narratives that predict imminent battle and cosmic conflict.[1] Within a Roman Empire, whose domination almost everywhere took military form, Jewish hope for freedom or relief not surprisingly saw itself in similarly militant terms. Thus, in the seventy years between 66 and 135 CE, intertwined religious and political aspirations fused more than once to produce messianic agitation among Jews, leading to three unsuccessful military campaigns against Rome. After that period, no Jewish insurrection or military campaign against Rome or another power is recorded for centuries.

But the second century posed even greater challenges to Palestinian Jewry and its leaders, for the political situation demanded Herculean efforts to preserve some unity among a dispersed Jewry—a need previously fulfilled by a belief in the centrality of the Land of Israel and Jerusalem, overlaid with a vibrant and hopeful messianism. My claim is that the Rabbis of the time sought vigorously to maintain the land's *religious* importance yet simultaneously to insist that messianism's *political* goals were beyond human reach, at least directly. By shifting agency to the divine, the Rabbis were able to turn an agitated and repeatedly violent Jewish nationalism, soaked in religious terminology and messianic hope, into a more quietistic posture. Contrary to the view of some social scientists, it is not whether, but *how*, God is brought into a conflict that determines the likelihood of a conflict inviting religious violence.

HISTORICAL BACKGROUND

If at some level, the second-century Rabbinic project was to decouple the political and religious understandings of Jewish nationalism, then it is helpful to go back to the Second Temple period to see how that integration was first achieved.

When Judeans were allowed to return from Babylonia to Jerusalem in 536 BCE, their political aspirations were primarily "restorative": to have once again an independent monarchy under a descendant of the Davidic line. While these returnees were able, with Persian support, to rebuild a temple in Jerusalem, their explicit political aspirations went unfulfilled, and they remained a vassal province of the Persian Empire. Alexander the Great's conquests in the fourth century BCE deferred those political aspirations once more, but by this time, most Jews, particularly in Judea, had made peace with their political reality. Sovereignty was not required; as long as the cult in Jerusalem could be maintained and the laws of the Torah generally observed, then the covenant could be largely fulfilled and the relationship with God sustained.

The spread of Hellenism, however, began to erode support among Jews for their distinctive cult and practices. The experience under the Seleucid Greeks, and especially under Antiochus Epiphanes (175–163 BCE), brought this internal conflict among the Jews to a head.[2] Hellenizers had occupied Jerusalem's Temple and converted it into a typical pagan site; coercion to Greek practices was apparently widespread. The Maccabees, a group of Judean rural priests, led a band of opponents of Hellenization and successfully expelled the Greeks from Jerusalem and rededicated the Temple. While some fought on for complete independence, others withdrew their participation from territorial expansion once the initial goals of cleansing Jerusalem and its Temple had been achieved.[3] This shows that while the political cannot be easily disengaged from the religious in ancient civilizations, they should not be utterly conflated.

The independent Hasmonean state lasted barely a century. Rome, the rising power in the Mediterranean, became involved in Judean affairs in 63 BCE, which ultimately resulted in direct Roman rule. Religious observance of the covenant and Jewish control of the Temple cult were once again in jeopardy; many Jewish groups believed that to ensure divine favor, Rome's oppression had to be stopped, even as they disagreed whether or not to pursue open confrontation.[4]

In the space of seventy years, between 66 and 135 CE, Jews staged three revolts in the eastern part of the Empire: the first in Judea and Galilee under the Emperor Vespasian (66–70 CE), the second in Northern Egypt under Trajan (115–117 CE), and the third in Judea alone under Hadrian, known as the Bar Kokhba Revolt (132–135 CE). Historians agree that in the background of each confrontation were a variety of conflicts, from tensions between Jews and their neighboring Greeks and pagans, to class war, to imperial Rome's efforts to unify the empire, particularly its eastern part—to which Jewish nationalist aspirations were a threat.[5] What is of greater interest to us, however, is the revolts' aftermaths; that is where one finds lingering effects, and it is the time during which a people absorbs the calamity into their collective consciousness. Obviously, all three revolts led to serious depopulation, dislocation, and a ruined economy. But if we look at each revolt independently—for certainly, the Jews of the time did not know there would be three failed revolts in such close succession—we begin to approximate the shift in thinking that likely occurred among some Jews.

The clearest outcome of the Revolt of 66–70 was the destruction of the Temple and Jerusalem. The symbol of Jewish pride was razed to the ground, and the city that served as a centralizing point for the Jewish diaspora was in ruins. The Jewish aristocracy was out of power, as were the priests, and little if any significant political and legal authority was vested in Jewish hands.[6] It is unlikely that Rome treated this Jewish revolt much differently from other native revolts in the empire,[7] although its being on the eastern fringe of the empire did make its situation more sensitive.

The revolt in Egypt about forty-five years later was the only major Jewish revolt outside of the Land of Israel for which we have evidence. Its suppression by local Egyptian forces was merciless. Contemporary historians use the term *extermination* to describe the Egyptian response; the hitherto populous Jewish community of Alexandria is not heard from after 117 until the end of the third century.[8]

Of the three revolts, the third—the Bar Kokhba Revolt—had some of the more severe consequences. Rome's ruthless response took an enormous human toll in death and enslavement, followed by a period of religious persecution initiated by Hadrian that led to sustained martyrdom.[9]

No doubt, some of these harsh decrees were nothing more than the traditional application of the status of *dediticii* upon a rebellious population, while others were simply the final stage of implementing Roman rule in the region by excluding Jews from all administrative positions. But the bans on public study of Torah and other religious practices appear to have constituted a deliberate assault on the Jewish faith. Jews were symbolically expelled from the region around Jerusalem, preventing them from visiting even their destroyed national monuments.[10] The period, albeit brief, was long enough to sear into Jewish memory the reality of martyrdom, a fate many Rabbinic scholars apparently suffered.

JEWISH REACTIONS TO THE DEFEATS

Admittedly, the scholar of this tumultuous period is frustrated by the absence of contemporaneous Jewish sources aside from Josephus. Nevertheless, Rabbinic literature attributes a fair number of statements to sages living within a century of Bar Kokhba, both in Palestine and Babylonia. Without granting greater or lesser historical veracity to a particular Rabbinic statement, I follow Isaiah Gafni that "the preponderance of allusions to a particular issue only from a specific generation or stratum within Talmudic literature . . . certainly suggest at least the possibility that a new reality had set in."[11] What I intend to show is that the later *tannaim* (second-century CE Palestinian scholars) and early *amoraim* (post-200 CE Palestinian and Babylonian scholars) engaged in a deliberate program to dampen or counteract the tendencies for large-scale violence contained in sacred Jewish texts and memory. This is not to say that the Rabbis were prescient, having figured out the recipe for long-term Jewish survival in a hostile or barely tolerant diaspora. There was no way for them to know how long their current situation would last. Rather, three failed revolts in relatively rapid succession led these Rabbinic leaders to see that a *different* response, an *alternative* hermeneutic, was required to enable the Jews to cope with their current reality.[12] Indeed, the very mounting of two revolts just decades after the Temple's destruction testifies to Palestinian Jewry's faith in the viability of violent resistance to Rome. After the Bar Kokhba debacle, however, many came to see that existing paradigms to interpret their situation and point toward options were failing them. While some Jews, no doubt, abandoned their faith, and some continued to cling to the idea of renewed revolt, the Rabbis chose to revise their interpretive frameworks.[13]

It is likely that the emerging Rabbinic view was in fact in the minority. A Temple in Jerusalem had been part of Jewish life for all but seventy of the past thousand years and for the past several centuries had served as both a religious center for a widening Jewish diaspora and a symbol of Jewish distinctiveness throughout the empire. Donations and pilgrimages reinforced among many Jews that they belonged to a larger collective and shared a group identity.[14] After 70 CE, expecting the Temple's rapid return was reasonable, whether through a Roman imperial change of heart or a Persian military victory that might permit Jews to rebuild their shrine as it had six hundred years earlier. The Temple was such an integral part of Jewish life both in the land and in the diaspora that few could imagine, or cared to envision, a Judaism without it. The canonized stories of the prophets and Ezra and Nehemiah meant that many Jews were familiar with exile and return, with destruction and rebuilding, so they could easily assimilate this *temporary* loss into the Jewish worldview. Alternately, the memory of the Maccabeean revolt fueled hopes that with divine assistance, an against-all-odds Jewish military campaign could succeed against Rome as it had against the Greeks 250 years earlier. The best posture was thus simply to hold on, not to make radical changes to a social or religious order that would be restored in short order,[15] and continue to hope that a Jewish king or messiah would rule (again) in Judea.

The hope for military victory likely kept Jews still hopeful for the reestablishment of a sovereign Jewish state on the lookout for signs of Roman weakness. It was probably the perceived vulnerability of Rome in the mid-110s, as her armies were busy battling Parthians on the Persian front, that led to Jewish messianic agitation in North Africa and Egypt.[16] The surprisingly vicious Greco-Egyptian response, led by local peasants and anti-Jewish incitement by Egyptian priests, obviously did not dampen messianic hopes in nearby Judea. Jews saw Hadrian's preoccupation with the east in the 130s as another opportunity to take advantage of a distracted (and weakened?) Rome. More critically, Hadrian's decision to violate the sanctity of the Temple Mount by erecting a temple to Zeus was almost certainly seen by many as a provocation akin to that of Antiochus Epiphanes' defilement of the Temple in the days of the Maccabees—and called for a similar radical response. Add to this the nearing of the "predetermined" seventy years that had separated the First and Second Temples and the mix was truly volatile. The past became an undeniable model for the present, and the messianic movement led by Bar Kokhba had the support of many Jews—including, according to most historians, many of the Rabbinic class who had remained in Judea.

As mentioned, the failure of this third revolt was not only military defeat, which left Judea essentially de-Judaized,[17] but the launch of years of persecution in Judea against Judaism's rituals and the public teaching of Torah. For those who put covenantal premium on observance, Jewish life was rendered unbearable. Whatever Jewish population remained—if they decided to remain within Jewish society at all—either moved north to the

Galilee where the revolt had had little impact, or to Jewish communities outside of Palestine, most notably in Babylonia.

After Bar Kokhba, one starts to detect the beginnings of a change in Jewish messianic attitudes within Rabbinic circles. My understanding of the Rabbinic project from the mid–second century on is that the Rabbis felt the need to balance two conflicting desiderata: maintaining a vibrant messianic hope that would unite a widely dispersed Jewry, yet taming that hope to prevent outbreaks of further violence. Whether this balance was preached to a wider or narrower audience in its time is immaterial; while I am partial to the more minimalist view of Rabbinic influence in the second century,[18] the literary legacy of the Rabbis imbued Jewish communities up to the modern period with the Rabbinic ethos and hermeneutical stances that made messianic violence less likely.[19]

In the next section I map out the variety of strategies adopted by the Rabbis (as remembered in their later texts) that attempt to achieve this delicate balance.

STRATEGIES OF PACIFICATION

Pacification strategies included theological approaches and supernaturalizing messianism.

Theological Approaches

For first-century Jews who had suffered or witnessed much bloodshed and the Temple's destruction, the commonly performed biblical texts offered ready solace: God's wrath was now "spent," preparing the way for consolation and good tidings—and also retribution against Israel's enemies:

> Awake, awake; rise up Jerusalem. You have drunk from the Lord's hand the cup of his wrath, drained to its dregs the bowl of drunkenness . . . therefore listen to this, in your affliction . . . thus says the Lord . . . who will plead his people's cause: "Look . . . you shall never again drink from the bowl of my wrath, I will give it instead to your tormentors and oppressors." (Isaiah 51:17, 21–23)

The historical precedent of the return from Babylonian exile only fifty years after the First Temple's destruction likely led to expectations that a chastened Judah would both imminently enjoy rapprochement with its God and witness its enemies' downfall—a view that animated Jewish messianism throughout its history.[20]

But the series of three debacles within seventy years likely prompted thoughts that history was not following the biblical "script"; the classical theodicy of the prophets that one could *expect* God's grace simply because the people had undergone enormous suffering apparently no longer obtained. The scope and scale of divine retribution had exceeded previous experience; three failed efforts to throw off Rome's yoke meant God was not yet prepared to forgive. Rome, like Assyria, Babylonia, and the Greeks before it, was merely God's instrument to punish a still-sinful Israel.

Such a theodicy had two important implications. First, it compelled an emotional acceptance of one's fate and a practical embrace of passivity. One could not obstruct the divine plan; indeed, resisting or not submitting to the "deserved" punishment only invited further suffering and delayed the ultimate redemption. This theological stance led to an utter transvaluation of Jewish violence: from Judah Maccabee's bold declaration that his armed struggle was an expression of divine will[21] to the Rabbis' even bolder claim that *the enemy* was the instrument of God's plan, not the Jewish resisters.

Second, shifting the conflict's arena from that between the Jews and Rome to that between Israel and its God offered the increasingly powerless Jewish community some sense of power: the errant nation could repent, be reconciled to their Father in heaven, who with divine omnipotence, would take care of the idolatrous, tyrannical, and haughty regime. The covenanted people were still covenanted, and thus still powerful: a potentially liberating notion to a thrice-defeated nation. As Jacob Neusner writes:

> The paradox must be crystal clear: Israel acts to redeem itself through the opposite of self-determination, namely by subjugating itself to God. Israel's power lies in its negation of power. Its destiny lies in giving up all pretence at deciding its own destiny. So weakness is the ultimate strength, forbearance the final act of self-assertion, passive resignation the sure step toward liberation.[22]

The transvaluation could not be stated more starkly.

But if redemption was now seen as contingent on the Jews' complete compliance with the covenant, it realistically might never arrive given the covenant's demands. The Rabbis in the century after Bar Kokhba clearly struggled with this fatalism, as this text attests:

> Rav said: there are no more [predetermined] endtimes; the matter [of the messiah's arrival] depends solely on repentance and good deeds. Samuel said: it is enough for the mourner to suffer in his mourning. [This debate] parallels a tannaitic debate: R. Eliezer said: if Israel repents, they will be redeemed, and if not, they will not be redeemed. R. Joshua said to him: [Is it

true that] if they do not repent they will never be redeemed? Rather, the Holy One Blessed be He sets up a king whose decrees against them are as difficult as Haman's, and Israel repents and resumes the proper path.[23]

The debates indicate the unease entailed in any seismic ideological shift. But as the views attributed to R. Eliezer and R. Joshua indicate, they concur that it is *Israel's repentance* that brings the messiah, not God's benevolence.[24] They differ over whether God will simply wait for Israel to be stirred to repentance on her own, or whether she will need a divinely ordained "kick in the pants"—a remarkable insistence that persecution is divinely ordained, and should be willingly accepted. For some Rabbis, God imposed a set of oaths on the Jewish people *not* to resort to violence against foreign powers, whether in Palestine or elsewhere.[25] The martyrdom faced by many during the Hadrianic persecutions was held up as the act of acceptance *par excellence*, to be endured with love. Martyrdom was to be suffered for the preservation of the law,[26] not for a nationalist cause, as the Zealots had done in 73 CE.[27] Many Rabbis were clearly encouraging a committed quietism that would turn suffering into a catalyst for improvement and repentance.

Supernaturalizing Messianism

To quell messianic activism, another Rabbinic strategy was to move messianism increasingly beyond human reach.[28] Through their exegeses and homilies, particularly of the messianic references in Isaiah and other canonized prophetic literature, the Rabbis dramatically reduced the human role in events leading up to the ultimate redemption. Comments that God would rebuild the Third Temple with fire,[29] and increasingly fantastic descriptions of the End of Days,[30] were part of a larger view of the utter supernatural character of the messianic age.[31] Passover, with its utterly miraculous redemption, became the paradigm of the future salvation, portraying Jews as mere bystanders to the marvels God would perform. The liturgy that evolved over the centuries for this ritual certainly stayed within this thematic arena.[32]

The Rabbinic emphasis on human passivity and divine agency in Jewish messianism force us to refine the conclusions of social scientists such as Mark Juergensmeyer, who claim generally that "when a struggle becomes sacralized . . . the use of violence becomes legitimated."[33] While he admits in the end that religion can also cure the violence by "deflect[ing] violence through its ritual enactment,"[34] the case of the second-century Rabbis also shows the possibility of taking a conflict *out of the human realm* and placing it in God's hands to be executed supernaturally. Therefore, we might say that what is critical in determining the role of religion in escalating or suppressing violence is a tradition's *view of human agency that accompanies* one's portrayal of a conflict in cosmic terms. If human beings have a role to play in the cosmic drama, then religious violence will be fostered; if human beings are to be bystanders, then religification of a conflict can actually quell the violence.

Transforming Precedent

How Jews read their own history had a profound effect on their messianic agitation. The Maccabees' successful insurgency no doubt served to inspire Judeans that they too could defy the odds, overcome the imperial forces, and again become an independent state. Part of the Rabbinic project was to shift the emphasis of this holiday from the military miracle to that of the pure uncontaminated oil lasting eight days in the Temple candelabrum. Scant attention is paid to the holiday in the Mishnah, the first major text of Rabbinic Judaism, and Rabbinic literature in general is curiously quiet about the Maccabees, who are often portrayed negatively when they are mentioned. Scholars have offered many explanations for this reticence, but whatever the cause, one clear effect was to prevent second- and third-century Rabbinic Jews from seeing the Maccabees as an example for their own political decisions.

The other dangerous precedent was, of course, Bar Kokhba's Revolt. Over time, peoples, especially downtrodden groups with little to inspire their hopes, tend to valorize the (few) victories of their failed saviors, mythologizing these figures to the point of hero worship. As Richard G. Marks carefully shows,[35] Rabbinic literature entertains two traditions about Bar Kokhba—false messiah and national hero—but makes clear within *both* traditions that the rebel leader's path was dangerous and brought about terrible consequences on the Jewish people. The Rabbis could not or would not expunge Bar Kokhba's place in the national memory, but they ensured that his legacy would not lead to imitation of his revolt, with its many attendant risks.

Rabbinic sources from this period also show that more ancient precedents began to be read through the prism of the new quietism, taming stories or episodes with potential for violent imitation. Thus, biblical figures such as Joshua and King David, whose military exploits are treated in biblical books (some, in rather graphic detail), are "converted" into proto-Rabbis, that is, figures whose main occupation is Torah study, but who occasionally go out (grudgingly?) to fight the necessary war. The second- and third-century Rabbinic emphasis on Torah study not only valorizes Torah but also sanitizes the biblical figures whose behavior might embolden militant nationalist elements in Judea. Instead, figures such as Jacob, who used appeasement and diplomacy in his encounter with his brother Esau (Genesis chap. 32–33), are held out as paradigms of how one should behave with a hostile—and clearly more powerful—adversary.[36]

The period we are examining is also when Jewish liturgy began to gel and reach greater standardization. While precise dating of the inclusion and formulation of prayers is impossible,[37] it is noteworthy that some themes and motifs are employed with much greater frequency. As already noted, the exodus from Egypt, with its clear portrayal of divine salvation and human passivity, was an obvious trope for the Rabbis and their quietistic agenda; it now becomes a central motif in the morning and evening prayers. The daily prayer's entreaties for national salvation are all worded to convey divine activity, not assistance, and lack any mention of human agency.[38] The prayer's final blessing that begs God to bestow peace on His people—even before the ultimate salvation arrives—echoes the Rabbis extolling of peace[39] and underscores their survival strategy of avoiding conflict.[40]

Muting the Territorial Dimension of Judaism

Scholars such as W. D. Davies have shown that over the course of the late Second Temple period and thereafter, the unambiguous emphasis on the Land of Israel in Judaism's theological tradition was attenuated by historical realities. As Davies presents it,[41] a strong diaspora community living Jewishly outside the land led to various strategies of reinterpreting the land's centrality, such as seeing Jerusalem and Zion in more transcendental terms.[42]

The Rabbinic tradition furthered these spiritualizing trends by articulating an alternative axiological nexus for the covenant between God and the Jewish People: the Torah and its expansion through Rabbinic exegesis. The essence of Judaism was the covenant, which subsumed both Temple and land within its parameters. Post Bar Kokhba, the Rabbis elevated Torah beyond all other values. This may have been by design, or it may have been merely a trajectory of earlier trends whose momentum increased when land and Temple ceased to exist. Regardless of the motives, these spiritualizing trends converged in the thinking of some Rabbis with the effect of dulling or checking the motivation for militant nationalism— but with the collateral effect of weakening the land's practical centrality.[43]

THE CENTRALITY OF THE LAND AND JERUSALEM

In the previous sections, we have seen how the Rabbinic tradition sought to pacify the more militant or violence-prone aspects of Jewish religious nationalism. It is important to conclude with the other side of the coin that we have thus far neglected: the complementary emphasis on the central-ity of the land and the Temple. For if we are right that the Rabbis focused on converting the *means* of redemption from human to divine agency, it was just as crucial to their project to keep the dream itself alive. Passivity could easily devolve into complacency, quietism into affirmative accept-ance. Thus, we find in Rabbinic literature an equal if opposite thread glo-rifying the land and the Temple and mourning their loss.

Daily prayer was a ready means of imprinting values and rehearsing priorities; although the requests for national restoration relied entirely on divine initiative, the fact remained that Rabbinic prayer had the Jew daily begging for restoration of multiple facets of national life: political, judicial, and religious. Jews were asked to pray toward Jerusalem wherever they were,[44] and not forget Zion's ruins at weddings.[45] Ritual life had the dou-ble duty of conveying the meaningfulness of its present forms, yet simul-taneously communicating the sense of incompleteness and deficiency of current religious life. Prayer was a clear substitute for the sacrifices that were no longer offered, but their language likely emphasized the aspira-tion for the ideal. Rituals of mourning the Temple's and Jerusalem's de-struction evolved, some entering the calendar to commemorate the events and deepen the sense of loss—such as the four fast days on anniversaries of Jerusalem's various tragedies—and others intended to impose restraints on otherwise joyful expressions, such as weddings or building houses.[46] Aggadic, homiletic statements—also dating from this post–Bar Kokhba era, when Judea suffered from severe Jewish demographic reversals—echo this glorification of the land.[47]

For the Rabbis, then, the balance to be struck was delicate: post Bar Kokhba, Jewish life had to go on to quell nationalist and messianic agita-tion; at the same time, daily Jewish life had to feel unfulfilled without a Temple and without Jerusalem, lest people reach a level of complacent ac-ceptance and cease wishing for the ideal's return.[48] That was the sensitive equilibrium many Rabbis of the second century sought to achieve in the wake of Bar Kokhba's Revolt.

CONCLUSION

Since the nineteenth century, scholars have noted the Rabbinic substitution of Torah for land and Temple, seeing it as a consequence of Jerusalem's de-struction in 70 CE. For some, it was a deliberate effort to free Judaism from the shackles of primitive cultism and territorial religion; for others, it was a grudging axiological exchange to prevent the complete collapse of Jew-ish society into despair. In this chapter, we show that in reaction to three cumulative defeats, the Rabbis undertook a more dialectical process of maintaining the axiological centrality of Israel and Temple, yet not allowing that commitment to translate into nationalistic agitation. They achieved that tactful, if fragile, balance by praying for redemption but insisting that it would come about by divine, supernatural intervention as did the exodus from Egypt; effective human agency from here on in was in the realm of punctilious ritual observance.

While I think many of the processes outlined here were Rabbinic reactions to the serial defeats, we must resist claims of Rabbinic prescience.[49] In all likelihood, many, if not all, Rabbis of that time felt that the restoration was indeed imminent: fully one-third of the Mishnah, Rabbinic Judaism's first major text, is devoted to legal material relevant only in Temple times, a proportion that remains stable in the Talmuds of Palestine and Babylonia.

Of course, the very "success" of the Rabbinic strategy may have been a self-fulfilling prophecy; Jewish passivity ultimately became the norm, dampening most militant impulses. Rabbinic Judaism made Jewish life meaningful without a Temple, thus sustaining and even nourishing diaspora centers of Jewish learning.[50] As it turned out the beast, once tamed, became a domesticated household pet, and was unlikely to scare or harm others—until it was retrained. But that is another story.

NOTES

1. Local Canaanite nations are the targets of biblically mandated destruction (e.g., Deuteronomy 7:2, 20:16) as are the Amalekites (Deut. 25:18, 1 Samuel 15). Apocryphal literature foretells the miraculous destruction of the Jews' enemies (2 Ezra, 1 Baruch); in the pseudepigrapha (2 Baruch, 4 Ezra, 3 Enoch), the messiah's functions almost always involve military achievements, as do the apocalyptic visions contained in the Dead Sea Scrolls.

2. See Bickerman (1976, 66–86).

3. Davies (1982, 61–67).

4. Davies (1982, 67).

5. See Millar (1993): "The extensive evidence for the two great Jewish revolts [of 66 and 132] . . . shows unambiguously that both gave rise to regimes which were clearly nationalist and sought the fulfillment of national traditions in independence from Rome" (337).

6. See Schwartz (2002, Part II, esp. chapters 3 and 4).

7. See Dyson (1971, 239–74).

8. Rabbinic tradition acknowledges the utter destruction of a large and wealthy Alexandrian Jewish community by Trajan; see Babylonian Talmud [henceforth BT] Sukkah 51b and variants. Both the Jewish revolt and the severity of the Egyptian response may be examples of religiously motivated violence; see Frankfurter (1992, 203–20, esp. n. 10).

9. Lieberman (1975, Hebrew section, 214–34); Herr (1968, 79–84).

10. This is attested to by Paulus Orosius, a Christian writer. See in general the appendix "Roman and Christian Writings on the Jewish Rebellion of 116–117 and the War of Bar Kokhba," Marks (1994, 209–14).

11. See Gafni (1997, 16).

12. The Rabbinic tradition seems to string the defeats together; see, e.g., Mishnah Sotah 9:14. Moshe Aberbach and David Aberbach (2000) see the Rabbinic emphasis on Hebrew literature and culture as a reaction to failed military and political strategies, although their claim presumes precise dating of Rabbinic sources; see below at n. 49.

13. Some scholars prefer to locate the change in Rabbinic attitudes to the Temple's destruction in 70 CE; see Bokser (1983, 37–61); Stone (1981, 195–204). Given the dating of most Rabbinic sources to the second century and beyond, I believe it is best seen as reaction to the cumulative tragedies of 66–135 CE rather than just to the Temple's destruction.

14. See Jaffee's helpful classification of Jewish commonality and diversity (1997, parts 1 and 4).

15. The traditions of changes implemented by Johanan ben Zakkai immediately after the destruction (e.g., mSukkah 4:1) were likely redacted later to highlight a Rabbinic prescience for the new reality.

16. Conflict on the scale of empires often led to messianic agitation; see Horbury (2003, 286). Certainly, the statement attributed to R. Elazar bar Avina, "If you see kingdoms battling one another, expect the Messiah's feet" (*Bereishit Rabbah* 42), is an echo of this attitude.

17. Cassius Dio claims 50 Judean fortresses and 985 villages were destroyed, and 580,000 Jews were killed in battle. Rabbinic sources give similarly inflated figures; see Palestinian Talmud (=PT) Ta'anit 4:8 (24a–b); BT Gittin 58a, and parallels in *Eikhah Rabbah*. While no doubt exaggerated, these numbers attest to the enormous depopulation in the wake of Bar Kokhba's Revolt.

18. Hezser (1993–94, 234–51); Shaye Cohen (1999, 3:922–90); Schwartz (2002, 110ff).

19. Less likely does not mean impossible. Sectarian Jewish movements in the Middle Ages, particularly messianic ones, occasionally produced their own violence. Gerson Cohen offers a typology of quietistic vs. activist messianism (1967, repr. 1991, 271–98). Elisheva Carlebach has recently challenged Cohen's cultural distinction in "Between History and Hope: Jewish Messianism in Ashkenaz and Sepharad," Third Annual Lecture of the Victor J. Selmanowitz Chair of Jewish History, Touro College, 1998.

20. Silver (1927; repr. 1978); Aescoly (1987).

21. "Victory does not depend on numbers; strength comes from Heaven alone . . . we are fighting for our lives and our religion. Heaven will crush them before our eyes. You need not be afraid of them." 1 Maccabees 3:19, 21.

22. Neusner (1993, 55).

23. BT Sanhedrin 97b. The tale of R. Joshua ben Levi meeting the messiah who announced to him that he would be coming "today"—*if* the Jews will hearken to God's voice (*ibid.*, 98a)—echoes this theme.

24. The view that the messiah would arrive if only Israel punctiliously kept two Sabbaths is attributed to R. Simeon bar Yohai, a mid-second-century tanna (BT Shabbat 118a).

25. BT Ketubot 111a. See Gafni (1997, chap. 3, esp. 72–77), who puts this Rabbinic view in the context of a third-century debate whether to live in Babylonia or the Land of Israel.

26. Many of the views about the conditions for martyrdom are attributed to mid-second-century tannaim and early amoraim. See BT Sanhedrin 73ab.

This shift—from martyrdom for nationalism to martyrdom for religion and observance of the law—is not so radical. Both religions and nations (or nation-building) are meaning-making entities, and thus rather uniquely provide meaning to both the killing of others and to self-sacrifice by helping members achieve a profound sense of fellowship. See Anderson (1991).

27. See Elazar's final speech as recounted by Josephus in *The Jewish War, Book VII* 8:6.

28. See Oegema (1998, 306), on the inability to systematize eschatological and messianic expressions.

29. BT Bava Kamma 60b.

30. BT Sanhedrin, 96b–99a.

31. In Babylonia, where we presume messianic agitation was minimal, early amoraim seem to take a less supernaturalistic approach to the messianic age; see Samuel's comment (BT Berakhot 34b). See also Neusner (1993).

32. Bokser (1983, 77f.) argues that post-70, the early tannaitic tradition (m*Pesahim* 10:4) that on Passover night, one expounds the biblical section of Deuteronomy 26:5–10 ("until the end of the entire portion") was not followed in practice, as the final two verses of that portion that referred to entry into the land were too painful to bring up at the annual commemoration of national birth, given the contrasting political reality. In the same vein, not reciting these verses also had the effect of dampening the Jewish desire to return to regain control of the land, particularly around holidays, when religious emotions normally run high.

33. Juergensmeyer (2000, 163).

34. Juergensmeyer (2000, 236). The work of René Girard is cited there, and deserves more treatment than I can give it here.

35. Marks 1994, *The Image of Bar Kokhba in Traditional Jewish Literature*, chapter 1. He concludes, "Readers are advised by both traditions to heed the guidance of the sages who, in the first case, expose the impostor's lies, and in the second, provide more effective leadership. . . . In this way both traditions about Bar Kokhba ask people to look beyond him, beyond his falsehood or his failings, and turn their eyes to heaven, from which alone would come redemption and the power to attain it" (56).

36. In an admittedly late midrashic collection (*Midrash Shocher Tov*), we find the following statement attributed to the late-second-century tanna R. Jonathan: "All who want to appease a king or ruler and does not know their ways or strategies, should study this portion [of Jacob's handling of Esau]." Similarly, *Breishit Rabbah* 75:6 presents the Galilean patriarch Judah I modeling himself on Jacob as he sent a communication to the Roman authorities.

37. Heinemann (1984) argues that topics addressed in prayer were standardized far before their actual liturgical formulation.

38. For instance, in all its variants, the blessing for rebuilding Jerusalem makes no mention of human agency in bringing this about. See Heinemann (1984, chap. 2, and esp. 48–51). Contrast the earlier prayer for Chanukah, "You delivered the strong *into the hands* of the weak," formulated according to scholars in the late Second Temple period.

39. See Bialik's and Ravnitsky's *Sefer Ha-aggadah*, under "peace." For a rather complete catalog, see *Otsar ha-Aggadah*, s.v. *shalom*.

40. Rabbinic tradition (BT Berakhot 48b) locates the origin of the fourth blessing after eating, *Ha-tov veha-meitiv* ("Who is good and Who does good"), in the Romans' permission to bury the corpses after Bar Kokhba's defeat. The blessing's motif of divine benevolence may have been intended to promote a quietistic counterbalance to the nationalistic themes of the second and third blessings.

41. Davies (1982, 61–67).

42. Davies' work details these strategies. Some communities, such as the Judean Desert communities, viewed the existing Temple and priesthood as corrupt and abandoned Jerusalem, thus rendering them a "diaspora" community of sorts. See also Gafni (1997, chap. 3), for a similar discussion of Jewish identity outside of Israel.

43. See Gafni (1997, *passim*), who claims that Babylonian Jewry subsequently took advantage of this trend to free itself of Palestinian religio-political hegemony.

44. Anonymous tannaitic source, BT Berakhot 30a.

45. The texts of the blessings at a wedding are attributed to the early amoraic period; see BT Ketubot 7b–8a.

46. Tannaitic source attributed to R. Joshua (early-mid-second century), Tosefta Sotah 15:5; BT Bava Batra 60b.

47. Gafni (1997, 70ff.) claims that this ideological glorification of the land was intended to reverse the trend and encourage Jews practically to settle there. The historical reality, in my view, may or may not have required this emphasis; the interest of many Rabbis to maintain an ideal of the land's centrality, however impractical, warranted promoting this ideal.

48. This might account for the increasing ascetic severity surrounding commemoration of the Temple's destruction throughout the Middle Ages. For instance, the original tannaitic limitation on meat and wine during the meal before the fast of the ninth of Av evolved into a weeklong restriction among segments of Jewry. As the Jewish community accepted the Temple's loss as normal, rituals intended to elicit appreciation of the loss had to deepen.

49. Moshe and David Aberbach (2000) are prepared to see in the Rabbinic reaction to Bar Kokhba a more complete break with the past and an embrace of a more radical form of cultural nationalism centered on the Hebrew language. I resist such grand statements; the Rabbinic project was multifaceted and of significant duration, and it is unwise to ascribe to so short a historical period the full range of activities among Rabbis for generations to come.

50. See Gafni (1997, 120f).

4

Violent Yearnings for the Kingdom of God: Münster's Militant Anabaptism

Charles A. McDaniel, Jr.

In February 1534 the city of Münster, Westphalia (present-day Germany) was overtaken by a zealous group of Anabaptists who forcibly expelled or "re-baptized" most of its Roman Catholic and Lutheran citizens and proclaimed the city to be the "New Jerusalem." Despite its biblical foundation, the "Anabaptist kingdom" of Münster was a violent, often decadent, and short-lived phenomenon. Efforts to reclaim the city for the Holy Roman Empire precipitated acts of unimaginable cruelty by Catholics and Anabaptists alike. When Münster was retaken by the forces of Prince-Bishop Franz von Waldeck in June 1535, several hundred of its inhabitants were slaughtered. Three of the rebellion's most radical leaders were later tortured and executed to dramatize Münster's "punishment";[1] their bodies were cut into pieces and entombed in iron cages, replicas of which have been suspended from the tower of St. Lambert's Church until the present day.

This chapter assesses the religious and sociological influences that prompted the Anabaptists of Münster to reject the commitment to nonviolence of their theological patriarch Melchior Hoffman and turn to the sword for preservation of domestic order and in defense against their external adversaries. Central to this inquiry are the roles of prophecy and eschatology in instigating aggressive behavior among adherents. Violent insurrection has been a rare event in Anabaptist history despite centuries of persecution. Thus, it is intriguing that the conflict at Münster was accompanied by a distinct shift in the millennial thinking of the city's leadership and by a politicization of institutions uncommon to Anabaptism. Münster offers a unique opportunity to assess whether these two factors may be decisive in mobilizing a religious community toward violence.

Emphasis on the internal life of the Anabaptist community is not intended to minimize the egregious acts perpetrated against religious "sects" by both Catholic and Protestant authorities in the Reformation era. Acts of religious violence are rarely reducible to individual causes nor are they singularly attributable to particular "sides." Identification of the probable causes of this atrocity in the pages that follow presupposes that a factor in the violent confrontation was the religious and legal ethos of sixteenth-century German culture that made adult baptism a capital offense. Yet the barbaric response to that ethos by Münster's theocratic order forced social interactions to a plane beyond reason. Governance by esoteric and eschatological prophecies fostered a rising tide of violent behavior within the community and an equally brutal reaction from those who desired to see it eradicated.

RISE OF THE ANABAPTIST KINGDOM AT MÜNSTER

Anabaptism is a form of Christianity that emerged from what has been described as the "Radical Reformation" of the sixteenth century in order to distinguish it from the "magisterial" reform movement inspired by notable figures such as Martin Luther and John Calvin.[2] The name "Anabaptists" or "re-baptizers" was derisively applied to this group to signify one of their defining doctrines—that the sacrament of baptism should only be administered to "true believers" who have reached the age of understanding. Anabaptists rejected infant baptism as practiced in the Roman Catholic Church and in the Lutheran and Reformed Protestant churches.[3] Anabaptism was also characterized by its separatist inclinations and, ironically, given the events at Münster, its pacifism.

Anabaptists condemned the magisterial reformers' perceived theological accommodations to the social order and sought to establish a separate identity vis-à-vis state and religious institutions, which led to near universal hatred of this group. Official condemnation of Anabaptism was issued from the Second Diet of Speyer (1529), which originated the term *Protestant* to describe those Lutheran princes who "protested" against renewed oppression by Holy Roman Emperor Charles V. Despite the enmity between Catholics and Lutherans at the Diet, they did achieve agreement on one issue: the need to exterminate Anabaptists. An edict, to which both sides agreed, stated:

Every Anabaptist and rebaptized man and woman of the age of reason . . . shall be condemned and brought from natural life into death by fire, sword, and the like, according to the person, without proceeding by the inquisition of the spiritual judges; and let the same [punishment be inflicted on the] pseudo-preachers, instigators, vagabonds, and tumultuous inciters of the said vice of Anabaptism.[4]

Although isolated "inquisitions" of Anabaptists by Catholic and Protestant authorities were conducted after 1529, the edict's implication that *this* heresy did not require formal trial by "spiritual judges" is intriguing in the context of this volume. Other heresies, like anti-trinitarianism, were aggressively prosecuted through the formality of inquisition, as in the famous case of Michael Servetus, who was pursued by John Calvin himself, along with Catholic inquisitors.[5] One explanation for this avoidance of theological engagement with Anabaptists was because their theology, according to Alister McGrath, "radicalized" the *sola scriptura* principle of the Reformation that Luther had initiated.[6] Extreme biblical literalism and unwillingness to "play by the rules of reason" in theological debate led Anabaptists to go beyond traditional bounds for such discussions, often calling into question the legitimacy of long-established institutions. The Anabaptists' rejection of state authority and calls for a Christianized social order distinguished them as more than theological innovators. As Hans-Jürgen Goertz has observed, "All in all, the Anabaptist theocracy saw itself as a 'counter-world' of the old Empire," which was viewed by imperial and Lutheran authorities alike "as a provocation of the entire society."[7]

The basis for Münster's Anabaptist theocracy is found in the writing and teaching of Melchior Hoffman, a furrier and evangelical lay preacher who visited Wittenberg and was influenced by Luther's teachings in the early 1520s.[8] By 1530, however, Hoffman had become disillusioned by what he perceived as the growing conservatism of the Lutheran reform movement. He traveled extensively throughout Scandinavia and northern Germany, preaching a mystical form of evangelical Christianity and wearing out his welcome in cities like Stockholm and Lübeck. Hoffman's theology was apocalyptic and radically subjective, as influenced by "spiritualists" such as Hans Denck and Sebastian Franck during his days in the theologically liberal and free imperial city of Strasbourg. Strasbourg was a melting pot of ideas authored by some of the most controversial figures of the Reformation, including Andreas Karlstadt, Michael Sattler, Pilgram Marpeck, and Balthasar Hubmaier.[9] However, Strasbourg took a conservative turn in the spring of 1530, ironically under the influence of the famed ecumenist and reformer Martin Bucer, and the radicalism of Hoffman and others fell out of favor with city authorities. In response, Hoffman left Strasbourg for the northern provinces, where his emotive preaching and mass baptisms in places like Emden and Amsterdam earned him fame as the "father of Dutch Anabaptism."[10]

But Hoffman's fame and theological radicalism had adverse consequences. He remained controversial, publishing tracts on baptism and the "sword" of government until his arrest by Strasbourg authorities in May 1533.[11] Historian Cornelius Krahn notes the significance of Hoffman's arrest and incarceration, as two diverse factions emerged that professed to follow his teachings. One group was largely pacifist and continued Hoffman's emphasis on a life of Christian discipline, "enduring all suffering for Christ until his expected second coming." The other group was led by Jan Matthijs and Jan van Leiden, two followers who were less inclined to Hoffman's pacifism and determined to help usher in the new millennium.[12]

This division between militant and peaceful factions would have fateful consequences. As the end of the appointed year 1533 approached, the Dutchman Matthijs assumed leadership of the Anabaptists. Matthijs recognized Münster as a city culturally predisposed to radicalism; its Catholic hegemony already was being challenged by the strong Lutheran presence on the city council. Moreover, a radical theological foundation for the arrival of the "prophet" Matthijs already had been laid by Bernard Rothmann, a native Münsterite who had also been involved in the religious ferment at Strasbourg.[13] These conditions inspired Matthijs to relocate the setting for the New Jerusalem from Strasbourg to Münster and to complete his vision by reappointing the date for the Second Coming to Easter 1534.

One of the first signs of an imminent confrontation at Münster was a change in the religious demographics of the city, which had begun even prior to Matthijs's arrival. Despite attempts by Bishop von Waldeck to control commerce and population movements, hundreds of Anabaptists arrived in Münster in 1532–1533, lured by leaflets authored by Rothmann and printed by local Anabaptist merchant Bernard Knipperdolling.[14] The messages espoused in these tracts were social and economic as much as theological. Private ownership was condemned as divisive and contrary to God's will: "God had made all things in common, as today we can still enjoy air, fire, rain, and the sun in common, and whatever else some thieving, tyrannical man cannot grasp for himself."[15] Münster's Catholic and Lutheran citizens, increasingly apprehensive at the growing power of the Anabaptists, left the city. Stayer cites Karl-Heinz Kirchoff's estimate that as many as two thousand non-Anabaptist citizens exited the city, while an influx of some twenty-five hundred Anabaptists took their places.[16]

This religious recomposition of Münster resulted in a transition of political power. The Anabaptists applied sufficient pressure to force new elections for the city council in March 1533. The result of that election was a split between the Anabaptists and a more moderate Lutheran faction that sought a peaceful solution to the city's problems. No peaceful solution to Münster's increasingly chaotic social situation was forthcoming, however. The bishop, who had rightful imperial claim to Münster, was increasingly angered by Rothmann's appeals to the "dispossessed" and the displacement of the city's Catholic citizens by "religious radicals."[17] One last attempt was made to mediate a truce at the bishop's palace at Telgte in February 1534. Von Waldeck, however, was so angered by the roguish delegation dispatched by the city council that he turned them away.[18] According to Anthony Arthur, the citizens of Münster "reacted gleefully to the assurance, at last, of an attack by the bishop that would confirm their apocalyptic expectations."[19]

Adding to the inevitability of carnage at Münster was the presence of lansquenets— "soulless" mercenaries who offered their killing services to the highest bidder.[20] They were employed on both sides, in particular by von Waldeck, who collected revenues for their payment through application of a tax on his subjects. Lansquenets were also present among the Anabaptist forces, having been secured previously by the Lutheran-dominated city council that feared an attack by the bishop as early as 1532. Moreover, there is evidence that some of von Waldeck's mercenaries defected to the cause of the Anabaptists when the bishop was unable to pay them.[21]

The majority of Münsterites who fought and died, however, did so at the behest of their religious leaders and not for material reward. Matthijs's prophecies were aided by social and historical events that gave them legitimacy. Stayer observes a turning point in the continuing cultural revolution at Münster that established Matthijs as a prophet and leader of the Anabaptist kingdom whose visions were worthy of ultimate sacrifices. This "political miracle" was the dissolution of Lutheran control of the city council and the emergence of the Anabaptist-dominated United Guild as the principal political authority in Münster in February 1534.[22]

Once the political reformation was complete, Matthijs initiated the expulsion of those Münsterites who refused to be rebaptized. He also issued prophecies that laid the foundation for a tyrannical monarchy founded on Old Testament principles. Hermann von Kerssenbrock, who was said to have witnessed events at Münster, testified to the brutality of Matthijs's reign. In one case, a burgher named Hubert Ruscher claimed that Matthijs was possessed of the devil, an accusation for which Ruscher was executed. Two notable citizens stepped forward to protest Ruscher's "execution without trial" and were promptly thrown into prison.[23] These acts were typical of the severity and arbitrariness of justice in the New Jerusalem.

Less than two months after Münster's political miracle, however, Matthijs faced a siege force assembled by the bishop that numbered in the thousands. On Easter Sunday 1534, Matthijs set out to realize his prophetic dreams. Wielding sword and lance, he led a small band into the besieging army, who obliged his valor by killing and beheading him. The severed head was supposedly paraded about by one of the bishop's mounted knights in mockery of those trapped inside, before being placed on a pole in front of the city gates.[24]

The death of Matthijs made room for the rise of Jan van Leiden as the sole prophet and unchallenged leader of the Münsterites. Van Leiden's status was reinforced on August 31, 1534, when, subsequent to a battle in which von Waldeck's forces were repulsed, Johann Dusentschuer acted on a vision and his interpretation of passages in Jeremiah and Ezekiel to proclaim van Leiden the "King of the New Zion."[25] King Jan instituted various practices that strained the sensibilities and social mores of the Anabaptist community. The "Christian communism" that was established by Matthijs was radically expanded under van Leiden, as citizens were told to bring possessions other than bare necessities to the city's warehouses for distribution. However, what amounted to a "vow of poverty" for most Münsterites did not extend to van Leiden or his "court."[26] Wealth and power were disproportionately concentrated among members of the "old order."[27] Moreover, this philosophy of communal sharing extended even to wives, as the handsome King Jan instituted polygamy as biblically ordained. Van Leiden took sixteen brides himself, the first being Matthijs's widow, Divara, whom he named as his "queen" in reinforcing his prophetic heritage. Terror repressed dissension and heightened apocalyptic expectation. At least one woman was executed for "refusing the marital duty" and van Leiden himself beheaded one of his wives for "disobedience."[28]

Of the aberrant social norms that developed in Münster during the siege, polygamy was the most contentious. Henry Mollenheck, a leader of one of the guilds and a respected citizen of the community, determined that polygamy exceeded the bounds of prophetic license and led around two hundred men in armed rebellion. On the evening of July 30, 1534, Mollenheck and those sympathetic with his cause stormed Münster's City Hall and captured Münster's triumvirate: van Leiden, Rothmann, and Knipperdolling.[29] The rebel force had no plan for reinstituting order, however, and even allowed the imprisoned leaders to appeal to followers from their cells. Not long after the capture of van Leiden and his court, a force of six hundred "loyalists" to King Jan converged on the center of the city with cannon and threatened to level it. They stormed the *Rathaus* and captured one hundred and twenty rebels, condemning forty-seven without trial and forcing the rest to prove that they had no role in instigating the rebellion. The condemned men were executed in the most brutal fashion; many had limbs cut off before being beheaded.[30]

Such brutality was applied not only to seditious persons, but to any Münsterite who violated the austere moral code instituted during the reign of van Leiden. The new king replaced the city council with the Council of Twelve Elders who "issued a decree stating their intention to govern according to the scriptures and citing scripture in an enumeration of crimes worthy of death. These were: (1) blasphemy, (2) disrespect for the government, (3) disrespect for parents, (4) disrespect for the head of the household, (5) adultery, (6) fornication, (7) avarice, (8) theft, (9) fraudulent business transactions, (10) lying, (11) gossiping, (12) quarrelsomeness, and (13) sedition."[31] This moral severity necessitated swift and ferocious enforcement. Executions were often carried out ceremoniously to demonstrate the means by which the "moral purity" of Münster would be imposed.

King Jan's brutal regime required the persistence of supernatural appeals for its legitimacy, much of which was provided by Bernhard Rothmann, whose calculations for the "end times" served to nourish the community's apocalyptic expectations. Rothmann perceived the "Restitution" as having begun under the magisterial reformers, but these "learned men" had abandoned the cause that the Münsterites were now called to complete.

Rothmann considered that the Church had been in a second "Babylonian Captivity" since the time of the apostles—a period of sustained corruption and decadence. He calculated the modern period of captivity at twenty times that during the time of Elijah, which was seventy years. According to Stayer, "Since Jesus was thirty-three or thirty-four at the time of the ascension, and since the true Church had lasted one hundred years and the fall of the Church for fourteen hundred years, the logic of the numbers put the Restitution around 1533 or 1534."[32]

Yet prophetic vision often clashed with the more immediate desire of some Münsterites to survive the bishop's siege. Van Leiden himself was caught up in the confusion of vision and reality, at times speaking rather meekly about the Anabaptists' wish to live as a society apart, without interference from other authorities, and, other times, talking aggressively about plans to expand the millennial kingdom.[33] He apparently reacted with sincere humility on the occasion of his "crowning" as King of the New Jerusalem, "throwing himself to the ground in prayerful humility."[34] In one episode during the siege, the bishop's forces attacked the Münsterites and attempted to enter the city. The Anabaptist army resisted them easily and won an overwhelming victory; yet, rather than pursuing the confused and retreating force in what likely was a decisive moment in the siege, the Münsterites were content to return to their city singing Luther's great hymn, "A Mighty Fortress Is Our God."[35] On another occasion, however, van Leiden "called into question Münster's status as the New Jerusalem by toying with the idea of abandoning the city for an

armed invasion of the Netherlands."[36] These alternating periods of inde-
cisiveness and visions of grandeur suggest that religious violence may at
times *require* an element of irrationality to sustain its energy and legitimacy. If van Leiden had appeared too calculated in his approach to the
war, it might have changed his image from the prophetic King of Münster
to a mere political manipulator and even jeopardized his prophetic hold
over the people.

Ceremonialism, especially as enacted through public execution, became increasingly important in binding the community to an ethos of
collective terror. After the Mollenheck uprising over the issue of
polygamy, any citizen who wished to participate in the executions of the
rebels was allowed to do so. By Stayer's account, "The King, too, performed executions, so as to make his right of the Sword unmistakably
vivid. In the last fearsome days of the siege the King's personal wielding
of the executioner's sword made Anabaptist terror so tangible that practically everyone preferred almost certain death at the hands of the enemy
to the risks of trying to organize an internal uprising."[37] Thus, Stayer perceives a community manipulated by terror and prophecy against its own
survival instincts.

In June 1535, after a siege of some sixteen months and the associated
deprivations that had decimated the population, the bishop's army entered Münster through the complicity of Anabaptist guards.[38] Mass
killings occurred over the next two days as both male and female Anabaptists were brought to the cathedral square, condemned, and executed. Three leaders of the rebellion, van Leiden, Knipperdolling, and
Bernhard Krechting, were tortured over several days with tongs heated to
glowing over coal fires. Executioners ended the leaders' lives by plunging
similarly heated daggers into their hearts.[39] Many of the native Münsterites who wished to remain in the city were offered pardons in exchange for renouncing their Anabaptist beliefs. However, one source suggests that few took advantage of the bishop's "magnanimity"; one year
after the city's reclamation for Catholicism, only 216 citizens who had re-
canted their "heresies" remained.[40]

THEOLOGY AS CATALYST TO REBELLION:
FROM PACIFISM TO BLOODLUST

Critical in Münster's growing appreciation for the legitimacy of violence
was the transformation of apocalyptic vision. Hoffman's millennial theology asserted that the "preaching of two witnesses, Enoch and Elijah," was
the extent of human participation in the Second Coming. Rothmann, on
the other hand, envisioned that the "elect" would be involved in "the

physical restoration of the kingdom of God on earth,"[41] as Münster's leaders assumed the role of Old Testament kings and prophets.

For both Rothmann and Matthijs, true believers served as *catalysts* in the advent of the Second Coming, differing markedly from the tacit involvement of Christians in the apocalypse noted by Hoffman. One observes a *layering* of apocalyptic doctrine that provided divine justification for violence. Rothmann validated the human element in the apocalypse while the "two Jans" offered the Old Testament archetypes by which it might be carried out. Once Matthijs assumed an Old Testament persona, his followers could envision the warlike nature of the ancient Israelites, and this collective self-image eclipsed the New Testament symbolism employed by Hoffman in Strasbourg. Van Leiden later identified Münster as the New Zion and himself as a Davidic king to carry forward this vision. Although Matthijs's suicidal charge into the bishop's forces undoubtedly disillusioned some Münsterites, it may have heightened expectations and the identification of a prominent role for Münster due to the sheer drama with which it was enacted.

One might suspect that prophetic failure, in combination with the moral austerity that was forced on the community by its theocrats, engendered internal dissension. However, Otthein Rammstedt believes that the *routinization* and *institutionalization* of all aspects of life in Münster reinforced its social and political structure within a pervasive climate of fear:

> Formerly spontaneous, extraordinary events became ordinary phenomena, became ritualized, and all that remained was fear for one's own life. To preserve their power positions and to prevent the disintegration of the congregation, the ruling minority regulated the life of the Anabaptists completely, making the life style of all uniform and confronting the subjects with the realities of war. The houses had to be left open, the style of clothing was prescribed, the days of the week were renamed, and the names of infants were set.[42]

Prophecy and ritualistic violence became communal expectations, as did the common ownership of property, uniformity in attire, and ultimately, although more begrudgingly, polygamous marriage.

In such an atmosphere, van Leiden's ability to "shock" the population into submission became more difficult. Ultimately, he resorted to the rather arbitrary execution of a fellow Anabaptist at the conclusion of a mass gathering of Münsterites. Even this "terrorizing act," Rammstedt concludes, "was a socializing factor, since through the counter impulse which was thus created the integration of the Anabaptists was heightened."[43] Moreover, the layering of prophecy resulted in an escalation and sensationalizing of the prophetic message that culminated in other acts of ritualistic violence. Jan van Leiden received one of his visions at a feast following a victory in which some of the bishop's soldiers were captured. He had one of the prisoners brought to the table where he was ceremoniously wined and dined. Jan announced his vision to those assembled, saying that he was to behead the prisoner and suffer the same fate himself if he had not freed Münster from the bishop's army by Easter 1535.[44] That vision would later be "revised" when it could not be fulfilled, disappointing the community's apocalyptic expectations.

Krahn perceives the scriptural reorientation of the basis for the entire community from the New Testament Christo-centrism of Melchior Hoffman to the New Jerusalem of Jan van Leiden as critical in fueling the fire of militant rebellion. This shift resulted from Jan van Leiden's "ambition to rule the world"; yet, while the vision remained eschatological, it was transformed from a New Testament orientation based on the Second Coming to a "self-centered messianic ambition" centering on the formation of the New Israel. The result was what Krahn describes as "a militant theocratic and secularized chiliasm."[45]

But does chiliasm in and of itself account for the turn to violence? One might expect "extreme" behavior as the anticipation of the millennium grew; however, why would extreme pacifism and even greater piety not be *as likely* or even a *more likely* outcome than hostility? In answering these questions, the differing roles for the human element in respective visions of the Second Coming articulated by Hoffman and Rothmann again appear significant, as was the evolving nature of Rothmann's apocalyptic theology. Rothmann's second theological tract, *Eyne Restitution*, produced in October 1534, offered a guidebook to the restoration of the church of the apostles. But it was followed in December of that year with *Van der Wrake (Concerning Revenge)*, which issued an apologetic for active defense of the Church.[46] According to Krahn, "This constituted a significant point in the development of the Melchiorite Anabaptist movement which had a very unusual record of suffering without revenge. Besieged by a strong army, the 'children of Jacob' now felt called not only to defend themselves but also to help God punish the 'children of Esau.'"[47] By the winter of 1534, Rothmann's theology had evolved to a position that justified communal aggression.

Without the theological sanction provided by Rothmann and reinforced through the prophetic visions of Matthijs and van Leiden, it is doubtful that the community would have strayed so far from its religious roots and the pacifism of Melchior Hoffman. However, once the theological basis for human involvement in the Second Coming had been established, almost any act, no matter how brutal or deviant from social norms, was justifiable.

SEPARATISM AND POLITICIZATION

A separatist religious community's existence apart from mainstream civilization often is perceived as a challenge to the established social order. Vogler cites the work of Hans Hillerbrand, Claus-Peter Clasen, and Hans-Jürgen Goertz in noting that separatism alone engenders hostility for its perception as both an "insult" and "threat" to the wider culture.[48] Sixteenth-century Anabaptism's separatist inclinations resulted from the desire to eschew the moral stain left by more than a millennium of Roman corruptions of the Church and the disappointingly incomplete program of restoration instituted by the magisterial reformers.

The attempt by Münster's Anabaptists to carve out a religiously pure society by force was a luxury possessed not even by German princes, who tried mightily to sustain religious homogeneity but were forced to deal with the messiness of nascent religious pluralism in the sixteenth century.[49] Leaders of the major German principalities may have resented the Münsterites' coercive and wholly impractical solution to the problem of religious conflict that plagued European society. Similarly, Luther and other magisterial reformers detested Anabaptists for the reason that Catholics often portrayed the situation at Münster as the inevitable *political* result of *religious* reform.

Perhaps the most unique characteristic of Anabaptist Münster was its political structure. Anabaptism's traditional aversion to state institutions has contributed to largely apolitical societies, extending to modern-day Amish and Mennonite communities. The political aspirations and institutional development of Münster, however, were its distinguishing features[50] and became integral to the conflict. Anabaptist political power commenced by attaining dominance of the city council, but its ultimate designs were more grandiose. And while it never achieved his vision, Jan van Leiden's "kingdom" evolved into something more than a figment of his imagination. The Council of the Elders that exerted strict legal and moral control over the city was dissolved in response to another of van Leiden's visions and power was transferred to his courtiers.[51] King Jan continued Münster's political transformation by appointing twelve dukes who would reign over various parts of Europe after the Anabaptists conquered their Catholic and Lutheran adversaries. Vogler offers a glimpse of Anabaptist Münster as a political entity: "Jan van Leiden as king had sword, scepter, and orb carried before him, a striking expression of the royal dignity he claimed. These and other attributes, on the one hand, showed Münster to be a theocracy, and, on the other, characterized it as a secular order with its own insignia, coat of arms, seals, and currency."[52]

This politicization of Münster contributed to an identity that posed an institutional threat to the established order of the Holy Roman Empire. Münster was a fortified city shaped by a biblical vision that combined the sixteenth-century institutions that were gaining strength and most directly threatening to imperial power: the city council and the trade guild.[53] Although the council was sacrificed for van Leiden's monarchical dreams, Münster continued to pose a rival political structure capable of emulation in neighboring cities and principalities. That threat is evidenced by a letter from von Waldeck to Philip of Hesse on January 20, 1535, stating that the rebellion would "make some progress with the common man and in other towns of our and neighboring countries."[54] The bishop's opinion that the effects of the Münster rebellion could not be contained within the city likely found a sympathetic ear on the part of Philip and other nobles to whom the bishop appealed. The German Peasants' War of 1525 was still vivid in the German memory for the cultural convulsion it precipitated and the carnage it inspired.[55] Moreover, peasant rebellion was associated with Anabaptism through the influence of charismatic "spiritualists" like Thomas Müntzer.[56] This collective memory was reenergized by the formation of tangible and replicable political institutions in Münster, which undoubtedly amplified the perceived threat of Anabaptist society in Europe.

SOCIOLOGICAL CAUSES AND CONSEQUENCES

Much of the older scholarship held that the Münster tragedy resulted more from socioeconomic than religious conflict as disenfranchised masses were stirred to resistance by religious zealots. In this view, the Anabaptists of Münster were merely third in a line of rebellious classes that turned to violence out of desperation to locate their place in postmedieval European society. Both the German Peasants' War of 1525 and the Knights' Rebellion of 1523 involved similarly disenfranchised groups that came to believe that violent resistance was the only means of collective self-preservation.

Karl-Heinz Kirchoff's studies have discredited this "impoverished" view of Münster, suggesting that its class structure and distribution of wealth were remarkably normal, vis-à-vis that of comparable German cities in the period.[57] Another interesting social dynamic in Münster's transformation that depreciates the socioeconomic view of the tragedy is observed in the contrast of the town's two convents. Historian Jonathan Grieser notes that Überwasser, a nunnery that housed women from the nobility, became more radicalized and supportive of the Anabaptist cause than its less affluent and socially inferior sister convent, Niesing.[58]

Grieser's observation serves as a caution against stereotyping religious radicalism and violence as smoke screens that mask underlying social tensions. The fact that the nuns of the lower social caste were generally more supportive of the status quo in Münster than their more affluent sisters at Überwasser suggests that, at least in this instance, social and economic rivalries may have been less important than other factors in the violence. This observation may temper somewhat Bruce Lincoln's contention in chapter 13, that the core of religious conflict is competition for scarce resources.

The fact that *some* association of religious radicalism with socioeconomic factors appears to have existed may be significant. But to explore the possible sociological causes of the Münster tragedy it is necessary to go beyond the city's walls. For a brief period, roughly 1527 to 1545, Anabaptism appears to have become markedly more aggressive in its relations to state authority and even other religious groups. Perhaps this is unsurprising when one considers the events at Speyer in 1529. Yet, in one notable event two years prior to the pronouncement of damnation at the Diet, a group of "sword bearing" Anabaptists (*Schwertler*) led by Balthasar Hubmaier took control of the town of Nikolsburg, in the present-day Czech Republic, imprisoning and eventually expelling many of the "pacifist" Anabaptists (*Stäbler*) who resided there. Hubmaier went on to institute a "state church" form of Anabaptism not unlike that which would later arise in Münster.[59]

Adding weight to the possible existence of social factors in the Münster uprising are the observations of historian Gary Waite that the period of 1535 to 1545 witnessed an abnormal degree of affinity by Dutch nobles for unorthodox religion, in particular Anabaptism.[60] Waite believes that this was spawned by the administrative centralization of Dutch society by the ruling Spanish Hapsburgs under Charles V. Especially interesting is Waite's observation that while, "on the whole [the Dutch nobility] did not suffer economically—signs of discontent among them were widespread."[61] This alliance between the nobility and Anabaptists even resulted in attacks on several Hapsburg towns in the Netherlands during this period. Two particular noblemen who participated with radical groups of Anabaptists in the attacks, Pieter van den Binchorst and Jan van Batenburg, had previously lost their respective positions as a bailiff and a mayor of Dutch towns following disputes with the Hapsburg government.[62] This fact seems consistent with Grieser's observation of the more intense religious radicalism by the socially affluent nuns at Überwasser vis-à-vis their counterparts at Niesing. It may signify that individuals who previously held some standing in society but become socially dislocated are often more predisposed to religious violence than individuals who are entrenched in the lower classes.

The work of Kirchoff and others in discrediting strongly socioeconomic explanations for the Münster tragedy opened the door to more in-depth analysis. Eschatology, social dislocation, the rise of pluralism, a pervasive climate of religious intolerance, and other as yet unknown factors all undoubtedly combined in some way to precipitate the carnage. Such an alienating combination of forces had the effect of convincing Münsterites that they had "nothing to lose" in their confrontations with the outside world. It remains for researchers to clarify these relationships in furthering our knowledge into the nature of religious violence.

CONCLUSION

Pervasive hostility toward Anabaptists in the sixteenth century and mainstream society's rationalizations for violence against them undoubtedly contributed to the carnage at Münster. Had the Holy Roman Empire and Lutheran principalities offered Anabaptists some refuge from the persistence of persecution, this tragedy may never have occurred. Yet *twentieth-century* tragedies suggest that prophetic and charismatic religious communities will continue to exist on the fringe of society and challenge traditional values based on unique theological formulations. It is just as certain that established social orders will continue to view such groups with suspicion and, often, hostility.

Münster was unique, however, in ways that illuminate specific characteristics of religious violence. Eschatology guided the city's political transformation and led to an escalation of violent behavior, suggesting a relationship between the extent of a religious community's "politicization" and the potential for conflict. Institutional development creates the vision of an alternative society that may amplify eschatological or other potentially contentious values that are already present in a group's theological core. It also establishes a more observable threat to outsiders, presenting a rival structure toward which external agents may target aggression. Institutionalization of prophecy and eschatology at Münster contributed to apocalyptic obsession, social volatility, and, ultimately, brutality by a Christian group that is today characterized by its pacifism. Recognition of these facts and the willingness to learn the lessons of history might help to lessen the frequency and magnitude of religious conflicts that, to this point, have been defining characteristics of Western culture.

NOTES

1. Estimates of the total number killed when Bishop von Waldeck retook the city on June 25–27, 1535, range from three to seven hundred. For more on the final days of Anabaptist Münster, see Krahn (1968, 158–64).

2. Stayer, Packull, and Deppermann (1975, 83–121) have argued for three distinct sources of origin for Anabaptism in the sixteenth century: Switzerland (Swiss Brethren), South Germany, and the Netherlands/North Germany (Melchiorites).

3. Anabaptists reject any biblical basis for infant baptism, which is a practice inconsistent with their desire to return Christianity to a more pristine form as that found in the "Church of the Apostles." For more on the institution of believers' baptism in Anabaptist communities, see Krahn (1968, 92–101).

4. Quoted in Arthur (1999, 10).

5. Ozment (1980, 369–71).

6. McGrath (1999, 9–10).

7. Goertz (1980); cited in Vogler (1988, 100).

8. Noll (1973, 48–49).

9. Noll (1973, 87–88).

10. See Krahn (1968, 87–91). Hoffman was jailed in Strasbourg in 1533 where he spent the final ten years of his life and was never able to visit Münster after the takeover. This too may shed light on the violence, to which Hoffman seemingly never would have consented. That Hoffman's pacifist theology required articulation by his followers in Münster implies that successive interpretation of theological ideas risks the possibility that critical principles may become "lost in translation."

11. Krahn (1968, 102–7).

12. Krahn continues by noting that "as far as [Hoffman] was concerned, he never approved of militant chiliasm, but expected that the second coming of Christ would usher in the Kingdom of God on earth." See Krahn (1968, 118).

13. Krahn (1968, 122–23).

14. See Arthur (1999, 21, 23).

15. Rothmann pamphlet quoted in Arthur (1999, 23).

16. Kirchoff (1963, 24); cited in Stayer, "Christianity in One City" (1988, 128).

17. Arthur (1999, 24–26) and Vogler (1988, 114–15).

18. Arthur (1999, 26–27).

19. Arthur (1999, 27).

20. Lansquenets, renowned for their drunkenness and lack of allegiance to particular religious or political causes, were also employed by Holy Roman Emperor Charles V in the sacking of Rome in 1527. Charles was angry with Pope Clement VII because of the latter's "lenient" treatment of Charles's rival Francis I, King of France. Clement was forced to flee for his life through Roman tunnels to escape the siege. See The Biblical Studies Foundation website at http://www.bible.org/docs/history/schaff/vol7/schaf183.htm; accessed on April 14, 2004.

21. Stayer (1972, 258–59).

22. Stayer (1988, 121–22).

23. H. von Kerssenbrock, *Anabaptistici furoris Monasterium inclitam Westphaliae metropolim evertentis historica narratio*, II. H. Detmer (ed.), *Die Geschichtsquellen des Bisthums Münster*, VI (Münster, 1899), 559–61; cited in Stayer, *Anabaptists and the Sword* (1972, 236).

24. Arthur (1999, 64–66).

25. Krahn (1968, 144–45).

26. Arthur (1999, 112).

27. Stayer (1988, 125).

28. *Berichte de Augenzeugen über das Münsterische Wiedertäuferreich*, ed. C. A. Cornelius, *Die Geschichtsquellen des Bisthums Münster*, II (Münster, 1853), 401; cited in Stayer (1972, 258).

29. Arthur notes that another leader of the city, Herman Schlachtscape, also was captured in bed "with his four wives" and taken to the stocks near the *Rathaus*, where angry women threw rocks and manure clods at him. They shouted, "Do you have enough women now?" Mollenheck was actually forced to rescue Schlachtscape from the angry crowd and lock him up with the other leaders. See Arthur (1999, 96–97).

30. "Gresbeck Story," in C. A. Cornelius, ed., *Eyewitness Reports of the Anabaptist Kingdom of Münster. Historical Sources of the Bishopric of Münster* (Münster, 1923), 78; cited in Arthur (1999, 101–2).

31. Stayer (1972, 259–60).

32. Stayer (1972, 247).

33. Stayer (1972, 264–65).

34. Yet his "acceptance speech" was filled with ambiguities, with Jan stating his unworthiness of the crown in one sentence and his duty to use the sword in the next. See Arthur (1999, 110).

35. Arthur (1999, 107–8).

36. Stayer (1988, 124).

37. Stayer (1972, 256).

38. Heinrich Gresbeck and Hans Eck abandoned their sentry posts a month prior to final battle and, in exchange for their lives, helped the bishop's army enter the city on June 24, 1535. See Krahn (1968, 159).

39. Arthur (1999, 176–78).

40. Krahn (1968, 159–60). Krahn cites Gerhard de Buhr, "Der Wiedertaufer Heinrich Krechting und seine Sippe," as one source for the few remaining Münsterites who were said to be "reformed" Anabaptists after the fall of the kingdom.

41. Waite (1988, 307).

42. Rammstedt (1966); quoted in Eichler (1981, 48).

43. Rammstedt (1966, 80); quoted in Eichler (1981, 49).

44. Arthur (1999, 123–24).

45. Krahn (1968, 140–41).

46. Krahn (1968, 139).

47. Krahn (1968, 139).

48. Hans Joachim Hillerbrand, *Die politische Ethik des oberdeutschen Täufertums: Eine Untersuchung zur Religions- und Geistesgeschichte des Reformationszeitalters* (Leiden/Köln, 1962); Clasen (1972, 358ff); Goertz (1980, 127ff); cited in Vogler (1988, 104).

49. The Peace of Augsburg (1555) embodied the principle *cuius regio, eius religio* (whose region, his religion) to designate that the princes would determine the religion for their respective subjects. In fact, rising religious pluralism rendered this principle unworkable and is often cited as contributing to the Thirty Years' War that ravaged Europe in the seventeenth century (Ozment 1980, 259–60).

50. Stayer (1988, 118).

51. Eichler (1981, 54).

52. Vogler (1988, 109).

53. Ozment (1975, 10–11, 123–25, 148–50).

54. Quoted in Carl Adolph Cornelius, ed., *Berichte der Augenzeugen über das Münsteriche Wiedertaüferreich* (Münster, 1853, 283); cited in Vogler (1988, 114).

55. For an intriguing assessment of the sociological characteristics of rebellion in sixteenth-century German society, see Scott (1979, 693–720).

56. Manchester (1992, 179–80).

57. Kirchhoff, "Die Taüfer in Münsterland," 35–44; cited in Stayer (1988, 125).

58. Grieser (1995, 45–46).

59. See "Biographical Notes" on both Hubmaier and Hans Hut in Baylor (1991, 263–65).

60. Waite (1992, 458–85) references Smit (1970) as another source exploring the relationship of Dutch noblemen and religious dissenters.

61. Waite (1992, 460).

62. Waite (1992, 460–61).

5

Imperial Christianity and Sacred War in Byzantium

Paul Stephenson

The topic of holy war in Byzantium has been discussed fairly compre-hensively in recent years.[1] The Orthodox Church, it has been main-tained by a majority of scholars, while recognizing the necessity of de-fending the Christian empire, was never responsible for declaring war, and rejected all calls to offer spiritual rewards to Christian soldiers. Both the declaratory role of a religious authority and the offer of spiritual rewards are key features of holy war in its mature Latin Christian and Islamic ar-ticulations. Spiritual rewards included remission of sins and, if one met with death in battle with the infidel, martyrdom.[2]Additional factors said to distinguish holy war from just war include: an overtly religious aim for the war, for example the delivery of a holy land from the infidel, and the pos-sibility, although not inevitability, of waging an offensive holy war, whereas just war is by definition defensive. Lacking these dimensions, it is argued, Byzantine warfare was just but never holy. But as Tia Kolbaba has shown in an important dissenting paper, there was more than one attitude to war in Byzantium, and the problem cannot be resolved—indeed it is neatly avoided—by speaking of *the* Orthodox Christian position.[3] As she concludes: "Instead of denying that wars fought by Christian soldiers in defense of a Christian empire against Muslims and polytheists were reli-gious wars, we might concentrate on other tasks: for example, describing and defining religion and the holy as understood by the Byzantines, then analyzing the relationship between such an understanding and the *im-perium.*"

An important study in that direction has been undertaken by Gilbert Dagron, which focuses on the office of emperor, although without paying particular attention to his military function. Dagron begins with the statement that "no one today would still speak about Church and state as two institutions," thus echoing the sentiments expressed by many contributors to this volume. However, he proceeds to demonstrate: the importance of understanding the relationship between the emperor as head of state, and the Church as an institution of state; the role of the emperor as quasi-priest, as manifested in and reinforced by ceremonial; and the distinctions between the Christianity of the emperor and that of the clergy. Dagron observes "that an imperial Christianity that was Old Testament in tone was confronted by the more New Testament-oriented Christianity of the clergy," and "realise[s] that the central problem, clearly posed but never truly resolved, was that of the sacerdotal nature of kingship."[4]

These two strands of Orthodox Christianity, the imperial and the clerical, remained intertwined but distinct, from Constantine I's conversion in the fourth century CE to the end of the Byzantine empire as a political entity in 1453. Throughout the Byzantine millennium, the two strands were ever in a state of tension, as ritual and ceremonial prescriptions demonstrated. On the major feasts of the Christian calendar, when the emperor entered the cathedral church of Hagia Sophia in Constantinople, "it was as if the ceremonial was designed to accentuate the differences between the two conceptions of Christianity before developing the strategy of an encounter between them."[5] Before the emperor passed from his palace, the seat of his "Old Testament" powers, into the realm of the "New Testament" clergy, he received their written instructions, and before he entered the church itself he removed his crown. Once and briefly during the liturgical entrance, unlike any other laymen, the emperor was permitted to enter the sanctuary, led by the patriarch, to kiss the altar cloth. Afterward, this area was off limits to him, and he conducted his role in proceedings from behind the chancel barrier. However, the initial entry into the holy of holies was understood by emperors to signify their quasi-priestly status.[6]

A fundamental difference between the imperial and clerical Christianities, as Kolbaba has observed, lay in their conceptions of warfare. Although the New Testament itself offers no clear guidance on the morality of war, "New Testament-oriented" clergy might more readily adopt a pacifist stance, following the early Church Fathers.[7] A favored authority, to which we return below, was St. Basil of Caesarea, whose thirteenth canon translates thus: "Our fathers did not reckon killings in wars to be among murders, it seems to me, giving pardon to those who defended on behalf of chastity and piety, but perhaps it is to be well advised that those whose hands are not clean be prohibited from communion alone for three years."[8] The approach of emperors, however, was distinctly militaristic. Many might profess to believe, like Leo VI (886–912), that the devil stirred man to war, and his natural state was to be at peace.[9] But when war was necessary, it was the emperor's duty to pursue it, as commander-in-chief of the armed forces, and as divinely inspired "Master of Victory." Christ himself was the ultimate "Master of Victory," who had triumphed over death and left behind the relics of his Passion as sources of power for those who followed his path. But the Old Testament provided more and better models for the conduct of righteous war, and these were emphasized with greater force at particular times. The seventh century was one such time, as we shall see below, and efforts by the emperor Herakleios (610–641) to portray himself as a new David may be reflected in the production of the famous silver David Plates.[10] The tenth century was also such a time, as we shall see subsequently, and the production of the famous Joshua Roll, which depicts the exploits of the eponymous Hebrew general, may be considered a parallel to the David Plates.[11] Many further examples and arguments could be adduced if space permitted.

If we follow Dagron, we must accept that the office of emperor remained fundamentally Davidic. Thus the emperor as the New David, rather than any individual holding that office, presided over a strand of the faith, which ran parallel to that cultivated by the leaders of the institutional Church. Such a revelation helps elucidate the numerous instances where emperors clashed with clerics, notably the patriarchs of Rome and Constantinople, over matters of faith, without recourse to the problematic notion of *caesaropapism*.[12] We must also accept that the office of emperor cannot be considered as purely secular, but that it was also quasi-priestly. The emperor declared and pursued war, therefore, both as secular authority and quasi-priest. Must we reconsider, then, the claim that war was never declared by a "religious" authority in Byzantium? And what of the second principle criterion of holy war, that participants be offered spiritual rewards?

It was the Byzantine emperor's task, as surely as any commander, to find means to inspire his troops to fight, to the death if necessary, in pursuit of imperial interests. Christianity, in its imperial form, was the most potent vehicle to this end, for as the editor of this volume notes, paraphrasing Rodney Stark, "Religions make claims and create rewards that motivate individuals to do extraordinary things in light of [their] truth claims and promises." And it is clear that emperors sought to make claims and offer spiritual rewards to those who fought and died for their causes. As we shall see, the idea of earning spiritual rewards through battle was not wholly absent from Byzantine thought, being called for by more than one emperor. Moreover, at a late stage it even permeated into clerical Christianity, when indulgences were offered to those who fought or died in righteous battle by the Patriarch of Constantinople Michael

Autoreianos (1208–1214), although this perhaps reflected the Western influences that prevailed during his pontificate.[13]

Christianity was always a galvanizing and motivating force for imperial troops, but during certain periods in the Byzantine millennium the conduct of war was increasingly sacralized at the initiative of emperors. The wars the emperor Herakleios (610–641) fought against the Zoroastrian Persians generated art and literature that suggest a developing Byzantine notion, if not of holy war, then at least of sacred war.[14] The recovery of the "true cross," upon which Christ had been crucified, and which had been captured in the Persian sack of Jerusalem in 614, was not an objective of these wars, and does not feature in literature composed between 622 and 628 (namely the *Persian Expedition* and *Heraclias* of George of Pisidia). However, after the negotiated recovery of the cross, its return to Jerusalem in 630, and its transfer in 635 to Constantinople ("New Jerusalem"), it became the central motif of the Herakleios story.[15] The cross was presented as the symbol of Christian victory in various historical works, in the later poems of George of Pisidia, and on Herakleios's coins.[16] This appears to have been the culmination of a process: in 591 the emperor Maurikios had ridden out behind a fragment of the true cross raised on a golden spear.[17] It has been argued that in the 420s, as war escalated between Byzantium and the Persians, Theodosius II (408–450) was inspired by his sister to recognize in the cross a guarantee of imperial victory, and have it placed on imperial coins held by a winged Victory, the so-called Long-Cross *solidi*.[18] At the same time, Theodosius "in imitation of the blessed Pulcheria" sent to Jerusalem "much money . . . [and] a golden cross studded with precious stones to be raised on the holy site of Golgotha," which symbolized Christ's own victory over death at that place.[19] Versions of the legend of Helena, mother of Constantine I, relate that she discovered the true cross and two nails, which she sent back to her son, and which he incorporated into his helmet and his diadem.[20] Representations of the cross, rather than the cross itself, had been used still earlier, indeed since Constantine had his vision at the Milvian Bridge in 312, fulfilling the command, "By this sign conquer."[21]

The rise of Islam in the immediate aftermath of the Byzantine-Persian wars brought a further protracted period of conflict before a *modus vivendi* was established between the Christian empire and the caliphate. The cross remained a potent symbol throughout this period, which was one of political and military retrenchment in Byzantium, and its significance was extended during Iconoclasm (726–787; 813–843), when the veneration of other holy images was officially banned.[22] Although there is some debate on the matter, it is likely that the Iconoclasts rejected the veneration of relics as well as icons; certainly, the defense of icon veneration rested heavily on the existence of *acheiropoietoi*, images "not made by human hand," which were both icons and relics.[23] Thus the great defender of icon veneration, "John of Damascus found himself compelled to write a justification for the cult of relics."[24] This cult flourished after the restoration of icons in 843, when a concerted effort was made to secure the salvific power of relics for the empire.

Our principal historical source for the period of Iconoclasm, Theophanes the Confessor (d. 818), was a staunch supporter of icon veneration. It is therefore with caution that we must approach his chronicle, which covers the first period of Iconoclasm (726–787) and was completed shortly after its terminal entry for the year 813, the year in which Iconoclasm was restored. Circumspection is necessary also when reading his account of the reign of Herakleios, although it draws heavily, but selectively, on extant and lost works by George of Pisidia. One can understand why, for example, Theophanes draws attention to the importance of an *acheiropoietos* icon of Christ in Herakleios's first campaign against the Persians in 620–621.[25] Similarly, one must approach with caution the suggestion that in 622–623, "Herakleios gathered his troops and gave them courage by assuaging them with these words of exhortation."[26]

> Be not disturbed, O brethren, by the multitude of [the Persian army]. For when God wills it, one man will rout a thousand. So let us sacrifice ourselves to God for the salvation of our brothers, may we win the crown of martyrdom so that we may be praised in future and receive our recompense from God.

This passage is believed to be derived from fragments of a lost work by George of Pisidia, and thus may indeed reflect words and thoughts expressed in the 620s.[27] If so, this is a remarkable imperial guarantee of spiritual rewards to Christian soldiers fighting against the infidel. But even if the words were never uttered, it is striking that Theophanes did not emend the text, that he believed Herakleios might have made such a statement, and that it would have been both legitimate and well received. Theophanes had attended the seventh ecumenical Church council of 787, spent much of his life as a monk, and is commemorated as a saint, but in the chronicle which bears his name he saw no reason to question or correct Herakleios's statement on the possibility of martyrdom and divine recompense for death in battle.[28]

The true cross remained the most potent harbinger of Christian victory, being both symbol and relic, through the ninth and tenth centuries. In the mid-tenth century it was prescribed that a cruciform reliquary (*staurothêkê*) containing the life-giving wood precede any emperor taking part in a military campaign.[29] The tenth-century Byzantine attitude, amplifying that which had gone before, is summed up in an inscription carved into an ivory reliquary of the true cross, now kept at the church of San Francesco of Cortona in Tuscany. It reads:

> In the past, Christ gave to the powerful emperor Constantine [I]
> The cross for [our] salvation
> And now our emperor Nikephoros
> Puts to flight the tribes of barbarians because he possesses it.[30]

The tenth century, like the age of Herakleios, is a period when the developments of earlier centuries were refined and amplified to produce a fuller articulation of sacred war.[31] At this time the disintegrating Abbasid Caliphate ceased to be a powerful centralized counterweight to its Christian neighbor. Consequently, conflict intensified across their mutual frontier as Muslim border warriors and fighters for the faith, operating without access to state resources, cohered around successful commanders, notably the charismatic Saif ad-Dawla (Sayf al-Dawla), Hamdanid emir of Aleppo.[32] Simultaneously, the rise of the Fatimids in North Africa threatened Byzantine interests in southern Italy and, later, the eastern frontier through Syria and Palestine.[33] Returning to the offensive, Byzantium entered a period of great military success, and one when Christian victory was increasingly associated not just with the cross, but with other symbols and relics of Christ's Passion.

A key feature of battle preparations was the harangue. Two tenth-century harangues, which were delivered to Byzantine troops on the eastern frontier, highlight the role of the true cross and other relics, particularly those of Christ's Passion.[34] The first harangue was delivered on behalf of Emperor Constantine VII (913/945–959) to praise a defensive force that had won victories over the rampaging army of Saif ad-Dawla. It was most likely delivered late in 950, as that force was disbanded for the winter and encouraged to reassemble promptly the following summer. A key passage reads:

> Therefore, have no fear, my men, have no fear, fill your souls with zeal and show the enemies who rely on the aid of Beliar or Mohammed what those who put their faith in Christ can accomplish. Be the avengers and champions not only of Christians, but of Christ himself, whom they wickedly deny . . . so let us put all our hope in him, and instead of our whole panoply let us arm ourselves with His cross, equipped with which you lately made the fierce soldiers of the Hamdanid the victims of your swords.

The crosses alluded to were not merely metaphorical, but the regular battle standard of the Byzantine army. These were not, of course, weapons but palladia, defending the defenders of the Christian empire. This had been the case since the reign of Constantine I, whose *labarum* standard acted as a shield to those who bore it. Constantine himself is said to have observed the death of those who relinquished the *labarum* to bear arms, while a soldier who grabbed it escaped javelins hurled at him, each one striking the narrow pole of the standard.[35]

The second extant harangue was delivered in different circumstances, not to a successful defensive force disbanding, but, on internal evidence, to a large expeditionary force comprising the armies of the east and west, with foreign mercenary units also present. It was, therefore, most likely delivered in September 958, on the eve of a dramatic Byzantine victory over Saif ad-Dawla at Raban. To ensure victory Constantine VII had sought the prayers of holy men and monks throughout the empire, and dispatched to the army "holy oil" (*myron*), which emanated from the most holy relics:[36]

> Behold that after drawing holy oil from the immaculate and most sacred relics of the Passion of Christ our true God—from the precious wooden fragments [of the true cross] and the undefiled lance, the precious titulus, the wonder-working reed, the life-giving blood which flowed from His precious rib, the most sacred tunic, the holy swaddling clothes, the God-bearing winding sheet, and the other relics of His undefiled Passion—we have sent it to be sprinkled upon you, for you to be anointed by it and to garb yourself with the divine power from on high.

This fascinating list of the relics gathered in Constantinople begins, as was meet in a military context, with the true cross. The relics of the Passion were housed in the imperial palace in Constantinople, the chapel of the Virgin (*Theotokos*) of the Pharos. They were joined by the "great cross" of Constantine I.[37] During the mid to later tenth century, three further relics of great consequence were brought to Constantinople and deposited in the Pharos chapel: the *mandylion* (in 944), the arm of John the Baptist (in 959), and the sandal of Christ (in 975). A fourth, the "holy brick" (*keramos*, *keramidion*), which had reputedly come into contact with the *mandylion* and thus been imprinted with the face of Christ, was transported from Hierapolis in Syria in 966, and deposited in the Church of All Saints in Constantinople.

Such potent relics as these, alongside the relics of the Passion, were required to defend the city from its myriad enemies, but that potency could be shared with the empire's troops through the dispatch of crosses blessed by them, or of oil drawn from them. Similar assistance was required from holy men and monks whose prayers were sought for all military undertakings. This is well summed up by the eleventh-century historian, Michael Attaleiates, who could look back on a century of spectacular monastic growth, much sponsored directly by emperors:

For it is fitting for him [the emperor] to look to the wishes of the founders
and to protect the holy establishments [i.e. monasteries] . . . so that the holy
men may commend their lives to God and offer prayers for their safety, and
for the raising of military standards, the campaigning and victory of the
army, the governance of the commonwealth and its spiritual welfare and
those things pleasing to God.[38]

By the time Attaleiates wrote his *diataxis*, the spiritual center of Byzantine monasticism was Mount Athos, and this owed much to the patronage
of a monastic founder, who was also a general and emperor; a man who
cut his military teeth against Saif ad-Dawla on the eastern frontier and
drove Arabs from the islands of Crete and Cyprus: Nikephoros Phokas.

Nikephoros II Phokas (963–969) is revered in medieval Greek historiography as the emperor who advanced the frontiers of the Byzantine empire after three centuries of retrenchment. His very name means "bringer of victory," but his preferred nickname was "Pale death of the Saracens." Both
were acclamations offered by the citizens of Constantinople as he processed
from the imperial palace to the cathedral church of Hagia Sophia.[39] Upon
his death, murdered by his wife and her lover, John Tzimiskes, Nikephoros
was celebrated as a martyr by the monks of Mount Athos. A liturgy was
composed at the Great Lavra Monastery, which had been founded with
booty from Nikephoros's conquest of Crete, offering prayers for his im-
mortal soul.[40] The manner of his execution ensured that Nikephoros entered the pantheon of Christian martyrs, but this status was denied the soldiers who fought and died in his armies.

At one point in his six-year reign, Nikephoros demanded a review of
Orthodox canons relating to death in battle, so that "those who fell in battle be honored equally with the holy martyrs and be celebrated with
hymns and feast-days." We do not know the date of the synod, as it is not
mentioned by Leo the Deacon, our principal source for the period, which
is itself a significant fact.[41] The aforementioned ruling of the fourth-
century Church father Basil of Caesarea was used by the synod to deny
the emperor's request. "How is it possible to number with the martyrs
those who fell in battle, whom Basil the Great excluded from the sancti-
fied elements for three years since their hands were unclean?" the synod
ruled.[42] Rather than gain spiritual rewards, Byzantine soldiers ran the risk
of losing rights to communion by killing in battle. It is notable that before
the synod drew attention to it, this patristic canon had not been enforced,
and what we have called the imperial view had come to dominate, particularly among those who fought and died on the frontiers.

On the basis of several military manuals (*taktika*) preserved from the
later ninth through tenth centuries, G. Dagron and H. Mihaescu have
demonstrated that the ruling of the synod was in direct contradiction to

what soldiers were told and believed.[43] These were beliefs which had been reinforced by a century of warfare in the eastern border regions against highly motivated *jihad* fighters. In the *Taktika* attributed to the emperor Leo VI (886–912), written c. 895, a clear understanding of the advantages that accrued to the empire's Muslim enemies is evinced. The Arabs, it is stated, assembled for war voluntarily, since the rich are interested in spiritual rewards and the poor also in the accrual of booty. Moreover, warfare is a collective effort, whereby all members of society share in the expenses, supplying the fighting men with arms and equipment, and hence also share in the spiritual rewards of warfare. This appears to be an acknowledgment of the efficacy of Islamic *waqf* foundations, and the contemporary Byzantine problem of assembling troops and financing campaigns centrally. Despite the usual insults leveled at Muslims, Leo considered the Islamic model to be one which the Byzantines should seek to emulate, and he realized that the cornerstones of this system would have to be replicated. That is, he stated (XVIII, 133), the Muslim enemy should be confronted bravely "for our spiritual salvation, sure that we are fighting for God himself, for our compatriots and for all our Christian brothers."[44] Moreover (XIV, 35), at the burial of "those who die in war," it should be noted that they will be "perpetually honored and blessed because they did not esteem their own lives above their faith and their brothers."[45] In effect, Leo was calling for a special liturgy for those who died in war which would ensure their special status as "perpetually blessed."

At the very end of the ninth century, Dagron suggests, "Byzantium was neither ready for holy war ('la guerre sainte'), nor organized for permanent warfare."[46] However, through the tenth century attitudes hardened and a new institutional framework was developed to pursue "permanent war," culminating in the reign of Nikephoros Phokas, when state finances were overhauled and ever more cash was directed to the war effort. Nikephoros shared Leo VI's views on the status of soldiers for the faith, and did his best to ensure that each Byzantine soldier was prepared to enjoy the same spiritual rewards as his foes, the *jihad* fighters of the emirates which had emerged at the fringes of the Abbasid Caliphate. *Kantatores*, heralds and chanters, were to remind soldiers of their duty to God and assure them that their sacrifices would be commemorated forever by compatriots.[47] But spiritual rewards were not to be bought lightly: each soldier had to be pure for his own salvation, and also for the collective efficacy of the fighting force. Thus three-day fasts were observed prior to engagements by all, with only a dry meal to be taken in the evening; hymns were sung and prayers of supplication were said en masse; pious utterances were orchestrated on the eve of battle and as combat was engaged; and special services were composed and conducted in the field. Moreover, troops were ordered to cry out "Lord have mercy" up to one hundred times on both the eve and morning of battle, and at the very moment of engagement to cry out "The cross conquers," or "Let the cross conquer."[48]

Nikephoros Phokas took great pains to ensure that all his troops participated in such services and prescribed that "whosoever is detected at the time of the litany attending to some other matter without thinking of putting all else aside to stand and offer his prayer in fear of the Lord, such a man is to be demoted from his office, is to be assigned to an inferior rank, is to be beaten, have his hair shorn and be publicly displayed."[49] Ultimately, therefore, each soldier was prepared for his own demise and redemption, and according to the *Taktika* of Nikephoros Ouranos, a military manual attributed to one of Nikephoros II's most trusted generals, the troops were to pray for the courage to fight to the death.[50]

> Have the command given to the army that, when the trumpets or other instruments cease to sound, they are to repeat, "Lord Jesus Christ, our God, have mercy on us, Amen," and "Come to the aid of us Christians and make us worthy to fight to the death for our faith and our brothers, strengthen our souls and our hearts and our whole bodies, the mighty Lord of battles, through the intercession of the immaculate Mother of God, Thy Mother, and of all the saints. Amen."

From this one might make a fairly obvious observation, but one that, to my knowledge, has not been made before. The demand that those who died in battle be accorded spiritual rewards was a necessary corollary to the call for troops to fight to the death. Both were practical considerations, and not motivated purely by knowledge of Muslim practices. That is to say, if those who were captured and died subsequently might receive the crown of martyrdom, or indeed be ransomed, what incentive was there to fight on rather than surrender? From a military perspective—and above all else, Nikephoros Phokas was a general—it may have seemed imperative to secure equal rights for the troops who fought on as those accorded to troops who surrendered.

How close, then, have we come to a vital criterion of holy war, that Christian troops be offered spiritual rewards for dying in battle? Rather close, suggests a unique religious service (*akolouthia*) preserved in a tenth-century document at St. Catherine's Monastery on Mt. Sinai.[51] The manuscript, *Sinai graecus 734–735*, contains a version of the Triodion, the liturgical book for the Easter cycle, and the service in which we are interested was to be performed on Meat-fare Saturday, the first of five All Souls Saturdays during Lent. Unlike other All Souls services, this one was devoted exclusively to those who had died in battle. In effect, it was a type of veterans' day service, but one which failed to become established in the Orthodox calendar and is therefore otherwise unknown. This is the type of commemoration service that Leo VI promised his troops in his *Taktika*, and which Nikephoros Phokas would have wanted for those who died in his armies. With it we are brought remarkably close—far closer than the ruling of the synod would allow—to acceptance that soldiers who die in battle, fighting for Christ, should thereby enter the kingdom of heaven. It is not automatic, being subject to God's dispensation, and the status of martyr is not mentioned. But there is a clear reference to remission of sins, and no mention that they died in a state of sin, as the canon of Basil of Caesarea stated.

CONCLUSION

War is violent, and every war fought by the Byzantine was religious in preparation and execution, if not always in motivation. So, the Byzantine millennium was one of unremitting religious violence. Yet, it has been noted that the use of the phrase *holy war* in a Byzantine context is misleading because *the* Orthodox conception of war failed to incorporate, or actively rejected, crucial aspects of related ideologies. Most notably, it rejected the declaration of war by a religious authority, and the guarantee of spiritual rewards for fighting and being killed, which are key to Latin Christendom and the Muslim ideologies of holy war. Such indulgences as remission of sins or, the ultimate reward, martyrdom, are indeed alien to the Orthodox tradition. However, careful scrutiny of surviving texts suggests that this was not always the case, and that at certain periods imperial Christianity prevailed. Then, warfare became increasingly sacralized, and, especially in conflicts with adherents of other faiths, those engaged in fighting were led to believe that they would receive spiritual recompense for their efforts. It is clear that in both the seventh and tenth centuries concerted efforts were made to extend spiritual rewards, up to and including the status of martyr, to those who fought the righteous war, suitably purified in advance and with the intention to defend their Christian brothers. These soldiers carried with them symbols of Christian victory and gained strength from blessings bestowed by relics of the Passion. In death they believed—because they were led to believe by emperors and generals, but also by priests who conducted the services in which they participated—that their sacrifice would be rewarded.

NOTES

1. Although it is a topic with some pedigree, renewed discussion of Byzantine holy war has accompanied the exhaustive coverage of Latin Crusade and Islamic

jihad. Much interest was provoked by the publication of Kolia-Dermitzaki (1991). See Laiou (1993, 153–77); Oikonomides (1995, 62–86); Haldon (1999, 13–33); Dennis (2001, 31–39).

2. Dennis (2001, 31–32). Walker (1977, 301–27) dispensed with the notion that a late tenth-century emperor set his sights on the liberation of the "holy land" through a "crusade."

3. Kolbaba (1998, 194–221, at 219).

4. Dagron (2003, 1, 103–4).

5. Dagron (2003, 97–98).

6. Dagron (2003, 84–95).

7. Taft (1995, 17–32, at 26–28); Miller and Nesbitt (1995, 1–13, at 8–9).

8. Viscuso (1995, 33–40) provides an overview of the vast literature on this canon.

9. Miller and Nesbitt (1995, 4).

10. Spain (1977, 217–37). And against this interpretation of the David plates, as reflecting a developing ideology of imperial victory, see now Leader (2000, 407–27).

11. Kresten (2001, 185–212), provides an exhaustive bibliography. It has been suggested that the tenth-century roll alludes to the exploits of Nikephoros II Phokas (963–969), and also that it is a copy of an original that celebrated the victories of Herakleios.

12. Arnason (2000, 39–69) highlights that this interpretation of authority is predicated on an inappropriate notion of the natural separation of church and state.

13. Oikonomides (1967, 113–45).

14. In summary, Haldon (1999, 20–21). In greater detail see now Kaegi (2003); Reinink and Stolte, eds. (2002).

15. Drijvers (2002, 175–90); Mango (1985, 105–18); Frolow (1953, 88–93).

16. *Chronicon Paschale* (1989, 169–70); Howard-Johnston (1994, 57–87); Whitby (2002a, 197–225); Whitby (2002b, 157–73).

17. *Theophylacti Simocattae historiae* (1887, 219–20); Dennis (1993, 107–17 at 108); Mergiali-Sahas (2001, 41–60 at 49–50).

18. Holum (1977, 153–72); Holum and Vikan (1979, 113–33, at 126–33).

19. Theophanes (1998, 135–36).

20. Kalavrezou (1997, 53–79 at 54) provides references and commentary.

21. Eusebius (1999, 81); J. Gagé (1933, 370–400).

22. Thierry (1981, 205–28); Kazhdan et al. (1991, I, 551–53).

23. Cormack (1985, 121–31).

24. Kazhdan et al. (1991, III, 1781).

25. Theophanes (1883, 303); Theophanes (1998, 436). This passage is derived from the poem *Expeditio Persica* by George of Pisidia, on which see Whitby (2002b, 162–67).

26. Theophanes (1883, 310–11); Theophanes (1998, 442–43); Kolbaba (1998, 206–7).

27. Howard-Johnston (1994, 67–72); Whitby (2002b, 167–73).

28. This point would be equally, if not more, valid for George Synkellos, who "stood very high in the ecclesiastical establishment," and whose work Theophanes edited and completed, perhaps adding very little of originality. See Theophanes 1998, xiii–xxiii.

29. *Constantini Prophyrogeniti imperatoris de cerimoniis byzantini, libri duo*, I, 484–85; Mergiali-Sahas (2001, 50–51).

30. Oikonomides (1995, 79). The second emperor it mentions, Nikephoros II Phokas (963–969), we shall turn to shortly.

31. Other definitions are possible, although rarely is a pertinent Greek phrase (e.g., *ieros polemos*) used in contemporary sources. Many historians, from as early as William of Tyre, have chosen to view the Byzantine wars of the early sixth century and later tenth century as "proto-Crusades." See Grousset (1934–1936, I, i–xxxii); Runciman (1951, 20–37); most recently, Regan (2001). Extending the notion of Crusade, which is difficult to pin down even in a Latin Christian context, to Byzantium is rather unhelpful.

32. McGeer (1995, 225–48); Canard (1951); Runciman (1929, 120–50).

33. Tibi (1991, 91–107).

34. McGeer (2003, 111–35).

35. Eusebius (1999, 97–98).

36. McGeer (2003, 133). See also Kolbaba (1998, 207).

37. Kalavrezou (1997, 55–57). A second fragment of the true cross was housed in the chapel of St. Stephen, also within the palace complex.

38. Gautier (1981, 4–143, at 81); Morris (1995, 107).

39. Liutprand of Cremona, *Legatio* (1910, 440–77, at 447). A second tradition vilified Nikephoros for parsimony, for which see the excellent study by Morris (1988, 83–115).

40. Petit (1904, 398–420); Kolia-Dermitzaki (1991, 254–58). On the foundation of the Great Lavra, see Life of Athanasios of Athos B (23–26); Noret (1982, 147–54).

41. Leo the Deacon, *Leonis diaconus Caloensis historiae* (1828). The synod is first noted in the late eleventh century by Skylitzes (1973, 274–75) and in the early twelfth century by Zonaras (1897, III, 506). See also Viscuso (1995, 37–39).

42. References and commentary are provided by Viscuso (1995, 33–40) and Kolbaba (1998, 204–07). See also Kolia-Dermitzaki (1991, 132–41) and Haldon (1999, 28).

43. Dagron and Mihaescu (1986, 284–86).

44. Dagron (1983, 219–43, at 221–23) paraphrases these important passages with pertinent commentary. See also Dennis (1997, 165–78); Haldon (1999, 28); Kolbaba (1998, 206).

45. Dagron (1983, 230–31).

46. Dagron (1983, 224).

47. Dennis (1993, 112).

48. Dennis (1993, 107–17); Viellefond (1935, 322–30); Dagron (1983, 225–32). One such service has been preserved: Pertusi (1948, 145–68, at 154–55). It has been dated to the reign of Leo VI (886–912), who ruled with his brother Alexander, but it could as easily be from the joint reign of Constantine VII (945–959) and his son Romanos II. See also Kolia-Dermitzaki (1991, 252–56).

49. McGeer (1995, 56–57).

50. McGeer (1995, 126–27); quoted by Dennis (1993, 116) and Haldon (1999, 27).

51. Détorakis and Mossay (1988, 183–211); Kolia-Dermitzaki (1991, 258–60). Taft (1995, 18), cites an unpublished dissertation on this manuscript, A. Quinlan, *Sinai Greek 734–735: Triodion*, Pontifical Oriental Institute (Rome, 1991), to which I have not had access.

II

THE MODERN WORLD

6

Founding an Empire of Sacrifice: Innocent Domination and the Quaker Martyrs of Boston, 1659–1661

Jon Pahl

An ostensible separation of "church" and "state" in the United States has obscured the productive interaction between forms of cultural authority in American history.[1] Although the First Amendment effectively disallows government establishment of sectarian religion, Jefferson's "wall of separation" has in fact been a highly permeable barrier. Most notably, various efforts to establish political dominance on the foundation of clear religious grounds have tended to be treated either as strangely mythological aberrations from the otherwise logical progress of a common faith in secular reason, or as the necessary political reduction of a howling wilderness to the millennial destiny of largely righteous, if occasionally misdirected, believers.[2] In fact, despite the best efforts of the founders of the Republic to separate religion from politics, a durable pattern can be traced to the Puritans: imperial control of land (and people) through the sacrifice of some unfortunate victims.[3] From the vantage of all but the millennially progressive, of either religious or secular estates, the religious history of the United States evidences recurrent pressure toward anti-intellectual conformity that produces material control of land and peoples under an assertion of innocence.[4] More succinctly, force has repeatedly been actualized in American history under religious pretenses of purity.[5] These paradoxical constructs of innocent domination cut across American institutions, unite church and state, and are effective precisely to the degree that their paradoxical relation cannot be admitted. In short, the most dominant empire in human history originated in a logic, psychology, and economy of sacrifice.[6] An excellent example of this paradox of innocent domination at work, and its manifestation in sacrifice, can be found in the execution of four Quakers on Boston Common between 1659 and 1661.[7]

EMPIRE BUILDING AND SACRIFICE:
FROM GIRARD TO CARRASCO

There is, of course, no consensus about the function of sacrifice in the history of religions. Fortunately, none is needed, although theory can help to clarify how sacrifice has played a central role in American history. One chief theorist of sacrifice has been René Girard. According to Girard, literary sources reveal that sacrifice stems from a form of desire that he variously dubs "mimetic desire" or "acquisitive mimesis." In Girard's sources, a subject observes another's desire, and from this observation *learns* desire. The subject's desire threatens, or actually produces, rivalry for the desired object. Girard calls this situation of rivalry a "crisis of differentiation." Religion arises as an effort to mitigate this crisis, in Girard's sources, through sacrifice. Sacrifice "solves" the crisis of differentiation when people react to rivalry by selecting a scapegoat whose death or expulsion temporarily defuses rivalry, uniting all against one, and thereby re-establishing order. Girard writes: "Sacrifice is primarily a collective action of the entire community, which purifies itself of its own disorder through the unanimous immolation of a victim."[8] This insight about the socially unifying, albeit ambivalent, logic of sacrifice is hardly unique to Girard, and his theory has more than a few shortcomings—especially as articulated by some of his devotees.[9] But the logic that implicates desire in violence, and that holds religion responsible both for containing and fueling that desire, has been considered plausible since at least Augustine, and surely since Freud—both of whom Girard acknowledges as influences.

Girard's "revelation" of the mimetic logic through which sacrifice both embraces and contains violence has been extended and given some empirical grounding in the recent work of R. Scott Appleby. For Appleby, people of faith, or those affiliated with what go by the name of "religions," have produced violence and peace, conflict and reconciliation. Violent believers Appleby describes variously as "extremists," "reactionaries," or devotees of "weak" religions, of which the preeminent examples are the global "fundamentalisms" that he traced in the five-volume project he co-edited with Martin E. Marty.[10] Emerging at the core of Appleby's historical analysis of religious violence is a psychological pattern that he calls "ecstatic asceticism." He characterizes this odd conjunction of terms as follows:

Traditional rituals and devotions that sacralize personal self-sacrifice become in extremist hands a means of preparing the devout cadres for physical warfare. . . . Such prescribed prayers and rituals, interpreted by an extremist preacher, locate the believer in a sacred cosmos that rewards martyrdom or imprisonment endured in a divine cause. . . . This ability of religion to inspire ecstasy—literally, to lift the believer psychologically out of a mundane environment—stands behind the distinctive logic of religious violence. As unpredictable and illogical as this violence may seem to outsiders, it falls within a pattern of asceticism leading to the ecstasy of self-sacrifice that runs as a continuous thread through most religions.[11]

This dense set of generalizations poses problems in almost every word, but it describes the general pattern that emerges from Appleby's empirical studies of many instances of religious violence around the globe. People find power, even ecstasy, in acts of self-sacrifice that might also involve violence against or sacrifice of others. That this psychological pattern might have a very peculiar *cultural* origin, quite close to the home of fundamentalism properly so-called, does not seem to dawn on Appleby.[12]

Finally, the most historically grounded study of the role of human sacrifice to date comes from Davíd Carrasco. Carrasco's field of study is the Aztec empire. According to him, "ritual slaughter within the ceremonial precincts of Aztec life was the instrument, in part, for educating adolescents about their social future, communicating with the many gods, transmitting cosmological convictions, as well as directing social change in the form of imperial expansion."[13] Aztec sacrifice—practiced repeatedly and publicly—was a means for the imperial city of Tenochtitlan to demonstrate control over the peripheries of its empire. Sacrifice was a tool in "the militarization of society."[14] If Girard identifies a logic of sacrifice, and Appleby a psychology, Carrasco sketches a sacrificial economy—in the broadest sense of that term, as a matter concerning the settling of a human community. Carrasco's work brings together three facets of historical study not often linked: attention to material *and* symbolic processes associated with human settlement and organization; attention to the integrative *and* destructive powers of ritual and religion; and attention to the way the history of religions itself as a discipline has developed a hermeneutic that both opens and forecloses avenues of investigation.[15]

The implications of this latter feature of Carrasco's work are especially significant for our purposes. Carrasco finds it stunning that previous theorists of religion "*completely ignored* the most thorough record of real, historical sacrifice while favoring either distant reports of animal sacrifices *or literary sacrifices* from Western Classics!"[16] In fact, however, the scandal may be even more pronounced. The history of religions developed as a discipline, as a number of recent works have clarified, alongside what Carrasco has called a "mass-sacrifice society," led by figures of the ilk of "'lord' Captain Cortes."[17] That this "mass-sacrifice" society planted itself here in the New World, where the discipline of the history of religions has also made its most secure home in the academy, is a further coincidence worth exploring. Indeed, what *is* one to make of the almost utter silence (with some notable exceptions) of American scholars of religion about *American* religious violence, over the same time span that U.S. military and economic dominance reached the point of empire?[18] In constructing a fetish of the "primitive" or foreign "other," and the sacrificial violence found there, historians of religion may have neglected some of the most powerful and significant *interactions* and *convergences* between forms of cultural authority around practices of sacrifice, in the history of the formation of the United States.[19]

MIMESIS IN MASSACHUSETTS, 1656–1657

As is well known, the colony of Massachusetts Bay was settled by Christians intent upon creating a holy commonwealth. Perry Miller long ago described in vivid prose the Puritan "errand into the wilderness" through which a public theologian such as John Winthrop could in all modesty arrogate to himself and his followers a "modell of Christian charity," on whom the eyes of the world were surely trained.[20] Such a modeling process presupposed, of course, an object to be admired and mirrored—a "charity" to be imitated and realized. "When God gives a special Commission," which Winthrop could obviously assume He had, "he lookes to have it strictly observed in every Article." Such mimesis, that could not deviate a jot or a tittle, was all but bound to produce strife. Indeed, strife (or at least the opposite of charity) was implicit in the injunction itself, not to mention in the wilderness that the Puritans imagined they were sent to settle.[21] Consequently, within a generation of their arrival among the Massachusetts Indians, the English resolved more prosaically, in the *Cambridge Platform* of 1648, that "idolatry, blasephemy, heresie, venting corrupt and pernicious Opinions . . . are to be restrained and punished by Civil Authority."[22] That made the matter clearer than Winthrop's noble theological rhetoric had, and it set the stage for the arrival of the Quakers in Boston in 1656—only four years after George Fox had seen the "inner light" and started his own controversial career as a lay preacher.[23]

The first two Quakers to arrive in New England were Mary Fisher and Anne Austin. Their gender did not help their cases.[24] Richard Bellingham, deputy governor of Massachusetts Bay, had received a warning that some enthusiasts were due in Boston Harbor. He consequently dispatched a few soldiers to detain the wayward women while still on board ship, and to search their shipping trunks. The soldiers confiscated about a hundred suspect books. The next day—in what must have been a panic—Bellingham managed to convene Boston's magistrates to pass a law prescribing the burning of any Quaker books, and the holding of Fisher and Austin in the Boston "gaol." The language of the law is instructive. Quaker ideas were "very dangerous, heretical, and blasphemous opinions." It replicated the language of the Cambridge Platform, thereby justifying through a self-fulfilling prophecy Bellingham's exercise of his civil authority to contain and punish the Quakers. Even worse, in the eyes of the law, the Quakers "do acknowledge . . . that they came here purposely to propagate their said Errors and Heresies." The letter of the law was thereby fulfilled: the Quaker books were burned the next morning by a hangman on Boston Common. But the spirit of the law, and the contagion of these errors that might be propagated, seemed to call for extraordinary measures: the women were thus strip-searched while in prison, "under pretence of searching whether they were witches," opined eighteenth-century Quaker chronicler Joseph Besse, and the window to the gaol was boarded up—to prevent all conversation with these dangerous propagators of contagious ideas. After five weeks of what must have been a long silence, Austin and Fisher were dispatched on a boat back to Barbados, from whence they had come, via England.[25]

Within days, eight more Quakers arrived in Boston. They were imprisoned for eleven weeks. The General Court at Boston was feeling besieged, and thus passed the second anti-Quaker law of the year 1656, mandating a fine of one hundred pounds to any ship commander who transported Quakers into Boston. Quakers themselves now would be not only subject to imprisonment and banishment, but also officially silenced by an explicit prohibition that none could be "suffered to converse or speak with them," which would obviously make any defense they might muster difficult. As the Puritan judges saw it, Quakers were contagious and needed to be contained. Quakers dared, the law put it, to "speak and write blasphemous opinions . . . [and were] seeking to turn the People from the Faith and gain Proselytes to their pernicious ways." Ironically, this law had the effect of directly *increasing* the flow of Quakers into Boston. Anne Burden, a widow, and Mary Dyer—well known to Massachusetts Bay authorities from her days as a supporter of Anne Hutchinson—were the next to inhabit Boston's prison. Mary Clark followed shortly thereafter, and a precedent soon to be enshrined in law was set when she received "twenty stripes of a three-corded whip on her naked back." A crisis of differentiation was under way in the wilderness. Winthrop's city on the hill was now beset by rival models of what Christian "charity" actually meant.[26]

Consequently, even stronger measures in defense of "charity" seemed necessary. A third law passed against the Quakers by the General Court at Boston clarified further what the magistrates thought was at stake. This was a crisis in language, about what words could be disseminated, and which needed to be contained. The punishments, in the characteristically magical mentality of conjuring a torture to fit the crime, followed suit:

> Every such Male Quaker shall for the first Offence [of coming to Boston, after having once been banished], have one of his Ears cut off . . . and for the second Offence, shall have his other Ear cut off. And every Woman Quaker that has suffered the Law here . . . shall be severely whipt, and kept at the House of Correction at Work. . . . And for every Quaker, he or she that shall a third Time herein again offend, they shall have their Tongues bored through with an hot Iron.[27]

Such threats to their abilities to hear or speak did not deter the Friends from visiting Boston; in fact, they came in droves: William Shattock, a shoemaker; Sarah Gibbons, Dorothy Waugh, and Horred Gardner—all suspected of witchery; Laurence, Cassandra, and Josiah Southwick—an entire family of heretics, along with various individuals—Joshua Buffum, Thomas Harris, and William Brend, among them. The latter was incarcerated in late 1657, and whipped nearly one hundred strokes, until "the Blood hanging as it were in Bags under his Arms, and so into one was his Flesh beaten, that the Sign of a particular Blow could not be seen."[28] The growing Puritan uncertainty about their errand into the wilderness, their undifferentiated frustration about exactly what kind of charity they were supposed to be modeling, was inscribed on the body of William Brend.

ECSTATIC ASCETICISM: THE DOMINATION OF DISCOURSE AND RHETORICAL INVERSION, 1658–1661

The earliest Quakers were, by the standards of their day, uncivil. They were engaged in what the most colorful of their original members, James Nayler, called "The Lamb's War."[29] It was a "lamb's" war because it was fought not with physical weapons but primarily with words, with silence, or with what has come to be called "civil disobedience." Quakers interrupted the preaching of established ministers, refused to attend established worship, or, when they did assemble, refused to use formal printed prayers or recognize clerical and gender hierarchies. In public life, they declined to participate in major rituals—such as the taking of oaths—and minor ones—the doffing of hats—thereby refusing to demonstrate deference to superiors. As the Puritan Commonwealth spun out of control and veered toward the Restoration of the monarchy in 1660, the Quakers were increasingly subject to persecution and repression throughout the trans-Atlantic world. In reaction, Friends demonstrated both an annoying tendency toward self-righteous assertions of innocence, and a surprising facility at crafting apocalyptically tinged curses. Juxtaposed to the Puritan laws that imposed a rhetoric of domination, or a domination of rhetoric, upon them, the Quakers developed corrosive rhetorics of inversion that demonstrated an ecstatic asceticism that magistrates understandably feared.[30] In England, the Edict of Toleration ended official persecution of Quakers in 1689. In Boston, the matter came to a more dramatic end—with four Quaker executions between 1659 and 1661. The mimetic crisis, and the existence of ecstatic ascetics willing to die as martyrs to solidify the social order, led to the practice of human sacrifice on Boston Common.

The first Quakers to feel the wrath of Boston's new laws were Christopher Holder, John Rouse, and John Copeland. All three were arrested for the second time in Boston in 1658. By then, Governor John Endecott had made the scapegoating of Quakers a primary feature of his administration. "The Quakers have nothing to prove their Commission by," he contended, "but the Spirit within them, and that is the Devil."[31] Endecott consequently presided as Holder, Rouse, and Copeland all had their ears cropped in a bloody private ceremony that deserves closer scholarly scrutiny someday.[32] In reaction, the Quaker trio suggested that for any who undertook such an act with malicious intent (as if there was any other way to wield knife against ear),"let our Blood be upon their Heads; and such shall know, in the Day of Account, that every Drop of our Blood shall be as heavy upon them as a Mill-stone."[33] This set the ritual pattern: official punishment (or threat of punishment) to reinforce and mark domination, retaliatory imprecation that rhetorically inverted power, and escalating conflict. It lasted for nearly four years.

The Puritan magistrates responded to being cursed with what, in hindsight, appears to be a lack of legislative restraint: they passed a fourth law against the Quakers now mandating "banishment upon pain of death." "By Word and Writing [the Quakers] have published and maintained many dangerous and horrid Tenets," the law redundantly stated. Such tenets were "insinuating themselves into the Minds of the Simple . . . whereby diverse of our Inhabitants have been infected." Such "infection" was no illusion. According to Besse, the new law barely passed by a vote of 13-12, and then only after strong argument in favor of it by Boston's ministerial leadership, notably John Norton, and an amendment stipulating that any case involving the death penalty against Quakers must be "tried by a special Jury."[34]

In response, the Quakers turned to even more exaggerated rhetoric that put them in the role of judging their judges. Humphrey Norton (no relation to Rev. John) had arrived in Rhode Island in 1657 and had promptly set out to preach his Quaker faith in Plymouth. There he warned the governors that if they harassed Quakers, God would punish them with pain "like gnawing worms lodging betwixt thy heart and liver."[35] His reward for such vivid anatomical detail was to be twice arrested and flogged, after which he fled Plymouth for New Haven in hopes of finding a more congenial audience. He didn't, but he did leave Connecticut with a new badge of honor: an "H" branded on his right hand to permanently signify his status as a heretic.

Norton had never set foot in Boston, but, after learning of the ear-cropping of the three Friends, he wrote to Massachusetts Bay Governor Endecott a letter that eventually was made public to a "great noise" in the city. The letter has the rhythm of an "imprecatory psalm," according to historian Frederick B. Tolles. "Accursed are thy rulers," the letter begins, "thou Town of Boston, for they are become the High Priests servants, and hath cut thy Saints right Ears." Norton in quick succession strung together curses against Boston's teachers, people, counsel, governor, and hangman:

> Cursed be the Tongue, that takes pitty on [the hangman], for he pittied not his own Soul, neither showed he mercy to the Saints of the most High. Double give him to drink for what he hath done. . . . Let not the earth be suffered to drink up his blood, but let it rot in his breasts, as an untimely birth: Vengeance for evermore is thy reward thou Manslayer. The irresistable curse swallow thee up for evermore.

And, of course, Norton did not withhold his judgment from Governor Endecott: "The curse of God rest upon thee, Joh. Indicott, for my brethren and Companions sake, the curse of God rest upon thee, thy deeds shalt thou answer for, as sure as ever thou consentedst to that deed, thou Son of a Murtherer." Norton's letter was published by the Boston authorities, with a foreword that asked the reader "to consider how consistent the Toleration of such persons is with the Subsistance of a Land."[36]

By October 1659 the Boston magistrates were ready to demonstrate just how far they would go to protect their subsistence. Quakers William Robinson, Marmaduke Stevenson, and Mary Dyer were arrested in Boston after having previously been banished. All three were summarily sentenced to death in a trial presided over by Endecott. On October 27, the three were marched to the gallows on Boston Common, accompanied by a large band of soldiers, including some on horses. John Wilson, pastor of First Church, Boston, was also in attendance, as was Captain James Oliver and Marshal General Edward Michelson. Besse narrates the scene:

> Now the procession began, and a Drummer going next before the Condemned, when any of them attempted to speak, the Drums were beaten. Glorious Signs of Heavenly Joy and Gladness were beheld in the Countenances

of the three Persons, who walked Hand in Hand, Mary being in the Middle, which made the Marshal say to her . . . "Are not you ashamed to walk thus Hand in Hand betwixt two young men." She replied, "No; this is to me an Hour of the greatest Joy I ever had in this World: No Ear can hear, no Tongue can utter, and no Heart can understand, the sweet Incomes or Influence, and the Refreshings of the Spirit of the Lord which now I feel." Thus going along, W. Robinson said, "This is your Hour, and the Power of Darkness;" but presently the Drums were beaten, yet shortly after, the Drummers ceasing, Marmaduke Stevenson said, "This is the Day of your Visitation, wherein the Lord hath visited you." More he spake, but could not be understood, because of the Drums beating again, yet they went on with great Chearfulness, as going to an Everlasting Wedding, and rejoicing that the Lord had counted them worthy to suffer Death for his Name's Sake.[37]

Then the two men were hanged. Dyer received a reprieve, due perhaps to an earnest letter written to Endecott by her more or less orthodox husband, and to the personal intervention of her son.[38] Besse goes on to record that as the large crowd dispersed after the executions, a drawbridge gave way under the weight, and "several were hurt, especially a wicked Woman, who had reviled the said persons at their Death." It was, no doubt, a sign that due to her injuries "the Flesh rotted from her Bones, which made such a Stink, that the People could not endure to be with her." In which "miserable condition," Besse concludes, "she died." The magistrates, Besse also notes well, naturally took no notice of the providential occurrence.[39]

As for Mary Dyer, after her October reprieve she managed to observe her banishment to Rhode Island for a full four months. In March, after sneaking away without her husband's knowledge, Dyer was arrested for the third time in the city. Now there would be no reprieve. As she was marched to the gallows "the drums [were] beaten before and behind her, and so continued, that none might hear her speak all the Way to the Place of Execution, which was about a Mile." At the gallows, she was given occasion to address the crowd. "I came [back] to keep Blood-Guiltiness from you," she altruistically began her defense, "desiring you to repeal the unrighteous and unjust Law of Banishment upon pain of death, made against innocent Servants of the Lord." This assertion of her innocence did not persuade the crowd, some of whom disputed with her, including one who taunted her to the effect that she must have really loved the Boston prison to visit it so frequently. To this taunt Dyer replied: "Yea, I have been in Paradise these several Days." Yet this paradise was nothing, she continued, compared to the place she would soon inhabit. Her destination was "the Will of my Father," and the real reason she came back to Boston was so that "in Obedience to his Will, I stand even to Death." "And more," Besse concludes, "she spoke of the

Eternal Happiness, into which she was now to enter. Thus Mary Dyer departed from this Life."[40]

Such ecstasy awaited one other Quaker—William Leddra, who was executed by Boston's authorities in January 1661. It followed the ritual pattern. Leddra knew the law, but defied it in an effort to recall for the leaders of the colony how they themselves had once been innocently accused and persecuted. "How have [you] defiled the Bed of Virginity," he accused the Puritans, "who once in a great Measure had escaped the Corruptions that are in the World through Lust!" As for their part, the Puritans had no trouble venting their lust on the poor Leddra, who claimed, if not ecstasy, to feel no pain or hear no torment in: "The Noise of the Whip on my Back, all the Imprisonments, Sound of an Halter, from their Mouth, who Jezabel-like, fat on the imperious Throne of Iniquity, did no more affright me, through the Strength of the Power of God, than if they had threatned [*sic*] to have bound a Spider's Web to my finger." Leddra felt the hangman's noose around his neck on January 14. Over the next few months, as many as twenty-eight Quakers were imprisoned at a time in Boston. Most were released. One more—Wenlock Christison—was sentenced to death. But on September 9, 1661, Charles II intervened, in a letter sent to a Salem Quaker, who carried it to Endecott. The letter mandated that "if there be any of those People called Quakers amongst you, now already condemned to suffer Death, or other Corporal Punishment, or that are imprisoned, or obnoxious to the like Condemnation, you are to forbear to proceed any farther."[41] With that, the killing of Quakers in early America came to an end.

Now, there is much that is curious about this set of events. First is the patent ineffectiveness of the Puritan effort at deterrence. The punitive laws passed by the Massachusetts General Court to threaten and exclude Quakers were matched by a corresponding escalation of Quaker presence in Boston. Such a presence mirrored the Puritan effort at domination with curses whose rhetorical effect was to invert and undermine the Puritan claim to power. Underneath this mimetic crisis, however, is the curious question of the early Quaker *mentalité*. What motivated and sustained these ordinary men and women to find such glory in their suffering, and to express joy in the face of brutal physical punishment and death? Finally, then, beneath both the crisis of differentiation and the ecstatic asceticism— if we may identify these curiosities with these categories—is the even more curious question of Puritan motive. Why did Endecott, Norton, Bellingham, and company imagine—so obviously wrongly—that the sacrifice of a few Quakers would help establish their holy commonwealth in New England? To get at the root of that question, we need to return to the project of empire-building and see the interaction between the Puritans and the Quakers in the larger context of settling the New World.[42]

SACRIFICIAL RITES AND
AN IMAGINED COMMUNITY, 1620–1776

In the prevailing historiography of American religions, the Puritans lost. Their effort to construct a holy commonwealth gave way—at one point or another, and scholars tellingly differ by centuries about exactly when that point was reached—to the flourishing of religious liberty, and the Yankee project of building a truly secular society.[43] I suspect, however, that the process was somewhat more complex than this progressive narrative can encompass. On the level of institutions—where historians for many decades earned their bread and butter—there is some truth to the shift from Puritan to Enlightenment modes of organization in America. But on the level of lived experience, or within the domain of culture, so-called, re-turning to this founding event in American history and tracing its trajec-tories can help us to see that the quest for holiness and the settling of the New World were not well-differentiated processes. In fact, the settling of the New World may have been far more consistent with the Puritan proj-ect than much recent scholarship seems willing to admit.

To recognize the continuities between the Puritan project of building a holy commonwealth and building a nation we can return, briefly, to the Aztecs. According to Carrasco, the Aztecs used public sacrifices to forge an economy based on military expansion. Sacrifices were a means for Aztecs, among other things, to communicate with the gods and to direct "social change in the form of imperial expansion." More specifically, sac-rifices were tools "in the militarization of society," and even more partic-ularly, a way to establish a "center" in the sacred city of Tenochtitlan that would radiate power outward to the peripheries of the empire, and thereby insure their loyalty and patronage.[44] The Puritan effort in killing Quakers may have served similar functions and stemmed from similar motives. Although the Quakers themselves were safe after 1661, the im-pulse that led to the burning of their books on Boston Common hardly vanished from American history. In fact, sacrifice may have become the very fuel of the economic order on which a new nation would arise, through a diffusion of "innocent" or "just" practices of domination in which capital punishment was only the most extreme.

That the Puritan effort to sacrifice Quakers was in the interest of con-trolling the peripheries of their imagined community is obvious enough.[45] As Jonathan Chu and Carla Pestana have demonstrated, the Quakers who were sacrificed came from outside of Boston, yet it was only *in Boston* that Quakers were put to death.[46] On the peripheries of Massachusetts Bay—in places such as Plymouth, Hampton, Kittery, and even nearby Salem—Quakers were, if not tolerated, at least never killed. As Chu suggests, in these localities community leaders were more concerned to establish *any*

English presence—even heterodox—than to regulate uniformity regarding the doffing of hats. In Boston, however, the advancement of the civilizing process, and the centralization of power, mandated an effort to extend the settlement process to the peripheries of the colony. As Rev. John Norton put it, the execution of Quakers was along the lines of "preventing of infection, and spreading contagion." "Impunity of the sinner encourageth others to do the like," the Rev. Norton went on, "but punishment speedily and seasonably inflicted, makes others more afraid of such evils."[47] Plymouth, Hampton, Kittery, and Salem—not to mention Rhode Island—were infected, and the preemptive sacrifices of a few Quakers in Boston would both demonstrate the proper medicine, and deter spread of the disease. That this deterrence was effective only in Norton's imagination did not matter in the least. His vision of a pure commonwealth now had the power not only of reason, but of physical force, behind it.[48]

Of course, the killing of the Quakers also had a theological rationale: the sacrifices preserved good commerce between the Puritans and their God. Rev. Norton again put it well. The execution of the Quakers "may be looked upon as an Act which the court was forced unto . . . in defence of Religion, themselves, the Church, and this poor State and People." It was not that God required a state to do his business, of course. He could just as easily have smote the Quakers immediately through some special Providence. But "that God makes use of Civil power, consequently of man, is not from his need of him, but his favor to him. Not from defect of power, but abundance of goodness."[49] Indeed, the Puritans killed the Quakers not only out of goodness, but in "all humility" and good "conscience," as Governor Endecott explained in a letter to the king.[50] The Puritans merely "held the point of the sword" toward the Quakers, who in their "desperate turbulency" wittingly went "rushing themselves thereupon." They were, after all, "blasphemers" who questioned the Trinity, defamed Christ's divinity, and undermined the scriptures with their dependence on an "inner light." To kill the Quakers was only to preserve "pure scripture worship," and to preserve the Puritan errand into the wilderness, for which they had forsworn the comforts of old England, and undertook to settle the "poor wilderness," surrounded by "the heathen." The Puritans were innocent in their domination, because they imagined themselves to be God's agents in settling the New World.

Such a claim was little different from the Quakers' own to possess God's "inner light," of course, as Quaker apologists quickly pointed out.[51] But between the two parties they were, rather obviously, engaged in a contest to define what vision of the New World would prevail, and which parties would participate in the economic project of settling it. Norton knew this on a personal level: he received a generous land grant as payment for completing his apology for the Quaker killings, sentimentally entitled *The Heart of New-England Rent*, from which we have already quoted at length.[52] In it, he contended (optimistically, and in direct contravention of the facts he was supposed to be explaining) that "all orders and persons amongst us respectively, sanctifie God according to the prescript of scripture, and that at such a time in the regular exercise whereof, we may secure ourselves of a greater blessing than the adversary threatens trouble." This was dubious Protestant theology—sanctification was a questionable doctrine at best, and to imagine that human works could "secure" any blessing from the sovereign God was to walk a narrow line indeed. But Norton's imagination was not, now, focused on salvation—at least not as salvation had been understood in classical Christianity. The current crisis was surely a "test" for his people, Norton admitted, but "though the Beast blasphemeth, the witnesses overcame." This was the classical argument of the victor, of course. When you kill your enemy, you get to describe how just your cause was. While the Quakers had been a pesky opponent, then, filled with zeal, out of the struggle Norton fully expected to "bring forth so much the more zealous and luculent a confession of the Trueth."[53]

And the "Trueth" involved was, finally, civil as well as theological, or rather, military as well as ecclesiastical. In a word, it was economic. The executions of the Quakers were civic rituals, accompanied by all the trappings of military technology that the Puritans could muster. Carla Pestana was the first to surface how the Quaker hangings were surrounded from beginning to end by "military maneuvers" that far exceeded the normal procedures in public executions according to common law.[54] The Boston jail holding Quaker prisoners was surrounded by a night-watch. A fence was built around the prison enclosure, both to keep out crowds and to contain communication with the prisoners. And, as we discuss above, fully armed soldiers, complete with drummers, accompanied the procession of the damned through the city to the Common in a public spectacle. The martyrdom of the Quakers in Puritan Boston was a show of military, as much as ecclesiastical, strength.

As such, it was no doubt reassuring to many citizens. Consequently, Norton could end his apology on a flourish. Having lined up the provinces, God, and the military to his cause, in his final effort to explain himself and his people, Norton clarified that nothing less than the entire project of Christendom was at stake in quelling Quaker dissent in New England:

> The Rule of doctrine, discipline, and order, is the Center of Christianitie. Sincere and grave Spirits are like grave bodies, they cannot rest out of their Center, ie. the Rule. Religion admits of no eccentrick motions. . . . It concerneth N.-E. always to remember, that Originally they are a Plantation Religious, not a plantation of Trade.[55]

By thus contrasting so starkly religion and trade, Norton opened the way—as Sacvan Bercovitch has so cogently demonstrated about jeremiads—to harmonize exactly the very forces he claimed to oppose. Thus he could lament, while yet celebrating: If New England, that "hath now shined twenty years and more, like a light upon a Hill, it should at last go out in the snuff of . . . Corn-fields, Orchards, Streets inhabited, and a place of Merchandize," then people will say, "New England is not to be found in New England."[56]

But, of course, this was that much easier for Rev. Norton to say now that he had his land grant. There was no contradiction between the Puritan sacrificial spirit and Yankee ingenuity. As Weber so long ago intuited, it was an innerworldly but still ecstatic asceticism of commerce, backed by a zealous militia and a ready hangman, which led to the founding of a new nation.[57] A recent flurry of scholarship has clarified how the revolutionary generation mobilized itself to engage in violence against the British precisely through rhetorical appeals to and economic practices of sacrifice.[58] To be sure, these sacrifices were conditioned by desires for glory, consumer baubles, and creature comforts, like land, shelter, and even tea. But it was the willingness of Yankees to *sacrifice* these comforts in various rituals—to hurl the tea into Boston harbor, or to burn it in bonfires on Boston Common—that may have motivated and united them in willingness to risk "sacrificing" themselves and the British in the battles that led to independence. And then these "sacrifices," of both tea and people, were enshrined in public memory as the heroic deeds of "patriots" and "founding fathers," if not "freedom fighters," against whom future generations would be measured, and whose sacrifices they would have to meet or exceed. Of course the object to be sacrificed shifted over time: from Quakers to Indians, or Quakers to slaves, or Quakers to Redcoats, or even Quakers to tea. But that did not change the basic economy. By creating a scapegoat—an enemy-threat-rival—and then executing what they could call a "sacrifice," the "blessing" of a free flow of commerce between God and humanity, and across the human economy, was secured. Between the burning of Quaker books, the hanging of four Quakers, and the bonfires of tea that all took place on Boston Common, the American nation was set on its trajectory as an empire of sacrifice.[59]

NOTES

1. I question whether the term *civil religion* is appropriate; see Fenn (2001). My own thinking is advanced by Richey and Jones, eds. (1974) and Bellah and Hammond (1980).

2. The two schools of thought are represented, respectively, by Richard Slotkin and Martin E. Marty. For Slotkin, America had a "myth" that produced violence,

but this had nothing to do with religion, and for Marty, America was ironically "righteous," but its empire was largely metaphorical (and the Protestants were, of course, waning in influence, anyway).

3. See my forthcoming work, tentatively titled *An Empire of Sacrifice: The Religious Origins of American Violence*, which traces the interaction of religion with various forms of violence throughout American history; see Douglass (1997) and Taves, ed. (1989).

4. Hofstadter (1963); Noll (1994). On innocence, see Hughes (2003).

5. On purity, see Douglas (2002).

6. To call the United States an empire is controversial. I intend to provoke reflection on the way various other categories ("American," "religion," "politics," "freedom") obscure how global markets and military might organize national interests. On empire, see Hardt and Negri (2000).

7. For one narrative history of broader examples of this process, shrouded today in the "innocence" of the judicial system, and where vengeance is sanitized, see Steelwater (2003).

8. Girard (1979, 9–19), as cited in Williams, ed. (2000, 11). See also Girard (1974).

9. Girard's theory can have the ironic outcome of scapegoating religious traditions other than Christianity. See, for example, Hamerton-Kelly (1992). Girardian thought has fostered an academic society, The Colloquium on Violence and Religion, which meets biannually, http://theol.uibk.ac.at/cover/, as cited.

10. Appleby (2000) developed the notion of "weak religions" to describe extremisms. His later work, Almond, Appleby, and Sivan (2003), uses the alternative metaphor of "strong" religion. For the five volumes on "fundamentalism," see Marty and Appleby, eds. (1991–1995).

11. Appleby (2000, 91).

12. Appleby dismisses too glibly the role of the nation-state in fostering religious extremism and violence. See Chomsky 2003.

13. Carrasco (1999, 3).

14. Carrasco (1999, 195).

15. Carrasco (1999, 5).

16. Carrasco (1999, 8).

17. See McCutcheon (2003) and (1997).

18. Hardt and Negri (2000) are helpful, although they overestimate the decline of nationalism in a globalizing, capitalist empire. For examples of scholars who have turned attention to sacrifice within American political power, see Jewett and Lawrence (2003); Linenthal (1993); Chernus (1986); and Albanese (1976). See also Lincoln (2003).

19. See Pahl (2003).

20. Miller (1956).

21. The 1838 edition of Winthrop's document is available online at http://history.hanover.edu/texts/winthmod.html, as cited 4/04/04. See Bercovitch (1978), on the paradoxical character of Puritan rhetoric.

22. The entire document is online at http://www.ucc.org/theology/cambridge.htm, as cited 4/04/04. Attention to the embrace of "discipline" by Puritans is perhaps the central insight of the most recent scholarship on the movement,

along with its indelibly trans-Atlantic character. See Bozeman (2004); Knoppers, ed. (2003); Round (1999); and Kamensky (1997).

23. On early Quakerism, see Barbour and Roberts, eds. (1973), and Barbour and Frost (1988). Still useful, and typical in its subtle anti-Quaker bias, is Worrall (1980).

24. See here Reis (1997), who traces how sin and evil were constructed in gendered terms in early America.

25. I follow Besse's account throughout. See Besse (1753, II: 177–78). Swarthmore College, Friends Historical Library. My gratitude to Christopher Densmore, curator of the collection, for his expert assistance in my research.

26. Besse (1753, II: 179–81).

27. Besse (1753, II: 183).

28. Besse (1753, II: 183–86).

29. On Nayler, see Damrosch (1996).

30. Lincoln (1994).

31. Besse (1753, 189). See the only extant biography of Endecott, written by an heir, Mayo (1936).

32. Ear-cropping, like other forms of punishment by way of public humiliation, was designed to "brand" the punished. The practice varied in its technical effect, from removal of the entire ear—leaving a gaping hole—to less dramatic alteration. The rationale for this punishment probably went well beyond mere magical sympathy or correspondence between the contagion of heresy and hearing. In an oral-aural culture such as the Puritans created, ears were vehicles of grace that when damaged marked the punished as a public reprobate. See Schmidt (2000).

33. The image of the millstone was well known to the Puritans. Jesus invoked this curse in the gospel of Luke 17:1–2.

34. Besse (1753, 190).

35. Tolles (1951, 416). Swarthmore College, Friends Historical Library.

36. Tolles (1951, 420).

37. On the significance of the drumming in early America, see Rath (2003).

38. The letter can be found in *Mary Dyer, Quaker* (1927?). Swarthmore College, Friends Historical Library.

39. Besse (1753, 204–5).

40. Besse (1753, 206–7).

41. Besse (1753, 215–19).

42. See the argument of Petersen (1997).

43. Two influential works that put dates on when the Puritan epoch in America ended are Ahlstrom (1972) and Handy (1971). Handy actually describes two "disestablishments." I think a third is needed. In an understandable (and absolutely necessary) effort to "unseat" the Puritan master-narrative, by means of which only dead white Protestant men received attention as agents in history, historians have obscured some of the complex violence done in the name of privilege and power by dead white men.

44. See here especially chapters 2 and 3 of Carrasco (1999, 49–114), "Templo Mayor: The Aztec Vision of Place" and "The New Fire Ceremony and the Binding of the Years: Tenochtitlan's Fearful Symmetry."

45. Throughout, I depend on the construction of nationalism by Anderson (1983).

46. See Chu (1985) and Pestana (1991).

47. Norton (1659). Swarthmore College, Friends Historical Library.

48. In that sense, the Puritans "won" this episode. Endecott and the magistrates stayed in power. No court or tribunal held them accountable. And, if anything, the link between purity and force has become an unquestioned assumption in American culture, through the rhetorical sleight of hand of "defense." For peace reform in America, see DeBenedetti (1980).

49. Norton (1659, 56).

50. The letter is reprinted in its entirety in Mayo (1936, 252–53).

51. Endecott's petition is quoted verbatim and answered point by point by Quaker apologist Burrough ([1660] 1939, 3). Swarthmore College, Friends Historical Library.

52. The terms of the commission are recorded in a *Resolution of the Massachusetts General Court*, 4 November 1659, Massachusetts Archives, 10:260A, State House, Boston, as cited by Chu (1985, 31).

53. Norton (1659, 57).

54. Pestana (1991, 34). Hall (1989) describes the usual procedures.

55. Norton (1659, 58).

56. Norton (1659, 58).

57. Weber (1958).

58. See, most notably, Purcell (2002) and Breen (2004).

59. To trace a cultural dynamic in a single episode like this is laden with historiographical risk. I explore more fully the continuities alluded to in this compressed conclusion in my forthcoming manuscript, *An Empire of Sacrifice: The Religious Origins of American Violence*. See note 3.

7

Holy Culture Wars: Patterns of Ethno-Religious Violence in Nineteenth- and Twentieth-Century China

David G. Atwill

Western historians have until recently paid only minor attention to Islam in China.[1] Although constituting about 2 percent of China's current population, China's population of twenty million Muslims exceeds that of any Middle Eastern country except Iran, Turkey, and Egypt.[2] Their diminutive demographic presence is belied, however, by the Chinese central government's intense concern over the Muslim population. Traditional interpretations by Chinese and Western scholars reflect this concern by emphasizing the political threat to the Chinese state posed by the Muslim Chinese. Few observers call attention to the competing religious, political, and cultural threads of their Islamic identity and the influence those threads had on the nature of anti-Muslim violence in nineteenth- and twentieth-century China.

This study probes the political, cultural, and ethno-religious tensions between Muslim Chinese (Hui)[3] and Han by tracing the pattern of anti-Muslim violence in the southwestern Chinese province of Yunnan from the mid-nineteenth to the late twentieth century. The investigation is framed historically by two especially violent periods in the Han-Hui relationship during the nineteenth and twentieth centuries. The first occurred between 1839 and 1873 when Han Chinese townspeople, local militia, and imperial officials jointly massacred tens of thousands of Muslim Chinese. The massacre sparked the Panthay Rebellion (1856–1873), a Hui-led rebellion against the Qing empire, which lasted nearly two decades and garnered significant multiethnic support before finally being suppressed by the central court in 1873. The second period—while not as sustained an upheaval as the first—began on July 29, 1975, with a seven-day assault on the Muslim Yunnanese town of Shadian by PLA troops, and continued sporadically into the early 1990s.

The heightened tensions between Han and Hui Chinese during these two periods underscore a commonality the Muslim Chinese conflicts have with many other ethno-religious conflicts in other parts of the globe.[4] As in the recent Arab-Israeli and Bosnian Muslim conflicts, "Muslim violence" in Yunnan is inextricably tied to nonreligious issues of majority-minority discord, friction over limited resources, and ethno-cultural differences. This is not to say that religion has no place in the investigation here, rather that it needs to be considered as one of several factors that shaped "religious violence." Religion is a central and incontrovertible dimension of Yunnan Hui identity. Yet, the term *religious violence* when applied in the borderland context of Yunnan is overly ambiguous and easily misconstrued.

In this chapter, I define *religious violence* in a manner similar to that of Natalie Zemon Davis, whose classic characterization described it as "any violent action, with words or weapons, undertaken against religious targets by people who were not acting *officially and formally* as agents of political and ecclesiastical authority."[5] Davis's focus on sixteenth-century France undeniably intimates a more religious framework than that of nineteenth- and twentieth-century China. It also suggests that the violence ultimately had a religious goal, which, as we will see, is not the case for the anti-Hui violence of Yunnan. Yet, her definition is useful to exhort us to emphasize the *targets* of religious violence over the *motivations* of such violence and thus that not all violence involving Muslims is inherently "Muslim violence."

THE RISE OF ANTI-HUI SENTIMENT IN QING CHINA

The Han-Hui relations within Yunnan Province date back to the thirteenth-century Mongol conquest of China. From that period until the onset of the Qing dynasty in the seventeenth century, the Yuan (1271–1368) and Ming (1368–1643) bureaucracies employed large numbers of Muslim Yunnanese as government administrators and soldiers throughout China, with the most famous being Admiral Zheng He, who led Ming voyages to Southeast Asia, India, and the eastern coast of Africa nearly a century before the voyages of Columbus.[6]

With the rise of the Qing in 1644, imperial attitude toward the Muslim population dramatically shifted. The Qing, far more expansionistic and militarily better equipped than their Ming predecessors, quickly expanded their control into the ethnically diverse but predominantly Muslim area of Central Asia. This process culminated in the late nineteenth century with the creation of a new administrative region designated as Xinjiang (literally the "new dominion"), nearly doubling the size of the Chinese empire.[7] The addition of Xinjiang next to the already heavily Muslim northwestern provinces of Gansu and Shaanxi created a sizeable "Qur'an Belt" that stretched across the empire's northwestern borderlands.

From the perspective of the court, Islam served as the common feature uniting the newly incorporated peoples of this region, and this perspective would color its interpretation of northwest China until the dynasty finally fell in 1911. From the outset, despite Xinjiang's considerable ethnocultural diversity (Kazaks, Kirghiz, and Tajiks[8] to name just a few), Chinese-speakers, including the Manchu Qing monarchs, uniformly referred to this region's population monolithically as Hui-hui or Huimin (Hui people).[9] Similarly, officials labeled the region as the "Muslim Border" (Huibu or Huijiang) and began speaking of the violence that occurred there as "Muslim uprisings" (Huibian).[10]

Revolts against the Qing in Xinjiang began soon after the Qing annexed the region in 1757 and continued virtually uninterrupted until Yakub Beg's Rebellion (1864–1877) ravaged much of Xinjiang.[11] The early Qing emperors hoped the newly subjugated peoples would gradually conform to Manchu rule and few of the Qing emperors strayed from the standard affirmation that the Muslims of the Northwest were "their children and thus to be treated equally in the eyes of the court."[12] But as Morris Rossabi has pointed out, the court overlooked the cultural and racial prejudices of its own officials.[13]

Qing officials tended to bring with them the orthodox concerns of central China, in particular, the desire to root out heretical Buddhist, Daoist, and, now under the Qing, Islamic sects. By the early 1800s, officials across northwest China began to report a growing concern over both overt physical resistance and "subversive" intellectual movements in northwest China. This caused the Qing court to erect distinct legal and intellectual categories for its Muslim population, sanctioning harsher punishments for Hui than for their Han counterparts.[14] Significantly, these legal shifts affected all Hui regardless of whether they lived in northwest China or in China proper (*neidi*) or what style of Islam they practiced.

Although intended to end social and political instability largely limited to the northwest, such policies spread Hui discontent across China. These laws reflected, even encouraged, a growing bias among Han against the Hui in society as a whole. Thus, an official and unofficial anti-Hui bias manifested itself throughout the empire, and in particular in the southwestern province of Yunnan.

YUNNAN HUI

When the Qing dynasty was founded in 1644, Muslim Chinese communities existed in every province of the empire, with one of the heaviest concentrations outside of northwest China in the southwestern province of Yunnan. However, unlike the Muslim population of northwestern China, the Muslim Yunnanese were a distinct minority constituting only 10 percent of the province's total population of ten million in 1850.[15] Significantly, it was the diverse non-Han population (including Miao, Yi, Zhuang), not the Han Chinese, who dominated the local landscape.

The majority of the Yunnan Hui by the early nineteenth century had been Chinese subjects for several centuries and across several dynasties. Thus, the Hui of Yunnan by the nineteenth century were quite unlike the Hui of northwest China, nor were they similar to the increasing numbers of Han Chinese migrating from interior China. Unlike Han immigrants who generally resisted adopting the local indigenous traits (e.g., dress, language, and cultural attributes), Yunnan Hui tended to adopt (or at least accept) indigenous attributes while retaining their distinctive religious beliefs, allowing them to emerge as key middlemen in Yunnan society.[16]

The Hui's lucrative position in Yunnan society drew scorn and contempt from the Han who were immigrating in increasing numbers by the early nineteenth century. Unfortunately while we can document such patterns of majority-minority conflict, it is difficult to pinpoint the actual source of the Han resentment of the Hui. In part, as Jonathan Lipman recently argued, the enmity toward Hui stemmed from the Hui's ability to simultaneously "acculturate to local society wherever they live and to remain effectively different from their non-Muslim neighbors."[17] Yet, often there was little rational or tangible foundation for the animosity.

If the source of Manchu-Han resentment is frustratingly ambiguous, its presence is not. Nearly ubiquitous in all Han and Qing official descriptions of the Yunnan Hui is a litany of disparaging or unflattering Hui attributes (often juxtaposed in official correspondence with flattering accounts of Han).[18] This remark of a top Yunnan official is typical: "The Hui's character has always been strong, and they make it a habit of mocking Han."[19] Another official compared Yunnan Hui's personality to an "animal; the more you try to appease it the more obstinate they become."[20] Underlying the majority of these accounts is the belief that the "Han are accommodating, while the Hui are obdurate."[21] If these examples reveal the bias officials felt comfortable including in their memorials to the throne, one can easily conjecture the derision the Hui encountered in daily interactions with Han that have gone largely unrecorded.

The attitudes endorsed by the state, embraced by its officials, and upheld in its law codes are even more striking when one realizes that by and large the Yunnan Hui did not fit the Qing stereotype. The Yunnan Hui were not extensively involved in the burgeoning opium trade, a cause of near perennial concern for the imperial court from the Opium War (1839) onward. Only a small minority of the Muslim communities in Yunnan adopted the Sufi teachings that had led to so much consternation in the northwest.[22] Until the Panthay Rebellion (1856–1873), there is no record of Hui-led disturbances except in direct retaliation for Han attacks. The number of Hui incidents paled in comparison to the more persistent Lisu, Dai, and Yi insurgencies occurring throughout the province during the same period. Yet, despite the absence of these traditional triggers of state response, the animosity toward the Yunnan Hui in mid-nineteenth-century China remained engrained in both popular and state attitudes toward the Yunnan Hui. The Muslim Yunnanese differed enough from the Han to be identifiable; they excelled commercially enough to be resented; and they were culturally supportive enough of Yunnan's multiethnic and multiregional orientation to be a threat to the Manchu Han's increasingly segregationist vision of China. As a result, by the 1830s a rancor quite different from the Qing court's original legal concern with orthodox religious beliefs in northwestern China emerged against the Yunnan Hui. This rancor expressed itself not in objections to ideas, actions, or beliefs, but in the wholesale extermination of a single ethnic group: the Muslim Yunnanese.

NINETEENTH-CENTURY HOLY CULTURAL WARS: BAOSHAN AND KUNMING MASSACRES

Early on an October morning in 1845, local Han militias marched into Baoshan, a prefectural capital on the far western border of Yunnan, on the pretext of preventing a surprise Hui attack. Local Han with the assistance and open consent of Qing civil and military officials massacred some eight thousand of the city's Hui population.[23] Despite the lack of any evidence to support the militia's claims the governor-general recommended that the local official's prescient and preemptive action should be considered for immediate commendation.[24] Muslim Yunnanese survivors, in a remarkable display of faith in the Qing system, dispatched four Hui to Beijing to file a grievance and seek proper compensation for the victims of the massacre.[25] As a direct result of their efforts, the emperor appointed a new governor-general, Lin Zexu. His investigation pieced together the basic sequence of events beginning with false rumors deliberately spread by Han Chinese and the militia's order to "slaughter all the Hui within the city—regardless of age or sex."[26] Despite his acknowledgment of the horrendous scope and scale of the massacre, Lin failed to pursue with any rigor the local officials involved.

Lin's report on the Baoshan Massacre is emblematic of a broader bias emerging among the Qing bureaucracy. Yunnan officials became progressively more concerned with Hui responses to Han attacks than with the initial Han aggression. In the wake of the massacre Lin and the other provincial officials faced a difficult situation. They had to rectify two seemingly irreconcilable demands: the throne's professed desire to carry out justice based on "separating the good from the bad, not the Hui from the Han," and the rising Han insistence that the Hui be eliminated. The officials placated both the throne and the Han, with neat but ultimately circular logic, by blaming the Hui for bringing the Han-initiated violence upon themselves.

In years leading up to and after the Baoshan Massacre, nearly all of Yunnan's top provincial officials admitted that the Han had sought to exterminate the Hui, but implied that the violence would not have occurred if there were no Hui.[27] Indeed, it would be nearly two decades before a court-appointed official in Yunnan finally called attention to the fact that it was the local Han, with the assistance of numerous Qing officials, who massacred eight thousand Hui in Baoshan, not the other way around.[28]

Increasingly, Qing officials posted to Yunnan emphasized the armed Hui responses to Han violence to justify their biased opinions and continued persecution of the Hui. In spite of a pervasive anti-Hui prejudice among Qing officials and a propensity to defend their actions with often specious claims, none of the officials characterized the "Hui violence" as religiously inspired. As local Han chauvinism united with the bureaucratic biases, an even greater wave of anti-Hui violence erupted.

On May 19, 1856, a massacre extraordinarily similar to that of Baoshan erupted in Kunming, Yunnan's provincial capital, killing over ten thousand Hui.[29] Like the Baoshan Massacre before it, the Kunming Massacre was a premeditated and carefully executed affair. The scope, however, was much larger, since provincial officials issued a circular permitting militias to form and kill Hui in every "prefecture, sub-prefecture, department and district" in Yunnan.[30] This spawned attacks on Hui communities in and around Kunming and throughout the province.

Official accounts of the massacres offer only gross exaggerations of the Hui character and make no effort to provide any legal motives for the extent of the violence. What makes the official and unofficial accounts intriguing is that both popular and official descriptions of the Hui treat them as an identifiable ethnic group, and not as Qing subjects who unlawfully adhered to heretical religious beliefs. The religious heterodoxy of the Hui beliefs is virtually never broached in the months and years following the Kunming Massacre.

If the highly biased official accounts do not characterize the violence in the nineteenth century as religiously incited, why do so many of the postrebellion accounts (up to the present) of these events characterize it as "Islamic violence"? This may be explained in large part by the fact that few of these treatments of the rebellion, and the violence leading up to it, examine sufficiently the level of official involvement that occurred in orchestrating the attacks.

Mary Wright's summary of the Panthay Rebellion is typical in this regard. She presents one of the few extended examinations of the rebellion in English. In her analysis she hints that a lack of Qing leadership was largely at fault for the rebellion's success: "Among the governors-general and governors of the period, one was murdered, one was a suicide, one lost his mind, one refused to enter the province to take up his duties, and several had to be recalled for gross incompetence."[31] What she and others omit in their scrutiny of that period is that it was, in fact, precisely the advocacy of anti-Hui policies by Yunnan's highest officials and the emperor (or those acting in his name) that ignited and fanned the flames of rebellion. It was not the officials' ineptitude but their meticulous proficiency in organizing anti-Hui violence that incited the rebellion.

A Manchu official, Shuxing'a, held the post of Yunnan governor at the time of the Kunming Massacre (the official later labeled by Wright as "insane"). He openly encouraged and defended the anti-Hui actions of those around him. In his few memorials to the throne, he never once mentioned the Kunming Massacre, only that he had suppressed a "Hui plot."[32] Even two months after the massacre, with the province spiraling out of control, he still attempted to place blame on the Hui by relying on stereotypes, such as "the Hui are suspicious and fierce by nature."[33]

One of the few opponents of the attacks on the Hui was Shuxing'a's immediate superior, Yunnan-Guizhou Governor-General Hengchun. The initial massacre occurred while he was out of the province on a military campaign suppressing another ethnic uprising. On his return Hengchun assessed the factors that led to the violence and advocated only limited use of military force. This approach, he hoped, would stem the spreading violence. Yet the court continued to support Shuxing'a's anti-Hui policy, denoting an even more pervasive prejudice against the Hui than hinted at by Wright and traditional treatments of the rebellion. The emperor instructed Hengchun to maintain the policy of "not distinguishing between Han and Hui and pacify them uniformly," and at the same time he dictated that the rebels were to be militarily subdued.[34] The contradiction inherent in these instructions implicitly called into question Hengchun's moderate policies.

Even more striking from the perspective of the rebelling Hui is the fact that the emperor never censured the Han militia and the lower officials for their roles in inciting the violence. Instead he admonished their one defender, Hengchun: "There are good and bad Muslim Yunnanese. If you do not suppress the bad leaders not only will the Han suffer but the good Hui will also languish."[35] These words expose the court's lack of concern with distinguishing between good and bad *Han*, only between "good and bad *Hui*."

The Hui-led Panthay Rebellion enveloped Yunnan province for the next eighteen years (1856–1874). The government victory in 1874 achieved the original goals of those who had pursued the extermination of the Hui in Baoshan more than two decades earlier. Of the approximately one million Hui residing within the province at the beginning of the rebellion, only a small fraction remained in 1874. The devastation of the Hui segment of Yunnan society was so complete that more than a century later the Yunnan Hui population has still not returned to the prerebellion level.[36]

TWENTIETH-CENTURY HOLY CULTURAL WARS: SHADIAN AND PINGYUAN UPRISINGS

In the early 1970s, almost exactly one hundred years after the brutal suppression of the Panthay Rebellion, a second wave of violence began in Yunnan. Political skirmishes of the Cultural Revolution (1966–1976), like many areas of China, racked Yunnan in the 1970s. The Muslim Yunnanese, along with the Buddhists and the Confucians, had been ordered to close down their places of worship and burn their religious books as part of the "Destroy the Four Olds" campaign. In 1968, in the southern Yunnan village of Shadian,[37] a propaganda team took up residence in the village mosque. There the team ate pork, threw the bones down the well used for ablutions before prayer, and repeatedly humiliated the local Hui religious leaders as a means of demonstrating their revolutionary ardor.[38]

In October 1973, a local Hui secondary teacher, Ma Bohua, outraged at the years of insults and desecration of the town's mosque, organized a drive to remove the propaganda team and reopen the mosque for prayer. The application cited their rights as an officially recognized ethnic group (*minzu*) to practice their religion. His efforts met with no perceptible effect. The party cadres refused to leave and attempts to secure support from the provincial leaders brought no changes. In a final attempt to resolve the situation, ten local Hui representatives took their request to Beijing, in an act strikingly similar to that of the Baoshan Hui in 1846.[39] Unlike their Baoshan forebears, their attempts to secure the support of the proper authorities were rebuffed. Their actions did not go unnoticed, for on their return to Yunnan matters quickly took a turn for the worse.

In mid-May 1975, several People's Liberation Army (PLA) units appeared outside of Shadian and took up positions. On May 17, the troops attempted to enter the town, but informally banded together Hui militia units composed of Hui from Shadian and the surrounding area repulsed them. The PLA accused the Hui of carrying out a "Counter-Revolutionary Insurgency," "Leftist Activities," and "Separatism." Their troops opened a seven-day attack on the Shadian Hui on July 29, 1975, "with artillery, flame throwers and incendiary bombs," killing nine hundred and wounding six hundred.[40] PLA units killed or wounded an additional three to four hundred Hui from adjacent Hui villages, including dozens of women, elderly, and children.[41] Fighting leveled the entire town of Shadian during the eight days of intense combat and forced the surviving residents to flee to neighboring villages.[42]

The following year (not insignificantly the year after Mao's death), provincial and national officials investigated the Shadian attack. The investigation advocated the full rehabilitation of the implicated Hui. The Yunnan Provincial Party, however, waited a decade and a half before finally issuing a document formally removing the counterrevolutionary status from the Shadian Hui.[43] In 1989 provincial officials erected a memorial in Shadian expressing regret at the "bloody suppression of the Shadian Hui" and at the same time explaining that now the leaders were following the "correct political course."[44] Officially the excesses were blamed on the political climate wrought by the Cultural Revolution and the Gang of Four. The betrayal of trust, the massacre, and the lingering prejudice against the Yunnan Hui remained indelibly marked on the Muslim Yunnanese collective memory. If there was any question that Han-Hui tensions remained on either side, subsequent events in Pingyuan confirmed it.[45]

Superficially, the Pingyuan Incident (1992) appears to be an anomaly among the other major Hui episodes. It, unlike the others, suggests the Muslim Yunnanese Pingyuan community did indeed invite a government attack, with the government demonstrating remarkable restraint both in its execution and subsequent adjudication. Yet, recent representations of the event reveal several disturbing omissions. What follows is how the incident unfolded.

Pingyuan is situated in the prefecture directly to the east of Shadian and is roughly 125 miles from Yunnan's border with highland Southeast Asia.[46] It is composed of a small town encircled by seven outlying villages. In a scenario similar to the three episodes examined above, a caravan of more than a hundred trucks left Kunming on August 30, 1992, carrying over two thousand public security officers and paramilitary policemen.[47] The forces arrived outside of Pingyuan that evening, and the soldiers quickly cordoned off all routes leading in and out of the city. The city secured, twenty armed teams entered Pingyuan early the next morning and arrested close to twenty Hui drug and gun dealers in what officials at the time described as a criminal syndicate. Almost immediately gunfire erupted. Two police officers and several Pingyuan Hui were killed. Fearful of a bloody repeat of Shadian, the Chinese law enforcement authorities hastily withdrew to their perimeter several miles distant and essentially besieged Pingyuan for the next eighty days.

When the Chinese authorities finally entered the city two and a half months later, they arrested more than 850 individuals, confiscated over two thousand pounds of heroin and opium, and seized nearly one thousand firearms. In the end, the only direct casualties of the crackdown were those of the initial assault on the first day. Over four hundred of the Hui who were arrested were accused of capital crimes. In the public trials carried out after the offensive, seven Hui received death sentences.[48] Chinese officials have repeatedly asserted ever since the incident that "the Pingyuan Problem is not a minority (*minzu*) problem, nor is it a religion problem; rather it is a problem of a serious criminal offence and the manifestation of class struggle under a new situation in some areas."[49] Yet, such efforts to spin the meaning of the campaign on Pingyuan as purely a drug-suppression campaign overlook several factors.

In the 1980s the average annual income in Pingyuan was under three hundred yuan (or roughly $35 USD).[50] Being a poor community in a peripheral province, the local Hui turned to their traditional role as middlemen in the cross-border trade between Southeast Asia and China. And the provincial and local authorities, ever mindful of the Shadian affair, trod delicately in affairs involving the Hui. The confluence of these trends resulted in Pingyuan emerging as one of the key nodes in a drug distribution network that extended from the Golden Triangle to Hong Kong and Shanghai. Pingyuan's reputation also fueled a provincewide perception of the Hui as drug peddlers. Predictably, negative stereotypes of all Yunnan Hui remained intense among local Han and provincial government circles.

A second factor concerns the publicity that attended the assault on Pingyuan. The two main trials resulting from the arrests of the drug dealers were public and attracted eight and twelve thousand spectators respectively. In addition, the crackdown itself was widely covered in the Chinese media with exposés repeatedly presented on television and in newspapers and the weekly tabloids, a deviation from the usually secretive approach employed by China's law enforcement authorities. This publicity as a tactic is clearly less violent than the massacres that occurred in the earlier episodes; however, it played on and reinforced the public impression that most Hui were drug traffickers.

Third, there is evidence to suggest that the Chinese government employed a double standard in its efforts to suppress the drug trade and treated the Hui differently than it did the Han and other ethnic groups. Although trumpeted as a key state victory against the drug trade, the

Pingyuan arrests represented only 1.5 percent of the more than twenty-eight thousand drug-related arrests in the province.[51] Yet, state accounts repeatedly point to the large number of Hui arrested for drug trafficking. What is not apparent in these state reports is the actual proportion of Hui involved in the drug trade as compared to the less publicized Han and non-Han involvement. Zhou Yongming, in his study of Chinese anti-drug campaigns, hypothesizes that "the standard of ethnic differentiation was set mainly according to the degree of potential threat posed to the authorities."[52] Chinese government authorities continued to perpetuate the myth of the "potential threat" posed by the Hui to defend their actions against the Muslim Yunnanese.

Finally, Susan McCarthy, in a recent article on the party-state participation in non-Han (or "minority" [*shaoshu minzu*]) affairs, traces the increasing frequency with which the government sponsored crackdowns on a variety of grassroots institutions. As she describes it, "The party-state's concern with modernization is tied to its desire for ideological control and to matters of legitimacy. The leadership fears the real or apparent destablizing effects of Falun Gong, underground Christianity, etc., and seeks to quell them."[53] In other words, the treatment of the Pingyuan Hui by the Chinese state, while implemented in an undeniably more standardized manner than in past incidents, retains many of the same societal biases and ethno-religious prejudices present in China for over two centuries.

CONCLUSION

Prominent in the incidents described above is the blurred relationship between religion and ethnicity. Dru Gladney recently remarked with regard to Islam in China: "As Islam makes no distinction between state and church, or politics and religion, to discuss it in the abstract in China without reference to minority identity would be to ignore the way it is experienced and practiced in the daily lives of Muslims today."[54] This ethno-religious convergence, although long acknowledged in anthropological and cultural studies, has rarely been examined from a more macro-religious perspective. As I recently argued, the term *Hui* in the Chinese context has long been misconstrued to mean a "Muslim" without any acknowledgment of its complex ethnic associations.[55] The events outlined above, because they occur in an area traditionally perceived as outside of the Islamic world, reveal the often ignored ethnic dimension of such violence.

The significance of interposing ethnicity into discussions of religion lies in the propensity of many observers to privilege religion over other categories of identity. Despite the solid repudiation of Fukuyama (1989) and Huntington (1993) in academic circles, there remains among Western and

Chinese observers the lingering and often overt implication that all violence involving Muslims is, a priori, caused by Muslims.[56] Even more disturbing is the inveterate notion that all violence involving Muslims is understood by Muslims to be part of a single struggle. Perspectives such as
this lead to conclusions like that of one commentator who asserts: "But in
the long run, there cannot be any definitive sorting out of good Muslim
states from bad ones. It is the Muslim umma as a whole that has harbored
this murderous movement within it, and it is the Muslim umma as a
whole that must somehow be persuaded to break with it."[57] Artificial constructions that posit a Muslim world in this way, without regard to historical depth or cultural context, seek to explain "Muslim violence" as a
consequence of religious beliefs.[58] The problem in both of these examples
is that this causal logic is applied without consideration for the many
other and often far more influential factors at work.

The convergence of these two popular assumptions not only supposes
a predisposition among Muslims toward violent acts, but categorically assumes all violence involving Muslims—regardless of whether they are the
aggressor or the victim—is "Muslim violence." This stubborn propensity
is notable in the consistent depiction of the Hui by the Han as deserving
of the violence brought upon them regardless of the political, social, and
religious contexts in which it occurred. Equally notable is the persistent
absence, in both Hui and Han accounts, of religious justification for the violence. Rather, the identification of the violence as "Islamic" occurs after
the fact with erroneous premises leading to an equally erroneous conclusion: since Hui are involved, and since Hui are Muslim, the violence must
be religious in nature (both in China and elsewhere).

The central purpose in comparing these four incidents is to propose
that previous attempts to analyze these events have privileged religion
over other categories of analysis that I offer above—Han chauvinism,
governance, and ethnicity. In Bruce Lincoln's recent work *Holy Terrors* he
calls for the "end results of our definitional efforts to problematize, and
not normalize" our renewed exploration of religion by reveling in the
"fierce historical struggles" that typically shape religious interaction.[59] As
the Baoshan, Kunming, Shadian, and Pingyuan violence highlights, the
causes of such violence are deeply imbedded in complex local, regional,
and national frames of reference. By exploring the characteristics of these
neglected lines of analysis—the complexity of ethno-religious tensions in
nineteenth- and twentieth-century Yunnan—the commonly held myth
that Muslim violence is the sole explanation for the blood that was shed
in those incidents is refuted both at its reputed roots and in its more recent manifestations. This study serves as a call to view non–Middle Eastern Muslim society not as minor or peripheral, but as central and representative unto itself.

NOTES

1. Jonathan Lipman's *Familiar Strangers* is a notable exception.

2. Gladney (2003, 145–61).

3. Throughout this chapter the terms *Hui* or *Muslim Yunnanese* are used interchangeably. Neither should be interpreted to mean simply "Muslim."

4. For a discussion of periodization in China see Ng (2003, 37–61).

5. Davis (1973, 52).

6. Yang Zhaozhun (1994, 86–88). For perhaps the best account in English of Zheng He's voyages, see Wade (2004).

7. As Perdue cautions, "What we now call 'Xinjiang' is a recent creation. The Qing created the name 'Xinjiang' (New Dominion) during their eighteenth-century conquests." See Perdue (2005, 32).

8. Cao [1830] 1972. Using the terms *Kazaks, Kirghiz,* and *Uyghur* for the pretwentieth century is anachronistic, yet following James Millward and many Chinese historians I use them here to refer to the Turkic-speaking peoples of the region in and around the Tarim basin. See Millward (1994, 428).

9. Lipman (1997, xxiii). The exact meaning of *Hui* in the late imperial context is highly contested. Yet, there is an indication that there were ethnic differences among the Hui with ethnonyms employed such as *Chantou Hui* (lit. Turban-ed Hui) and *Sala Hui* (the group today identified as the Salars).

10. *Huijiang* often referred specifically to the "eastern circuit" (*nanlu*) of Xinjiang but documents from the era often employ it in a much broader (and inconsistent) sense.

11. For an excellent study of this rebellion and its impact on the region, see Kim (2004).

12. Lipman (1997, 94).

13. Rossabi (2004, 4–6).

14. For an insightful look at this change in the Qing law codes, see Lipman (1999, 253–75).

15. *Qinding Pingding Huifei Fanglüe* (hereafter QPHF), 9:19b; QPHF 19:18a–b; see also *Yunnan Tongzhi* 1835, 30:1a.

16. For the best study of this phenomenon to date, see Ma Weiliang (1999, 101–143).

17. Lipman (2004, 22). For a study that shows a similar evolution of tensions between old-timers and newcomers, see Reardon-Anderson (2005).

18. *Dengchuan* 1855, 4:3b; QPHF 4:2a, 3:14a; *Dali Xianzhi Gao* 24:42b.

19. QPHF 14:16b.

20. QPHF 10:10a.

21. QPHF 15:4a.

22. Ma Tong (1986, 126–28); Bai (1992, 27).

23. Lin (1935, 7:13b–14b).

24. He (1882, 11:13a–4b, 11:40a). See also Li (1953, 4–5).

25. Li (1953, 6).

26. Lin (1935, 7:13b–14b).

27. Lin (1935, 3:7b); Li Xingyuan [1865] 1974, *Li Wengong,* 4:28a.

28. Yun-Gui governor-general Pan Duo, in 1862, estimated the number of deaths at 8,000, see QPHF 14:16b.

29. Rocher (1879, 39); Cordier (1914, 153). One witness states nearly 20,000 were killed; see Wang (1953, 300).

30. It is unclear who ordered this, although it was likely either Shuxing'a or Huang Cong. QPHF 2:6a, 5:13b–14a, 6:19a–20a, 8:4a; Ma Guanzheng (1953, 294). *Dali Xianzhi Gao*, 9:17a; Rocher (1879, 36–37).

31. Wright (1957, 114).

32. QPHF 1:7a–9b.

33. QPHF 1:11a–b.

34. QPHF 4:2b.

35. QPHF 3:18a.

36. The Hui population in Yunnan today is roughly 600,000. The Hui population declined from disease, military casualties, and purges at the end of the rebellion, as well as out-migration to other parts of China and Southeast Asia.

37. Shadian is located at the south of the provincial capital and today has a population of 13,638, 90 percent of whom are Hui.

38. Dillon (1999, 165). Sources and accounts vary on the type of this desecration, "Shadian Tongshi."

39. "Yunnan Shadian Shijian Beiwen" (A memorial to the Yunnan Shadian Incident), erected December 1989.

40. Dillion (1999, 166); "Yunnan Shadian Shijian Beiwen."

41. Ma Shaomei (1989, 15), quoted in Israeli (1997, 24).

42. Matsumoto (1998, 5).

43. Ma Shaomei (1989, 15).

44. "Yunnan Shadian Shijian Beiwen."

45. There are in fact many instances of increased friction. An excellent account of more recent Han-Hui tensions in Yuxi is recorded by Lipman (2004, 19–20). In a recent visit to Najiaying, a wealthy township near Tonghai, an incident in late 1996 requiring police intervention was also related to me.

46. Also referred to in some accounts as Pingyuanjie.

47. Zhou Yongming in his study of this incident indicates that the caravan's movements were so out of the ordinary (and secretive) that American State Department officials initially were concerned that the convoy indicated an escalation of tensions with Vietnam (Zhou 1999, 161–67).

48. Luo (1993, 20–24); Yang and Zhao (2002); Zhou (1999, 161–67).

49. Luo and Zhang (1998, 28).

50. Yang and Zhao (2002).

51. It is not clear that all those arrested were charged with drug-related charges, so 1.5 percent represents a liberal estimate. See Qin Heping, "The northeastern Burma border drug threat towards China," 208.

52. Zhou (1999, 167).

53. McCarthy (2004, 47).

54. Gladney (2003).

55. Atwill (2003).

56. Huntington (1996).

57. Jack Miles (2002, 96). See also Inglehart and Norris (2003, 70–73).

58. Such definitions of the "Muslim World" ignore the multiple, or overlapping, nature of identity in such Muslim communities and of those Muslims who reside there.

59. Lincoln, *Holy Terrors* (2003, 2–3).

8

Femicide as Terrorism:
The Case of Uzbekistan's
Unveiling Murders

Marianne Kamp

In the late 1920s, the Soviet state witnessed a wave of murders in Central Asia. The murderers, Uzbek men, attacked Uzbek women who had unveiled at the behest of Communist activists. About 2,500 women were murdered in connection with unveiling between 1927 and 1930. The officially atheist Communist Party pushed for a radical social change, one that intervened in Uzbek family life. Many Muslim clergy denounced these efforts, and called upon fellow Uzbeks to attack and kill unveiled women.

In this chapter, I seek an explanation for femicide. In Uzbekistan, many murderers of unveiled women claimed that their actions were a defense of honor; this explanation highlights patriarchal structures that empower men to limit women's actions. I argue that these were not "honor killings"; rather, they were cases of religiously inspired gender terrorism. The murder wave in Uzbekistan took place in the context of a struggle for control of the state between groups whose religious ideas shaped their politics and a government that forcefully promoted secularism. Clergy who spoke in the name of Islam incited religiously sanctioned femicide, terrorism designed to force women to conform to a social order that the religious leaders proclaimed to be divinely willed.[1] Without religious incitement, there might still have been murders of women for unveiling in Uzbekistan, but not on such a large scale. Although this chapter examines only Uzbekistan, similar religiously incited forms of femicide and rape have taken place in other conflict zones, most notably in Algeria in the 1990s.[2]

In Uzbekistan, Islam is the religion of the community where violence occurred, and the religious ideas that promoted and justified that violence were grounded in interpretations of Islam that denied any public roles to women. Those with power (males) made a brutal effort to enforce an unequal social order (a gender hierarchy) through violence by terrorizing an entire group. Certain scholars would argue that this use of "terror," "violence intended to instill fear in a large audience," is too broad.[3] However, even in the 1920s, those who described the murders of Uzbek women called the wave "terrorism."

An Uzbek woman activist for unveiling, Saodat Shamsieva, recalled: "The father, husband or older brother of every woman or girl who threw off the paranji in the mahalla [urban neighborhood] or village would, having killed her, come to us saying, 'I killed her because I did not want her to uncover and to cause me shame.'"[4] The murders thus seem to be "honor killings," which most scholars relate to control of women's sexuality and to other forms of domestic violence, rather than to political agendas. In some Islamic societies and some non-Islamic societies, honor killing is a means of social control.[5] Honor killings are almost always explained as "not part of Islam," but rather "cultural," as if that somehow makes them more acceptable, or at least saves Islam from the taint of association with them.[6] Whether Islam condones or condemns such murders, the discourse that promoted the unveiling murders in Uzbekistan used appeals to Islam to convince men to murder women in their families and communities. However, "honor killing" is not a sufficient explanation for these waves of murder.

The targeted murders of women showed a degree of organization that went beyond individual action; murders were committed not only by family members, but also by groups of acquaintances or strangers. This wave of murders was not an enduring cultural phenomenon, but rather a burst of political violence that eventually subsided, even as women abandoned traditional veiling. When the incitement decreased, due to radical social upheaval and government suppression, so did the murders.

The unveiling murders and rapes in Uzbekistan mixed both intimate and stranger violence, complicating analysis. Violence against women is often explained through reference to enduring cultural attitudes, such as male proprietariness of women or sexual jealousy.[7] Even when this violence appeared to be intimate, such murders were motivated by a religiopolitical struggle, not by an enduring cultural tradition. In Uzbekistan, where the Soviet state tried to change women's status, rapidly and coercively, in ways that were not accepted by the majority of Uzbek men, men's violence against women became a conscious enactment of opposition to the state and its ideology, and a violent enforcement of what those men believed to be God's desire. Juergensmeyer notes that terrorist acts "can be both *performance events*, in that they make a symbolic statement, and *performative acts*, insofar as they try to change things."[8]

After discussing this wave of religiously incited violence against women and the factors that contributed to it, I ask, what causes such bursts of violence to subside? When violent actors use religion to challenge the state, what are potential state responses?

From 1927 to 1930, the three main years of the Hujum, or "Attack [on the old ways]" campaign (a Party program that promoted women's unveiling), more than 2,500 women were murdered in connection with unveiling.[9] The Communist Party regarded the murders as "crimes of everyday life," a category that included polygyny and minor marriage, and thus as evidence of Uzbek society's need for the Party's intervention in family life. More recently, scholars have argued that the Party prematurely or wrongly initiated the Hujum, thus stimulating a wave of violence against unprotected women.[10] Anthropologist Shirin Akiner writes: "For Central Asians, [the Hujum] was a defeat and a brutal rape; the honor and dignity of the community was suddenly and monstrously violated. No other measure of Soviet policy . . . provoked such violent and outspoken resistance. . . . More than a thousand unveiled women were murdered."[11] Both the Party's regard of murders as "crimes of everyday life," and scholarship that sees the Party as provoking the murder wave, assume that in Central Asian society, violence against women, including murder, was natural. Neither Party nor scholars question why men would respond to state offenses by harming women.

The Soviet state launched radical changes, but to focus on the state's role as provocateur is nonetheless one-sided: the state did not murder or rape women; Uzbek men did. The temporal and cultural contexts for these murders help explain them; even more important are questions about the purposes of the murderers.

Culturally, this burst of violence against women was an anomaly. Although ethnographic sources documented intimate violence against women, I have found no evidence that Uzbeks interpreted codes of honor as necessitating killing disorderly women.[12] Among Uzbeks, patriarchy ordered gender relations, but the idea that became widespread during the Hujum, that women who unveiled should be killed for that sin, was startlingly new. The campaign's initiators did not anticipate this response.

Murders of women for unveiling were not spontaneous crimes of passion; they were premeditated and often involved groups of people. Uzbek men who killed Uzbek women expressed hostility toward the individual victim and her decision to enter the public by unveiling, going to school, or getting involved with the state's programs. Murders also expressed coordinated opposition to the state and the Communist Party, enacted on the bodies of women, demonstrating that the local community, not the state, had authority over women's actions and their bodies. These murders were political in intent, designed to challenge the state; and they also

served to terrorize other women. Many murders were deliberately gruesome, involving cutting, dismemberment, and the disposal of the body
with symbolic dishonor.

Political violence was widespread in 1920s Uzbekistan, as the Soviet
government disrupted community structures and removed traditional
authority figures who opposed Communism. After 1918, resistance
groups, the so-called basmachi, fought the Red Army for control of rural
regions. The antiveiling campaign followed a decade of violence. However, there is a difference between state coercion and citizen violence.
While the state coerced women to unveil, the coercion to reveal one's face
in public cannot be made the moral equivalent of murder or rape. I refer
to state actions in forcing women to unveil as *coercive; violence* is a term I
reserve for brutal physical attacks.

Carroll Smith-Rosenberg's analysis of violent social relations in times of
rapid change offers an insight into gendered violence. Smith-Rosenberg
suggests that, when experiencing rapid change, hierarchical societies that
"insist on rigid dress codes and rules of physical decorum" will regard
"physical and sexual disorder as particularly threatening." In this context
such societies will see behavior that disrupts the rules as "sexually dangerous and physically polluting," and will make "stern efforts to control"
those who act outside the boundaries of the acceptable.[13]

Uzbek society was hierarchical, and Uzbek women's bodies were
bounded by the *paranji* and *chachvon* (a head-and-body-covering robe and
a face-veil). Rapid, forced changes in Uzbekistan included the Hujum,
which was a state attack on men's authority over women and on Uzbek
separateness from Russians, but also campaigns against religion and private property, which attacked nearly all socially prominent actors—the
wealthy landowners, the merchants, and the clergy. In this context,
women's unveiling was magnified as socially polluting. Murders of unveiled women were physical attempts to reassert one social boundary, to
enforce at least one aspect of a social order that was under a full-scale assault.

Finally, and importantly, most Muslim clergy opposed unveiling, and
many incited violence against the unveiled.[14] Uzbek society was divided
over the Soviets' sweeping social engineering. While some (including
some women) supported the Party's plans to redistribute land, to crush
the Muslim clergy,[15] and to "liberate" women through new laws, programs, and the unveiling campaign, other Uzbeks saw their entire world
under attack.

But what translated this discontent into terrorist attacks on women?
When the Communist Party made women a trigger for social change by
unveiling them, differences in religious interpretations among the Uzbek
clergy sharpened. During the Russian colonial period (1865–1917) the

Sunni clergy of Central Asia developed modernizing and traditionalizing trends. The Jadids, or modernists (including religious scholars and secular voices), advocated rethinking Islam and condemned their foes as "qadimists"—essentially, obscurantists. By the 1920s, the advocates of a modernized Islam believed that they shared ground with Communists who called for land reform and women's rights; they thought that the traditionalizers depended on the people's ignorance for maintaining their own authority. The traditionalizers opposed both the Communist order and those who supported it, seeing both as destroying religion. Some modernist clergy vocally supported unveiling, declaring that Islamic law did not require women to wear the *paranji* and *chachvon*. Many clergy condemned unveiling as a sin deserving of hell, declared that unveiled women were prostitutes, and began to preach violence against the unveiled.[16] While Islam did not create the context for this wave of femicide, I argue that the latter group of clergy incited murder by their preaching, thus translating men's anger over government intervention in family life into terrorist acts.

In 1927, the Communist Party adopted unveiling as the symbol of its social and cultural revolution in Uzbekistan. Earlier, in Uzbekistan's cities, a few Uzbek women unveiled as a symbol of their own commitment to social change. These women mainly were associated with the Uzbek progressive movement, with modern education, and with the Communist Party's program for women. The Party appropriated the symbol, believing that unveiling could serve as a mechanism to bring women out of the home and to change the whole dynamic of family and social life. The Hujum campaign featured Party-initiated mass unveiling meetings for Uzbek women, along with social reform measures, a revised code of family law, literacy schools for women, and efforts to bring women into the workforce. Some of the women who participated in public unveiling meetings wanted to unveil, but many were coerced.[17] Following the Party's highly publicized International Women's Day unveiling meetings on March 8, 1927, a wave of attacks began. For example, in Shahrixon, near Andijon, the Uzbek Women's Division director, Hadija-xon Go'ibjon qizi, convinced a number of women to unveil on March 8, 1927; one week later she was murdered, and so was her husband. Party members in Shahrixon, when asked about women who unveiled, said that unveiled women were all prostitutes, and that respectable women would not unveil. As a result, "all eighteen women who unveiled have now reveiled."[18] Many of the unveiled quickly resumed veiling as murders of unveiled and activist women increased.

The Hujum coincided with other dramatic programs. In 1927, the Party attacked Islam in Central Asia by closing the major religious Islamic institutions: *maktabs* (lower level schools), *madrasas* (schools of higher learning), Sharia courts, many mosques and shrines, and *waqfs* (foundations that provided income to Islamic institutions). This policy deprived the Muslim clergy of positions and income, as well as denying the importance of their religious understanding of life. During the 1920s and 1930s, the government arrested, exiled, and executed many Muslim clergy.[19] Land reform, which started in 1925, brought the arrest and dispossession of wealthy landowners, and redistribution to the poor. As the Hujum continued, the Soviets were also nationalizing businesses and began agricultural collectivization. All of these programs threatened the property, social influence, and lives of the wealthy and the religious leaders.

Uzbek society understood the Hujum as one element in a huge social upheaval. An ordinary farmer told his neighbors: "The Soviet government carried out land reform and now carries out reform on the woman question, taking second wives from those who have them and giving them to the landless peasants. Removing the paranji is one of the means of the Soviet government to carry out this reform."[20] While old elites lost their sources of capital and social power, new, pro-Soviet classes took control.

Partly in response to Russian colonial rule (1865–1917), Uzbek community boundaries were established through religious ritual and the rhetoric of proper behavior and separation from Russians. Those boundaries were threatened by social change before the revolution, but at the time of the Hujum, the Soviet government was ridding Uzbek society of the structures that maintained community boundaries. Unveiling women was part of this larger program.

Before 1927, there were Uzbek women who unveiled individually, and they faced harassment and opposition, but not murder. The murders for unveiling began after the Communist Party started the Hujum, turning unveiling into a political act that seemed to demonstrate women's support of the Party. When mass unveilings began, popular stories associated unveiling with prostitution, reports of the rape of unveiled women became rampant, and many clergy members not only opposed unveiling but encouraged men to "punish" unveiled women. The state used the secret police (OGPU) to collect reports of anti-unveiling violence.[21]

In Bukhara, Muslim clergy who saw women in headscarves said, "Look at how Muslim women have debased themselves. . . . They want the whole people to become infidels. Muslim women are throwing away their religion and turning to another." Some preached that neighboring states would attack the Soviet government for the unveiling campaign. In Tuda-Maidon, a religious leader collected false evidence about the unveiled wife of a village council representative, claiming that she was a prostitute. Under pressure, she reveiled.[22]

Widespread libel-mongering had serious implications in Uzbek society. A student at the medical technical school, Pulatova, committed suicide because her classmates insulted her, calling her a prostitute for unveiling.[23] Family members of unveiled women had to endure aspersions. Some men divorced unveiled wives. Some of the murders of women were undoubtedly responses to public stigma; that is, they were attempts to restore family honor by killing women who were blamed for bringing shame on their relatives.[24]

In many villages, social leaders (the wealthy and the clergy) called on the population to oppose this new, unwanted government intrusion by attacking everyone involved. In Andijon, police reports noted that farmers used the same language of opposition to unveiling that the rich and the clergy used. They said, "God forbids it," "I forbid it," and "She'll become a prostitute." In Qashqa Daryo, a rich man, Krimjon o'gli, declared: "The government demands unveiling women ever more strongly. We will kill them if they uncover, both our wives, and those who put them up to it. And then, finally, we will tell the government not to mess with our lives."[25] Elderly women whom I interviewed, both those who had supported unveiling in the 1920s and those who reported unveiling under duress, remembered hearing clergy members declaring that unveiled women should be killed.[26] This language, advocating killing unveiled women and their supporters, was widespread, and may have made murder seem normal or even ethically proper.

Husbands, fathers, and groups murdered women for unveiling and activism. The OGPU collected a long list of murders that took place between January and August 1928. Usually women were stabbed or beaten to death.[27] In Xorazm twelve murders of women were reported in three months. The police noted that murderers often claimed that murder was not a response to unveiling:

> It is characteristic in cases of the murder of women that the physical murderer (husband or brother) presents as his reasons for murder purely family reasons (jealousy, dishonoring the family), rejecting a political element to the murder. But the conditions accompanying the murder (in most cases the victim was planning to unveil or was unveiled) give reason to suspect that not only family and daily life relations played a role in the murder. These murders . . . reflect "that work" that is being carried out by groups who are our enemies, against the liberation of women, and is a direct result of their "work."[28]

The OGPU included in their report notice of a letter, signed by eighty people, declaring they would kill the unveiled and their helpers.[29] Arrests in unveiling murder cases often included not only the individual murderer, but also a number of accomplices.

Although it was evident to Uzbeks that some clergy incited the murders of the unveiled, and that much of Uzbek male society opposed the

Party's efforts to change women's social roles, numerous Uzbek Communist Party members, police, and local government officials also harassed, insulted, raped, and murdered women. While a few Communists supported unveiling, many more were upset that the Party charged them with enforcing the unpopular Hujum campaign. Some refused, and others undermined the Hujum and actively harmed women.

OGPU records show that government workers, village chairmen, and Party members made indecent proposals to unveiled women, scorned them, and called them prostitutes. In some villages, men in public roles preyed on the unveiled, and especially on those who turned to the government for help, and there were many reports of rape.[30] Women were easy targets; without government representatives protecting women, it almost seemed that rape was acceptable. One police report observed, "Thus, the people say that the Party wants to unveil women so they can rape them."[31] In Bukhara, a Party member murdered his wife, Adolat Burkhanova, age eighteen, four days after Bukhara's first mass unveiling. He forbade her to enter school, but she tried to enroll anyway, and he killed her.[32]

The Hujum Commission relied on Party members to unveil their wives and to lead community unveiling. Party members' only reward for taking on this task was possible promotion if they could demonstrate success. The Party members who planned the Hujum campaign, a group of five widely respected Uzbek Party members and two Russians, leaned on men whose motives for joining the Communist Party varied, and who often had reason to value the local support of traditional elites. The Uzbek membership of the Party increased rapidly in the 1920s, as the Party sought supporters by opening membership while exercising little training or oversight of members.[33] Most public officials and Party members took the same attitude toward unveiled women that other men in their communities did.

When many of these Party members were unwilling to carry out the radical step of unveiling women, and worse still, some attacked those very women, the Party interpreted this disloyalty in the same terms that religious people use to defend the abuse of their religion's name. Just as many Muslims would say that those who attack women in the name of God are not real Muslims, the Communist Party leadership regarded those who did not support the Hujum as "not real Communists," but as enemies who deserved dismissal.[34]

The Hujum's leaders did not anticipate that women who unveiled would be murdered. They attributed a swift rise in murders to provocation by the clergy and the wealthy. The fact that even Party officials and government workers attacked women thus demands explanation. Several factors were at work in making this femicidal wave possible: commonly held patriarchal understandings of women's proper place, public discourse from religious authorities who declared the unveiled impure and demanded their suppression, community pressure against men whose wives or sisters unveiled, and a broad awareness of state weakness. In the first year of this wave of attacks, prosecution was minimal, the attitude that one could kill a woman and get away with it was pervasive, and there was little to deter rape and murder. Party members acted under the same conditions as nonmembers, faced the same community pressures, heard the same religious incitement, and could use their limited local authority either to support the unpopular campaign or to inhibit women's activism.

Why did so many men murder women for unveiling during the Hujum? Jacquelyn Dowd Hall's scholarly work on antilynching activism in the United States argued that lynching "was a drama that helped to cement the entire southern social order. The dramatic spectacle of each lynching taught all southerners, male and female, black and white, precisely where in the social hierarchy they stood."[35] Anti-unveiling murders in the Hujum served the same purpose. Women who transgressed the patriarchal social order, defying both family and religious norms, were murdered. Religious leaders incited and validated murder, and murderers were told and believed that their actions would "restore honor." In addition, brutal murders taught other women a lesson: they should not unveil, and they should not join forces with the Soviet state. To murder unveiled women was to attempt to restore a rapidly eroding social order, by terrorizing other women back into submission. Murdering women, while it did not make any change to Communist domination of Uzbekistan, did express religiously framed hostility to the Party's fiercely antireligious agenda.

However, in the records of these murders, the perpetrators often had to be convinced to carry out their acts. Even in cultures where "honor killings" are a practice of social control, murders are incited, killers are put under social pressure to avenge honor, and there is planning and calculation.[36] In Uzbekistan, religious incitement to murder played an important role in normalizing the idea that it was appropriate to kill women who unveiled; as James Wellman notes in the introduction to this volume, religion provides a "teleological suspension of the ethical."

Murdering women terrorized others very effectively. Women who had unveiled, willingly or unwillingly, reveiled out of fear for their personal safety. Unveiling activists tried to convince women to risk not only their reputations, but also their lives for the sake of going into public places with uncovered faces. Uzbek women activists called for stronger legal protection for the unveiled, but legal protection relied on judges, police, and local administrators, none of whom were reliably pro-Hujum.

Local law enforcement remained inadequate for preventing crimes, but laws defending victims of unveiling-related violence were enhanced. In August 1928, Uzbekistan's criminal code was amended to declare that "killing a woman or severely wounding her on the basis of religious and daily life crimes connected with her liberation carries a sentence of not less than 8 years severe isolation. Carrying out lesser attacks on a woman brings not less than 2 years severe isolation."[37] Publicity of the law encouraged women (at least those who survived attacks) to bring charges against attackers.

In 1928, Women's Division workers raised the idea of banning veiling; Uzbek women activists vociferously supported the ban through demonstrations, petitions, and print media.[38] They believed that if unveiling was legally required, then women would happily unveil, and men would cease holding women individually responsible for dishonor and sin.[39] However, both the republican-level government and the U.S.S.R. Communist Party's Women's Division rejected a ban on the veil as unenforceable, and as a misunderstanding of Party policies and goals. In 1930, the Party reduced Hujum efforts when the struggle over unveiling became a distraction from the Party's economic revolution.

Although the Party reduced attention to unveiling, the state increased prosecution of the murderers of unveiled women. After April 1929, murdering a woman for unveiling, or for activism, was no longer simply a "crime of everyday life," with relatively minor penalties; instead, Statute 64, which allowed death sentences for acts of anti-Soviet terrorism, could be applied when men murdered their unveiled wives.[40] In 1930, the U.S.S.R. government went even further, declaring that liberation-related murders of women were counterrevolutionary crimes.[41] These legal changes showed a change in government attitude: the government defined these murders as acts of defiance against the state, not as family crimes. The Soviet state's increasingly harsh treatment of its opponents in the late 1920s, combined with an ever stronger presence of state authority to the Uzbek countryside, produced state ability to combat the murder wave, and murders of women for unveiling and activism decreased (but did not cease altogether), even as unveiling increased.[42]

Juergensmeyer, along with some other analysts of terrorism, delineates a spectrum of state responses to terrorism. States may negotiate; terrorists may capture the state; terrorist groups may fragment and hence lose their effectiveness; former terrorists may be partially incorporated by the state, and thus either empowered or defanged; or the state may seek to crush them entirely.[43]

In the case of Soviet Uzbekistan, the Party reduced attention to unveiling. But the state also attacked wealthy community leaders and clergy, arresting, exiling, or shooting them. In the Soviet Union, the Communist Party established a one-party state and did not negotiate. While murders of unveiled women continued (decreasingly) into the 1930s, open religious incitement ceased, murderers were more likely to face prosecution, and the state had the capacity to deter murder.

CONCLUSION

In Uzbekistan, unveiled women represented a threat to the boundaries of communities that were under the strain of rapid economic change and heightened government intrusion. Members of Uzbek communities murdered unveiled women, thus making what Smith-Rosenberg calls a "stern effort to control" all women. In this murder wave, Muslim clergy used ideas that they claimed were Islamic to incite and justify the murder of unveiled women. Some clergy, whom the state deemed "progressive," supported women's unveiling.[44] Most clergy opposed it, with arguments grounded in Islam. This conflict over veiling alone did not produce violence. Rather, when the state chose to make unveiling a symbol of its modernizing project, and to pressure women to unveil, then this religious discourse, condemning unveiling as sin, and unveilers to death, was married to an already active antigovernment movement, making murder seem ethically acceptable.

Although the Soviet state pushed a radical program for the liberation of women, the state did not incite the murders of women. It was religious discourse in the context of political struggle that made women the target of murder. In Uzbekistan, men turned their attention toward women's actions, and by killing and terrorizing women, demonstrated their opposition to the state.

NOTES

This chapter is adapted from the University of Washington Press publication titled *The New Woman in Uzbekistan: Islam, Modernity, and Unveiling under Communism* by Marianne Ruth Kamp.

1. *Femicide*, in explicit contrast with *homicide*, emphasizes that in these cases, men (mainly) murdered women because they were women (Skilbeck 1995, 43–54; Russell and Harmes, eds. (2001).
2. On religiously incited systematic rape and murder of women in the Algerian Civil War, see Turshen (2002), Bennoune (1995), and Burgat (2003). Burgat, an academic who sympathized with the Islamist side in the war, tried to explain these murders as intimate violence or honor crimes (102–16).

3. de la Roche (2004, 22: 1–4). de la Roche differentiates terrorism from lynching in terms of "system of liability" and "degree of organization" (1996, 97–128).

4. Solieva (1988, 20–22).

5. In the Middle Eastern, South Asian, and Balkan context, these incidents are called *honor killings* or *crimes of honor*. In the Mediterranean, European, Latin American, and North American context, *crimes of passion* is the term for the same phenomenon. Amira Sonbol's work shows that during colonial rule in the Middle East, European administrators who codified and modified Islamic law in Middle Eastern colonies drew on the European crime of passion understanding to validate local practices in law. In recent times, murders of women for "crimes of honor" may be more prevalent among Muslims than in other societies and have certainly received more media coverage. (Sonbol 1996; 2003).

6. The argument that culture, not Islam, sanctions honor killing is based in an understanding that religion is a set of ideas, and not the real-world practices of its followers; if murderers justify their acts religiously, their justification is dismissed as a misunderstanding. However, following Bruce Lincoln's definition of religion, which includes a set of discourses and practices, I argue that when Muslim religious leaders defend a practice using religious reasoning, we must assume that their audience also associates that practice with Islam. Fadia Faqir emphasizes that honor killing does not conform to Quranic dictates, and yet she also notes that Islamic religious authorities argued that changing current Jordanian law that permits honor killing would violate Sharia (Islamic law) (Faqir 2001; Lincoln 2003, 5–7).

7. Studies focus on intimate and domestic violence (Dobash and Dobash, eds., 1998; Russell and Harmes, eds., 2001).

8. Juergensmeyer (2000, 124).

9. Bibi Pal'vanova (1982, 197).

10. Uzbek historian Dilarom Alimova concurs with Party analysts from the late 1920s who argued male Uzbek Party members were unprepared for the unveiling campaign (Alimova 1991, 25, 76). The authors of a recent official Uzbek history argue that the campaign sparked violence because mistakes and injustices provoked the people whose whole worldview was challenged by this Communist effort (Jo'raev et al., eds., 2000, vol. 2, 379–84). Keller (2001) essentially agrees. Northrop (2004) treats murders as the Communist Party sources do, as one of the "crimes of everyday life."

11. Shirin Akiner (1997, 271).

12. The Nalivkins noted that girls who lost their virginity might be forced into an undesired marriage, but evidence for many regions of Uzbekistan is lacking. Anecdotally, this is still the way that some Uzbek families deal with female inchastity and the dishonor it brings (Nalivkin and Nalivkina 1886).

13. Smith-Rosenberg (1985, 48–49).

14. Most clergy opposed the Hujum; some demonstrated, some murdered activists, and several hanged themselves (Keller 2001, 116, 126). Northrop (2004, 92, 202) notes clergy agitation for violence against the unveiled.

15. In this chapter, *clergy* means Muslim religious leaders, including *imam*s and *khatib*s (local preachers), *mullah*s (educated Muslims who taught in Quran schools), *Ishon*s (men who led Sufi orders or were leaders of Friday mosques), and *qazi*s (judges in Sharia courts).

16. Keller (2001, 116–17).

17. I explain the roots of the unveiling movement and women's decisions in the Hujum in *The New Woman in Uzbekistan*. Most of the Uzbek women who unveiled voluntarily adhered to the modernist side of a Muslim religious debate in Central Asia, and believed that the Quran did not require veiling in the *paranji*.

18. RGASPI f. 62 d. 883, ll. 52–53 (Russian State Archive of Socio-Political History, formerly the Communist Party Archive, Moscow), "Sharixonda yana bir yavvoiliq," *Qizil O'zbekiston*, March 22, 1927, 2. Northrop interprets Party members reveiling their wives in Shahrixon as evidence of their "primary loyalty" to "Uzbek Muslim culture" (2004, 224).

19. Keller (2001).

20. RGASPI f. 62, d. 1691, l. 3–4.

21. The OGPU later became the KGB. Rarely do OGPU reports give details on the clergy whose words or actions they record; all that can be assumed about the inciters of violence is that they opposed women's unveiling. While Communist Party members often connected anti-unveiling rhetoric and incitement with "black," "qadimist," "obscurantist" clergy, they also distrusted the "Red" clergy who supported unveiling.

22. RGASPI f. 62, op. 2, d. 1503, ll. 47–48.

23. RGASPI f. 62, op. 2, d. 1691, ll. 7–10.

24. RGASPI f. 62, op. 2, d. 1503, l. 49. 1928.

25. RGASPI f. 62, op. 2, d. 1691, ll. 75–85, 6–8. January to August 1928.

26. Oral History interviews: Mafrat-hon M. (b. Kokand, 1914) April 1993, Rahbar-oi Olimova (b. Tashkent, 1908) May 1993, Aziza I. (b. Marg'ilon, 1910) May 2003.

27. RGASPI f. 62, op. 2, d. 1691, ll. 5–13, 68–93.

28. RGASPI f. 62, op. 2, d. 1691, l. 109.

29. RGASPI f. 62, op. 2, d. 1691, l. 50.

30. RGASPI f. 62, op. 2, d. 1391, ll. 9–10. Reports from February to October, 1928. Northrop (2004, 359–63) includes a translation of one such collective report.

31. RGASPI f. 62, op. 2, d. 1691, ll. 5–15; f. 62, op. 2, d. 883, ll. 39–40.

32. RGASPI f. 62, op. 2, d. 1503, ll. 49–50.

33. The Communist Party in Uzbekistan (or the Turkistan ASSR) expanded from 1,700 members and candidates in 1923 to 7,538 in 1924. In 1928, the Party numbered 31,133, with 14,285 Uzbek members, 379 of whom were women. *Kommunisticheskaia Partiia Uzbekistana v tsifrakh: sbornik statisticheskikh materilov, 1924–1977 gg.* (Tashkent: Uzbekistan, 1979, tables 2, 3, 13, 21, 26, 37, 42).

34. Northrop (2000).

35. Brundage (1997, 11); describing Hall (1993).

36. Some journalists and researchers examining "honor killing" have given attention to community pressures and incitement (Feldner 2000, 41–50; Moore 2001, A1; Mojab 2002).

37. RGASPI f. 62, op. 2, d. 1691, l. 93.

38. Rali, "Dekret chiqarilsin!," *Yangi Yo'l* 1929, 2, 4, and "Xotinlar majlislari nima deydi," *Yangi Yo'l* 1929, 5, 25. In *Qizil O'zbekiston*, "Paranji yopinishni man' qiladurg'on qonun chiqarilsin," April 2, 1929, 4, and "Xotinqizlar parnjiga qarshi," April 11, 1929, 3. Interview, Rahbar-oi Olimova. Saodat Shamsieva, "Na sluzhbe

delu partii," *Probuzhdennye velikim Oktiabrem*, ed. I. Finkel'shtein (Tashkent: Gos. Izdat., 1963), 186–93.

39. Women who support the French ban on the veil, both Muslim and non-Muslim, use similar arguments.

40. "Xotinqizlarni himoya qilish yo'lida," *Qizil O'zbekiston*, April 3, 1929, 1. Uzbekistan State Archive, f. R-86, d. 4450, l. 14.

41. Karryeva (1989, 126); this triggered the use of Article 8 of the criminal code and demanded the death penalty.

42. Mojab (2002, 7) argues that "one cannot expect an end to honor killing in a state which has no respect for citizens' right to life." I would argue that a state's ability to stop honor killing may be more related to its intent and its means to do so, than to its respect for citizens' rights. While in the ideal world an expansion in state respect for rights would create conditions leading to the outlawing of honor killing (by making penalties for this sort of murder the same as for other murders), nonetheless, the state's ability to enforce the law is related to the state's reach, its personnel, and its monopoly of the means of violence. The Soviet Union had little respect for citizens' rights in the 1920s and 1930s, but its harsh laws against the murder of unveiled women did have a deterrent effect.

43. Juergensmeyer (2000, chap. 11).

44. Some of the clergy who supported unveiling even tried to promulgate a fatwa declaring that women did not need to veil in *paranji* and *chachvon*. However, the Party was overtly antireligious, and did not want to grant religious voices any authority by giving official sanction to a fatwa, even to one that supported the Party's position. See Kamp (2006), *The New Woman in Uzbekistan*, chap. 7.

9

Monks, Guns, and Peace:
Theravāda Buddhism and
Political Violence

Charles F. Keyes

In the wake of September 11th, the intensification of the conflict between Palestinians and Israelis, the war in Afghanistan, and the war in Iraq, we have all become acutely aware of the role of Abrahamic religions—Judaism, Christianity, Islam—in justifying political violence and war and responding to these justifications and in questioning social injustice and responding to such questioning. But little is heard of the other major world religion—Buddhism—regarding these matters.

Buddhism, in contrast to the Abrahamic religions of Judaism, Christianity, and Islam, is often understood by Westerners as being a religion of radical world-rejection. The image of Buddhism is that it is a religion centered on meditation, a discipline that aims at achieving detachment from the world and, ultimately, transcendence of worldliness. A religion of radical world-rejection would seem unlikely to generate moral discourses regarding political violence and social injustice comparable to those found in the Abrahamic religions. Buddhism as practiced in countries where Buddhism is dominant has, however, contrary to Western images of the religion, in fact always been situated in and embroiled in the politics of the countries in which it is found and has even, on occasion, been the source of violence as well as the target of violence. This has been the case even as leading Buddhists have also sometimes generated radical questioning of power and its use. In this chapter I discuss how the transformation of the Theravādin world by forces of modernity led to the rise of Buddhist modernism and its derivatives, Buddhist nationalism and Buddhist fundamentalism. As with the rise of religious nationalisms and fundamentalisms elsewhere, this transformation has been associated with violence in the name of religion as well as violence against religion.

First, I need to say briefly what I understand by *modernity*. The "modern" subsumes the radical political transformations that have occurred because of colonialism and the rise of nation-states; it subsumes the increasing integration of local economies into a global economy; it has entailed the confrontation between different religious traditions and between religion and secular worldviews; and it has been associated with the spread of scientific technologies and medical therapies. While there are similarities between Theravāda Buddhism and other religions in the response to modernity, there also have been significant differences that I stress in this chapter.[1]

Although the theories of Marx, Freud, and Durkheim that provided the foundations for twentieth-century social science made a compelling case for religion declining in significance as societies became modern, by the late twentieth century it was inescapably evident that religion had not only not declined, but that a large proportion of the world's population was turning to new and revitalized religions in their search for means to accommodate to the modern world. Many scholars who seek to understand the dynamic role of religion in presumed modern as well as modernizing societies have turned to Max Weber, the other major theorist of the late nineteenth and early twentieth centuries. Although Weber's ideas about "rationalization" have sometimes also been interpreted as supportive of the thesis that "evolution" toward modern society leads to a decline in religion (see, for example, Bellah 1965), the dominant position among Weberian scholars over the past two decades is that "charisma," as well as rationalization, contribute the "developmental" transformation of society (see, for example, Schluchter 1981 and the essays in Lash and Whimster 1987; also see Keyes 2002). That is, even in societies in which much sociopolitical and socioeconomic action can be traced to the rational choices people make in the pursuit of their own interests, people still often act in accordance with values that are compelling because they are asserted or exemplified by those who are deemed to have direct links to a transcendental power. The evocation of charismatic authority can, even in the twenty-first century, redirect the course of historical processes. It is critical, thus, to understand how religious practices and beliefs remain relevant to social action in modern societies, rather than assuming that these practices and beliefs are vestiges of a premodern past.

Notable among the efforts to retheorize the relationship between religion and modernity has been the one that subsumes many diverse religious movements under the rubric of "fundamentalism." The monumental project headed by Martin Marty at the University of Chicago in the late 1980s and early 1990s brought together scholars working on all of the world religions (see Marty 1988; Marty and Appleby 1991, 1993a, 1993b, 1994, 1995; Marty, Appleby, Ammerman, Heilman, Piscatori, and Frykenberg 1994). These scholars agreed that there is commonality among practitioners of diverse religions who when faced with the conditions of modernity emphasize in a self-conscious way what are taken as "fundamental" truths and seek to reshape the world with reference to these truths. These truths have been derived, however, from very distinct and contrasting religious traditions, and very different social, political, and economic implications are based on them. Like many other scholars, I do not see all self-conscious turning toward the "fundamentals" of a religious tradition as "fundamentalism."[2] For the Theravādin tradition, I prefer to use the term *modernist* Buddhism to subsume all types of such self-conscious affirmation of religious fundamentals and, following other scholars, to use the term *Buddhist fundamentalism* to refer specifically to those sects and movements that take a constricted approach in asserting that only their understanding of these fundamentals is true.[3]

Each of the diverse Buddhist modernist movements has been shaped by the particular historical legacy recognized by its followers. To understand Buddhist modernism it is necessary first to understand the roots of the relationship between Buddhism and authority because it was a crisis of authority, in modern times, that led to the rise of Buddhist modernism. The roots for the societies in which Theravāda Buddhism became dominant—today subsumed within the nation-states of Sri Lanka, Burma, Thailand, Cambodia, and Laos—lie in the symbiotic relationship between monarchy and Buddhist monkhood (the Sangha) that is traceable to the third century BCE.

TRADITIONAL THERAVĀDA RELIGIO-POLITICAL ORDER

Although Buddhism has often been characterized in Western writings as a religion of radical world-rejection, the Way, the Dhamma, discovered by the Buddha sometime between the sixth and fourth centuries BCE, has never been separate from the social world in which Buddhists live.[4] The members of the Sangha, those who both exemplify the Dhamma in their practice and teach the Dhamma to others, have always needed the economic support of the laity and the protection offered by rulers. In the third century BCE, the first great ruler of India, Aśoka (r. 268–232 BCE), became an adherent of Buddhism. Aśoka was first and foremost a great military leader who used force to unite the people of India under his rule, but he was also the exemplary patron of the Buddhist religion. He convened a council of members of the Buddhist clergy, the Sangha, and oversaw their ensuring the accuracy of the Buddha's teachings. He also promoted disseminating relics of the Buddha, who had been cremated after death, to new followers.[5]

The followers of Theravāda Buddhism credit Aśoka not only with the spread of Buddhism to Sri Lanka and Southeast Asia where this tradition of Buddhism became dominant, but also with the establishment of a model of Buddhist sociopolitical order. This model, known as the "Two Wheels of the Dhamma," makes the laity, and especially a lay ruler, as equally responsible for the perpetuation and dissemination of the teachings of the Buddha as the Sangha (see Reynolds 1972; Smith 1972; Reynolds and Clifford 1987).

The Aśokan legacy was emulated in all Theravādin societies, although it only became fully realized in the period between the thirteenth and nineteenth centuries (Sirisena 1978; Gombrich 1988; Tambiah 1976). During this period, rulers of Buddhist kingdoms provided an example for all laypersons in their monetary support for the Sangha. The monarch also intervened from time to time to ensure that the Sangha adhered properly to the discipline and to prevent schisms within it. In turn, the Sangha, by participating in royally sponsored rites, conferred legitimacy on the monarch.

The societies ruled by Buddhist monarchs between the thirteenth and nineteenth centuries were hardly without conflict. The island of Sri Lanka was beset by almost perpetual wars throughout this period, and on at least two occasions the political turmoil led to the nearly total disappearance of the Sangha (see Gombrich 1988; Kiribamune 1978; Malalgoda 1976; Paranavitana 1932; Seneviratne 1978). In mainland Southeast Asia, following the collapse of the empires centered on Pagan and Angkor in the thirteenth century, there was almost constant warfare between the Burman and Siamese empires and between these empires and the smaller principalities that surrounded them (Prince Damrong Rajanubhab 1955, 1957, and 1958; 2001; U Kyaw Win 1997; Sunait Chutintharanond 1997; Lieberman 1993).[6] These conflicts in Sri Lanka and the wars in Southeast Asia came to an end only in the nineteenth century with the British conquest of Sri Lanka and Burma and the incorporation of Laos and Cambodia into French Indochina. The colonial era proved to be the crucible for forging new relationships between Buddhism and power.

BUDDHIST REFORMATION IN RESPONSE TO COLONIAL DOMINATION AND WESTERN INFLUENCE

Beginning in Sri Lanka in the eighteenth century, lower Burma in the early nineteenth century, and the remainder of the region throughout the nineteenth century, Theravādin traditions began to be challenged by new political and economic influences associated with the expansion of Western colonialism and capitalism and by new cultural influences associated with Christianity and Western science. Taken together, these influences constituted a crisis of authority and the responses to this crisis resulted in the resituating of Theravāda Buddhism within a modern world.

In Sri Lanka and Burma, the traditional sociopolitical order subsumed under the "Two Wheels of the Dhamma" was radically devalued when British colonial governments in both countries abolished the indigenous monarchies and ended government patronage of the Sangha. In both Cambodia and Laos the French colonial government retained indigenous monarchies under nominal protectorates, but in both countries, the reality of rule by non-Buddhist Frenchmen reduced the relationship between monarchy and Sangha to empty rituals.[7] In Siam the crisis of authority began not with colonial domination by an outside power, but through a radical redefining of monarchy to meet the colonial threat. Siam also undertook its own "internal colonialism" by extending the authority of Bangkok over what had been previously autonomous Buddhist polities. Rulers of these polities were replaced by officials under a new bureaucracy modeled on that of nearby colonial domains. Moreover, in the early part of the twentieth century the Bangkok monarchy issued an edict that placed all monks throughout Siam under a single institution.

In their reaction to the crises of authority of the colonial period, many people in the Theravādin countries turned to charismatic religious and political leaders whom they believed could restore the traditional sociopolitical order. In many cases they followed their leaders in violent reactions against the new orders. In Sri Lanka, and even more in Burma, supporters of the traditional monarchies fought strongly against the British forces sent to "pacify" the countries. Violence did not end with pacification, however. In the first decades of the twentieth century in Siam, French Laos, and British Burma, thousands of people died or were injured after having joined Buddhist millenarian movements to resist—unsuccessfully—the extension of new types of authority over them.[8]

By the 1920s Buddhist millennialism had begun to be replaced by nationalisms that were also shaped by Buddhism. Buddhist nationalism, in contrast to Buddhist millenarianism, was predicated not on traditional Buddhist ideas about sociopolitical order but on ones that derived from Buddhist reform movements in each of the countries.

The first charismatic leaders of Buddhist reform movements in Sri Lanka, Burma, and Siam were Buddhist monks who found themselves confronted with challenges to their religious commitments posed by Protestant missionaries. These missionaries brought with them ideas that were very different from those of the Catholic missionaries that had preceded them in the sixteenth to early nineteenth centuries. The Protestant missionaries laid great emphasis on establishing schools that offered instruction not only in religion but also in secular subjects. The Protestant-run schools and the Catholic ones that soon emulated them became the primary institutions whereby some indigenous peoples could enter into the colonial civil service in Sri Lanka and Burma. Protestant missions also sponsored hospitals and clinics. Through both these institutions and their schools, the Protestant missionaries made some of the local elites aware that they drew a clear distinction between religious knowledge and secular knowledge. This was not a distinction known in traditional Buddhist societies.

In Siam the man who would establish a reformist Buddhism was a princely monk who would later leave the monkhood and become King Mongkut (r. 1851–1868). During his twenty-seven years as a monk Mongkut acquired a critical perspective on Buddhism as currently practiced, in part because of his own intensive study of the Pāli texts and in part because of his extended conversations and study sessions with the few Westerners in the country, most of whom were Protestant missionaries.[9] From the missionaries Mongkut learned of the distinction made in the West between natural and divine law. He also acquired some knowledge, especially from those missionaries who had also been trained in medicine, of Western science as well as of Christian theology. If Buddhism, he came to think, was to be maintained in a world where powerful Westerners justified their actions with reference both to Christianity and to science, then it was necessary to focus on the essential teachings of Buddhism and to ignore or even discard many traditional practices.

Because he was a high-ranking prince and would subsequently become king, he was able to establish a new order of monks, one that followed his reformist understandings. This order, subsequently named the Dhammayuti-nikāya (Thai, Thammayut-nikāi), the order which adheres strictly to the Dhamma, mirrored Protestantism in the eschewing of ritual and accentuating ethical practice in everyday life. The Dhammayuti-nikāya would become in the reign of Mongkut's son, King Chulalongkorn (1868–1910), a primary vehicle for the creation of Buddhist nationalism in Thailand.[10]

Mongkut's reforms also contributed, although probably not seminally, to the reformist movement in Sri Lanka as he corresponded in Pāli with several Sinhalese monks. In Sri Lanka, Buddhist monks also encountered Protestant missionaries. In their efforts to counter the proselytizing efforts of the missionaries, some leading monks had begun to accentuate what they considered to be the essential teachings of the Buddha and to deemphasize many traditional practices (Malalgoda 1976, 220ff). These monks laid the groundwork for what has been termed "Protestant Buddhism" in Sri Lanka (Gombrich and Obeyesekere 1988).

This modernist Buddhism came subsequently to be epitomized by Angārika Dharmapāla (1864–1933). Don David Hewavitarana, as Angārika Dharmapāla was originally known, had been influenced in his teen years by two of the leading monks of the Buddhist reform movement in Sri Lanka. At sixteen he met the two leaders of the Theosophist movement, Colonel Henry Steele Olcott and Madame Helena Petrovna Blavatsky, and under their guidance he underwent a spiritual transformation. His commitment to a Theosophically inflected Buddhism led him to adopt a new role, one which was neither monk nor layperson, that of Angārika, "the homeless one." He also adopted a new name, Dharmapāla, the "upholder of the Dhamma." Gananath Obeyesekere has characterized Dharmapāla as being responsible for infusing Sinhalese Buddhism "with the puritan values of Protestantism" (Obeyesekere 1975, 250; also see Obeyesekere 1995, and Gombrich and Obeyesekere 1988, chapter 6, and Roberts 1997).[11]

In Burma King Mindon (r. 1853–1878), a contemporary of Mongkut, had also contributed to the development of a reform movement in his country through convening a council of monks in 1871 to ensure, in the Aśokan tradition, that the scriptures were being transmitted without corruption. Given that the British controlled Lower Burma at the time and would, shortly after Mindon's death, conquer Upper Burma, some leading monks who attended the council recognized that if Buddhism were to survive, monks must also confront the challenge of the West. During the latter part of the nineteenth century, the most prominent monk to promote a reformist Buddhism was the Ledi Sayadaw (1846–1923)—the revered master of Ledi.[12] Like Mongkut, Ledi Sayadaw made meditation central to Buddhist practice; he also disdained many traditional practices, and emphasized the importance of the study of the Buddhist scriptures, although he gave greater emphasis to the *Abhidhamma*, Buddhist metaphysics, than did Mongkut. Although the Ledi Sayadaw was at the forefront of the first nationalist confrontation with British rule, a confrontation that arose over the refusal of soldiers in the British army to take off their boots when entering a Buddhist monastery, the leadership of Burmese Buddhist nationalism was assumed by another monk in the early twentieth century.

U Ottama (1879–1939), a contemporary and very comparable figure to Angārika Dharmapāla, shaped Buddhist reformist ideas into an ideology that was at once nationalist and fundamentalist.[13] He was well educated, first in an Anglo-Burmese school, then in the Sangha as a novice where he acquired a good knowledge of Pāli and Sanskrit, and finally in Western schools in India. He drew on this education and on his experiences while traveling in India and Japan to formulate a Buddhist fundamentalism that was both opposed to the colonial order, which was seen as evil, and also critical of traditional religious practice. U Ottama in many ways established the paradigm of an activist monk who provides legitimation for violence in defense of the religion.

MODERNIST BUDDHISM

Although each of the Buddhist reformed movements had their own distinctive characteristics, they all perpetuated certain fundamental Buddhist doctrines while situating understandings of these in ways that reoriented Buddhism toward the modern world.[14] Modernist Buddhism retains the fundamental doctrine of Buddhism that all born into the realm of sentient existence (*saṃsāra*) will experience *dukkha*. Although *dukkha* is usually translated as "suffering," it also is understood today, as it was in earliest Buddhism, to be the cessation of pleasurable experience. Again, modernist Buddhism has retained unchanged the original Buddhist doctrine that *dukkha* is the consequence of *kamma*, morally significant action. Buddhism contrasts with the Abrahamic religions in making an impersonal "law" rather than a volitional being—God or Yahweh or Allah—the basis for moral or religiously efficacious action. The Law of Kamma posits that human action produces consequences in accord with the moral intention with which it was undertaken. Morally positive actions produce "merit" (*puñña*) that will be manifest as reduced suffering, while morally negative acts produce "demerit" (*pāppa*), which entails increased suffering.

The major difference between reformist and traditional Theravāda Buddhism relates to the fundamental Buddhist doctrine of *kamma*.[15] In traditional or "cosmological" Buddhism one was understood not only to have disabilities and beauty that were products of kamma from previous existences, but one was also thought to be relatively fixed in social status by virtue of previous kamma. One could, nonetheless, improve one's likelihood of being born to a higher status with less suffering if one used one's wealth to "make merit" through offerings (*dāna*) to support the Sangha and build image halls and stupas. Males could also improve their kammic heritage by serving as members of the Sangha for at least temporary periods of time. Reformist Buddhism has reinterpreted the legacy of kamma from previous existences as being far less determinative of one's conditions in the present life. One's kammic heritage, as I was told by a modernist Buddhist monk in Thailand, is fundamentally the same as one's genetic heritage. Reformist Buddhism also offers a different interpretation of kammically significant acts during one's lifetime. While ritualized merit-making remains important, reformist Buddhism also emphasizes that merit is also acquired from positive acts of generosity to needy laypersons, as well as to members of the Sangha.

Moreover, modernist Buddhism gives much attention to the importance of controlling the desires (*tanhā*) that if acted on generate demerit. Although in traditional Buddhism the "taking of the precepts"—which entail refraining from actions that lead to taking of life, stealing, deceit, and sexual impropriety—was an element of nearly every ritual, modernist Buddhism has given much more emphasis to making these the ethical basis of everyday life.

To control such desires, modernist Buddhism has accorded much more emphasis than traditional Buddhism to meditation. Hundreds of centers have been established by monks throughout the Theravādin world and far more monks than in the premodern world live in forest retreats where they follow very strict regimens centered on long periods in meditation. As a number of studies have shown, forest monasticism seems to have been particularly significant in the period following major sociopolitical and socioeconomic transformations in the Theravādin world in the first three-quarters of the twentieth century.[16] The rise of what can only be termed meditation movements in Sri Lanka, Burma, and Thailand reflects, as Taylor (1993, 316) has concluded, the fact that such monks are acutely aware that "wider social, political and economic changes—as *kammic* consequences—were inevitable" in the modernizing societies in which they live. While some meditation monks have sought to withdraw from the world to pursue their religious goals, many more have become teachers of meditation to lay people who reside in forest retreats or meditation centers for short periods of time. For these lay practitioners, and for many monks, meditation is not seen as a means to achieve enlightenment; rather, it is seen as a means to effect detachment from desire so that one can act effectively in the world without being driven by desire.

While some monks in modern Theravāda Buddhist societies attempt to withdraw from the world to forest retreats to devote themselves to meditation, most modernist monks teach that the quest for ultimate transcendence of suffering—that is, the quest for *Nibbāna*—can be, even should be, pursued while remaining in the world. In the words of Buddhadāsa *Bhikkhu* (1970), the most famous theologian of twentieth-century Thailand, "Nibbāna is in *saṃsāra*"—that is, one can realize ultimate transcendence—even if only momentarily—while remaining in the experiential world.[17]

Although some monks and laypersons—particularly in Burma where outside influences have been much more limited than elsewhere in the Theravādin world—continue to practice Buddhism following premodern understandings of religious doctrines, in all Theravādin countries—including Cambodia and Laos—there has been a significant reconstrual of Buddhism with reference to modern conditions. Foremost among these are the nation- and state-building projects undertaken by the postcolonial rulers of these countries. In pursuit of these projects states have often used violence as an instrument of power, or reactions to these projects have prompted violent resistance. In the modern Theravādin world, Buddhism has sometimes been evoked in support of violence and has sometimes been the target of violence. And while most Buddhist monks have denounced violence, others have offered religious justifications for its use. In all Theravādin countries, the use of violence and the consequences of violence have been subjects for religious reflection, ethical debate, and action advocacy.

MODERNIST BUDDHISM AND VIOLENCE IN SRI LANKA, CAMBODIA, AND THAILAND

The crises of authority first begun during the colonial period did not disappear in the postcolonial period. Nationalisms predicated on modernist Buddhism have continued to shape visions of authority that result in conflict and violence. I here focus on postcolonial crises that have entailed significant violence in Sri Lanka, Cambodia, and Thailand.[18]

The origins of a militant form of Sinhalese Buddhist nationalism can be traced to Angārika Dharmapāla. In particular he used the story of a Sri Lankan king—Dutugemunu/Duthagāmani, who reigned in the second century BCE—as the justification for a religious war with the Tamils. King Dutugemunu, the story goes, led his forces against non-Buddhists, brandishing a spear with a relic of the Buddha embedded in it. He was accompanied by Buddhist monks and after the battle was consoled by Buddhist saints who told him that since those who were killed "were unbelievers and men of evil life . . . not more to be esteemed than beasts," he had committed no sin in taking their lives (Obeyesekere 1975, 236[19]). This myth, in Dharmapāla's retelling of it in many forums, has provided a justification for a holy war against non-Buddhists in Sri Lanka.[20] By equating the unbelievers who were attacked by King Dutugemunu with the Tamils of today, the myth becomes a charter for holy war. As Tambiah has written: "Here then we have the transmission over time of an *ideology* that was enshrined and objectified as historical memory in the monkish chronicles, and which periodically, from the first centuries CE right up to our own time, was available for invocation, resurrection, and manipulation by zealots and political activists of different centuries, caught in differing circumstances, and following objectives relevant to their times" (Tambiah 1986, 94).

When Ceylon became independent in 1948, it was a plural society with marked diversity. While nearly 70 percent of the populace were speakers of Sinhala and most of these were followers of Buddhism, the other 30 percent consisted of Tamil Hindus and Tamil Muslims, other Muslims, and a small but politically very significant Eurasian segment. In the first years of independence, the government, led by an English-educated elite of diverse backgrounds, promoted a civil order in which diversity was recognized. However, in 1956 S. W. R. D. Bandaranaike, the leader of the Sri Lanka Freedom Party (SLFP), became prime minister after his party won a majority in Parliament. Bandaranaike, who had been educated at Oxford, was a convert to Buddhism and, like Angārika Dharmapāla, became zealous in his linking of religion and politics. He introduced a number of new policies that were to accord a privileged position to the Buddhist Sinhalese: (1) Sinhala was recognized as the only national language to the exclusion of English and Tamil; (2) the national history as taught in government schools accentuated the history of Buddhism in the country; and (3) the state undertook to support Buddhism beginning with the celebration of 2,500 years of Buddhism in 1955–1956. Bandaranaike had the strong support of many Buddhist monks for these policies (see Bechert 1978).

Bandaranaike's connection to Buddhism proved, however, to be a double-edged sword; in 1959 he was assassinated by a monk. Although the monk proved to be insane, the assassination was, nonetheless, the beginning of an increased association between Buddhism and political violence in Sri Lanka.

Although Sri Lanka had long been an ethnically complex society, the primary conflict that has its roots in the linking of Sinhalese nationalism and Buddhism has been that between Tamils and the Sri Lankan state. The relegation of non-Buddhists to second-class citizenship in Sri Lanka led to growing tensions within the country and finally to open conflict beginning in the 1980s. In 1983, the Sri Lankan government either backed or tolerated a pogrom-like attack by security forces and many ordinary Sinhalese on Tamils living in the capital of Colombo as well as in the highlands. Tamils subsequently turned in increasing numbers to a movement led by the radical and militant Tamil Tigers ("Liberation Tigers of Tamil Eelam"). Because the Tigers were pioneers in the use of suicide bombings and have killed many more noncombatants than Sri Lankan soldiers, they have been branded as a "terrorist" organization by India, the United States, and other countries as well as by the Sri Lankan government. The Sri Lankan government has been at war with the Tamil Tigers for over twenty years, with over 65,000 people on both sides having died.[21]

In 2002 the Tigers declared a cease-fire and entered into negotiations with the Sri Lankan government headed by President Chandrika Bandaranaike Kumaratunga, the granddaughter of S. W. R. D. Bandaranaike. However, the negotiations collapsed, in part because of controversy over the distribution of aid in Tamil areas following the tsunami in late 2004 and then the assassination of the country's foreign minister Lakshman Kadirgamar by a sniper in August 2005. President Kumaratunga has been pressed by the National Buddhist Front, an organization of many monks, to continue the war and even ban non-Buddhist NGOs from working in the country.[22] Buddhist nationalism has been a major factor for the tragedy of Sri Lanka, a tragedy that as yet does not seem to have an end.

The tragedy of Cambodia has been even more horrendous than that of Sri Lanka. On the surface it would seem as though Cambodia's ordeal was the product not of Buddhist nationalism but of a radical secularist ideology, that of the Khmer Rouge led by Pol Pot. However, as I discovered when I sought to understand the origins of the Khmer Rouge, the ideology of the Khmer Rouge has unequivocal roots in a version of reformist Buddhism (Keyes 1994).

The first imagining of a Khmer nation was spurred by the founding of the Buddhist Institute in 1930. The French had founded the institute "to lessen the influence of Thai Buddhism (and Thai politics) on the Cambodian Sangha and to substitute more Indo-Chinese loyalties between the Lao Sangha and their Cambodian counterparts" (Chandler 1991, 18). Suzanne Karpelès, a French Buddhist scholar who was placed in charge of the institute, recruited as her chief associates a number of ex-monks, several of whom subsequently founded the Khmer Communist Party. Pol Pot, the nom de guerre of Saloth Sar, who had also been a novice for a period of time, was one of the recruits to the Party.

Pol Pot and his close associates conceived of the Party, which they called Angkar, "the organization," in ways that were very similar to the Sangha. Those who became members subjected themselves to a discipline to subordinate themselves to the organization. Hinton has shown how the Khmer Rouge concept of "revolutionary consciousness" is linked to the Buddhist conception of "mindfulness" (Hinton 2005, 195ff). Even more perversely the Khmer Rouge took the conception of "cutting off one's heart" (*dach chett*), which in Buddhist practice meant cultivating detachment from worldly desires, and utilized it to promote among cadres a detachment from emotion when taking the lives of those deemed to be "enemies" (Hinton 2005, 262–63). But while the Angkar promised a future to Khmer that was an earthly Nibbāna, its actions actually led to a marked increase in suffering.

One of the first actions of Angkar after the Khmer Rouge took control of Cambodia in April 1975 was a move to eliminate the Buddhist Sangha. Monks and novices, even those in the base areas which the Khmer Rouge had controlled before April 1975, were compelled to disrobe. Being sent for re-education often meant being sent to be killed. In 1980, it was estimated that five out of every eight monks were executed during the Pol Pot regime. Major temple-monasteries were destroyed and lesser ones were converted into storage centers, prisons, or extermination camps. The only monks who survived were those who fled to southern Vietnam.

The Khmer Rouge reign of terror resulted in at least two million deaths out of a population of about nine million. Every survivor of the Khmer Rouge is haunted by the ghosts of those who died. In the late 1980s, the regime that came to power after the Vietnamese forced the Khmer Rouge to flee to the peripheries of the country erected monuments at sites of some of the worst killing—Tuol Sleng in Phnom Penh and Choeng Ek on the outskirts of the city.

The government under Hun Sen, himself a former Khmer Rouge, has supported the restoration of Buddhism and since the early 1990s Buddhism has become once again the religion of the state. The memories of the Khmer Rouge, however, raise for many Khmer fundamental questions about how a Buddhist society could have spawned such violence. Because these questions have been very difficult to answer, some have turned away from Buddhism and embraced Christianity. Even more Khmer have been attracted to millenarian and magical Buddhist sects that have sprung up in the late twentieth and early twenty-first centuries (see Marston and Guthrie 2004). The most respected senior monk, Maha Ghosananda, and many of his followers, some belonging to Buddhist nongovernmental organizations, have promoted active efforts to ensure that a Buddhist message of peace is clearly articulated.

Thailand has escaped the great tragedies that have beset both Cambodia and Sri Lanka, but there was a period when a militant Buddhist nationalism came close to contributing to the justification of violence that threatened to split apart Thai society. In the mid-1970s, after the military dictators, Field Marshals Thanom Kittikachorn and Prapas Charusathien, had been forced by a student-led movement to go into exile and King Bhumipol Adulyadej had overseen the establishment of a new constitution and parliament, a marked division in the Thai political system developed. Right-wing forces supported by elements of the military and police began to use intimidation and death squads to regain control of power. Many in the student movement, on the other hand, began to see the Communist Party of Thailand (CPT) as the best vehicle for ensuring a more just distribution of wealth in the society. The divisions were exacerbated by Thai reactions to the takeover in 1975 of the governments of South Vietnam, Cambodia, and Laos by Communist parties.[23]

In this context, a very prominent Buddhist monk, Kittivuddho Bhikkhu, began to preach that Communists were less than human and, thus, to kill them would not be a "sin"—that is, would not lead to "demerit"—in Buddhist terms.[24] Although many Buddhist monks and laypersons strongly denounced Kittivuddho for this position, the Ecclesiastical Council made up of the most senior monks in the Thai Sangha refused to reprimand him.

When the patriarch of the Buddhist Sangha agreed to preside at the ordination of Thanom Kittikachorn, the former military dictator, thereby enabling him to return to the country, it seemed clear that the established Sangha had sided with the right wing.

On October 6, 1976, right-wing paramilitary groups backed by units of the police staged a vicious attack on student protestors at one of the main universities in Bangkok. Many students were brutally killed and their bodies mutilated. In the wake of this event, the military once again took control of the government, while hundreds of students who escaped went to the forests up-country to join a Communist-led insurgency.

For nearly three years, Thais were at civil war with each other. The CPT—which had a close relationship with the Khmer Rouge—did not come to power, however. In part this was a consequence of the disenchantment of many of the students who had joined the insurgency with the rigidity of the Party leadership. It was even more the consequence of a decision taken by senior members of the Thai army who had taken control of the government to offer unconditional amnesty to those who had joined the CPT. This decision implied a rejection by these men of both militancy and militant Buddhism in the pursuit of their political objectives. No members of the Sangha, including Kittivuddho himself, provided renewed justification of a militant Buddhism.[25]

In the wake of this decision, the CPT collapsed and Thai society has become one of the most open in Asia. At the same time, many Thai, including many in the elite, have turned away from Buddhist nationalism. There are today a number of competing and quite distinctive Buddhist movements in Thailand. Even more striking is the emergence of a large sector of the populace that I call "post-Buddhists" (see Keyes 1999b). That is, there are many—mainly in the urban middle class—who still think of themselves as in some way connected to Buddhism, but who participate in rituals only rarely and who have limited contact with monks. Such people live very secular lives.

In the 1980s and 1990s there was strong popular support for moves by the government and King Bhumipol to expand Thailand's civil society to be inclusive of minorities, including religious ones. This inclusiveness was legitimated in a new constitution promulgated in 1997. This constitution redefined the term *sātsanā*, previously used primarily to designate Buddhism, to mean "religion" in a broader sense so that those following Islam and Christianity could also be considered to be full citizens of a nation based on the three pillars of monarchy, *sātsanā*, and Thai-ness (defined primarily as having competence in the national language). The promotion of inclusivist policies led to greater integration of Muslims, including the large Malay-speaking Muslim population of southern Thailand, into Thai society (see Chaiwat Satha-Anand and Suwanna Satha-Anand 1987; Chaiwat Satha-Anand 1988; and Bonura 2003).

This process was radically reversed in the early twenty-first century. Thaksin Shinawatra became prime minister in early 2001, when his Thai Rak Thai (Thai love Thai) was elected on a populist platform. Thaksin began promoting a more constricted nationalist approach after the World Trade Center Bombing in September 2001 and agreed to send a small contingent of Thai troops to participate in the war in Iraq. This move was strongly protested by Thai Muslims. In early 2004 violent confrontations erupted in the Malay-speaking provinces of Thailand's far south. Since then, violence has escalated with Thai government troops killing a large number of Muslim youth in a mosque, causing the deaths of many more who suffocated after having being piled on trucks by security forces, and insurgents assassinating many local officials, teachers, and even Buddhist monks and novices. Religious violence has become a painful reality in Thailand. After a coup led by the military headed by a Muslim general in September 2006, a new government was appointed with a clear mandate to implement the recommendations of a National Reconciliation Commission, which had been ignored by Thaksin. Although the violence continued, there was now hope that efforts to promote dialogue rather than confrontation (see Chaiwat Satha-Anand 2003) would prevail.

CONCLUSION

As I show in this chapter, despite the image so prevalent in the West of Buddhism as exceptional among world religions in being regarded as a religion of peace, violence undertaken in the name of Buddhism and against Buddhism has also been evident in those countries belonging to the Theravāda Buddhist world. As with other world religions, Theravāda Buddhists have turned to what are taken as the fundamentals of their religion in response to the political-economic and sociocultural transformations associated with the rise of modern nation-states. While a few of these responses have sometimes provided the legitimation or justification for extreme violence, most modernist Buddhists, even while stressing the need for religious renewal, have not embraced the type of militant fundamentalism associated with the Abrahamic religions.

There remains an inherent difference between societies in which Theravāda Buddhism is the dominant religion and those associated with Abrahamic religions. Whereas for followers of Christianity, Judaism, and Islam the fundamental religious responsibility is to seek to know and act on the will of God or Allah, for Buddhists the essential religious responsibility is to seek to control in oneself the "desires" that if acted on will increase *dukkha* ("suffering"). There is no equivalent in Buddhism of a vengeful Allah or a God of wrath. Fundamental Buddhist doctrine, as expressed in the first of the precepts taken by lay Buddhists and the first of the rules of training to which a member of the Sangha submits himself, stresses that the taking of life leads to suffering. This doctrine has not prevented some monks and laypersons from justifying violence as a means to protect the religion from unbelievers. Moreover, it did not prevent the leaders of the Khmer Rouge, who had themselves once been Buddhist novices or monks, from turning this premise on its head. Nonetheless, the more convincing religious voices in Theravāda Buddhism are those that advocate the cultivation of mindfulness, often through the practice of meditation, to enable the follower of the Buddha to reduce and eventually eliminate the anger in him or her that conduces to violence.

The most revered monk in Thailand in the second half of the twentieth century was Buddhadāsa *Bhikkhu* (1906–1993). Through his sermons, his published work, and his "spiritual theater" at his residence at Suan Mokh in Chaiya in southern Thailand, Buddhadāsa sought to make the Dhamma relevant to those confronting the temptations and the conditions of the modern world. He went even further—in his advocacy of "Dhammic Socialism"—in maintaining that a Buddhist should not only seek to act in ways that will ensure a reduction in *dukkha* in future lives, but should also act to help reduce suffering for all with whom one shares a social world in this life (see Buddhadāsa *Bhikkhu* 1986; Swearer 1973).

Those who follow Buddhadāsa see themselves as part of an international movement of socially engaged Buddhists, a movement that strongly advocates nonviolence. This movement has coalesced around such loose organizations as the Buddhist Peace Fellowship and the International Network of Engaged Buddhists. INEB is under the patronage of the Dalai Lama and Thích Nhất Hạnh, a famous Vietnamese Zen Buddhist monk who resides in France.[26] In many ways the monk who most epitomizes this movement today is the Cambodian monk Maha Ghosananda,[27] a ranking monk who was outside of Cambodia when the Khmer Rouge took over. Maha Ghosananda has devoted himself through leading marches through Cambodia to restoring Buddhism as a refuge for peace. While there remain in Sri Lanka some monks committed to militant Buddhist nationalism, the role of socially engaged Buddhists appears to be gaining ground throughout the Buddhist world. Socially engaged Buddhists have also joined with members of other religions who emphasize the nonviolent implications of their religious heritages in offering quiet ripostes to the shrill voices of those who justify violence in the name of or against religion.

NOTES

1. This chapter is one element of a long-term project on how those adhering to Theravāda Buddhism, especially in Thailand, have adapted to the transformations brought about by the influences of "modernity" on the societies in which they live. See Keyes (1971, 1975, 1977, 1978, 1983a, 1990, 1991, 1992, 1999b).

2. Marty and his colleagues sought to find more commonalities among "fundamentalisms" than what I describe here, but scholars involved in the project, including myself, who work in East and Southeast Asia are skeptical of more expansive definitions of fundamentalism.

3. I am grateful to Frank Reynolds (personal communication, February 3, 2005) for pushing me to rethink my use of "Buddhist fundamentalism." See also my discussion in Keyes (1993) and Swearer's (1991) key article.

4. The Theravādin tradition places the death of the Buddha at 543–544 BCE. Recent scholarship strongly indicates that the Buddha's life was confined to the fourth century BCE (see Bechert 1991–97). On the way in which Buddhism as understood in Western countries was a construction of Western scholars of Buddhism, see Welbon (1968) and Lopez (1995). Schopen (1997, 2004) has been at the forefront of scholars who have used actual historical evidence as distinct from interpretations of the *Tripiṭaka*, the collection of texts that long have been considered to constitute the Buddhist canon, to show how Buddhism became an established religion only through a symbiotic relationship between laity and members of the Sangha.

5. The role of Aśoka in the establishment of Buddhism as a religion with the patronage of a monarch has been the subject of considerable study. The main sources for understanding his role are his "edicts" that were inscribed on stele throughout India (see Nikam and McKeon 1959). On the history of his patronage of Buddhism during his reign, see Basham (1987) and Gokhale (1948). And on the transmission of the Aśokan legend among Buddhists, see Strong (1984). On dissemination of relics of the Buddha, see Strong (2004).

6. The Siamese wars with the Burmese have recently re-entered Thai social memory in influential ways with the release in the early twenty-first century of the immensely popular films *Bang Ra-chan* and *Suriyothai*. These films, like many other Thai historical films, depict very bloody battle scenes, including ones involving Buddhist monks.

7. Archaimbault's (1971) description of the role played by the prince of the small Lao principality of Champasak in the New Year ritual is particularly revealing of the emptiness of royal rituals in the wake of the crisis of authority generated by colonial rule.

8. On the related movements in Siam and Laos, see Ishii (1975), Keyes (1977), Murdoch (1974), Gunn (1990), and Wilson (1997). On those in Burma, see Solomon (1969), Maung Maung (1980), and Herbert (1982).

9. Two studies by Lingat (1926, 1958) and a still unpublished dissertation by Craig Reynolds (1973) remain the best accounts of Mongkut's religious reforms. Also see Wilson (1971); Craig Reynolds (1976); Butt (1978); and Kirsch (1973).

10. The Thammayut order also would subsequently gain followers in both Laos and Cambodia. In the early part of the twentieth century, the French rulers of

these two countries sought to counter the influence to the Thammayut monks by creating a Buddhist Institute that also promoted a type of reformist Buddhism.

11. I am grateful to Professor Obeyesekere who heard my presentation at Harvard for some clarification on the early religious life of Angārika Dharmapāla.

12. *Sayadaw*, from *saya*, "teacher," is a term of respect accorded to a monk who has become a senior elder by virtue of spending ten years in the monkhood and who has achieved a reputation for knowledge or practice of religion. The term typically is used in association with the name of the monastery or community where the monk resides (Mendelson 1975, 374). The Ledi Sayadaw, or Pandita U Maung Gyi, was a highly respected monk who resided at the Ledi-tawya monastery in upper Burma. See "A Life Sketch of the Venerable Ledi Sayadaw," in Ledi Sayadaw (1961, 86). Although some of the Ledi Sayadaw's writings on Buddhist meditation (Ledi Sayadaw 1961, 1971) have been translated into English, his life is only sketchily recorded in a number of scattered sources in English.

13. All English accounts of U Ottama cite as their source *Sayadaw U Ottama: Lutlatye Seikdat Myozicha thu* (Sayadaw U Ottama: He Who Sowed the Seeds of Independence) by Bama Khit U Ba Yin (Rangoon: Thamamitta, Djambatam, n.d.). The most extended account in English is to be found in Mendelson (1975, 200–206). I have discussed U Ottama at greater length elsewhere (Keyes 1993).

14. The best study of the reforms and their social consequences in Sri Lanka is that by Gombrich and Obeyesekere (1988); also see Seneviratne (1999). For Burma see Mendelson (1975), Sarkisyanz (1965), and Spiro (1970). For Thailand see Reynolds (1973), Tambiah (1976), Jackson (1989), and Keyes (1971, 1992). For comparative perspectives see Swearer (1991, 1995) and Keyes (1993).

15. I draw here, in part, on my introduction to *Karma: An Anthropological Inquiry* (Keyes 1983b).

16. In Sri Lanka, forest monasticism that had become very significant in the post–World War II period (Carrithers 1983) appears to have markedly declined since the mid-1980s when the country was plunged into intense conflict over the status of Tamils. In Thailand, forest monasticism expanded rapidly in the post–World War II period, led primarily by the followers of the Ajarn Man Phurithat (Bhūridatto Thera) (1870–1949), a monk thought by many to have been a "saint" (Taylor 1993; Tambiah 1984; Kamala Tiyavanich 1997). By the late twentieth century forest monks had, however, become as much known for their social activism, especially in promoting forest conservation, as for their religious accomplishments (*Phra* Phaisan Visalo 1990; Taylor 1991, 1996; *Bhikkhu* Sumedho 1999). In Burma, although meditation centers have less often been located in the forests than in either Thailand or Sri Lanka, they have had a profound influence (Byles 1962; King 1964; Houtman 1996, 1999). Also see Kornfield (1977) for biographical sketches of a number of meditation masters in the Theravādin world.

17. In Burma some modernist monks also proposed a comparable reevaluation of *saṃsāra* (King 1965).

18. I had intended to also include Burma in my comparison, but space limitations preclude my doing so. I would observe, in lieu of a fuller discussion, that Buddhist nationalism has contributed to the long-standing conflicts between the Burmese state and ethnic minorities (Taylor 1986, 1988; Gravers 1993; and Matthews 1993). More recently the military junta that has ruled Burma since 1988

has justified its rule by evoking Buddhist nationalism, while the supporters of the opposition to the junta, led by Daw Aung San Suu Kyi, have drawn inspiration from other interpretations of modernist Buddhism (see Aung San Suu Kyi 1991, Schober 1997, and Houtman 1999).

19. Obeyesekere updated and revised this article as Obeyesekere (1995).

20. On Dharmapāla's vision of an exclusivist Sinhalese Buddhist nationalism, also see Roberts (1997).

21. For some examination of the role of Buddhist nationalism in the Tamil-Sri Lankan conflict, see Manor (1985), Tambiah (1993), Roberts (1995), and Bartholomeusz and De Silva (1998).

22. On the direct involvement of monks in the election of 2004 as well as the advocacy of some monks for the violent suppression of Tamil ethnonationalism, see the article "Powerful Buddhist Monks Enter Sri Lanka's Election Race" issued by Dow Jones news service on March 2, 2004 (http://framehosting.dowjonesnews .com/sample/samplestory.asp?StoryID=2004030207260015&Take=1).

23. There is a large literature on the political crisis in Thailand in the 1970s. Among the most relevant sources for understanding the emergence of militant Buddhism in the period are the following: Girling (1981); Morell and Chai-anan Samudavanija (1981); Anderson (1977); and Thongchai Winichakul (2002).

24. I have discussed Kittivuddho's advocacy of militant Buddhism at some length elsewhere (Keyes 1978). His most extended justification of militant Buddhism is found in Kittivuddho (1976). Also see Somboon Suksamran (1982) for further details.

25. Although Kittivuddho escaped any censure from the Thai Sangha hierarchy, he later became involved in scandals concerning the illegal import of Volvo automobiles and promoting projects that entailed questionable fund-raising. He never renounced his militant interpretation of Buddhism, but he also never repeated it. He died in January 2005 at the age of sixty-nine (*Bangkok Post*, January 22, 2005).

26. See the following websites for information on this international network of socially engaged Buddhists: Buddhist Peace Fellowship (http://www.bpf.org/ html/home.html); International Network of Engaged Buddhists (http://www .bpf.org/html/resources_and_links/think_sangha/ineb/ineb.html). For analyses of this movement, see Bobilin (1988); Gosling (1984); Kraft (1992); Nhat Hanh (1993); Sulak Sivaraksa (1990); Swearer (1992); Thai Inter-Religious Commission for Development and International Network of Engaged Buddhists (1990).

27. On Maha Ghosananda, see the following websites: http://www .buddhanetz.org/engaged/engaged3.htm and http://www.buddhanet.net/s_ img052.htm. Also see Harris (1999, 2005), and Skidmore (1996).

10

Avoiding Mass Violence at Rajneeshpuram

Marion S. Goldman

From 1981 to 1986, American media, government experts, and a handful of scholars foretold bloodshed at Rajneeshpuram, the communal cult city in central Oregon. However, violence never escalated to the point of mass murder, suicides, or large, collective internal or external attacks. The Rajneesh case provides a fruitful context to explore the question: *How is potential religious violence averted?* I consider research on Peoples Temple and the Branch Davidians with Rajneesh data in order to explore processes that can diminish large-scale collective violence, engaging religious group members and/or the surrounding society.

PREVIOUS RESEARCH

Sociologists examined deviant cases like the Branch Davidians or Peoples Temple to develop models about the structural conditions and group dynamics contributing to intense religious violence (Hall 1987; Lifton 1999). The relatively isolated community of Rajneeshpuram met many of those structural conditions and group interactions associated with violence. In 1984 the cult seemed poised for dramatic collective confrontation with outsiders and among dissident internal factions. Moreover, leaders had stockpiled weapons, as well as accumulated some knowledge of biological warfare. Despite a confrontational context and the means for large-scale violence, none occurred. This case may further refine existing models, indicating the mixture of conditions mitigating large-scale violence.

Some violence occurred at Rajneeshpuram and toward external communities, but it was minimal in relation to dire predictions. I define extreme collective violence as involving most cult members, with lasting physical and emotional effects on victims. Beyond the standard of extreme collective violence lies a long arc of cult-associated violence.

Sociologists differ in their definitions of *significant* religious violence (Lalich 2004, 261–74). Most conceptualize mass violence as a large number or major segment of movement members and/or outsiders who perish because of faith-based controversy (Stark 2001). However, beatings or routine psychological punishments contained within a group are not always framed as extreme violence, so long as individuals or small groups are victimized in relative isolation.

There are academic disputes about whether ineffectual or moderate attacks on outsiders signify intense collective brutality. Accepted scholarship on Rajneeshpuram did not define isolated murder attempts or targeted biological attacks that had no lasting physical effects as intense collective violence (Carter 1990; Palmer 1994; Goldman 1999). Thus, I am concerned with why violence did not occur.

From 1981 through 1985 a small number of devotees and a handful of Oregon state leaders worked to avoid violence at Rajneeshpuram. I examine how they diminished possibilities of widespread bloodshed in a context poised for confrontation. After briefly describing my sources, I develop a framework for understanding cases in which extreme collective violence develops. Then I describe the Rajneesh movement and its philosophy during the 1980s, in order to ground postulates concerning how violence is negated. After that, I consider the two *key* elements diminishing possibilities of violence within cults and between cults and their host contexts in the United States: life-embracing, individualistic doctrine and affirmation of the rule of law grounded in the Establishment Clause of the Constitution, which separates church and state.

SOURCES

In the early 1980s, Bhagwan Shree Rajneesh and about 2,500 of his sannyasins created the communal city of Rajneeshpuram on the Big Muddy Ranch in Wasco County, Oregon. The group, mostly from North America and Western Europe, traveled from India to Oregon to blend spirituality and materialism while building an intentional community. During the Rajneesh sojourn in Oregon, I interviewed forty-four sannyasins in the course of a total of thirty days spent at Rajneeshpuram between fall 1984 and fall 1985. Formal interviews of eleven men and thirteen women ceased when the commune verged on collapse and residents no longer believed that their intentional community would last forever (Carter 1990). Between 1999 and 2001 I also interviewed ten individuals active in local Wasco County resistance to Rajneeshpuram.

In 1997, I taped a set of interviews with former Oregon attorney general David Frohnmayer, who played a decisive role in averting violence at Rajneeshpuram. I re-interviewed Frohnmayer in 2004. In 1996, I interviewed Bill Bowerman, the former University of Oregon track coach who had cofounded Nike, and his son, Jon, a nearby rancher who mobilized nonviolent opposition to Rajneeshpuram, through the environmental group Thousand Friends of Oregon. In 2004, I interviewed Ma Anand Sheela, Rajneesh's former personal secretary, now known as Sheela Biernstiel. She served two-and-one-half years in federal prison for her role in attempted murders and other criminal activities at Rajneeshpuram. She left the United States in December 1988, before more charges could be filed against her, and resides in Switzerland, running two convalescent homes. This was the first time an American researcher had interviewed her since she departed for Europe.

PREDICTING MASSIVE CULT VIOLENCE

I compare the sannyasins in Oregon with two massively violent groups, which, like the Rajneesh movement, were primarily American: the 1978 Jonestown, Guyana, Peoples Temple, where more than nine hundred people died at the behest of their leader, Jim Jones, and the Branch Davidians in Waco, Texas, where a bloody shootout between government agents and group members took place in 1993.

Unlike the Peoples Temple or the Davidians, both groups with roots in the United States, the Rajneesh movement originated in India in the early 1970s. The Rajneeshees, mostly Americans and Western Europeans by 1975, established headquarters in central Oregon in 1981. The Oregon phase of the movement was widely known because of Rajneesh's collection of more than ninety Rolls Royces and because of sannyasins' abortive attempt to recruit homeless individuals to join their community and vote in Wasco County elections in order to place their sympathizers in charge of local land use decisions.

By 1984 the group had amassed means for violence far greater than either the Peoples Temple or Branch Davidians. Rajneeshpuram housed a huge, formally registered arsenal of semiautomatic weapons, rifles, and machine guns (Fitzgerald 1986, 343–44); but none of the weapons were used against insiders or outsiders.

During the Rajneeshpuram years, individual movement members engaged in or were targets of personalized psychological or physical violence, and outsiders suffered at the hands of a few of Sheela's cadre. However, individual attacks did not pave the way for collective outbreaks. Such personalized violence or deprivation may be a predisposing condition, as it was at Jonestown, but it is not in itself sufficient for collective violence.

Devotees of groups ranging from Tibetan Buddhists to fundamentalist Christian communities frequently submitted to and also engaged in violence toward other individual members that did not lead to collective outbreaks. Jacobs (1989) observed that devotees often left groups like Divine Light Mission after being physically disciplined. And physical deprivation and emotional abuse were commonplace among several generations of members of the Bruderhhof, a pietistic evangelical sect living in closed, authoritarian communities along the eastern seaboard in the United States (Rubin 2002). Neither of these groups engaged in mass violence, nor did members of other groups where extreme discipline was commonplace.

Individualized violence may make members less sensitive to their own and others' suffering, but it rarely leads *directly* to collective violence within a movement or between movement members and outsiders. Melton (1992) notes that groups like the Children of God, Hare Krishna, Synanon, and Scientology engaged in discrete incidents of aggression carried out secretly by a handful of members toward hostile outsiders, but they never escalated to significant violence involving the majority of the group. These cults' charismatic leaders did not publicly advocate collective violence toward dissident factions, group suicide, or attacks on large numbers of critical outsiders.

Sociological theories about cult violence directed toward outsiders and/or groups of insiders suggest that a combination of internal group processes and environmental conditions must converge to ignite massive collective hostilities in a religious cult (Robbins and Anthony 1995, 237). Wallis (1976) asserts that the interaction of exceptional internal movement deviance and external social suppression produces a cycle of members' alienation, increased external suppression, and finally intense religious conflict. Dawson (1998, 128–57) and Hall et al. (2000) develop similar, but more detailed theories of communal religion and extreme violence.

Members' intense identification with a cult along with collective withdrawal from the larger society are central to the interactive theory of collective violence that John Hall and his coauthors mapped out in *Apocalypse Observed* (2000). They chart the development of apocalyptic belief systems within communal religious contexts. Scenarios foretelling dramatic religious violence that are developed in isolation from possible empirical disconfirmation contribute to potential violence. When law enforcement officials confront the group, as in the cases of Jonestown or the Branch Davidians, members may view the first confrontation as a signal that all-out war and Armageddon will soon follow.

RAJNEESH IN OREGON

While working as a professor in the 1960s, Rajneesh traveled around India delivering scathing critiques about Indian electoral politics, sexuality, and spirituality. He gained a loyal off-campus following of wealthy merchants and businessmen seeking consultations about their spiritual development and daily life (Mehta 1979). As his following grew and diversified, Rajneesh quit the university and assumed the expansive title of "Bhagwan," signifying enlightened or awakened individual (Carter 1990).

In the early 1970s, visiting Westerners outnumbered Indians attending Rajneesh's lectures, meditation camps, and individual sessions. Rajneesh's criticisms of Indian traditions, his eclectic philosophy, and the many privileged Western devotees' flouting of Indian conventions all combined to generate tension with the surrounding culture. In 1974, he moved headquarters from an airy apartment in Bombay to Pune (Poona), one hundred miles southeast of that city. With considerable Western backing and additional financial support from longtime Indian devotees, Rajneesh acquired a six-acre enclave and adjoining real estate in an elite suburb. Over the next five years, the Shree Rajneesh Ashram grew to include a meditation hall where Rajneesh could lecture to several thousand people, a smaller auditorium, and facilities for a multitude of human potential therapy groups, a medical clinic, cottage industries, restaurants, shops, classrooms, and housing for sannyasins who were permanent residents.

At the movement's peak around 1976, close to 30,000 Westerners visited the ashram yearly, and the worldwide movement included over 25,000 sannyasins (Milne 1987, 23; Carter 1990, 59–60). After 1976, however, recruitment stagnated. There was greater competition in the American spiritual and self-actualization marketplaces, Western economies were constricting, and some influential figures in the human potential movement, like Richard Price of Esalen Institute, publicly denounced physical assaults as a means of "getting in touch with anger" within Rajneesh therapy groups (Anderson 1983, 299–302).

Rajneesh lectured to his devotees about the Buddhafield, a spiritual community built around him and his teachings, but no regional governments in India were willing to permit a Rajneesh commune. In July 1981, Rajneesh representatives purchased the 64,229-acre Big Muddy Ranch in Central Oregon for $5.9 million, and they immediately started building the Buddhafield, the communal city of Rajneeshpuram that ultimately housed about 2,500 residents in quarters ranging from cramped townhouses and trailers to luxuriously spacious apartments and freestanding houses. Boutiques, cafés, bars, and restaurants were available to affluent sannyasins and moneyed visitors alike.

Even devotees with private incomes toiled twelve hours a day, doing Rajneesh's version of karma yoga, in which work became a vehicle for worship and personal growth. All community members received free housing, free clothing, medical care, and possibilities of building a permanent city grounded in Rajneesh's presence and philosophies. Rajneesh retained his vow of silence for three years, appearing only for a daily afternoon drive. Otherwise, the guru retreated from public view, speaking only to his personal secretary, his physician, his companion and former lover, and his dentist. Ma Anand Sheela, his personal secretary, became organizational head of Rajneeshpuram.

From the moment the sannyasins settled in Oregon, they challenged established laws and customs, generating opposition throughout the state. Some adversaries to the Rajneeshees used the media, others the courts, and others proposed vigilante action. The land was zoned as restricted farmland, and until the community disbanded, environmental groups like Thousand Friends of Oregon issued press releases, filed civil lawsuits, and encouraged government investigations of land use and building code violations.

On a national level, the Federal Immigration and Naturalization Service closely investigated Rajneesh's status from his first application for a one-year visa, involving American medical treatment. He later requested visa extensions because of his work as a religious teacher. After legal disputes with Rajneesh attorneys, INS rescinded an earlier deportation order (Carter 1990, 161–65). But federal agencies continued to investigate all foreign nationals at Rajneeshpuram (Carter 1990, 150–52).

In autumn of 1984, Sheela and her inner circle bused in hundreds of homeless individuals, mostly men, recruited in cities in the western United States. Sheela instituted a program of "rehabilitation," with the underlying purpose of ensuring hundreds of pro-Rajneesh votes in the forthcoming November election, in which sannyasin candidates competed for seats on the Wasco County Commission. Massive negative publicity, state monitoring of voter registration, and legal opposition doomed the plan. When external opposition to the election grew, Sheela encouraged Rajneeshpuram residents and visitors *not* to vote. By the end of 1984, almost all of the estimated 1,500 homeless visitors had departed.

A month before the election, Rajneesh abandoned his vow of silence, explaining his resumed lectures as the result of improved personal health and his own spiritual growth. There are conflicting narratives about whether or not Rajneesh knew of Sheela's doomed election plan, but its failure and the community's mounting debt coincided with his new involvement with daily operations at Rajneeshpuram.

Less than a year after the "Share a Home" debacle, Sheela and her inner circle fled Rajneeshpuram for Europe. Rajneesh publicly accused Sheela and her cadre of a wide variety of "recently discovered" crimes, including their secret mass salmonella poisoning of at least 750 individuals in almost a dozen restaurant salad bars located in the Wasco County seat, The Dalles. Sheela and a handful of sannyasins had designed it as a test run for a more massive effort that could temporarily incapacitate large numbers of anti-Rajneesh voters on election day (Carter 1990, 224–26). The existence of laboratories and salmonella cultures at Rajneeshpuram was supported by sannyasins' testimony, documentary records, and, in the case of the secret laboratories, my own later tour of hidden rooms at the ranch.

Rajneesh also accused Sheela and her circle of drugging dissident sannyasins, wire-tapping, arson, and embezzling Rajneesh movement funds. A number of these charges eventually led to convictions and imprisonment of Sheela and members of her inner circle. In the wake of FBI and state investigations of these allegations, dozens of devotees received subpoenas to testify before a grand jury. All evidence suggested that Sheela and her small circle were responsible for these dangerous activities, but whether or not Rajneesh knew remains in dispute. However, for the past twenty years, Sheela has sworn that Rajneesh directed every criminal and violent move.

Rajneesh himself was subpoenaed after Sheela fled, and soon afterward federal marshals in Charlotte, North Carolina, captured him, when two Lear jets carrying Rajneesh and a handful of sannyasins stopped to refuel en route to Bermuda. He was taken back to Oregon, where his attorneys posted bond so he could return to his communal city. Rajneesh departed the country less than a month later, after filing no-contest pleas to two counts of immigration fraud and paying fines and prosecution costs of $400,000 (McCormack 1985, 116).

Bent on saving face by flight rather than confrontation, Rajneesh also protected his devotees from the consequences of collective confrontation. In the wake of deportation, the guru and his new staff shifted all responsibility onto Sheela and most sannyasins accepted that explanation. Rajneesh traveled all over the world seeking asylum and meeting rejection from a number of countries until his representatives bargained with the Indian government and he resettled in the old Pune ashram.

As the INS and the FBI moved closer to Rajneesh in 1984, the Oregon attorney general successfully challenged the incorporation of Rajneeshpuram itself as an unconstitutional merger of church and state. His opinion asserted that the Buddhafield violated the Establishment Clause of the Constitution. That legal opinion foretold discontinuation of all state services to Rajneeshpuram, and key actors on both sides of the controversy interpreted the opinion as the beginning of the end.

The Oregon attorney general and his staff consistently emphasized the importance of due process, refusing to label the movement as enemies of the state or act on then-spotty evidence about the salmonella poisonings. This reliance on law facilitated successful mediation leading to Rajneesh's plea bargain and ultimate return to India. The relatively peaceful disintegration of Rajneeshpuram also reflected the fact that sannyasins had no desire to die for any cause. Collective violence might have been possible if Rajneesh had been tried and convicted, but even then, the life-affirming, individualistic philosophy at the heart of Rajneesh's teachings militated against mass violence. Sannyasins wanted to enrich their current lives on earth, and physical risk was not on their individual or collective agendas.

INDIVIDUALISM AND OPTIMISM

In almost six hundred books, most of which were transcriptions of his lectures and initiation talks, Bhagwan Shree Rajneesh discussed almost every major religious and philosophical tradition. These varied approaches came together in a spiritual stew dominated by Zen Buddhism and spiced by exhortations to fully enjoy every aspect of life. The eclecticism led to contradictions in philosophy, but it also allowed sannyasins very personal, individualistic, and idiosyncratic interpretations of Rajneesh's wishes.

Rajneesh spoke repeatedly of his vision of a new man, synthesizing the worldly and the godly. His ideal was "Zorba the Buddha," a consummate being with the spiritual focus of the Indian mystic and the life-embracing traits of the materialistic Westerner. Zen, Tantra tradition, and Reverend Ike's message came together in a vision that enticed many privileged Americans. Rajneesh relished this fusion of materialism and spirituality. He stated:

> A new human being is needed on earth, a new human being who accepts both, who is scientific and mystic. Who is all for matter and all for spirit. Only then will we be able to create humanity, which is rich on both sides. I teach you the richness of body, richness of soul, richness of this world and that world. To me that is true religiousness. (Rajneesh 1983, 14)

Becoming a sannyasin was also individualistic, and in addition it was easy. From the early 1970s through 1990, prospective devotees checked a box on their application forms to note whether they wanted to keep their old first name, which would now be prefaced with Ma or Swami followed by a brief name such as Prem (Love), or whether they wished to receive an entirely different, Hindu-style name. After taking sannyas, in the 1970s and 1980s, devotees were supposed to meditate at least once daily, wear sunrise colors (which included a whole spectrum of red-based shades), don a mala of 108 beads with a locket housing Bhagwan's likeness, and become vegetarian. But even these minimal requirements were subject to individual's whims, and outside Rajneeshpuram, sannyasins often ignored them.

In most of his writings and lectures, Rajneesh defined his ultimate charismatic success in terms of influencing individuals and bringing a new spiritual consciousness to the world. He constructed his goals as broad, sustained global cultural influence, without any specific targets or timelines.

The brief summary of Rajneesh philosophy is important because it highlights the central ways in which the internal Rajneesh movement implicitly discouraged collective violence. The movement's organization was always flexible and directed toward sustaining itself. It was engaged in producing personal growth rather than following a set of abstract precepts. Rajneesh suggested that devotees find their pleasures in the here and now, reiterating the popular American Zen emphasis on living in and enjoying the present moment. He consistently encouraged individualism in both the practice of his brand of spirituality and also the quest for personal enlightenment. Most important, the guru had no coherent apocalyptic vision.

NO IMPLOSION/NO EXPLOSION

Until 1982, when sannyasins took over the town of Antelope near Rajneeshpuram, they remained relatively friendly with many Oregon neighbors. An experienced Rajneesh public relations force and a group of hired lobbyists countered mounting tensions by meeting with local elites, cultivating legislators in the state capital, and providing carefully orchestrated tours of the communal city. Rajneesh public relations officials attended gatherings of local American Civil Liberties Union chapters and nurtured media and entertainment industry contacts. In its first two years, Rajneeshpuram had a number of public supporters, including large businesses selling the group lumber, heavy equipment, and luxury cars. In April 1983, however, Sheela printed a letter in the *Rajneesh Times* that was quoted in newspapers throughout the state. She laid out possibilities for religious violence: "We are tired of this uncivilized, barbaric, and unsophisticated and violent way of trying to intimidate a religious minority. Once and for all, we wish to make it clear that we are in Oregon to stay at whatever cost. If that means that some of our blood is spilled, or some of our property is vandalized, then this is the price we are prepared to pay" (Fitzgerald 1986, 337).

Some sannyasins agreed with her paranoia, but most did not, defining Sheela's vitriolic comments as both means to attract publicity and also mechanisms to build solidarity within the movement. Sannyasins could dismiss Sheela's words because they did not come directly from Rajneesh himself. Devotees also avoided total dependence on Sheela's framing because they retained sources of rewards outside the cult. The mean adult age at Rajneeshpuram was thirty-four years old, and sannyasins were predominantly drawn from the upper and middle classes. Their ages, social class, and sustained connection to family, former colleagues, and old friends allowed devotees to retain some of the social and cultural capital that they could use to minimize conflicts with the outside. Their outside ties also made them less dependent on the group.

Many sannyasins had abandoned lucrative professional careers, business investments, or established relationships to join in the utopian experiment (Goldman 1999). A contingent had law degrees, and they formed a network that tried to placate local law enforcement agencies and limit confrontation to the courtroom. Until 1983, Rajneesh attorneys had relatively cordial informal interaction with the Oregon attorney general and his staff. Rajneesh representatives talked with attorneys from the U.S. Office for Civil Rights about their fears of harassment. They also held secret talks with the Oregon attorney general and the United States Department of Justice Mediation and Conciliation Service.

Throughout the sannyasins' sojourn in Oregon, law enforcement at local, state, and federal levels monitored their activities and by and large tried to calm insurgent local opponents. A handful of Rajneesh opponents posted signs about "Rajneesh Hunting Season," but this was symbolic, rather than an actual call to arms. The local gun culture centered around hunting and from an early age, gun owners were taught to raise guns only when they planned to use them. One rancher whose land bordered the communal city urged other locals to follow him in locking his firearms in a bank vault.

The fact that there was no dominant local religious tradition and that there were large numbers of unaffiliated individuals in central Oregon (Hout and Fischer 2002) also impeded development of unified, intense opposition. Land use groups, local residents, and churches had different reasons for opposing Rajneeshpuram, but they failed to unify into overwhelming, influential opposition.

As Sheela rose to power, she ostracized vocal dissidents within the movement. Some formed sects of the Rajneesh movement, such as "The Wild Geese" or "The Camels." These dissidents, however, rarely criticized Rajneesh or his desire to build a communal city. Instead, they blamed Sheela and continued to support Rajneesh's vision of Zorba the Buddha (Goldman 1999, 248–68; Franklin 1992). Groups of apostate sannyasins never publicly suggested that they or other devotees had been brainwashed, nor did they solicit external intervention. Thus, they never joined with the wider anti-cult movement in stirring negative media coverage or exhorting law enforcement to act precipitously.

In 1984, as sannyasins reeled from disclosures of the group's overextended finances and Sheela's growing irrationality, the Oregon attorney general issued the legal challenge to the city of Rajneeshpuram itself, arguing that the community represented the unconstitutional merger of church and state. The Federal District Court enjoined the City of Rajneeshpuram to cease exerting governmental power in December 1985, after the Big Muddy Ranch was already up for sale once again.

The Oregon attorney general worked to minimize possibilities of violence, emphasizing the need to keep open lines of communication with sannyasins, to coordinate law enforcement at all levels, and to fly beneath Sheela's radar. In a 1997 interview Frohnmayer noted:

> I had persons from central Oregon who were ready to go right over the river [into Rajneeshpuram] with guns blazing. Part of our job was still to keep the peace with people who agreed with the legal position we took, but were impatient and even furious with the slow pace of the courts. . . . And not withstanding [the sannyasins'] extreme reaction to my opinion, within hours of its issue, my assistants were on the phone to Rajneesh officials saying, "Above all, we've got to keep the peace with this!" (Rajneesh Manuscript Collection, UO Library Special Collections 1997)

Much of the negotiation between state, local, and federal authorities remains confidential. However, published accounts indicate that the attorney general's stance consistently upheld a rule of law involving centralized procedures informed by the Bill of Rights. The focus on due process safeguarded both the rights of sannyasins and also the interests of their opponents.

In the cases of Waco or Peoples Temple, sudden government intervention precipitated religious violence. The reliance on the rule of law allowed opponents to meet privately and defused a number of possibilities for violence.

AFTERMATH AND IMPLICATIONS

Sannyasins began to reframe their Oregon history in immediate response to criminal charges in the United States and the disestablishment of the city of Rajneeshpuram, blaming Sheela and her circle for all of the Oregon crimes and failures. Their later historical reconstructions minimized the importance of the Oregon experiment altogether and emphasized the importance of continuity from 1974 through the present in Pune. Rajneesh and his new inner circle banished Sheela and her aides. After their failed five-year Oregon experiment ended and sannyasins resettled the movement's old ashram estate in Pune, Bhagwan Shree Rajneesh became known as Osho. He died in 1990. The ashram was recently renamed Osho Meditation Resort, offering luxurious spiritual services to an affluent, worldwide clientele. Rajneesh's formerly controversial movement continues with a small core of several dozen committed devotees guiding a larger movement, whose affiliates are engaged with Osho and often with other spiritual organizations (*Sannyas News Website,* December 2004).

Learning from the Oregon debacle, the guru created a council of leaders, so that no single individual emerged as his successor. He encouraged the council to continue after his death, without conferring complete authority on any one person. There are now numerous Osho Centers throughout the world that remain loosely affiliated with the Pune ashram. A handful of former sannyasins have established their own followings. Diversification has also accelerated the process of inclusiveness, where individuals may be sannyasins and still practice other faiths as well.

The contemporary Osho Rajneesh movement has transformed itself into a broad-based corporate spiritual enterprise, with neither motive nor means to engage in religious violence. It conforms to the axiom that the more loosely organized and eclectic the religious movement, the less likely it will engage in collective violence.

Despite these significant changes in the group, the case of Rajneeshpuram remains more than an isolated point on the map of Oregon or Rajneesh movement history. It represents a case where a heavily armed religious group that was in high tension with the surrounding culture neither exploded outward in mass violence nor turned inward to group suicides or selected inside murders.

The relatively peaceful demise of Rajneesh's communal city reflected interactions of external environmental variables and internal movement characteristics. The movement remained connected to the outside society and cultivated enough positive relationships to mitigate violent verbal or physical attacks against it. In turn, law enforcement officials gave the movement time and space and did not force confrontation.

The Rajneesh case illustrates that collective cult violence is generally *rare* and is also a case that could provide guidelines to assess and minimize potential cult violence. A number of internal and external characteristics usually combine to generate relatively peaceful solutions. Despite superficial similarities with other contemporary new religions that were devastated by collective violence, the Rajneesh case demonstrates two *major* dissimilarities that are most important both in developing strategies to avert collective religious violence and also in assuaging ungrounded fears that may actually contribute to violent confrontations. *Externally, the Oregon attorney general's focus on a rule of law grounded in the constitutional separation of church and state and internally, the Rajneesh movement's life-embracing doctrine were the key variables permitting a peaceful resolution to a situation fraught with danger.*

Issuing an opinion on the ostensibly limited question of whether or not the City of Rajneesh could control or prevent travel on county roads, Attorney General David Frohnmayer addressed a number of constitutional issues. He asserted that the separation of church and state was ultimately more important than individuals' rights to free exercise of religion. Thus, he limited the Rajneeshees' power to force their priorities on outsiders. This position effectively controlled the Rajneeshees' influence in Wasco County and affirmed the efficacy of the rule of law (Frohnmayer 1985). It also limited the role of law enforcement agencies in forcing confrontation with sannyasins at Rajneeshpuram, which could have precipitated violence.

The internal violence to individuals, the stockpiled arms, and the 750 nonfatal poisonings in The Dalles, all indicated credible possibilities for collective violence. However, as a group, the sannyasins had *no* desire to die. *A number of internal variables militated against the possibilities for violence, but the most important of these was the overall philosophy of embracing the material world.* Rajneesh's affirmation of sensual comfort and personal growth was opposite from apocalyptic prophecies, such as those that shaped events at Jonestown and Waco. His affirmation focused on individualism, and that provided ways for sannyasins to disengage from Sheela's confrontational stance. Apocalyptic prophecy is considered to be central to current religious violence (Lifton 1999). Rajneesh's doctrine of life as comedy, not tragedy, was the single most important internal variable in mitigating violence at Rajneeshpuram.

In 2004, Sheela Biernstiel (formerly Ma Anand Sheela) laughed at her role at Rajneeshpuram, disclaiming any malevolent attentions. Addressing the issue of whether something like Jonestown could have happened at Rajneeshpuram, she noted, "Bhagwan was life positive. His whole movement was life positive. Where [a] life negative situation happens you can see suicide happening" (Sheela Biernstiel Interview, August 2004).

Using data from the case of Rajneeshpuram, I have identified a number of variables contributing to peaceful solutions amid violent possibilities. I have built on theories about how collective cult violence develops, particularly drawing on Wallis (1976) and Hall et al. (2000).

When faced with similar crises, law enforcement officials ought to consider the importance of approaches grounded in constitutional protections for members of alternative religions and also their opponents. Also, outsiders and movement members might each consider how apocalyptic beliefs fit with the doctrines of specific movements. Unlike most cases where religion and violence are examined, the case of Rajneeshpuram serves as a positive example of peaceful resolution in the face of potential collective violence.

11

"Obliterating an Idol of the Modern Age": The New Iconoclasm from the Twin Buddhas to the Twin Towers

Joel Black

A year before the attacks of September 11, 2001, Mark Juergensmeyer observed that religious, in contrast to political, terrorism has less to do with strategic calculation than with ritual performance and symbolism. "What is striking about religious terrorism," he wrote, "is that it is almost exclusively symbolic, performed in remarkably dramatic ways."[1] And in a chapter titled "Theater of Terror," Juergensmeyer noted that in "virtually every . . . recent example of religious terrorism, the building, vehicle, structure, or locale where the assault took place has had symbolic significance." With respect to the location of the assault, the symbolism may either be specific, as in American pro-life activists' bombings of abortion clinics or Islamic terrorists' attacks on Egyptian tourist sites, or general, as in the case of the explosions of the World Trade Center in 1993, the Oklahoma City federal building in 1995, or the USS *Cole* in 2000—targets that represent "the power and stability of the society itself." By staging spectacular attacks on these particular structures, terrorists attempt to create the impression "that the movements perpetrating the acts have enormous power and that the ideologies behind them have cosmic importance."[2]

Juergensmeyer's observations into the symbolic character of acts of religious terror were dramatically confirmed a year after his book appeared with the 9/11 attacks on the World Trade Center, the Pentagon, and presumably the White House. These highly visible structures respectively represented the economic, military, and political might of the United States, and more broadly, of secular modernity. As bin Laden himself acknowledged two months after 9/11, "The September eleven attacks were not targeted at women and children. The real targets were America's icons of military and economic power."[3] Yet while these targets may have been chosen for their symbolic value, the violence directed against these "false deities" of a "godless" society also savagely took the lives of thousands of people. Holy wars tend to be more brutal than secular warfare because their commanders are more concerned with religious (or irreligious) symbols than human lives. The icon's symbolic value is an incentive—even an invitation—to commit acts of devastating violence that are anything but symbolic.

As secular critics have traced eruptions of religious violence like that of 9/11 back to the violent imagery of war, suffering, persecution, and martyrdom that abounds in religious texts, religious conservatives blame much of the brutality of modern, secular society on the violent imagery in the commercial mass media. Yet many of the same critics who hold Hollywood responsible for real-life violence find nothing wrong with hyper-realistic violence when it is presented in a religious (or specifically, a Christian) context. Thus the graphic (rather than symbolic) depiction of Christ's physical torment in Mel Gibson's 2004 film *The Passion of the Christ* not only served the political end of rallying the religious right in support of America's military presence in Iraq, but it performed a vital symbolic function in linking George W. Bush's "war on terror" to the original Christian Crusade, or "war of the cross," a millennium ago when, as James Carroll suggests, "the bloody crucifixion began to dominate Latin Christian imagination," and a "theology narrowly focused on the brutal death of Jesus reinforced the primitive notion that violence can be a sacred act."[4] Events like the release of Gibson's film focusing on Christ's physical suffering, and the prosecution of Bush's war on terror in the guise of a Christian Crusade, suggest that the idea of violence as sacred and redemptive as well as retributive is hardly a "primitive" notion in a historical sense but is every bit as compelling today as it was in antiquity or the Middle Ages. On the one hand, nothing inspires religious enthusiasm in people like the spectacle of violence. On the other hand, nothing seems to incite people to engage in acts of violence like religious images.

Such highly charged imagery cuts both ways, however. If Gibson's graphic images of Christ's persecution served to rally the Christian faithful against nonbelievers at home and abroad, the infamous Abu Ghraib photographs that surfaced three months after the film's release (one of which seemed an unwitting parody of the crucifixion) inflamed Islamic extremists. Within days these images of American prison guards torturing and humiliating Muslim detainees in Iraq were followed by the Internet spectacle of terrorists beheading an American hostage. (Both the prison photos and the "snuff" webcasts served as effective Islamist recruiting tools.) A similar instance of media-mediated violence occurred two years later, when caricatures of the prophet Mohammed by Danish cartoonists triggered riots throughout the Muslim world.

If graphic or symbolic religious imagery doesn't necessarily prevent violence but often provokes it, this may be because its ritual dramas are hardly as harmless or healing as they are believed to be. Indeed, to an even greater extent than Juergensmeyer and other commentators suggest, issues of representation—specifically related to questions of realism and symbolism—lie at the heart of much religious violence. It's surprising in this regard that recent studies of religious terror have failed to address the type of violence most profoundly connected to representational issues since it is *directed at the image itself.* Inasmuch as religious terrorism is a matter of rituals and symbols, it's impossible to ignore the topic of iconoclasm—the defacement or destruction of artifacts belonging to a rival religious tradition, and especially of images symbolizing rival divinities themselves. In this primal form of religious violence, symbolic representation is itself the issue.

For centuries, iconoclasm has played a major role in Jewish, Christian, and Islamic religious history. The phenomenon that archaeologist Eberhard Sauer calls "image destruction and religious hatred" is a tradition that appears to be as old as religion itself.[5] Thus in the Old Testament, God not only prohibited the making of graven images, but he ordered the destruction of pagan altars, the leveling of sacred groves, and the smashing and burning of the stone and wooden images of the pagan gods. As Christianity struggled to establish dominance in Europe between the fourth and the seventh centuries, the Jewish destruction of pagan relics was taken over by "Christian image-haters." Subsequent "episodes of image destruction" occurred in the Byzantine Empire during the eighth and ninth centuries, and later in northern Europe during the Protestant Reformation.[6] The phenomenon also has a long history in Asia, as in the destruction of Buddhist artifacts in fifth-century China, and of the persecution of Buddhist image makers—and even image worshipers—by the Northern Wei emperor T'ai-wu.

In all these instances of traditional religious iconoclasm, the image breaker is compelled to deface, behead, and destroy idols because they are perceived as religious rivals that threaten to seduce worshipers away from the true deity.[7] Although they are false gods, idols are a good deal more than mere images. The very fact that they *are* representations—made by man, as Isaiah said, *with his own hands*—signifies that they are not deities but demonic impostors with godlike powers that must be exposed and destroyed. Indeed, the reason that monotheism and violence seem to "go hand in hand"[8] is that idols are an intolerable affront to believers in a God—be it Jehovah or Allah—who created man in his own image but who is Himself unrepresentable by man.[9] Behind every act of iconoclasm lies a paradoxical principle: the supposedly true believer in an unrepresentable divinity also believes at some level in the quasi-divine power of the image he condemns as a false god. In their visible, iconic form, false gods are rival divinities and, as such, remain godlike beings for the iconoclast. No one takes idols more seriously than the iconoclast who seeks to destroy them.

By emphasizing religious and sectarian issues, studies of the great iconoclastic movements in history have tended to overlook key aesthetic factors that shed light on this specific type of religious violence. Especially in the modern era when images are everywhere, aesthetic issues are involved at least as much as matters of religion in acts of iconoclastic violence. After all, iconoclasm is not always motivated by religious beliefs, nor is it always directed against specifically religious artifacts. In such instances of what I call *secular* iconoclasm, the religious nature of the icon—its explicit claim to divinity *as* an idol—is not the primary reason for its mistreatment.

Two forms of such image destruction can be distinguished. First, there's a *purely* secular iconoclasm directed against nonreligious artifacts and/or motivated by nonreligious interests. Examples would include cases of plundering and vandalism, such as the removal of the Buddhist statuary in the early twentieth century from the Yungang and Dunguang cave temples in China by Western archaeologists and antique collectors, or in present-day occupied Iraq where biblical history "is being pillaged on an epic scale."[10] Or one could cite the willful disfigurement of bodies and insignias in the late Middle Ages that served the political purpose of challenging illicit authority,[11] or the intentional destruction of ancient religious artifacts during the Cultural Revolution in China, or the presumably unintentional but wanton damage done in Babylon and other ancient sites by U.S.-led coalition forces during their occupation of Iraq. Although the desecrated icon in such instances may be without religious value, it is often politically or symbolically significant, as in the toppling of the Berlin Wall in 1989, or of Saddam Hussein's statue by American troops entering Baghdad in 2003. But there's also another kind of secular iconoclasm in which the drive to destroy a nonreligious—and often nonanthropomorphic—artifact is religiously motivated to some degree. In such instances, a secular icon is invested by the iconoclast with a profound religious meaning despite—or because—of its profane character. As will be seen, this was the case in the 9/11 attacks.

Ironically, the neglect of the aesthetic issues connected with secular—and even traditional forms of religious—iconoclasm are themselves part of a general iconoclastic tendency. For as destructive as the prohibition against graven images, or *Bilderverbot*, was for countless artifacts that were considered idols or visual representations of the sacred, the supposedly progressive development of modern secular culture has had a secondary iconoclastic effect. In the sixteenth and seventeenth centuries, Protestant iconoclasm made possible an aesthetic, and ultimately philosophical, appreciation of the artifact as an object of contemplation rather than veneration.[12] And in the eighteenth century, the emergence of aesthetics itself as a scholarly discipline led to a deeper appreciation of the beauty—rather than divinity—of natural and artistic objects. To be sure, the new museum culture provided a refuge for artworks from religiously motivated iconoclasm, which rapidly came to be associated with superstitious zealotry in opposition to progressive Enlightenment ideals. Yet as Gary Shapiro reminds us, "Before the era of art and the rise of the museum, the questions associated with iconoclasm were much more pressing."[13] Images of religious figures "were icons, not representations"—holy images that were far more powerful than artistic images because, as objects of worship, they could alternately inspire veneration or incite violence.

Visual images, in short, were accorded much greater power in religious cultures, where they were esteemed for what Walter Benjamin called their "cult value," than in secular society where, as works of art, they were prized for their "exhibition value."[14] Since the Enlightenment, the spread of modern museum culture in the West has led many with an aesthetic education to take the intrinsic artistic and cultural value of religious artifacts for granted, and to neglect the periodic resurgence of iconoclastic movements in much of the world. And so it was a shock for many Westerners to learn of a contemporary instance of iconoclasm, as happened in March 2001 with the Taliban's destruction of the 1500-year-old giant rock-cut Buddhist statues in Afghanistan's Bamian valley.[15]

The Buddhas' destruction was ordered by a true iconoclast. The Taliban leader Mullah Mohammed Omar, as Shapiro notes, was "not really a mullah," and

> has a complex relation to the visual: he has only one eye (one was lost in fighting the Soviets), and he refuses to be photographed, since he believes that the traditional Islamic exclusion of images extends to photography and video; in this respect his position is more radically iconoclastic than that of his associate Osama bin Laden, who allows himself to be photographed and videoed and who apparently does not discourage the widespread distribution of his image.[16]

Ordering the demolition of the Bamian Buddhas was one way for the fanatical iconoclast Mullah Omar to achieve his goal of establishing Islamic law or Sharia in Afghanistan. Welcoming the al Qaeda leader bin Laden, and providing him with a base in Afghanistan from which he could plan and direct a global campaign of religious terror, was another.

The shock with which many Westerners responded to the destruction of the Bamian Buddhas kept them from situating this contemporary resurgence of religious violence in its proper historical context. As horrific as the Taliban's destruction of these ancient colossal statues may have been from a historical or cultural perspective, the deed offers a revealing glimpse into the mindset of religious hatred that once was commonplace, and now appears to be making a comeback. The destruction of the Buddhas by Islamic extremists provides illuminating parallels with the activities of seventh-century Christian iconoclasts whose European campaign against pagan relics was getting under way at the very time that the prophet Mohammed appeared in the Arabian peninsula and introduced the tenets of what would become the new religion of Islam. Some five centuries later, Muslims would pursue their own iconoclastic campaign, deliberately beheading and mutilating Buddhist statues during their eastern advance into India in the twelfth and thirteenth centuries.[17] Thus Mullah Omar's call for the destruction of the Bamian Buddhas was hardly unprecedented.

Religious zealots engaged in iconoclastic campaigns do not regard their actions as wanton destruction. As Sauer describes, the late Roman Christians who sought to eradicate all traces of paganism considered their iconoclastic acts to be "a religious duty" that would enable them to convert nonbelievers to their creed. Sauer's reconstruction of the reasons behind seventh-century Christian image breakers' systematic destruction of pagan artifacts like the ancient Roman bronze statues at Bregenz—which were "beyond human ability at the time to produce," and whose "destruction marked a cultural revolution which broke the link of the people with their past"[18]—provides some insight into the motivations that led twenty-first-century Muslim extremists to destroy the Bamian Buddhas. For these modern-day iconoclasts, not only was there nothing about Buddhist artifacts that was "worth preserving," but their "destruction was a necessary step in the process of 'freeing' the world" from false and "dangerous demons."[19]

The destruction of the Bamian Buddhas differs in one important respect from older acts of this kind—namely, in the ability of modern iconoclasts to use far more powerful means of destruction. Sauer notes that while "iconoclasts in earlier periods of history depended on basic tools and manual labor which saved at least the colossal monuments partially or completely, such as Dendara [in Egypt] or Bamian [before the Taliban], modern explosives could turn whole countries into cultural deserts within days."[20] Despite their hostility to modernity, the Taliban didn't hesitate to use modern explosives, which enabled them to achieve their iconoclastic aims far more effectively than their predecessors in previous centuries. No wonder Sauer is prompted to warn that as "war today is so much more destructive than it has ever been before in world history, so the prospect of a renewed wave of image destruction has become much more frightening than at any previous point in history."[21]

Yet as horrified as modern Westerners profess to have been by the Taliban's iconoclastic acts—practices Shapiro describes as "holdovers from before the age of art"[22]—and as troubled as archaeologists and art historians are by the prospect of a new epoch of iconoclasm and the destruction of religious artifacts on a far greater scale than anything we have experienced in the past, we now know that the violence can get a good deal worse. When Sauer reflects that an earlier act of mutilation at Bamian in 1999, in which the head of the smaller statue was blown off, ought to have been "a loud warning signal to the world of what was to come,"[23] it now seems almost quaint that the catastrophe he had in mind was the explosion of both statues two years later. We now realize that the destruction of the Bamian Buddhas *itself* was a loud warning signal to the world of far greater devastation that was on the way—the 9/11 attacks six months later, and the loss of thousands of lives planned by al Qaeda militants in the haven provided by the Taliban. In today's world, religious iconoclasm is often a prelude to terrorism and secular (albeit religiously motivated) iconoclasm on a grand scale.

Unfortunately, the signal of the Buddhas' destruction was not loud enough. The connection between the Taliban's local act of iconoclasm and the possibility of a spectacular act of Islamic terrorism on U.S. soil was never made, or at least not taken as seriously as we now know it should have been. Even today, the September 2001 al Qaeda attacks on the Pentagon and the World Trade Center have so vastly overshadowed the Taliban's destruction of the Bamian Buddhas six months earlier that the connection between the two events continues to be missed.[24] Beyond the endless inquiries into possible links between terrorist groups and nations that give them support or cover, we need to ask whether there is a more fundamental relation between terrorism and iconoclasm as two kinds of religious violence. As there was an undeniable association between the Taliban and al Qaeda, there is also an unmistakable connection between the destruction of the Buddhas ordered by the former and the 9/11 attacks organized by the latter. This connection highlights the potentially explosive relation between art (statuary and architecture) and religion, and points to the need to formulate a theology of the image or an aesthetics of iconoclasm as a way of approaching the subject of religious violence.

What I'm suggesting is that there's more than meets the eye in the case of the terrorist attacks of 9/11. Or rather, more than the issues of religion and ideology, it's precisely the aesthetic issue of *what* meets the eye that needs to be considered. That's because 9/11 is an example of the type of secular iconoclasm mentioned earlier in which a nonreligious icon becomes the target of an act of aesthetically, as well as religiously, motivated violence, and in which the icon, precisely because of its profane character, is invested by the iconoclast with a profound symbolic meaning. This was clearly the case in the 9/11 attacks in which an iconoclastic—and ultimately, an aesthetic—motivation lay behind the decision to target the World Trade Center Towers.

Such aesthetic considerations were already evident in the first attempt to destroy this landmark in 1993. The original idea of targeting the Twin Towers is attributed to the blind Egyptian Islamic scholar and one-time theology professor Sheikh Omar Abdul Rahman. As revealed in a disciple's notebook, Rahman envisioned an expanded notion of jihad that focused less on killing and injuring the enemy than it did on inflicting spectacular visible damage to the enemy's "infrastructure." Rahman's vision of jihad called for the

> breaking and destruction of the enemies of Allah. And this is by means of destroying exploding, the structure of their civilized pillars such as the touristic infrastructure which they are proud of and their high world buildings which they are proud of and their statues which they endear and the buildings which gather their head[s,] their leaders, and without any announcement for our responsibility of Muslims for what had been done.[25]

Two years later in August 1992, as Daniel Benjamin and Steven Simon have described, "Rahman decided that the time had come to topple the 'civilized pillars.'"[26] He contacted a young engineer named Ramzi Yousef who, the following February, set off the explosion that became the first attempt to lay low the Twin Towers. He was captured in Pakistan in 1995 before he could pull off his crowning performance planned for later that year: Project Bojinka, involving the destruction of eleven American passenger planes above the Pacific Ocean.

The following year, another engineer named Khalid Shaikh Mohammed combined Yousef's separate schemes to bring down the Twin Towers and blow up multiple airliners in his own plan that called for trained pilots to fly planes into buildings inside the United States. Mohammed's "planes operation," approved by bin Laden three years later and culminating in the 2001 attacks on the World Trade Center and the Pentagon, had all the hallmarks of an iconoclastic act. Instead of a direct attempt at conquering the infidels' territory, the 9/11 attacks sought to bring about a global mass mobilization of the faithful, and even a conversion of the infidels, by staging a spectacular display of martyrdom, retribution, and revelation. As described by bin Laden in the video that aired three months after the attacks, the deeds of the nineteen hijackers were "speeches that overshadowed all other speeches made everywhere else in the world. The speeches are understood by both Arabs and non-Arabs—

even by Chinese. . . . In Holland, at one of the centers, the number of people who accepted Islam during the days that followed the operations were more than the people who accepted Islam in the last eleven years."[27] In the face of the vastly superior military might of Western nations, the only means to restore the caliphate was through a spontaneous mass conversion that would supposedly follow a daring, unexpected, and unforgettable strike against the enemy—a rapid succession of symbolic attacks against multiple targets.

The 2001 attacks on the Bamian Buddhas and the World Trade Center were both iconoclastic acts motivated by fundamentalist perceptions of the Buddhas and the towers alike as "civilized pillars" that were an offense to Islam. Indeed, the idea of targeting twin Buddhas in Afghanistan and twin towers in New York City was already presaged in the 1998 bombings of two east African embassies and by the 1993 explosion at the Twin Towers; in 2004 the idea was reprised with the near simultaneous bombings of two Russian airliners. In each case, the idea was to bring down *two* structures, thereby highlighting their symbolic, architectural significance *as* pillars—like those dislodged by Samson in the biblical story that brought down the temple, crushing himself along with his enemies—and heightening the aesthetic impact of their destruction.[28]

Despite the similarities of the destruction of the twin Buddhas and of the Twin Towers as acts of religious violence, some key differences should be noted. Most obviously, the Taliban's destruction of the Buddhas was a purely symbolic act that did not entail a loss of life, while al Qaeda's coordinated attacks on the World Trade Center, the Pentagon, and presumably the White House were directed against human as well as symbolic targets. Hiding out, supposedly in the Hindu Kush, after escaping the American assault at Tora Bora, bin Laden is only the latest "Old Man of the Mountains" in a long line of Islamic leaders from the time of the Crusades who sent out bands of thugs on murderous missions.[29] But whereas the assassins, or *hashshashin*, of former times were hopped up on hashish to help them commit their deeds, bin Laden's minions were intoxicated with religious doctrine, Marx's opium of the masses.

As for the particular object of their attacks, while the Taliban leader Mullah Omar targeted a specifically religious symbol in the case of the Bamian Buddhas—or as Sunni insurgents in 2006 destroyed the golden dome of a Shiite mosque in the Iraqi city of Samarra—bin Laden had a broader vision that involved attacking large, symbolic, secular targets like the World Trade Center. (Novelist Martin Amis has even speculated that bin Laden's reluctance to target a nuclear power plant on 9/11, which could have turned "large swathes of the Eastern seaboard into a plutonium cemetery for the next seventy millennia [that is, until the year 72001], may have been its lack of 'symbolic value.'"[30]) While Mullah

Omar was motivated to destroy the twin Buddhas because of their cult value as sacred objects, bin Laden seems to have been provoked by the Twin Towers' exhibition value.[31] Such flagrant exhibitionism seemed to call forth a spectacular iconoclastic response. After all, the sensational act of piloting a jetliner into the North Tower was planned for "maximum visibility"—as the ultimate pornographic spectacle for all the world to see.[32] For Taliban purists, the ancient twin Buddhas may have been sacrilegious idols, but at least they were quasi-spiritual objects. In contrast, the modern Twin Towers—that showpiece of New York City, viewed by bin Laden and much of the Arab world "as a city of Jews and the capital of world finance"[33]—represented a far more offensive profanation of the sacred by the West, which, especially after the 1990 deployment of U.S. troops in Saudi Arabia to protect it from Saddam Hussein's "Muslim" army, was perceived to be steadily encroaching upon Islamic society and culture.[34]

Bin Laden's obsession with the World Trade Center as a secular Western icon, and his determination to destroy it in "a symbolic act that speaks for itself,"[35] was matched by the zeal of his lead hijacker Muhammad Atta, although for slightly different reasons. This young Egyptian's academic training was not in religion like Sheikh Rahman, medicine like Ayman al-Zawahiri, economics like bin Laden, or engineering like bin Laden, Ramzi Yousef, and Khalid Shaikh Mohammed. Rather, Atta was a student of architecture and urban preservation. His dissertation, written two years before the attacks at the Hamburg-Harburg Technical University in Germany and entitled "Urban Renewal in an Ancient Islamic City," contrasted the Syrian city of Aleppo's old souk and sprawling, interconnected neighborhoods with modern projects to build Western-style highrises in their place.[36]

Such a conflict between Eastern and Western cultures, and between religious and aesthetic values, seems not to have concerned the bin Laden family's business empire. Since its founding by Osama's father, the Saudi Binladen group has been involved in a variety of major secular as well as religious projects. As proud as Osama was of his family's role in renovating the three holiest sites of Islam, he could not have been pleased with the firm's construction in the 1990s of a U.S. military base in Saudi Arabia, or its alliance with Western business partners like General Electric and Citigroup. Nor can he be expected to take much pride in the fact that since 9/11, his family's company has demolished the 230-year-old Ottoman fortress in Mecca in order to make way for new high-rises and a luxury hotel.[37]

Osama's loathing for such visible signs of urban development and its desecration of Islamic society was no doubt shared by Muhammad Atta. More than the international alliance of economic interests represented by the New York City towers, however, he was obsessed with the growing numbers of skyscrapers in the Middle East that he believed were defacing the horizons of Arab communities.³⁸ For Atta, this was an intolerable situation, as he perceived the vertical structures of Western skyscrapers as modern Towers of Babel—especially the World Trade Center Towers where a cacophony of global languages was spoken—that were "an unforgivable challenge to the sovereignty of heaven."³⁹ Like the Khobar Towers in Saudi Arabia, the New York City towers' conspicuousness as "civilized pillars" made them particularly offensive. The secular towers of commerce clash with the horizontal lines of the desert landscape and are an affront to the modest height of the ancient souks and minarets they increasingly overshadowed.⁴⁰

While some have noted how Atta's deeply ingrained religious "dialectic of purity and pollution led him to the 'noble obligation' of martyrdom,"⁴¹ I would instead emphasize his aesthetic obsessions, and specifically his perception of skyscrapers as a profanation calling for an iconoclastic response. In Atta's eyes, the distinction between Mullah Omar's act of religious iconoclasm in the case of the destruction of the Bamian Buddhas, and Osama bin Laden's project of secular iconoclasm in the case of the planned destruction of the World Trade Center and the Pentagon, ultimately merged into an iconoclastic aesthetic. This convergence of an aesthetic and a terrorist education that led him and the eighteen other "lions," as described by the Islamist website azzam.com, to "graciously glide into the tower[s], obliterating an idol of the modern age," has not received adequate recognition. Current plans to erect an even taller, 1,776-foot tower at the site of Ground Zero—a by no means arbitrary or functional, but purely symbolic, measurement—seem less a sign of America's resilience and resolve than a deliberately provocative gesture. As Daniel Benjamin has argued, "Dangling an iconic and indefensible target in front of terrorists is inconsistent with a strategy of reducing our vulnerabilities wherever possible." As "an even more powerful symbol of American might and values" than the World Trade Center, the Freedom Tower can be expected to "become a top target for Islamic terrorists as soon as it is occupied."⁴²

Besides the connection I've made between the Taliban's religiously motivated destruction of the Bamian Buddhas and the secular iconoclasm represented by the 9/11 attacks, a further connection should be noted between the destruction of the Buddhas in Afghanistan and the numerous instances of religious as well as secular iconoclasm that followed the United States–led invasion of Iraq in response to the 9/11 attacks. The looting of priceless antiquities in the National Museum in Baghdad and elsewhere in the country, the bombing of Shiite mosques by Sunni insurgents and of

Sunni shrines by Shiite militias, and the damage done by coalition forces themselves to Iraq's ancient cities and cultural sites, led the World Monuments Fund to place the whole country on its list of one hundred most-endangered sites. "It's the first time we've listed an entire country in danger," said the group's president.[43] Such wanton and widespread acts of destruction—whether committed intentionally or inadvertently—are inseparable from the ongoing violence and loss of life plaguing that country. In the aftermath of the destruction of the Bamian Buddhas and the pillaging and unrestricted trade in Afghan art during the Taliban regime, and amid the looting and vandalism of ancient artifacts in Iraq both before and after the U.S. occupation,[44] there is an urgent need to review the relationship between a nation's claim to its cultural heritage and the international community's interest in artistic preservation. In debates about whether international agencies have the right to intervene in war-torn nations or iconoclastic regimes in order to preserve historical artifacts, it's becoming increasingly clear that calls for such intervention need not, and probably cannot, be made exclusively on cultural grounds or in the name of art. Rather, they need to be made on humanitarian grounds and in the name of human lives.[45]

The primacy of human over historical considerations became especially evident in the case of the Bamian Buddhas. Despite the general outrage at the demolition of these ancient statues, no nation or international alliance thought seriously of taking military action against the Taliban for what it did—certainly not in the manner that military action *was* taken against that regime after the World Trade Center and Pentagon were attacked. And it isn't surprising that in the heat of the invasion of Iraq, no plans had been made by coalition leaders to protect the antiquities in that country's museums, or to safeguard the treasures of Babylon and other archaeological sites. Today we can see that the wanton pillaging of antiquities that was allowed to occur presaged the ongoing violence and loss of life that continues to plague that country. In all these cases, violence against art (iconoclasm) and violence against life (terrorism) aren't the separate issues that art connoisseurs and military planners in Western secular societies assume them to be. On the contrary, in predominantly religious societies iconoclasm and terrorism would seem to be inextricably related, and the destruction of artifacts is a fairly reliable sign of imminent violence against human beings themselves.[46]

Much as the worst acts of human violence in the twentieth century have frequently been preceded by the systematic, regime-sponsored destruction of books and libraries,[47] such wanton acts of twenty-first-century iconoclasm as the destruction of the Bamian Buddhas need to be recognized as early warning signs of even more brutal violence about to be (if not already) directed against human beings. While the United States is

closer than ever to making the purely symbolic, and ultimately inconse-
quential, gesture of adopting a flag desecration amendment to the Constitution, the desecration of irreplaceable cultural monuments and artifacts in the name of religious or ideological purity continues to be largely
ignored, even though such acts of violence against the world's cultural
legacy and artistic patrimony are often the first step on a path that is likely
to lead to violence against human lives and entire peoples. Had the close
relation between art and life been generally recognized, a more compelling case could have been made that the destruction of the Bamian
Buddhas was a monumental crime against culture and humanity that
called for timely intervention by the international community *before* religiously sanctioned, iconoclastic violence could escalate into all-out terrorist violence against human beings.[48]

NOTES

1. Juergensmeyer (2000, 217).

2. Juergensmeyer (2000, 131–33).

3. Cited by Peter Bergen, "The Long Hunt for Osama," *The Atlantic Monthly*
(Oct. 2004), 88–100; 90.

4. James Carroll, "The Bush Crusade," *The Nation* (Sept. 20, 2004), 14–22; 17.

5. Sauer (2003). See also Besançon (2000).

6. Sauer (2003, 9, 10, 14).

7. Thus Kugel (2003, 72) suggests "that the Bible's purpose in outlawing the
making of such images was primarily to block off one easy way in which Israelites
might be led into worshiping these other gods." See also Halbertal and Margalit
(1994).

8. Benjamin and Simon (2002, 421). On the problematic relation between
monotheism and iconoclastic violence, see Schwartz (1997). The recent statement
by a prominent Saudi cleric that "killing a soul without justification is one of the
gravest sins under Islam; it is as bad as polytheism," prompted an incredulous Fa-
reed Zakaria to ask, "So polytheism is akin to murder?" ("The Saudi Trap,"
Newsweek [June 28, 2004], 32).

9. Reza Aslan notes that as "the god who had created the heavens and the
earth," and "who had fashioned human beings in his own image," Allah was even
for pre-Islamic Arabs "the only god not represented by an idol in the Ka'ba" (*No
god but God: The Origins, Evolution, and Future of Islam*, rev. ed. [New York: Random
House, 2006], 8).

10. Melinda Liu and Christopher Dickey, "Unearthing the Bible," *Newsweek*
(Aug. 30, 2004), 33–36; 34. The authors report that more than 8,000 pieces looted
from the Iraqi National Museum after the American invasion "are still missing, of
which almost 30 are considered of unique historical and artistic importance" (35).

11. See Groebner (2004). Although many of Groebner's examples are instances of
secular iconoclasm (in which the illicit political authority of the image is challenged)

rather than of religious iconoclasm (in which the image's false divinity is discredited), the aesthetic effect of the image itself needs to be given greater significance.

12. See Belting (1994, chap. 20) and Koerner (2005).

13. Shapiro (2003, 3); see especially the discussion in section 6 of Nietzsche's archaeology of the visual and his analysis of pre-artistic cult objects. Sauer (2003, 17) notes the tendency of classical art historians to regard damaged artifacts, whatever the cause of their defects, as objects to be restored to their "original splendour"; consequently, "the visitor to the modern museum will not notice that [they] had been damaged at all, let alone be able to differentiate between deliberate and accidental damage." In contrast, ravaged locations like Bamian are unlikely to be reconstructed "since rebuilding ancient sites is frowned upon by archaeologists and preservationists" (Lawler 2004, 32).

14. Benjamin (1969, 242).

15. Five years later, Westerners were similarly surprised by the Muslim world's violent reaction to Danish cartoonists' "blasphemous" representations of Mohammed.

16. Shapiro (2003, 395n6). Amid the escalating violence in Afghanistan, however, the Taliban has lifted its ban on human images, and even launched its own video unit.

17. Sauer (2003, 162). As Sauer observes, however, a significant difference between Christian and Islamic iconoclasm is that image destruction in Islam was never really balanced by "image veneration" as was the case in Christianity. As a result, Islamic hostility to images would seem to be potentially more violent and extreme.

18. Sauer (2003, 13–14).

19. Sauer (2003, 14).

20. Sauer (2003, 163).

21. Sauer (2003, 163).

22. Shapiro (2003, 4).

23. Sauer (2003, 162–63).

24. One connection was made by the artist J. Otto Seibold who playfully proposed rebuilding the World Trade Center towers and the Bamian Buddhas, but switching their locations. In this curious instance of crossculturalism, the restored giant Buddhas would grace lower Manhattan while replicas of the towers would be found nestling in the two huge rock caves of Bamian. See Calvin Tomkins, "After the Towers," *The New Yorker* (July 15, 2002), 63.

25. Cited by Benjamin and Simon (2002, 6).

26. Benjamin and Simon (2002, 7).

27. Cited by Benjamin and Simon (2002, 159).

28. Although only a single charge was detonated in the 1993 World Trade Center bombing, Ramzi Yousef planned for "one tower to topple into the other, killing everyone inside" (Benjamin and Simon 2002, 14).

29. Bin Laden's "first known long-distance attack" occurred in 1991 when he sent an assassin disguised as a reporter on an unsuccessful mission to murder the deposed king of Afghanistan (Max Rodenbeck, "Their Master's Voice," *New York Review of Books* [March 9, 2006], 4–8; 6).

30. Martin Amis, "The Last Days of Muhammad Atta," *The New Yorker* (April 24, 2006), 152–63; 156.

31. Bin Laden appears to have advanced the date of the attacks, however, after Israel's opposition leader Ariel Sharon's provocative September 2000 visit to two Muslim holy sites atop Jerusalem's Old City.

32. I am deliberately appropriating Linda Williams's term "maximum visibility" from the spectacle of pornography to that of terrorism (1989, 48). Whether or not it was bin Laden's intention, the sixteen-minute interval between the airliners' collision into the North and South Towers assured maximum media coverage of the second impact.

33. Benjamin and Simon (2002, 160).

34. Since secular Westerners "have no religion" and are not alive but "just moving like dead bodies," according to an accomplice in the 1993 World Trade Center bombing (Juergensmeyer 2000, 69), there would be nothing sinful about killing such soulless beings who were already corpses.

35. Ferguson (2004, 122). Alluding to Joseph Conrad's depiction in his novel *The Secret Agent* of a terrorist plot to bomb the Greenwich Observatory, Ferguson observes that a "hundred years ago the 'fetish of the hour' was science; hence the attack on the observatory. In 2001 the 'fetish of the hour' was economics or, to be precise, economic globalization; hence, it might be argued, the attack on the World Trade Center" (122).

36. In fact, Atta had traveled to Aleppo twice in the mid-nineties, leading the FBI and the CIA to seek Syria's permission to begin intelligence-gathering operations in that city just weeks after the September 11th attacks. See Seymour M. Hersh, "The Syrian Bet," *The New Yorker* (July 28, 2003), 32–36; 33.

37. Benjamin and Simon (2002, 95–96).

38. Richard Lacayo notes that while skyscrapers in Western countries have steadily "been losing ground as a symbol of power, wealth, and importance . . . elsewhere in the world, extreme verticals are still entirely in fashion, especially for developing nations looking to announce themselves" ("Kissing the Sky," *Time* [Dec. 27, 2004–Jan. 3, 2005], 173). Nowhere has this trend been more evident than in Dubai where three of the world's tallest buildings have been erected in the past five years, while two others are in the planning stages, including the Burj Dubai, which will be well over 2,000 feet.

39. Benjamin and Simon (2002, 37).

40. The ideal of a pure Islamic architecture had already been called into question by T. E. Lawrence, whose 1936 book *Crusader Castles*, based on his 1910 Oxford thesis, claims Western influences on Eastern buildings as early as the twelfth-century Crusades.

41. Jonathan Raban, "Rebels with a Cause," *The Guardian* (March 4, 2002).

42. Daniel Benjamin, "The 1,776-Foot-Tall Target," *New York Times* Editorial (March 23, 2004).

43. Bonnie Burnham, quoted in *Newsweek* (July 11, 2005), 23.

44. The looting of Iraq's antiquities had already begun during Saddam Hussein's rule. See Lauren Sandler, "Thieves of Baghdad," *The Atlantic Monthly* (November 2004), 175–82.

45. Efforts at artistic and historical preservation need not be separate from human rescue missions. UNESCO's Christian Manhart describes how scientists coming to Bamian to preserve what was left of the caves protected homeless families they found living there from government officials who wanted to evict them and turn the caves into a tourist site: "Culture is not just monuments. It's a living thing. Without people these caves are dead" (Lawler 2004, 36).

46. Cf. Jon Pahl's discussion in chapter 6, this volume, of the Quaker executions following the burning of their books on the Boston Common.

47. See Knuth (2003).

48. See Lentricchia and McAuliffe (2003).

12

Is War Normal for American Evangelical Religion?

James K. Wellman, Jr.

In a March 2003 visit to Venice, Florida, just after the U.S. invasion of Iraq, I walked past the First Baptist Church and witnessed a bold statement of evangelical support for the war. Along the sidewalk in front of the church placards read, "God Bless America," "Pray for Our Troops," and "Jesus, The Supreme Commander." It made me ask a simple question: Was this sort of public display of political sentiment and support of war typical of evangelical Christianity?[1] If so, what are its historical and ideological roots?

Many leaders in the evangelical community quickly came to support the Iraq war.[2] Indeed, white evangelical Christians and the Southern Baptist Convention came out publicly in favor of the invasion of Iraq; the Roman Catholic Church and mainline Protestant denominations advocated against it. Of course, there is little evidence that evangelicals or contemporary Christians of whatever stripe seek, encourage, or applaud outright violence.[3] Nonetheless, state-sponsored violence of various forms is supported by many Christians. I found in my 2004 survey of twenty-four of the fastest growing evangelical churches in the Pacific Northwest, only fifteen out of 298 clergy, lay leaders, and new members did not support the war in Iraq.[4] Indeed, in the first months of the war, white evangelicals strongly supported the military action in Iraq.[5]

Of course, not all evangelicals supported the war—there were pockets of evangelical leaders who opposed it, including Jim Wallis, editor of *Sojourners* magazine; Tony Campolo, professor of sociology at Eastern University; and Philip Yancey, a popular evangelical writer.[6] On the other hand, leaders of the religious right (e.g., Jerry Falwell, Pat Robertson, and

Ralph Reed) were activists for Bush's reelection and policies. Moreover, there are documented instances of a rhetoric of revenge from leaders of the religious right, blaming various liberal advocacy groups for 9/11 and suggesting that America's moral lapses are to blame for the violence against her.[7] At the grassroots level, however, evangelical support of state-sponsored violence centers on the idiom of fighting and deterring evil—a central plank in the ideological worldview of evangelicals (Green 2003, 15). Ideologically then, the question is not whether *conflict* is normal for Christianity—I argue that it is. The question is, rather, is *war* normal?

THE RELATION OF RELIGION, CONFLICT, AND VIOLENCE

The relationship between religion and violence is problematic and complex. I argue elsewhere that this relation is long overlooked and that the *"symbolic and social boundaries of religion (no matter how fluid or porous) mobilize individual and group identity in conflict, and sometimes violence, within and between groups"* (Wellman and Tokuno 2004). Tension and conflict are functional for religion, creating moral identities for individuals and solidifying group identities over against what can be called out-groups or negative reference groups (Smith 1998; Coser 1956). Religion creates a moral worldview for groups and a part of maintaining that identity is marking what one is *not* like—which behaviors are immoral, wrong, and even evil. Thus, the conflict of religious groups with outsiders (and even in internecine conflicts) is normal;[8] this does not always lead, however, to physical violence or state violence.

Christian Smith argues that American evangelicals thrive because they engage and are in tension with a wider, secular American culture (Smith 1998). Deploying subcultural identity theory, Smith argues that in an open religious market and modern pluralistic culture, evangelicals create meaning in relationship to out-groups. This tension is the source of evangelical success, Smith argues, giving evangelicals a distinctive identity and group dynamism. Smith finds that evangelicals have no interest in militant strategies as they engage American culture; they remain benign in their interaction with secular culture, preferring the conversion of one person at a time (Smith 2000, 46).

Yet subcultural identity theory, which predicts the creation of negative reference groups, can also explain how evangelicals come to support war, sponsored by the American state, as an avenue of engagement with global opponents. Nations that stand against America are out-groups and opponents of free government, who threaten the cultural, economic, and political interests of the United States. These out-groups, along with nonstate "terrorists," are labeled "enemies" and therefore must be deterred by state violence.[9]

The support of state-sanctioned violence is relatively consistent among evangelicals. Most evangelicals approve of capital punishment[10] even as they stand against abortion;[11] moreover, they support state violence that deters what they label as "evil." Thus, in general evangelicals tend to find conflict normal,[12] seek to distinguish good and evil, create out-groups that are labeled "evil" (or at least "unsaved"), and are willing to support the state when it fights to deter evil and to spread religious and political freedom. Each of these evangelical characteristics solidifies evangelical identity and mobilizes evangelical action. Thus, as the Protestant evangelical subculture grows in numbers and political power, one can predict that evangelicals would support a strong national defense to deal with out-groups, whether on a national or global basis.

HISTORICAL SOURCES OF EVANGELICAL CIVIL RELIGION

Civil religion is the ideological rationale for group social life based on transcendental warrants and powers. The common evangelical transcendental warrants, or what has been called a "civic gospel," include the beliefs that evangelical conversion will address and solve social problems; the government should protect America's religious heritage; the United States was founded as a Christian nation; it is hard to be a political liberal and a Christian; democracy should be promoted around the world; the U.S. should advocate for economic, religious, and political liberty; and by extension of these last two, the war in Iraq must be supported (Kellstedt and Green 2003, 553).

The linkage between religion and state for American evangelicals is not natural but is culturally and historically constructed. The interchange of religion and culture is, however, inevitable. As David Martin has explained, "politics and religion are isomorphic" (2005, 47). That is, there is a necessary relationship between the two because one cannot be "in" a religion without being "in" a political culture, and of course modernity by definition puts one "in" a nation. This was true for Christianity from the beginning, as it established its identity in relationship to what the gospels called the "world"; and in the time of European Christendom, Christianity was the world. It is a relation that has always been fraught with tension, conflict, and sometimes violence, both against Christians and by Christians against those "outside" the Christian realm. Christian prophets, from the right and left, have called for more and less separation from the "world," depending on context, history, and culture.

Like other historical moments, the relationship and elective affinity between evangelical Christianity and U.S. conservative politics is complex. The link has long historical and ideological roots in the Anglo American evangelical tradition (Noll 2001, 2002; Ward 1992). The nineteenth century featured a homogeneous American evangelical culture that centered on scripture but assumed that Christianization, Americanization, and civilization were homologous forms (Carpenter and Shenk 1990; Marsden 1982; Stanley 1990). By the turn of the twentieth century it was taken for granted by American politicians that America was a Christian nation (Hughes 2003). The trauma of the First World War cast doubt on whether Western civilization was truly Christian or whether the West was the vanguard of cultural progress. The nineteenth-century postmillennial optimism was overshadowed by a premillennial realism, derailing goals of social reform and prioritizing the need to "save" souls from a perishing world.

The rise of American fundamentalism in the 1910s captured this individualistic emphasis, totalizing scripture as "inerrant" and rejecting social reform as liberal accommodation to the social gospel (Marsden 1982). Fundamentalism went underground, building a grassroots network, led initially by northerners but blossoming in southern soil. The later "southernization" of the national evangelical movement was accomplished by immigration. By 1970 more than 75 million southerners had gone north and west to establish evangelical enclaves outside the South (Dochuk 2005; Harvey 2005).

In the aftermath of the Civil Rights movement, white southerners, disenchanted with Jimmy Carter in particular and the Democratic Party generally, turned to the Republican Party, forming the grassroots of the Christian Right (Wilcox 2000). This movement sought not only salvation of souls, but it expanded its early moral conservativism and anticommunism to a broader social, economic, and political platform. It advocated for conservative causes on the family and sexual morality and eventually against abortion and gay marriage. The capitalist predilection was signaled early on by the sponsorship of *The Fundamentals* in the 1910s by the Sun Oil Company's J. Howard Pew, along with other free enterprise conservatives, aligning a conversionist impulse with a free enterprise culture to expand the domain of Christ and commerce (Carpenter 1997; Marsden 1982). Finally, the prominence of southerners in the military knitted together evangelicalism and the American military, producing the strong support of evangelicals for America's military goals and the vision of the United States as a "beacon" of democracy and freedom in foreign policy (Loveland 1996; Martin 1999; Marsden 2006).

At midcentury, the liberal Protestant establishment complained that evangelicals had retreated from the world. To some extent this was true.

But in the 1970s, following the loss of Bible reading and prayer from schools in the 1960s, and the passage of *Roe v. Wade* in 1973, the public muscle of the evangelical grassroots movement awakened and today numbers more than fifty million American adults. In current surveys, American evangelicals believe their faith informs their politics by nearly two to one relative to mainline Protestants; they are by similar proportions more committed to "transforming" society than mainline Protestants. Furthermore, they believe, by more than 90 percent, that religious people should "fight evil." Self-identified fundamentalists and evangelicals no longer believe in "separation" from the world, but that the world must be engaged, transformed, and converted (Green 2003, 15, 18; Smith 1998).

This engagement is not shy in using the state to resist evil, spread freedom, and advocate American forms of democracy. The evangelical historian George Marsden wrote:

> [Evangelicals] as compared to other Americans . . . are more likely to sanction state-sponsored warfare. Perhaps most important, despite their sharp critiques of some aspects of modernity and their deep suspicions of many of the pretensions of governments, they often appear almost wholly uncritical of the immensely powerful modern ideology of nationalism when it is manifested in their own nation. So they seem more than willing to endorse raising the United States to sacred status. (2006, 9)

As Marsden makes clear, evangelicals do not seek a theocracy, although there is a minority who are political Reconstructionists. In the main, however, American evangelicals are deeply committed to religious liberty, influenced by the Baptist tradition and shaped by the Enlightenment that emphasized personal autonomy and the separation of church and state (Smith 2000). Thus, their politics are a complex mélange of moral rectitude; the advocacy of liberty and freedom; the expansion of economic and religious markets here and abroad; and a commitment to security and the deterrence of evil.

The elective affinity between evangelicals and American conservative politics has historical roots that have combined a religious vision with a social, economic, and political strategy that is perceived as "natural" and "normal." The isomorphism between American evangelicals and the American state is not a given but a result of a century of cultural and political development. What makes this religious vision powerful is that its construction is portrayed as self-evident. This alienation from its human constructions is an effect made plain by Peter Berger in *The Sacred Canopy* (1969). Berger may have been wrong about how modernity leads inevitably to secularization, but the way in which he describes how religion erases its past and mythologizes its origins is potent and applicable in this case. The plausibility structures that religions create manufacture core expectations about history, conflict, the interpretation of the Bible, and finally the theology of war.

THE EVANGELICALS' EXPECTATIONS OF
HISTORY AND CONFLICT

Ronald Reagan's election in 1980 was a turning point for the Republican Party and for evangelical Christian politics. Reagan defeated the Southern Baptist Jimmy Carter, sealed the transformation of the South from a Democratic to a Republican stronghold, and galvanized the evangelical community to believe that their cultural revolution could have political impact (Bruce 2003; Edwards 1999). Moreover, Reagan inspired Christian evangelicals by using moral language to describe the political landscape. Reagan's calling the Soviet Union an "evil empire" created a moral rhetoric that evoked the spiritual conflict between good and evil that could be played out in historical terms. Some have suggested that the evil empire was a direct allusion to millenarian ideas that the Soviet Union was fulfilling the role of Gog from Ezekiel 38 (Boyer 1992)—a prophecy that a great army would come from the north to destroy Israel and to inaugurate the coming battle between the Antichrist and Jesus at the Battle of Armageddon.[13] It is difficult to know to what extent Reagan believed in the Second Coming of Christ or whether he shaped foreign policy based on it, but what is critical is that for evangelicals history is the context for God's work of salvation. History has a divine destination and a goal shaped by the revelation of scripture; within this trajectory the conflict between good and evil is expected and normal. George W. Bush has capitalized on "moral politics" by using the binaries of good and evil more than any other president in American history (Lakoff 1996; Domke 2004). Indeed, Bush combines this expectation of conflict in history with a long tradition that espouses an American role in deterring evil and leading the forces of good to liberty, democracy, and freedom.[14]

Bush's vision of American leadership to deter evil and spread freedom resonates with an American grassroots culture that abounds in millennialist and apocalyptic thinking. Seven out of ten American adults believe in the Second Coming of Jesus, and half of all adults believe in some form of the apocalypse (Kosmin and Lachman 1994). Tim LaHay and Jerry Jenkins's *Left Behind* series of novels based on premillennial dispensational theology has sold more than sixty million volumes since its inauguration in 1995. Amy Johnson Frykholm's *Rapture Culture: Left Behind in Evangelical America* (2004) portrays the evangelical culture of readers as responding with fear to what they feel is a general moral decay in American culture, taking comfort in the hope for a future release, and finding joy in the identity that comes from this subculture of fellow evangelical readers. As Frykholm points out, some evangelical leaders dispute the theology of the books, but this premillennialist worldview offers a plausible bridge between the personalism of evangelicalism and evangelical ambitions in the public sphere.

The apocalyptic parts of Christian scripture provide a resource for the evangelical support of war by the state and for viewing conflict with evil as normal and expected. Satan remains active in the world, working to seduce the world toward destruction. Rodney Stark argues that Judaism, Christianity, and Islam developed traditions of "dualistic monotheism— each teaches that, in addition to the existence of a supreme divine being, *there also exists at least one evil, if less powerful, supernatural being*" (author's italics) (Stark 2001, 25). This tradition solves the problem of evil by making this less powerful supernatural being responsible for it. For the evangelical believers I have interviewed, there is a battle between good and evil that must be fought each day—internally for individuals and externally relative to groups and nations. The translation of this battle onto a wider historical and political field is expedited when leaders distinguish between good and evil in the political realm. What is consistent for the broad evangelical community is the supposition that there is a historical battle between good and evil, which entails pervasive suspicion of international bodies, the need to resist non-Christian worldviews, the importance of deterring evil, and support for the spread of religious freedom.

I saw this illustrated in my study of evangelical churches. In nearly all of the churches I examined, strong moral rhetoric was used to attack the moral relativism of liberal culture. Nearly half of the 298 respondents mentioned gay marriage and abortion as markers of moral decay and cultural "sin." Moreover, the strong moral rhetoric by pastors was consistently met with applause (both literally and figuratively) by laypeople in the churches. The most common comment: "Thank God our pastor is standing up for what is right." The tendency to see conflict in historical terms was aptly illustrated in a March 2004 newsletter article from a pastor in an evangelical Presbyterian Church (U.S.A.) in Oregon, one of the first churches that I studied. He put the matter in bold terms: "There are three primary ideologies competing to shape the future of humankind: militant Islam, Western European secularism and socialism, and American Judeo-Christianity accompanied by democracy. The first is being spread both peacefully and violently, the second is being spread peacefully, and I'm afraid the third is not being spread."

In subsequent churches I studied, respondents were divided in their estimation of the Oregon pastor's perspective. But of those who disagreed, they asserted that the centers of conflict are broader and more diverse than these three. Of course, the Oregonian pastor did say that only 10 percent of

Muslims are willing to use violent means; nonetheless, the supposition remains that European secularists and Muslims in general both seek to dominate global culture. The pastor painted a desperate situation for American Christian children: "Our children are overwhelmingly educated by people who believe Europe's values, not ours." The instruments of European domination are said to be the "United Nations, the European Union and international institutions such as the International Court. . . . Neither Judeo-Christian nor capitalist values are secure in America."

Even as the Oregon pastor asserts that neither moralism nor legislation offers ultimate answers, he encourages Christians to fight politically to transform the culture. The number one strategy, however, is the conversion of individuals to Jesus Christ. It is through these conversions that Christians work to restore the absolute moral values and truths of Christianity against the "moral relativism" of modern liberalism. Personal conversion is always the main goal, although the transformation of the culture, government, and world is an important correlate. The evangelicals I interviewed understood that this transformation will lead to conflict, and that this tension is often seen as a sign of religious faithfulness.

Evangelical ideology portrays socialists, Muslims, and liberals as negative reference groups, out-groups that must be overcome, or at least converted. The ideological construction of out-groups galvanizes evangelical churches and solidifies their identity. The Bible provides the lens to identify who is in and out; to interpret the history of salvation for Christians; why Christians must expect conflict; and how the task of government is to deter enemies and spread freedom as an instrument in the progress of salvation history.

THE BIBLE AND THE EXPECTATIONS OF GOVERNMENT

The Bible is pivotal to the evangelical worldview. From it evangelicals gain examples of how conflict is inevitable between the forces of good and evil and how government plays a role in history, conflict, and war. In contrast to the evangelical hermeneutic of Christian scripture, liberal Christians assert that their interpretation is more faithful to the intent of the Bible (Spong 1991; Bawer 1997). Liberals tend to disregard individual salvation, God's role in history or government, or the expectation of God's supernatural intervention in the future (Borg 2003, 175). Liberal Protestants reinterpret the word *salvation* as a process of personal transformation that calls them to focus on the work of social justice. If God intervenes in history at all it is in the spiritual lives of individuals to bring them peace and inspire them toward egalitarian goals (Wellman 2002). Evangelicals make the case that their theology more closely mirrors the major themes in Christian scriptures—the Old and New Testaments—arguing that history is the context for salvation, government is given specific obligations in the economy of salvation, and eschatology is a consistent and even dominant theme in the Bible.[15]

Evangelical interpretation of scripture comes out of what Michael Cavanaugh has called an "empiricist folk epistemology" (Marsden 1991, 166). This epistemology, which has its origins in the Scottish Common Sense empiricist tradition of the eighteenth and nineteenth centuries, asserts that what humans observe in the external world is what is actually there. The human mind does not contribute anything to what we observe but mirrors the objective world. This fact-based epistemology extends to the Bible. The "plain" meaning of scripture is believed to be trustworthy because God's word is inspired and given by the spirit. The historical critical method of biblical analysis, coming from early nineteenth century Germany, is thus contested because it suggests that the Bible is historically determined and culturally constructed, enabling interpreters to prioritize one aspect of scripture over another (Hutchison 1992). This is precisely what evangelicals reject. They require that interpreters must submit to the whole of the Bible and the full spectrum of its demands. This assertion of "inerrancy" and rejection of human agency in the creation of scripture is precisely the "alienation" to which I referred to earlier with Berger, which allows the believer to "forget" the historical and cultural origins of "sacred" scripture. Thus plausibility is established because the human origins of texts and traditions are "erased," "hidden," and "obscured." Thus the "believer" is secure in knowing that the scriptures are without error, because they come from God.

The Bible, coming out of the evangelical point of view, presents the facts from which one can deduce a series of propositional "truths" about God and human beings. Evangelicals observe that God is good but that humans have fallen and are in need of redemption. They deduce from scripture that one can expect God to work in and through historical events, principally through Jesus Christ, to redeem human sin and to renew the world. Jesus, as God's son, came to earth, lived in perfect obedience to God the father, and was killed at the hands of sinners. But out of this death comes the victory of redemption from sin and eternal life for those who profess Jesus Christ. The dilemma is that the world remains in the hands of Satan and it is only in the Second Coming of Christ that Satan will be defeated. In the meantime, the church disciplines Christian believers, evangelizes the world, and waits for its final redemption. The task of government is to deter evil brought on by human disobedience and the ravages of the evildoer—Satan. For evangelicals it is plain that the Bible speaks about God's intervention in history, Jesus' own battle with Satan, the proper tasks of government, the expectations of Christ's return, and final triumph foretold in the Revelation to John.[16]

The majority of evangelicals claim that they are biblical literalists, and surveys consistently show that more than a third of all Americans read the Bible literally (Gallup and Lindsay 1999, 35). The broader evangelical community, however, is split between those who profess to read scripture literally—word for word—and those who assert that it is inspired and never mistaken, although not always to be taken literally in matters of science and historical reporting (Hunter 1987, 24). Moreover, evangelicals are clear that symbolic language is not interpreted literally but is appropriately read in relation to its literary genre.

Evangelicals use typological interpretation to understand the apocalyptic literature of the Bible. This literature is the main source for biblical prophecy and includes the Books of Ezekiel and Daniel, the "Little Apocalypse" of Mark 13 and, most important, the Revelation to John.[17] For example, the "little horn" in Daniel 8:9 (for evangelicals) is not literally a horn but a symbol for the Antichrist, who is coming to rule a ten-nation confederation, symbolized by the statue's ten toes (Boyer 1992). Historical representations of the Antichrist have ranged from Benito Mussolini during World War II to Saddam Hussein in the present era. Particularly when it comes to biblical prophecy, literalism constitutes not a direct correspondence between word and event but a belief that the scripture (typologically understood) points toward actual events and agents in history (Crapanzano 2000).

Evangelicals, even those who are neither pre- nor postmillennialists, take scriptural prophecy and apocalyptic literature in the Christian Bible as a part of the overall revelation of God. This literature often points to growing conflicts, rumors of war, and natural disasters as anticipatory warnings of the Second Coming of Christ. In this act of return, Jesus Christ is not the gentle prophet of peace (so often portrayed by liberal Christians), but the strident warrior-king who comes to defeat the Antichrist: "Jesus Christ emerges from heaven in full battle array, mounted on a white steed. His eyes are as flaming fire; he wears a blood-stained vestment; and his heavenly soldiers follow him, also riding white horses. This is the warrior-king . . . avenging the world's accumulated injustices" (Boyer 1992, 41). Based on the evangelical reading of the Revelation to John, Christ is not the one who unconditionally forgives but instead does the work of vengeance on behalf of a just and holy God. Thus, conflict in history and culture are natural to the human condition and expected as a part of salvation history.

EVANGELICAL THEOLOGY AND WAR

Evangelical theology does not directly advocate war; however, it supports and defends war by the state, whereby evil is deterred and freedom is sustained. In *Does Christianity Cause War?* David Martin says that Christianity rarely becomes the engine of war, although "Christian symbols can defend the pomp of power and be woven into themes of protest and autonomy. They can go with the flag or against it" (Martin 1997, 58). The scriptural resources of the Christian tradition are plastic, depending for interpretation on culture, context, and ideological perspective that guides and shapes the use of Christian symbols. Of course, a notable example of this flexibility is the Civil War, in which theologians rationalized scripture for and against slavery, depending on the side on which they found themselves (Noll 2006).

So how do evangelicals interpret scripture relative to war, and what is the role of the state in confronting evil? Rick Warren, the senior pastor of the 15,000-member Saddleback Church in California, is a leading figure in the evangelical movement and an exemplar of how evangelicals approach issues of war and peace. He has written *The Purpose Driven Church* (1995) and the *New York Times*–best-selling *The Purpose Driven Life* (2002). Warren is a Southern Baptist and, like many evangelicals, downplays his denominational affiliation and uses popular culture through worship and teaching to evangelize and engage the wider culture. Warren's beliefs mirror the broader evangelical community; he believes in the inerrancy of scripture, the centrality of personal conversion, mission activism, the substitution atonement theory of Christ's death on the cross, Christ's Second Coming, and a strong moral agenda on social issues.[18]

Warren's sermon "When Is It Right to Fight," preached in 1991 in support of the first Gulf War, elaborates the evangelical approach to war from a biblical-based perspective that I found mirrored in my research on evangelicals in the Pacific Northwest.[19] His evaluation of the Iraq wars centers on the personal sins of "greed" and "selfishness." Because Saddam Hussein wanted more than what he had and was selfish and cruel toward his own people, he deserved punishment. This doctrine of deterrence of evil originates for Warren in Romans 13:4: "Government is there to serve God for your benefit. If you break the law however, you may well have fear. He does not bear the sword for nothing. He is God's servant, an agent of justice to bring punishment on the wrongdoers."[20]

From these and several other verses Warren derives the key points that humans live in a fallen world and that each person has sinned or will sin. Thus, government is ordained by God to punish wrongdoing and to bring about justice. This has two consequences. First, government preserves freedom. Second, it deters and reduces evil in the world. Government cannot save one from sin, but it can deter sin and uphold societal order. Most importantly, government can defend freedom, thus allowing Christians to do the work of proclaiming the gospel and saving souls. Evangelicals argue that effective government is one that preserves broadly Christian social values, underwrites a market economy, sustains a liberal democracy, and values the individual as a consumer of goods and services—religious and otherwise.[21]

Evangelicals bring this moral and political view to global conflicts. Consistent with subcultural identity theory, evangelical ideology specifies what is good and evil, distinguishes order and disorder, rationalizes the need to defend the moral order, and brings freedom to those who are oppressed. This cultural and political freedom creates the space and possibility for preaching of the gospel of Jesus Christ. Thus, state conflict that deters evil and spreads freedom is deemed morally necessary. This rationale is similar to Reinhold Niebuhr's mid-twentieth-century Christian realism, which prodded Christian ethicists to face the communist threat with force in order to deter evil and protect the innocent. For Niebuhr, Christian nonviolence capitulated to sin and sacrificed innocents for lofty ideals. Niebuhr noted, however, in *The Irony of American History* (1952) that governmental power is often unaware of its limits and the unintended consequences of power. Likewise, evangelicals also pinpoint the limits of government as an agent of salvation; government can only deter evil and preserve freedom.[22]

For evangelicals, governments and even the saints are limited in what they can do to bring about peace. Thus, when Warren asks in his sermon, "Will peace ever be permanent?" the answer is "No." For Warren and most evangelicals, neither the United States nor the United Nations can bring about peace; only Jesus in his Second Coming can bring true and permanent peace. Peace is desirable, but before the final victory of Christ, war will inevitably be the world's fate.

In response to those who call Jesus a pacifist, Warren emphasizes that "twice [Jesus] cleansed the Temple by force. . . . One time he told the disciples to sell their coat and buy a sword" (Luke 22:36). Based on these two texts, Warren puts aside the Christian traditions of nonviolence. From his perspective, the Christian scriptures emphasize the importance of resisting evil. Moreover, God's people are to preserve freedom, protect the innocent, and deter the spread of evil. For these evangelicals, the idea of preemptive war makes sense based on biblical principles. Evil and sin are real and powerful, such that the primary reality of life is "war." Warren says at the end of his sermon, "War exists not only between nations but in the self, a war between Satan and Christ. You must choose Christ, rebuke Satan, and become a soldier for Christ in the world."

Warren expands on the meaning of this by referring to biblical prophecy: "Yes, we may be in the end times, but Jesus himself says 'We know neither the time nor the place.'" Avoiding predictions, Warren reasons, "Isn't it interesting how the [disciples] asked a question about prophecy and [Jesus] turns the question to evangelism? They want to talk about when He's coming back. He wants to talk about winning the world. . . . Why hasn't Christ come back yet? Because He's waiting until everybody He wants to hear the gospel has heard it. Once everybody He wants to hear has heard it, He's coming back."

This is the evangelical motivation to go out and win the world for Jesus Christ. The engine of evangelicalism as a social movement is driven by the belief that if one wants Jesus Christ to return, one must go tell people about him. But it is also the quintessential testament of a personalist religion with growing public ambitions, mediated by the promise of supernatural intervention. The saints will not bring the kingdom by force or by war—God will. War is only the penultimate reality, for in the end permanent and everlasting peace will be given to those who choose Christ and come into his everlasting kingdom.

CONCLUSION

For many Americans, the worldview of evangelicalism renders the world understandable and able to be negotiated with a sense of inner peace. This is so precisely because it is predictive about what happens in history; it anticipates forms of conflict and struggle, and—in the end—it pronounces that this is the condition that one should expect. The ambiguity that is promoted by liberals (whether Christian or otherwise) is rejected by evangelicals. For evangelicals, moral absolutes flow from scripture and defend and preserve the moral order. This rational system of thought is based on specific axioms from which one can infer principles that predict events and actions in the world. Although evangelical religion is based on assumptions (the presence of God, the hope of salvation, and coming supernatural intervention of Christ) that are empirically unverifiable, neither can they be disproved. Thus, many are willing to take on an "extended exchange relationship" with a God who offers enormous rewards and a predictable future (Stark and Finke 2000).

The American evangelical worldview creates negative reference groups that galvanize group identity and sustain evangelical growth. Evangelicals, as they have become numerically more successful, have expanded their public ambitions and seek an active role for government in deterring evil and preserving freedom. This is not new to Christianity. The Christian religion has followed this pattern from the beginning—successfully seeking governmental support and coming to support state-sponsored violence. Thus, for evangelicals conflict is normal and to be expected. State violence, and even war, is at times useful precisely because it can deter what they designate as evil, it can expand political freedom, and it can preserve social order for the sake of preaching the gospel and preparing the way for the Second Coming of Christ.

It is of course this very "normalcy" that disturbs those who take a different point of view. The normalcy of an American evangelical religion that supports state-sponsored war is neither natural nor self-evident. It is a cultural and historical construction. Critical analysis of ideological systems uncovers the tendency to "alienate" us from our human assumptions and forces us to awaken to what "we" have created. This goes for both sides of the ideological spectrum. A fair debate on religion, politics, and war disallows these kinds of hidden assumptions. Otherwise we are thrown back on false necessities and dubious conclusions.

NOTES

1. Debate continues over the exact makeup of American evangelicals. I find the best indicator is self-identification; in surveys self-identified evangelicals include more than fifty million Americans (Kosmin, Mayer, and Keysar 2001). Evangelicalism is not a denominational category. Evangelicals attend nondenominational churches, traditional evangelical denominations, Pentecostal and charismatic churches, and sometimes mainline Protestant and Catholic congregations. Evangelicals generally emphasize conversion, missionary activity, biblicism (scripture is without error), crucicentrism (the cross of Christ is the only redemption for sin), and an exclusivist soteriology (Jesus is the only way to heaven). The major support of evangelicals for the Iraq war is generated by white evangelicals that affiliate with fundamentalist, Pentecostal, independent, and traditional evangelical denominations.

2. A 2002 survey of 350 evangelical leaders by the Ethics and Public Policy Center found that 70 percent agreed that Islam "is a religion of violence," and that 59 percent thought the United States should use military force against Iraq; 19 percent disagreed. Richard Land, the president of the Ethics and Religious Liberty Commission of the Southern Baptist Convention, said, "In this administration, they call us. They say, you know, 'What do you think of this?'" (Bumiller 2003, 4).

3. I define violence as acts of emotional and physical injury or destruction. The movement from conflict to violence and finally to war is a complex process, involving leadership, cultural context, and ideological rationale (Bromley and Melton 2002).

4. This research examines twenty-four of the fastest growing evangelical congregations in the Pacific Northwest. We interviewed clergy, lay leaders, new members, and missionaries on their identity and theology and their views on culture and politics. Another fifteen respondents expressed ambivalence about the war; nonetheless, those who were against the war or were ambivalent toward it were unanimous in their support of President Bush (Wellman forthcoming).

5. The March 19, 2003, Pew Research Center survey showed that 77 percent of white evangelicals strongly favored military action against Iraq; by a similar number they believe that war is sometimes morally justified (Kohut 2003). In general, we know that African Americans are generally theologically and socially conservative, although on political issues they tend to lean toward the liberal spectrum (Lincoln and Mamiya 1993).

6. *Sojourners* sponsored a petition in autumn 2004 entitled "God Is Not a Republican. Or a Democrat." The petition stipulates that authentic Christian priorities should center on helping the poor, caring for the environment, being peacemakers, truth-telling, support of human rights, refusing to label other groups as evil-doers, and supporting a consistent pro-life position—including an anti–capital punishment position.

7. See the transcript of Pat Robertson's interview with Jerry Falwell, broadcast on the 700 Club, September 13, 2001 (Lincoln 2003, 104–107).

8. Of course, these kinds of cultural tensions are hardly exclusive to religious groups; other cultural identities are sustained and concretized by creating out-groups and negative reference groups. Religion is often overlooked in using conflict to create group identity (Avalos 2005).

9. Conflict with "enemies" is applied not just to out-groups, whether as nations or terrorists, but for evangelicals dealing with "adversaries" is a part of daily spiritual and human interaction, whether against spiritual agents (Satan) or human others (individuals that tempt one to sin).

10. White evangelicals favor the death penalty by 76 percent compared with 64 percent of the general American population (Lugo 2003).

11. See Juergensmeyer (2000, 20–23) on Christians who bomb abortion clinics. Evangelical Christians have participated in attacks on abortion clinics, although these are exceptional and condemned by evangelical leaders.

12. An evangelical Anglican dean in Australia asserted that evangelicals "pray knowing that wars and rumors of wars are normal in the last days. Wars are not abnormal; peace is abnormal" (Jensen 2003, 35).

13. Reagan was said by his closest associates and by his official biographer "to be hooked on Armageddon," and to have a "fundamentally religious nature," to believe that "maybe it's later than you think" (New 2002, 61, 69; Morris 1999, 668).

14. See Mark Noll, Nathan Hatch, and George Marsden's evangelical critique of the relationship between the American state and Christianity, *The Search for Christian America* (1989).

15. Keillor (1996, 305), an evangelical Christian scholar, writes an examination of American history using classical Christian eschatology to critique secularism and secular but spiritual movements. He argues that "Christ's return is the one sure, final, unchangeable event which alone provides the final meaning."

16. A heated debate is ongoing in evangelical circles between *futurists* and *preterists*. The former are those who believe that Christ's Second Coming occurred spiritually in the fall of the Second Temple in 70 CE. Satan's rule ended and the millennial reign of Christ occurred spiritually. This is a minority position and depends on "figurative" interpretations of scripture. Preterists, led by Tim LaHaye and John MacArthur, take the majority and traditional view for evangelicals,

which asserts that the seven-year Tribulation and Christ's return are in the future (LaHaye and Ice 2003).

17. Early Christians used a historicist hermeneutic to interpret apocalyptic literature, offering specific dates for the Second Coming. Augustine's fifth-century allegorical treatment asserted that Christ had spiritually come already (Boyer 1992). In Catholic circles thereafter, date setting for the Second Coming was downplayed and early Christian historicism was dampened.

18. Rick Warren asserted that the key issues for Christians in the November 2004 election included: (1) abortion, (2) stem cell research from embryos, (3) homosexual marriage, (4) human cloning, and (5) euthanasia (Warren 2004).

19. See Rick Warren's sermon "When Is It Right to Fight," 1991.

20. MacArthur, a well-known evangelical pastor, makes a parallel case to Warren's defense of war against terrorism (2001). MacArthur argues that the Bible is an instruction book that clarifies the purpose of government as deterring evil, and on the right uses of war.

21. Research shows that evangelical pastors (both traditional and independents) are "monotonously predictable" in their support of Republican politics and a conservative moral agenda (Guth et al. 2003, 512).

22. Stanley Hauerwas, a well-known Christian ethicist, is harshly critical of state-sponsored violence of any type (1983). He asserts that Niebuhr's ethics lacked any biblical basis. Jean Bethke Elshtain, another social ethicist, has defended the Christian ethical basis of the recent American war on terrorism (2003).

13

On Political Theology, Imperial Ambitions, and Messianic Pretensions: Some Ancient and Modern Continuities

Bruce Lincoln

I

If we are to improve on journalistic, popular, even presidential discourse concerning religion and violence, we can begin by offering a more rigorous—also, more probative—definition of what we mean by *religion.*[1] To that end, I would suggest that religion typically involves and depends on the misrecognition and misrepresentation of human speech, practice, subjects, communities, and institutions as something more than human, partaking of the eternal, transcendent, metaphysical, sacred, or divine. Such an operation constitutes a claim to exceptional authority and an assertion of ontologic privilege that enhances or elevates anything to which it is attached, as when the distinctly human injunction "It's a good idea not to fool around" is recoded as "God spoke these words, saying . . . 'Thou shalt not commit adultery'" (Exodus 20:1 and 14).

In principle, such metadiscursive markers as that of Exodus 20:1 ("God spoke all these words") can be applied to virtually any act of speech, transforming its status in the process. Many, perhaps most of the propositions that receive such enhancement in any given tradition or culture are (or have become so thoroughly habituated as to seem) relatively uncontroversial and benign, as in the case of the Decalogue or even the Boy Scouts' Oath. Indeed, one could imagine weary parents deploying the same formulaic marker in other contexts: "God spoke these words, saying . . . Eat thy peas . . . Go to bed . . . Be nice unto thy sister." In all events, the specifically religious preamble marshals support for principles that might prompt some practical resistance, but against which few truly principled objections are likely to be raised.

One begins to appreciate the power of religious discourse, however, not in cases like these, but when preambles of the same sort are attached to otherwise dubious propositions. Take, for example, the story on which Kierkegaard based his argument concerning "the religious suspension of the ethical." "God tested Abraham, and said to him . . . 'Take your son, your only son Isaac, whom you love, and go to the land of Moriah and offer him there as a burnt offering'" (Genesis 22:1–2).[2] Or the passage that portrays the same deity—he who also proclaimed "Thou shalt not kill" (Exodus 20:15)—as having instructed Saul: "Thus says the Lord of hosts, ' . . . Go and smite Amalek, and utterly destroy all that they have; do not spare them, but kill both man and woman, infant and suckling, ox and sheep, camel and ass'" (I Samuel 15:2–3).

Just before presenting this divine injunction, the biblical text asserts that at God's command, Saul had been ritually anointed as first king of Israel.[3] This recalls an earlier scene: "Then Samuel took a vial of oil and poured it on [Saul's] head, and kissed him and said, 'Has the Lord anointed you to be prince over his people Israel? And you shall reign over the people of the Lord and you will save them from the hand of their enemies round about'" (I Samuel 10:1). Anointment marks Saul the same way the preamble "God spoke these words" marks any subsequent discourse. Believers would say that such ritual gestures and scriptural formulae "consecrate" the things to which they are attached, while critical analysts, with an important shift in nuance, would describe the same operations as "constituting" the objects in question "as sacred." At issue is whether the marker effects a change in ontological status or changes the way its object is regarded by some relevant audience. But in either case, anointment announces Saul as king and invests him with two responsibilities: reigning over Israel and defeating Israel's enemies.[4] Military action is thus defined as a task undertaken, from the very origins of the kingdom, at God's behest. The divine command to slaughter the Amalekites builds on this, but goes beyond, since it calls not only for the death of soldiers, but of women, children, infants, and livestock; acts difficult, if not impossible, to justify or contemplate did the command not (purport to) originate with God. In such moments as this, we recognize the virtually unique capacity of religious discourse, to legitimate—even animate—practices that the decent people of any group might otherwise find repellent, by investing them with a sacred warrant.

II

The discussion above has obvious implications for questions concerning "terrorists" and "terrorism," but I will leave it for others to pursue this theme. One should not, however, dismiss or condone the violent acts of those who operate outside and against the state, even if one objects—as I do—to the tendentious way the states they challenge characterize such groups and use these characterizations to advance their own purpose. "Terrorist" groups are real and dangerous, and one can measure their danger by: (a) the degree to which they authorize lethal violence with discourse that (mis)represents their acts as serving a transcendent purpose; (b) the size of their membership and the fervor with which they embrace such views; (c) the amount of lethal force they have at their disposal.

As should be obvious, these same criteria can be applied not just to "terrorist" bands, but also to states and empires, which—at least on the last criterion—far exceed any nonstate actors. Only insofar as these remain more inhibited about using the force at their disposal do they remain more benign than their adversaries. And when they relax or shed those inhibitions, they become infinitely more dangerous. I propose to look at the most dangerous actors in their most dangerous moments by examining two great world empires as they discovered how to use religious discourse to motivate and justify their defining projects of conquest.

III

The first of these is the Achaemenian empire of ancient Persia, which was founded by Cyrus the Great (r. 558–530 BCE) and which endured until its overthrow by Alexander of Macedon (330 BCE). The earliest text we possess is known as the "Cyrus Cylinder," which was written shortly after the Persian king's troops took Babylon in 539 BCE. Ostensibly a building-foundation text based on Akkadian models, at the most superficial level it celebrated the new ruler's restoration of certain temples. More pointedly, it was designed to discredit Nabonidus, Babylon's last king (r. 556–539 BCE) and to generate enthusiasm for the new ruler.[5] Of Nabonidus, it said:

> An unworthy man has been installed in the kingship of his land . . . in Ur and the other cult cities, inappropriate rituals, unholy sacrificial displays. . . . Daily he spoke without reverence and in hatefulness he let the sacrificial rules be suspended and he ruined the cult. . . . He established the worship of Marduk, king of the gods, in the cult cities, but ended it in his own. Daily he did evil against his city. . . . His people under the yoke without rest, he ruined them all. Upon their complaints, [Marduk], the lord of the gods became enraged and [left] their region.[6]

Most of the information contained in this passage parallels similar charges in Babylonian texts authored by the priests of Marduk, traditional patron of the city, who felt Nabonidus had ignored their god and temple in favor of more exotic deities.[7] In all likelihood, some form of collaboration helped this information flow from the Marduk priests to Cyrus's agents, as the two produced a narrative in which the Babylonian god and the Persian king both figure as heroes.

> (Marduk) searched all lands, seeking a righteous ruler according to his heart's wish, whose hand he would grasp. He pronounced the name of Cyrus, king of Ans≠an (= Persia). He proclaimed his name for kingship of all the world. . . . Marduk, the great lord, who leads his people, looked joyfully at [Cyrus's] good deeds and righteous heart. He ordered him to go to his city, Babylon. He set him on the road to Babylon and marched at his side like a friend and companion. . . . Without conflict or battle, he let him enter Babylon, his city. He saved Babylon from oppression. Nabonidus, the king who did not worship, fell into his hands. All the people of Babylon, those of Sumer and Akkad, all the great men and the dignitaries bowed down before him and kissed his feet. They rejoiced at his kingship. Their faces shone. The lord, whose assistance had raised the dead, who preserved each of them from annihilation and distress—they all blessed him. They worshipped his name.[8]

Some excellent studies have been devoted to the difficulties of Nabonidus's religious policies and his struggle with the Marduk priesthood.[9] In the present context, however, our concern is not the Babylonian king, but Cyrus and the way he represented himself as Marduk's darling, thereby attempting to ingratiate himself with the Babylonian people. As evidence that he enjoyed this god's favor, he also emphasized the fact the highly fortified city fell to his troops without siege or battle (12 October 539 BCE).[10]

Military victory was thus facilitated and consolidated by discursive operations that addressed the thorniest problem attending the creation of empire. To wit, how can one justify—to one's self and to the ethnic/national others who are fast becoming one's subjects—the conquest, absorption, and exploitation of these foreign peoples? In its attempt to reorder the relations of conqueror and conquered, the text thus deconstructed the signifier "Babylon" into three previously integrated, but logically separable parts. These were: (a) Marduk, the city's god; (b) its people; and (c) Nabonidus, its king. In place of the traditional sentiments of affinity that bound these to one another, the text then described estrangement, even hostility among them, such that the king's repeated failure to observe accepted religious practices had turned the deity against him. Angered, Marduk sought a more righteous ruler, going outside Babylon (both spatially and ethnically) to do so. Having found Cyrus admirable in all respects, the god elevated him to a new level of power by investing him with a new, extraordinary title that transcended prior borders of nationality: "He pronounced the name of Cyrus, king of Ans≠an

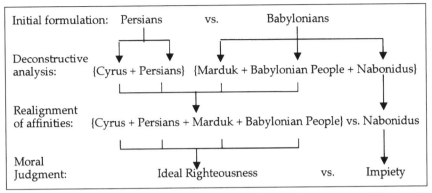

Figure 13.1. Discursive reorganization of the parties to the conquest of Babylon in 539 BCE, as accomplished in the Cyrus Cylinder

(= Persia). He proclaimed his name for kingship of all the world."[11] It was in this capacity—as imperial monarch, and not tribal chief—that Cyrus received the great city from the hands of its god.

The project undertaken by the Cyrus Cylinder was thus the discursive reorganization of social sentiments and political relations, such that the Persian king and his troops were portrayed as the true, if unexpected ally of the Babylonian god and people in their struggle against Nabonidus. The effect was to (mis)represent imperial conquest and subsequent domination as an act of liberation: a restoration of all that is holy and thus, a cause for rejoicing (see fig. 13.1).

IV

The Cyrus Cylinder, written late in 539 or early 538 BCE, is the earliest evidence for the way Persian rulers employed religious themes in their imperial discourse. With our analysis of this text as background, let us briefly consider a chronologically distant, but thematically related datum: the State of the Union address delivered by George W. Bush on 28 January 2003, in which he made the case for war with Iraq, based on unfounded charges concerning weapons of mass destruction and covert ties to al Qaeda. In addition, the president marshaled another argument, deploying a discourse of "compassion" as a justification for war. As in many previous speeches, he introduced this theme as a centerpiece of his domestic policies.

Our fourth goal is to apply the compassion of America to the deepest problems of America. For so many in our country—the homeless, the fatherless, the addicted—the need is great. Yet there is power—wonder-working power—in the goodness, and idealism, and faith of the American people. Americans are doing the work of compassion every day—visiting prisoners, providing shelter for battered women, bringing companionship to lonely seniors. These good works deserve our praise . . . they deserve our personal support . . . and, when appropriate, they deserve the assistance of our government. I urge you to pass both my faith-based initiative and the Citizen Service Act—to encourage acts of compassion that can transform America, one heart and one soul at a time.[12]

Mr. Bush's stress on "the goodness, idealism, *and faith* of the American people" announces the religious nature of this passage, as do several allusions. Thus, the phrase "wonder-working power" slyly references a gospel hymn: "Would You Be Free?" (also known as "Power in the Blood") by L. E. Smith, the chorus of which fervently proclaims, "There is power, power, wonder-working power / In the precious blood of the Lamb." Similarly, the list of good works Mr. Bush attributed to Americans is reminiscent of Matthew 25:34–36, where Christ welcomes the righteous into heaven with the following words: "O blessed of my Father, inherit the kingdom prepared for you from the foundation of the world: for I was hungry and you gave me food, I was thirsty and you gave me drink, I was a stranger and you welcomed me, I was naked and you clothed me, I was sick and you visited me, I was in prison and you came to me." Beyond these rhetorical gestures lies a view the president has frequently voiced, whereby faith is understood to be causal of compassion, while compassion is recognized as faith's outward expression; also a sign and vehicle of God's grace.[13] As a result, acts of compassion-grounded-in-faith have the power to save the souls of those who experience this blessed quality as its subjects and objects alike. While those who show such compassion are—in his view—typically Americans, those who receive and benefit from it can be of any nation.[14] This last point was the pivot on which Mr. Bush turned his attention from domestic to international politics.

The qualities of courage and compassion that we strive for in America also determine our conduct abroad. The American flag stands for more than our power and our interests. Our founders dedicated this country to the cause of human dignity—the rights of every person and the possibilities of every life. This conviction leads us into the world to help the afflicted, and defend the peace, and confound the designs of evil men. In Afghanistan, we helped to liberate an oppressed people . . . and we will continue helping them secure their country, rebuild their society, and educate all their children—boys and girls. In the Middle East, we will continue to seek peace between a secure Israel and a democratic Palestine. Across the earth, America is feeding the hungry; more than 60 percent of international food aid comes as a gift from the people of the United States. As our nation moves troops and builds alliances to make our world safer, we must also remember our calling, as a blessed country, to make this world better.[15]

Here again, we find good works reminiscent of Matthew 25 (feeding the hungry, clothing the naked, comforting the afflicted), also the beatitudes of Matthew 5:9: "Blessed are the peacemakers, for they shall be called sons of God." American actions—including the troop movements mentioned in the passage's closing sentence—are thus construed not only as moral and benevolent, but as nothing less than the nation's response to "our calling, *as a blessed country*, to make this world better" (§99). For the American vocation—in the fullest theological sense of the term—is, as the president revealed in the closing paragraphs of his address, to serve God by advancing the cause of "freedom," that vaguest, most appealing, most elastic, and (therefore) most useful of signifiers.

> Adversity has revealed the character of our country, to the world, and to ourselves. America is a strong nation, and honorable in the use of our strength. We exercise power without conquest, and sacrifice for the liberty of strangers. Americans are a free people, who know that freedom is the right of every person and the future of every nation. The liberty we prize is not America's gift to the world, it is God's gift to humanity. We Americans have faith in ourselves—but not in ourselves alone. We do not claim to know all the ways of Providence, yet we can trust in them, placing our confidence in the loving God behind all of life, and all of history. May He guide us now, and may God continue to bless the United States of America.[16]

In other passages, Mr. Bush contrasted the United States to an adversary he characterized as an "outlaw regime" (§145), "a brutal dictator, with a history of reckless aggression" (§177), a tyrant comparable to Hitler and Stalin (§§149–52), whose "ambitions of cruelty and murder have no limit" (§150). In sum, "If this is not evil, then evil has no meaning" (§235). Against such colossal maleficence, he said "we are called"—presumably by the Almighty—"to defend the safety of our people, and the hopes of all mankind" (§154). And so, in the culminating moment of his address, Mr. Bush cast the coming American invasion as nothing less than an act of salvation. "Tonight I have a message for the brave and oppressed people of Iraq: Your enemy is not surrounding your country—your enemy is ruling your country. And the day he and his regime are removed from power will be the day of your liberation."[17]

With these ringing phrases, Mr. Bush pursued much the same discursive strategy as was set forth in the Cyrus Cylinder. Thus, after deconstructing "the United States" and "Iraq" into bipartite compounds (God plus the American nation on the one hand, an evil leadership and a brave, oppressed people on the other), he realigned these entities. Three of them

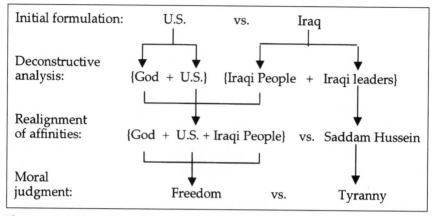

Figure 13.2.   Discursive reorganization of the parties to the Iraqi War, as accomplished in §§236–37 of Mr. Bush's State of the Union address

(God, the United States, and the Iraqi people) supposedly share an interest in "freedom," and thus have a previously unrecognized affinity for each other. It is this interest, moreover, that sets them in opposition to the remaining element: the freedom-hating Iraqi leaders, who on this basis are estranged from God and, what is more, from their own people (fig. 13.2).

For all that the discursive strategies employed by the Persian king and the American president were remarkably similar, there is one difference of detail that merits attention. Thus, where Cyrus aligned himself with a specifically Babylonian god, it is hard to imagine the ridicule and outrage it would have provoked had Mr. Bush made similar claims regarding Allah. Conversely, a straightforward claim that he served the Christian (or Judeo-Christian) god would have prompted the charge that his "liberation" of Iraq was simply a renewal of the Crusades.[18] Given this bind, Mr. Bush remained fairly vague concerning the identity of the deity whose work he was doing. In truth, he did not mention the divine until he reached the very end of his speech (§264 out of 268). There, he revealed that liberty is "God's gift to humanity," then identified the eminently inclusive deity in question as "the loving God behind all of life, and all of history" (§266). Presumably, this same generic God stands behind all peoples, nations, and faiths, but such an inclusive theology is undercut by the more exclusive claims implied in Mr. Bush's closing benediction: "May he guide us now and may God continue to bless the United States of America" (§267).[19]

V

The Persian conquest of Babylon also figures in several books of the Hebrew Bible written after 586 BCE, when Nebuchadnezzar conquered Judah, destroyed the Temple, ended the Davidic dynasty, and deported much of the Jewish population to his city.[20] Prophets like Isaiah and Jeremiah interpreted this catastrophe as God's chastisement for Israel's failings, but anticipated the day when God would make Babylon fall, restore the Jews to their home, and place their kings once more on the throne. Such expectations gained force as the Persians under Cyrus conquered first the Medes (550 BCE), then the Lydians (546 BCE), and emerged as the greatest threat to Babylon's power. The critically important chapters 40–55 in the Book of Isaiah (so-called Second or Deutero-Isaiah) are commonly understood to have been written in the years after 546 BCE, but before 539 BCE, since their prophecies of Babylon's fall erroneously anticipated a violent battle for the city.[21]

Whereas the discursive project undertaken by the Cyrus Cylinder was to appropriate Marduk for Cyrus, Deutero-Isaiah—a text written by Babylonian Jews in collaboration with Persian agents—worked in converse fashion to appropriate Cyrus for YHWH. Thus, it systematically constituted the anticipated Persian triumph as the fulfillment of YHWH's covenantal promises to Israel. The task was complicated, however, since the instrument through which God would accomplish this was not the rightful Hebrew heir in the line of David, as was normally expected, but a foreign king previously unknown to Israel. To normalize this anomalous (and potentially destabilizing) turn of events, the text thus has YHWH introduce Cyrus, saying, "He is my shepherd, and he shall fulfill all my purpose" (Isaiah 44:28). More fully, the Lord instructs both Cyrus and the reader:

> For the sake of my servant Jacob,
>   and Israel my chosen,
> I call you by your name,
>   I surname you, though you do not know me.
> I am the LORD, and there is no other,
>   besides me there is no God;
>   I gird you, though you do not know me,
> that men may know, from the rising of the sun
>   and from the west, that there is none besides me;
>   I am the LORD, and there is no other.
> I form light and create darkness,
>   I make weal and create woe,
>   I am the LORD, who do all these things.[22]

Beyond this text's repeated insistence that there is no other god than YHWH (and thus no other divine agency that could account for Persian success), two of its details deserve particular comment. First, the specification that YHWH bestowed a "surname" on Cyrus (45:4) employs the verb CNH, which means both "to betitle" and "to give an epithet or cognomen."[23] Recently, numerous commentators have preferred the former, more technical sense, translating, for instance, "I bestow on you a title of honor."[24] The verse thus bears an assertion much like that found in the Cyrus Cylinder, where Marduk "pronounced the name of Cyrus, king of Persia, to become the ruler of all the world."[25] In both cases, the royal title of greatest scope and deepest significance is the one bestowed by a foreign god, as a result of which Cyrus has a secret affinity with the people normally associated with that deity. Second, YHWH's assertion that he is responsible for the creation of light *and* darkness is a way to differentiate him from the dualistic traditions of Iran, where the qualities of light and darkness precede creation itself.[26] The result is clear: although Persian by birth, Cyrus has effectively been adopted by Israel.

To further mark Cyrus as his elect, YHWH grasps him by the right hand (Isaiah 45:1), marches before him (45:2), girds him for battle (45:5), grants him victory (45:1–3), calls him by name (45:4), and invests him with titles (45:4), including the same one used of Saul and David, that is, "[God's] anointed" (45:1). This is the title that marks the legitimate heir to Israel's throne as God's elect, moreover, as one who has been purified, filled with the Holy Spirit, and rendered ever-victorious.[27] At the time Deutero-Isaiah was written, the term was reserved for the savior-king who would restore Israel from captivity in Babylon.

Israel's liberation was accomplished with Cyrus's victory, after which Babylon ceased to be a political power. Within Christian and Jewish apocalyptic, however—above all, in the books of Daniel and Revelation, written when Israel was subjugated by the Seleucids and the Romans, respectively—the name of this once-great city became the trope for all evil empires and the worst states of impiety and corruption. Conversely, "*the* anointed" became the chief title of the hero expected to overthrow the conditions associated with this metaphoric "Babylon" and to establish not just the Kingdom of Israel, but the Kingdom of God. It is in this literature that this title acquired its eschatological and messianic significance. Quite often, the term we translate as "the anointed" is simply transliterated, by which process Hebrew ma–s≠IflahΩ becomes "the Messiah," while its Greek equivalent xristooow becomes "the Christ."[28]

VI

At the heart of Mr. Bush's speech was the message that with God's help he would free an oppressed people in the region between the Tigris and Euphrates. As he and his chief speechwriter (Michael Gerson, who holds a degree in theology from Wheaton College, "the Evangelical Harvard"[29]) surely knew, the president's words would inevitably prompt many of his supporters to recall Israel's liberation from Babylon.[30] Most of those who in-

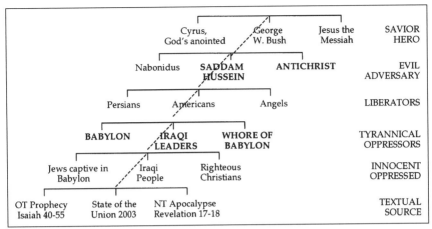

Figure 13.3.   Patterns of identification suggested by Mr. Bush's announcement of his intention to "liberate" the Iraqi people (§§236–37). Implied comparisons that are particularly encouraged appear in boldface.

terpreted Mr. Bush's speech and his Iraqi War through the lens of scripture were evangelical Christians fascinated, above all, by the New Testament's book of Revelation and its vivid if cryptic eschatology.[31] For such an audience, it was easy to imagine Saddam Hussein as Antichrist, Iraq as Babylon, and the war as the prelude to the Last Days. Somewhat more difficult was the question of how to interpret Mr. Bush himself, for even his strongest supporters would find it an act of scandalous—indeed, idolatrous—overreaching to read him as the coming Messiah. For his part, Mr. Bush preserved a prudent silence on the issue, although rumors circulated that he felt he had been chosen by grace of God to lead the country after September 11.[32] Association with Cyrus, however, yielded a more distant and respectful, but still recognizable (if subtle and deniable as necessary) relation to Jesus; one that was mediated through the Messiah's typological antecedent: Cyrus, YHWH's Anointed (see fig. 13.3).[33]

VII

There is much more that could be said about the conjunction of religion and violence in Achaemenian Persia and the contemporary United States, but a systematic and thorough discussion goes far beyond what is possible in this chapter. By way of summation, let me identify three recurrent themes that these and other empires have deployed to telling advantage.

The first of these is dualism: the sense that nations and people are starkly divided between the forces of Good and Evil, with little room in between, while the world constitutes the battleground and stake of victory between them. Insofar as one can identify one's enemies and would-be prey with the "Sons of Darkness," the exercise of force is construed as an urgent moral duty.

Second is the theme of election: the conviction that God intervenes in history through select human agents. Insofar as one successfully identifies one's self, one's compatriots, coreligionists, and the military forces of one's nation as chosen, whatever acts one pursues—however morally dubious they might be—are thereby justified as the execution of a divine mission.

Third and most complex is a soteriological sensibility, which assumes responsibility for perfecting the world through the exercise of one's power. Spreading freedom, establishing law, converting the heathen, and bringing history to an end are all variants on the theme of recovering some Paradise Lost. In such fashion, the project of empire—conquest, domination, indoctrination, extraction—is systematically, even if sincerely, misconstrued as advancing the work of universal salvation.

As I hope to show in a forthcoming book,[34] these themes form the core of Achaemenian religion and politics alike, if indeed the two are separable. The same themes continue to resonate beyond antiquity, however, and one finds them in the rhetoric and ideology of other empires, including the most contemporary. Such recurrence, I suspect, is not simply the product of vestigial influence or historic memory, but has a more pragmatic explanation. Dualistic theologies, doctrines of election, and soteriological missions are regularly reinvented, redeployed, and reaffirmed by would-be empires because they provide the best solution to a very difficult, eminently practical, and structurally recurrent problem: how to animate and justify violence sufficiently massive, brutal, and terrifying to effect imperial conquest.

NOTES

1. For a fuller discussion, see Lincoln (2003, 1–8).
2. Kierkegaard (1983).
3. I Samuel 15:1: "And Samuel said to Saul, 'The Lord sent me to anoint you king over his people Israel; now therefore hearken to the words of the Lord.'"
4. That warfare was the chief function expected of kings is made apparent by the narrative that describes how Israel demanded a king to protect itself against stronger enemies and how Saul was elected for this purpose (I Samuel). See, for instance, 14:47–48.
5. The text was discovered in lacunary form in 1879, but important sections were more recently added to it. For these, see Berger (1975, 192–234). A full translation of the restored text is available in Lecoq (1997, 181–85). The most important

literature includes Harmatta (1971, 217–31), Soden (1983, 61–68), and Kuhrt (1983, 83–97).

6. My own translation, CB §2–3 (lines 3–9).

7. The most important texts are the "Nabonidus Chronicle," for which see Grayson (1975, 104–11), and the "Verse Account of Nabonidus," a translation of which is found in Pritchard (1969, 312–15). Also relevant is the memorial written for Nabonidus's mother, Adda Guppi, available in Pritchard (1969, 311–12).

8. My own translation, CB §§4–6 (lines 11–18).

9. Consideration of Nabonidus's policies depends on establishing the chronology of the primary evidence relevant to his reign, for which see Tadmor (1965, 351–63). The most important studies at present are Beaulieu (1989), Kuhrt (1990, 117–55), D'Agostino (1994), and Schaudig (2001).

10. The testimony of CB §§5–6 that Babylon fell without a struggle is confirmed by the *Nabonidus Chronicle* 3.14–15 and the archaeological record. Herodotus 1.191 attributes this to a ruse, rather than divine favor, and Daniel 5—the story of Belshazzar's Feast (Belshazzar being the son of Nabonidus and his sometime regent in Babylon)—makes YHWH, not Marduk, the god responsible for delivery of the city. The peaceful entry of Cyrus's troops may not reflect their acceptance by Babylon, since two days earlier Babylonian troops fought the Persians on the banks of the Tigris and were soundly defeated, as reported in the *Nabonidus Chronicle* 3.12–13.

11. My own translation, CB §4 (line 12).

12. The full text of this speech is available at http://www.whitehouse.gov/news/releases/2003/01/20030128'19.html. The portion quoted represents §§67–72 of Mr. Bush's remarks and the ellipses are in the original.

13. Mr. Bush adopted a theologically complex understanding of *compassion* from Marvin Olasky and made it a centerpiece of his gubernatorial and presidential campaigns. See Olasky (1992, 1996, 2000). Mr. Bush offered extended discussions of compassion in his second Inaugural Address as governor of Texas (January 1999), his Inaugural Address as president (20 January 2001), his speech at the National Prayer Breakfast (1 February 2001), his Commencement Address at Notre Dame University (20 May 2001), his Philadelphia speech on the "Faith-based Initiative" (12 December 2002), and numerous other occasions. Most of these speeches can be accessed via links available at http://www.whitehouse.gov. See also Bush (1999, 10–11 and 226–36).

14. These points emerge from a careful reading of Mr. Bush's Inaugural Address, on which see my contribution to Rüpke and Makrides, eds. (2005).

15. George W. Bush, State of the Union 2003, §§92–99, available at http://www.whitehouse.gov/news/releases/2003/01/20030128'19.html. Ellipsis in the original.

16. George W. Bush, State of the Union 2003, §§261–67, available at http://www.whitehouse.gov/news/releases/2003/01/20030128'19.html.

17. George W. Bush, State of the Union 2003, §§236–37, available at http://www.whitehouse.gov/news/releases/2003/01/20030128'19.html.

18. On September 14, 2001, in impromptu remarks upon his return to the White House, Mr. Bush said, "This crusade, this war on terrorism is going to take a while." His use of the term *crusade* sparked a firestorm of criticism, and he has not uttered the word since in public.

19. Use of the lowercase *h* in the phrase "May he protect us now" is from the text made available by the White House and signals some of the same unresolved tension regarding the nature and strength of the religious claims the Bush administration wanted to advance.

20. Among biblical allusions, one should note Ezra 5–6, Psalm 137, Jeremiah 42:11–12, 50–52, Isaiah 14, 48, Daniel 5, and Revelation 14:8, 16–18.

21. Thus, for instance, Isaiah 45:1–2 has God promise to assist Cyrus in breaching the gates of the city.

> Thus says the Lord to his anointed, to Cyrus . . .
> "I will go before you
> > and level the mountains,
> I will break in pieces the doors of bronze
> > and cut asunder the bars of iron."

On the Cyrus Oracle of Isaiah 44:28–45:7, see Kittel (1898, 149–62), Haller (1923, 261–77), Simcox (1937, 158–71), Jenni (1954, 241–56), Smith (1963, 415–21), Koch (1972, 352–56), Kratz (1991, esp. 1–32), and Laato (1992, esp. 177–87), in addition to the standard commentaries on Isaiah.

22. Isaiah 45:4–7.

23. Brown, Driver, Briggs et al. (1952, 487). The verb occurs in two other verses, Job 32:21 and Isaiah 44:5, a verse closely related to the passage under consideration. Here, after promising the demographic restoration of Israel (44:3–4), YHWH prophesies the appearance of messianic figures, who will assume various titles representing themselves as chosen by the deity and bound to the nation.

> This one will say, 'I am the Lord's,'
> > Another will call himself by the name of Jacob,
> And another will write on his hand, 'the Lord's,'
> > And surname (CNH) himself by the name of Israel.

24. Childs 2001, 345. Cf., inter alia, Oswalt (1998, 198),"I title you."

25. CB §4 (line 12, op cit. n. 11).

26. Consider, for instance, Zad Spram 1.1–4, my own translation.

Now, in the Religion, it is revealed thus: "Light was above and darkness below, and in between the two was openness." Ohrmazd was in the light and Ahriman in the darkness, and Ohrmazd was aware of the existence of Ahriman, and also that he was coming to battle. Ahriman was not aware of the existence of the light and of Ohrmazd. Ahriman always went down in the direction of darkness and shadows. Then, by chance he went up. He saw a ray of light and for the sake of its difference from his nature, he strove to arrive at it and to exercise power over it like he did over the dark realms. When he came to the border [between them], in order to repel Ahriman from his own realm, Ohrmazd went forth to give battle. And with a pure, holy speech, he made him stupefied and threw him back into the shadows. For the sake of protection from the Lie, in the highest realm, he spiritually created the spirit of heaven, water, earth, plant, cattle, man, and fire and he preserved [them] for three thousand years.

Cf. Greater Bundahis≠n 1.1–4 (TD² MS. 2.11–3.4), my own translation.

It is revealed thus in the good religion: Ohrmazd, highest in all knowledge and goodness, for boundless time always exists in the light. That light is the seat and place of Ohrmazd, which he calls "Endless Light." All that knowledge and goodness exist in boundless time, just as Ohrmazd, his place and religion exist in the time of Ohrmazd. Ahriman exists in darkness, within after-knowledge, love of destruction, in the station of the depths. And his crude love of destruction, and that place of darkness are that which he calls "Endless Darkness."

27. The most important passages in the Hebrew Bible for understanding the significance of this title prior to its use in apocalyptic are Leviticus 21:10–17, I Samuel 16:6–13 and 26:9, II Samuel 1:14 and 22:51, I Kings 1:32–35, II Kings 11:9–12, I Chronicles 16:22, Psalms 2:1–9, 20:6, and 89:20–23. Only a small, select set of heroic figures are referred to as anointed: Aaron (Exodus 29:7 et al.) and his sons (Exodus 30:30 et al.), Saul (I Samuel 12:3 and 24:6 et al.), Solomon (I Kings 1:34), and above all, David (II Samuel 22:51, Psalm 18:50, 132:17 et al.).

28. On the history and significance of this terminology, see most fully and most recently, Schreiber (2000) and Waschke (2001). Mowinckel (1956) remains fundamental.

29. Regarding Mr. Gerson, see Zoroya (2001), available at http://www.usatoday .com/life/2001'04'11'bush'speechwriter.html.

30. Among biblical allusions, one should note Ezra 5–6, Psalm 137, Jeremiah 42:11–12, 50–52, Isaiah 14, 48, Daniel 5, and Revelation 14:8, 16–18.

31. Web activity that sought to interpret the Iraqi War in light of biblical prophecy and vice versa is almost impossible to calculate. A Google search in July 2003 under the heading {Babylon prophecy Iraq War} yielded 46,800 hits. Books on the subject appeared rapidly, including Charles Dyer (2003), Erasmus (2003), Hitchcock (2003), Intrater (2003), and Evans (2003). Pate and Hays (2003) make an attempt to refute these views while working within their presuppositions regarding scripture and prophecy.

32. As reported, inter alia, Lawson (2003, 396), where White House staff adamantly denied the rumor.

33. Mr. Bush is not the first American president to style himself after Cyrus. Woodrow Wilson was hailed as the new Cyrus upon his arrival in Europe after World War I (Melander 1919) and Harry Truman is said to have asserted in all seriousness, apropos of his role in the creation of Israel: "I am Cyrus. I am Cyrus" (Merkley 1998, 190–92).

34. Provisionally titled *Religion and the Logic of Empire: Achaemenian Persia and the Pursuit of Paradise.*

References

Aberbach, Moshe, and David Aberbach. 2000. *The Roman-Jewish Wars and Hebrew Cultural Nationalism*. Houndmills: MacMillan Press, Ltd.

Aescoly, Aaron Zeev. 1987 [1956]. *He-tenu`ot ha-Meshihiyot be-Yisrael*. Jerusalem: Mossad Bialik.

Ahlstrom, Sydney E. 1972. *A Religious History of the American People*. New Haven: Yale University Press.

Akiner, Shirin. 1997. "Contemporary Central Asian Women." In *Post-Soviet Women: From the Baltic to Central Asia*, ed. Mary Buckley. Cambridge: Cambridge University Press, 261–304.

Albanese, Catherine L. 1976. *Sons of the Fathers: The Civil Religion of the American Revolution*. Philadelphia: Temple University Press.

Albenda, Paula. 1998. *Monumental Art of the Assyrian Empire: Dynamics and Compositional Styles*. Monographs on the Ancient Near East, 3/1. Malibu: Udena.

Alimova, Dilarom. 1991. *Zhenskii vopros v srednei Azii: istoria izucheniia i sovremennye problemy*. Tashkent: Fan.

Allen, James P. 1994. "Reading a Pyramid." In *Hommages à Jean Leclant*, ed. Catherine Berger, Gisèle Clerc, and Nicolas Grimal. Bibliothéque d'étude, 106. Le Caire: Institut français d'archéologie orientale, 5–28.

Allès, Elisabeth. 2000. *Musulmans de Chine: Une anthropologie des Hui du Henan*. Paris: Èditions de l'Ècole des Hautes Ètudes en Sciences Sociales.

Almond, Gabriel A., R. Scott Appleby, and Emmanuel Sivan. 2003. *Strong Religion: The Rise of Fundamentalisms around the World*. Chicago: University of Chicago Press.

Anderson, Ben[edict R. O'G.]. 1977. "Withdrawal Symptoms: Social and Cultural Aspects of the October 6 Coup." *Bulletin of Concerned Asian Scholars* 9.3:13–30.

Anderson, Benedict R. O'G. 1991. *Imagined Communities: Reflections on the Origin and Spread of Nationalism*. London: Verso.

Andre, W. 1947–1952. "Der kultische Garten." *Die Welt des Orients* 1:485–94.

Anklesaria, Ervad Tahmuras Dinshaji. 1908. *Bûndahishn, Being a Facsimile of the TD Manuscript no. 2.* Bombay: British India Press.

Anonymous. 1986. "Dianhui Jiluan" (A record of the Muslim Yunnnaese rebellion). In *Yunnan Huimin qiyi shiliao* (Historical documents from the Yunnan Hui uprising), ed. Jing Dexin. Yunnan Minzu Chubanshe, 270–311.

Anonymous. n.d. "Shadian Tongshi" (The painful history of Shadian). http://jy28.myrice.com/yslqt/hn.htm (accessed March 15, 2003).

Appleby, R. Scott. 2000. *The Ambivalence of the Sacred: Religion, Violence, and Reconciliation.* Lanham, MD: Rowman & Littlefield.

Arai Takashige. 1990. *Chûsei akutô no kenkyû.* Tokyo: Yoshikawa kôbunkan.

Archaimbault, Charles. 1971. *The New Year Ceremony at Basak (South Laos).* Ithaca, NY: Cornell University Southeast Asia Program, Data Paper, 78.

Arnason, J. "Approaching Byzantium: Identity, Predicament and Afterlife." *Thesis Eleven* 62 (2000):39–69.

Arthur, Anthony. 1999. *The Tailor-King: The Rise and Fall of the Anabaptist Kingdom of Münster.* New York: St. Martin's Press.

Aslan, Reza. 2005. *No God but God: The Origins, Evolution, and Future of Islam.* New York: Random House.

Assmann, Jan. 1975. *Zeit und Ewigkeit im alten Ägypten: ein Beitrag zur Geschichte der Ewigkeit.* Heidelberg: C. Winter.

——. 2002. *The Mind of Egypt: History and Meaning in the Time of the Pharaohs.* New York: Metropolitan Books.

Atwill, David. 2003. "Blinkered Visions: Islamic Identity, Hui Ethnicity, and the Panthay Rebellion in Southwest, 1856–1873." *Journal of Asian Studies* 62 (4):1079–1108.

Aung San Suu Kyi. 1991. *Freedom from Fear and Other Writings.* Ed. Michael Aris. Harmondsworth, Middlesex, UK: Penguin/Viking.

Avalos, Hector. 2005. *Fighting Words: The Origins of Religious Violence.* Amherst, NY: Prometheus Books.

Bahrani, Zainab. 2003. *The Graven Image: Representation in Babylonia and Assyria.* Philadelphia: University of Pennsylvania Press.

Bai Shouyi. 1992. *Huizu renwuzhi (Qingdai)* (A collection of Hui biographies, Qing era). Yinchuan: Ningxia Renmin Chubanshe.

——, ed. 1953. *Huimin qiyi* (Hui rebellions). Shanghai: Zhongguo shenzhou guogang chubanshu, 2:109–20.

Barbour, Hugh, and Arthur O. Roberts, eds. 1973. *Early Quaker Writings 1650–1700.* Grand Rapids, MI: Eerdmans.

Barbour, Hugh, and J. William Frost. 1988. *The Quakers. Denominations in America, Number 3.* New York: Greenwood Press.

Barnett, R. D. 1970. *Assyrian Palace Reliefs in the British Museum.* London: British Museum.

Bartholomeusz, Tessa J., and Chandra R. De Silva, eds. 1998. *Buddhist Fundamentalism and Minority Identities in Sri Lanka.* Albany: State University of New York Press.

Basham, A. L. 1987. "Aśoka." In *The Encyclopedia of Religion,* vol. 1, ed. Mircea Eliade. New York: Collier Macmillan Publishers, 466–69.

Bawer, Bruce. 1997. *Stealing Jesus: How Fundamentalism Betrays Christianity.* New York: Three Rivers Press.

Baylor, Michael G., ed. 1991. *The Radical Reformation.* Cambridge Texts in the History of Political Thought Series. Cambridge: Cambridge University Press.

Beard, M. 2003. "The Triumph of Flavius Josephus." In *Flavian Rome. Culture, Image, Text,* ed. A. J. Boyle and W. J. Dominik. Leiden: Brill.

———. 2004. "Writing Ritual: The Triumph of Ovid." In *Rituals in Ink. A Conference on Religion and Literary Production in Ancient Rome,* ed. Barchiesi, Rüpke, and Stephens. Franz Steiner Verlag, 115–26.

———. forthcoming. *The Roman Triumph.* Cambridge, MA: Harvard University Press.

Beard, M., J. North, and S. Price. 1998. *Religions of Rome.* Cambridge: Cambridge University Press.

Beaulieu, Paul-Alain. 1989. *The Reign of Nabonidus, King of Babylon 556–539 B.C.* New Haven: Yale University Press.

Bechert, Heinz. 1978. "S. W. R. D. Bandaranike and the Legitimation of Power through Buddhist Ideals." In *Religion and the Legitimation of Power in Sri Lanka,* ed. Bardwell L. Smith. Chambersburg, PA: Anima, 199–211.

———, ed. 1991–1997. *The Dating of the Historical Buddha.* Nos. 189, 194, and 222 in Abhandlungen der Akademie der Wissenschaften in Göttingen. Göttingen, Germany: Vandenhoeck & Ruprecht.

Bellah, Robert N. 1965. "Epilogue: Religion and Progress in Modern Asia." In *Religion and Progress in Modern Asia,* ed. Robert N. Bellah. New York: Free Press, 168–229.

Bellah, Robert N., and Philip E. Hammond. 1980. *Varieties of Civil Religion.* San Francisco: Harper and Row.

Bello, David. 2003. "The Venomous Course of Southwestern Opium: Qing Prohibition in Yunnan, Sichuan, and Guizhou in the Early Nineteenth Century." *Journal of Asian Studies* 62:4 (November): 1109–42.

Belting, Hans. 1994. *Likeness and Presence: A History of the Image before the Era of Art.* Trans. Edmund Jephcott. Chicago: University of Chicago Press.

Benjamin, Daniel, and Steven Simon. 2002. *The Age of Sacred Terror.* New York: Random House.

Benjamin, Walter. 1969. *Illuminations.* New York: Schocken.

Bennoune, Karima. 1995. "SOS Algeria: Women's Human Rights under Siege." In *Faith and Freedom: Women's Human Rights in the Muslim World,* ed. Mahnaz Afkami. Syracuse, NY: Syracuse University Press, 184–208.

Bercovitch, Sacvan. 1978. *The American Jeremiad.* Madison: University of Wisconsin Press.

Berger, P.-R. 1975. "Der Kyros-Zylinder mit dem Zusatzfragment BIN II Nr. 32 und die akkadischen Personnamen im Danielbuch." *Zeitschrift fur Assyriologie* 64:192–234.

Berger, Peter. 1969. *The Sacred Canopy: Elements of a Sociological Theory of Religion.* Garden City, NY: Doubleday.

Bersani, Leo, and Ulysse Dutoit. 1985. *The Forms of Violence: Narrative in Assyrian Art and Modern Culture.* New York: Schocken.

Besançon, Alain. 2000. *The Forbidden Image: An Intellectual History of Iconoclasm.* Trans. Jane Marie Todd. Chicago: University of Chicago Press.

Besse, Joseph. 1753. *A Collection of the Sufferings of the People Called Quakers, For the Testimony of a Good Conscience, from the Time of their being first distinguished by that NAME, to the time of the act, commonly called the Act of Toleration, granted to Protestant Dissenters in the first Year of the Reign of King William the Third and Queen Mary, in the Year 1689. Taken from Original Records and other Authentic Accounts.* 2 vols. London: Luke Hinde.

Biblical Studies Foundation. Website available at http://www.bible.org/docs/history/schaff/vol7/schaf183.htm (accessed April 14, 2004).

Bickerman, Elias J. 1976. "The Maccabean Uprising: An Interpretation." In *The Jewish Expression,* ed. Judah Goldin. New Haven: Yale University Press, 66–86.

Bidmead, Julye. 2002. *The Ak•tu Festival: Religious Continuity and Royal Legitimation in Mesopotamia.* Piscataway, NJ: Gorgias Press.

Black, Jeremy, and Anthony Green. 1992. *Gods, Demons, and Symbols of Ancient Mesopotamia: An Illustrated Dictionary.* Austin: University of Texas Press.

Bobilin, Robert. 1988. *Revolution from Below: Buddhist and Christian Movements for Justice in Asia—Four Case Studies from Thailand and Sri Lanka.* Lanham, MD: University Press of America.

Bokser, Baruch. 1983. "Rabbinic Responses to Catastrophe: From Continuity to Discontinuity." *Proceedings of the American Academy of Jewish Research* 50:37–61.

Bonura, Carlo. 2003. Political Theory on Location: Formations of Muslim Political Community in Southern Thailand. Unpublished Ph.D. dissertation, University of Washington.

Borg, Marcus J. 2003. *The Heart of Christianity: How We Can Be Passionate Believers Today.* New York: HarperCollins Publishers.

Boyer, Paul. 1992. *When Time Shall Be No More: Prophecy Belief in Modern American Culture.* Cambridge, MA: Harvard University Press.

———. 2003. *The Chronicle of Higher Education,* February 14.

Bozeman, Theodore Dwight. 2004. *The Precisianist Strain: Disciplinary Religion and Antinomian Backlash in Puritanism to 1638.* Chapel Hill: University of North Carolina Press.

Breen, T. H. 2004. *The Marketplace of Revolution: How Consumer Politics Shaped American Independence.* New York: Oxford University Press.

Brennan, T. C. 1996. "Triumphus in Monte Albano." In *Transitions to Empire: Essays in Greco-Roman History, 360–145 BC, in honor of E. Badian,* ed. R. W. Wallace and E. M. Harris. Norman: University of Oklahoma Press.

Brilliant, R. 1999. "'Let the Trumpets Roar!' the Roman Triumph." In *The Art of Ancient Spectacle,* ed. B. Bergmann and C. Kondoleon. New Haven: Yale University Press.

Bromley, David G., and J. Gordon Melton, eds. 2002. *Cults, Religion and Violence.* Cambridge: Cambridge University Press.

Brown, Francis, S. R. Driver, Charles A. Briggs, Edward Robinson, and Wilhelm Gesenius. 1952. *A Hebrew and English Lexicon of the Old Testament.* Oxford: Clarendon Press.

Bruce, Steve. 2003. *Politics and Religion.* Cambridge: Polity Press.

Brundage, W. Fitzhugh, ed. 1997. *Under Sentence of Death: Lynching in the South.* Chapel Hill: University of North Carolina Press.

Brunner, H. 1954–1955. "Die Grenzen von Zeit und Raum bei den Ägyptern." *Archiv für Orientforschung* 17: 141–45.

Buddhadāsa *Bhikkhu* (Phutthathāt *Phikkhu*). 1970. *In Samsāra Exists Nibbāna*. Trans. Thawee Sribunruang. Bangkok: Sublime Mission.

———. 1986. *Thammikasangkhomniyom/Dhammic Socialism*. Ed. and trans. Donald K. Swearer. Bangkok: Munnithi Komonkhimthong.

Bumiller, Elisabeth. 2003. "Evangelicals Sway White House on Human Rights Issues Abroad." *The New York Times*, October 26, section 1, page 1, column 1.

Burgat, François. 2003. *Face to Face with Political Islam*. London: I. B. Tauris.

Burrough, Edward. 1939. *A Declaration of the Sad and Great Persecution and Martyrdom of the People of God, Called Quakers, in New England for the Worshipping of God*. London: Robert Wilson (1660), in *Three Quaker Writings by Edward Burrough*. Occasional Papers, Reprint Series No. 6. San Francisco: California State Library.

Bush, George W. 1999. *A Charge to Keep: My Journey to the White House*. Ghostwritten by Karen Hughes. New York: William Morrow.

Butt, John W. 1978. "Thai Kingship and Religious Reform (18th–19th Centuries)." In *Religion and Legitimation of Power in Thailand, Laos, and Burma*, ed. Bardwell L. Smith. Chambersburg, PA: Anima Books, 34–51.

Byles, Marie Beuzeville. 1962. *Journey in Burmese Silence*. London: George Allen and Unwin.

Canard, M. 1951. *Histoire de la dynastie des H'amdanides de Jazîra et de Syrie*. Algiers.

Cao Zhenyong. [1830] 1972. *Pingding Huijiang Jiaoqin Nifei Fanglüe* (A record of the pacification and anti-bandit suppression campaigns of the Hui-border region). Taipei: Wenhai chubanshe.

Carlebach, Elisheva. 1998. "Between History and Hope: Jewish Messianism in Ashkenaz and Sepharad." Third Annual Lecture of the Victor J. Selmanowitz Chair of Jewish History, Touro College.

Carpenter, Joel A. 1997. *Revive Us Again: The Reawakening of American Fundamentalism*. New York: Oxford University Press.

Carpenter, Joel A., and W. R. Shenk. 1990. *Earthen Vessels: American Evangelicals and Foreign Missions, 1880–1980*. Grand Rapids, MI: Eerdmans.

Carrasco, Davíd. 1999. *City of Sacrifice: The Aztec Empire and the Role of Violence in Civilization*. Boston: Beacon Press.

Carrithers, Michael. 1983. *The Forest Monks of Sri Lanka*. Delhi: Oxford University Press.

Carter, Lewis F. 1990. *Charisma and Control in Rajneeshpuram*. New York: Cambridge University Press.

Chaiwat Satha-Anand. 1988. "Of Imagination and the State." In *Ethnic Conflict in Buddhist Societies: Sri Lanka, Thailand, and Burma*, ed. K. M. de Silva, Pensri Duke, Ellen S. Goldberg, and Nathan Katz. London: Pinter Publishers; Boulder: Westview Press, 27–41.

———. 2003. *Āwut mī chīwit? Nāēokhit choeng wiphāk wāduai khwāmrunrāēng* (Do weapons live? Perspective on violence). Bangkok: S.Ph. Fā Diaokan.

Chaiwat Satha-Anand and Suwanna Satha-Anand. 1987. *Struggling Dove and Plastic Lotus: Peacemaking in Thai Society*. Bangkok: Pridi Banomyong Institute, Occasional Papers, No. VI.

Chandler, David. 1991. *The Tragedy of Cambodian History: Politics, War, and Revolution since 1945*. New Haven: Yale University Press.

Chernus, Ira. 1986. *Dr. Strangegod: On the Symbolic Meaning of Nuclear Weapons*. Columbia: University of South Carolina Press.

Childs, Brevard S. 2001. *Isaiah*. Louisville: Westminster John Knox Press.

Chomsky, Noam. 2003. *Power and Terror: Post-9/11 Talks and Interviews*. New York: Seven Stories Press.

Chronicon Paschale, 284–628 AD. 1989. Trans. M. and Mary Whitby. Liverpool: Liverpool University Press.

Chu, Jonathan M. 1985. *Neighbors, Friends, or Madmen: The Puritan Adjustment to Quakerism in Seventeenth-Century Massachusetts Bay*. Westport, CT: Greenwood Press.

Citarella, A. O. 1980. "Cursus triumphalis and sulcus primigenus." *PP* 35: 411–14.

Clasen, Claus-Peter. 1972. *Anabaptism: A Social History 1525–1618*. Ithaca, NY: Cornell University Press.

Coarelli, F. 1968. "La Porta Trionfale e la Vie dei Trionfi." *DArch* 2:55–103.

Cohen, Gerson. 1967/1991. "Messianic Postures of Ashkenazim and Sephardim." *Leo Baeck Memorial Lecture* #9; repr. in Cohen, *Studies in the Variety of Rabbinic Cultures*. Philadelphia: Jewish Publication Society of America, 271–98.

Cohen, S. J. D. 1982. "Josephus, Jeremiah, and Polybius." *History and Theory* 21, 3:366–81.

Cohen, Shaye. 1999. "The Place of the Rabbis." *Cambridge History of Judaism*. Cambridge: Cambridge University Press, 3:922–90.

Collon, Dominique. 2004. "Dance in Ancient Mesopotamia." *Near Eastern Archaeology* 66:96–102.

Constantini Pophyrogeniti imperatoris de cerimoniis byzantini, libri duo. 1879. Ed. J. J. Reiske, CSHB, 2 vols. Bonn.

Cooper, Jerrold. 2000. "Assyrian Prophecies, the Assyrian Tree, and the Mesopotamian Origins of Jewish Monotheism, Greek Philosophy, Christian Theology, Gnosticism, and Much More." *Journal of the American Oriental Society* 120:430–44.

Cordier, Georges. 1914. "Les Mosques du Yunnanfu." *Revue du Monde*.

Cormack, R. 1985. *Writing in Gold. Byzantine Society and Its Icons*. London: Oxford University Press.

Coser, Lewis. 1956. *The Function of Social Conflict*. New York: The Free Press.

Crapanzano, Vincent. 2000. *Serving the Word: Literalism in America from the Pulpit and the Bench*. New York: The New Press.

D'Agostino, Franco. 1994. *Nabonedo, Adda Guppi, il deserto e il dio Luna: Storia, ideologia, e propaganda nella Babilonia del VI sec. A,C*. Pisa: Giardini.

Dagron, G. 1983. "Byzance et le modèle islamique au Xe siècle, à propos des *Constitutions tactiques* de l'empereur Léon VI." *Comptes rendus des séances de l'Académie des Belles-Lettres*. Paris, 219–43.

———. 2003. *Emperor and Priest: The Imperial Office in Byzantium*. Cambridge: Cambridge University Press.

Dagron, G., and H. Mihaescu, eds. and trans. 1986. *Le traité sur la guérilla (De velitatione) de l'empereur Nicéphore Phocas (963–969)*. Paris: Editions du Centre national de la recherche scientifique.

Dali Xianzhi Gao. 1915. (Revised Gazetteer of Dali District), comp. Zhou Zonglin.

Dalley, Stephanie. 1995. "Ancient Mesopotamian Military Organization." In *Civilizations of the Ancient Near East*, ed. Jack M. Sasson. New York: Scribner, 413–22.

———. 2002. "Evolution of Gender in Mesopotamian Mythology and Iconography with a Possible Explanation of *ja rΣ jΣn*, 'the Man with Two Heads.'" In *Sex and Gender in the Ancient Near East. Proceedings of the 47th Rencontre Assryiologique Internationale, Helsinki, July 2–6, 2001*, ed. S. Parpola and R. M. Whiting. Helsinki: Neo-Assyrian Texts Corpus Project, 117–21.

Damrong Rajanubhab, Prince. 1955, 1957, 1958. "Our Wars with the Burmese." Trans. U Aung Thein (Phra Phraison Salarak). *Journal of the Burmese Research Society*, 38.2:121–96; 40.2:135–240; 40.2(a): 241–346.

———. 2001. *The Chronicle of Our Wars with the Burmese: Hostilities between Siamese and Burmese When Ayutthaya Was the Capital of Siam*. Trans. Phra Phraison Salarak, Thein Subindu (alias U Aung Thein); ed. and intro. Chris Baker. Bangkok: White Lotus.

Damrosch, Leo. 1996. *The Sorrows of the Quaker Jesus: James Nayler and the Puritan Crackdown on the Free Spirit*. Cambridge, MA: Harvard University Press.

Davidson, Donald. 1999. "On the Very Idea of Conceptual Scheme." In *Language, Truth, and Religious Belief: Studies in Twentieth-Century Theory and Method in Religion*, ed. Nancy K. Frankenberry and Hans H. Penner. Atlanta, GA: Scholars Press, 280–91.

Davies, W. D. 1982. *The Territorial Dimension of Judaism*. Berkeley: University of California Press.

Davis, Natalie Zemon. 1973. "The Rites of Violence: Religious Riot in Sixteenth-Century France." *Past and Present* 59:51–91.

Dawkins, Richard. 1976. *The Selfish Gene*. New York: Oxford University Press.

Dawson, Lorne L. 1998. *Comprehending Cults: The Sociology of New Religious Movements*. New York: Oxford University Press.

DeBenedetti, Charles. 1980. *The Peace Reform in American History*. Bloomington: Indiana University Press.

de la Roche, Roberta Senechal. 1996."Collective Violence as Social Control." *Sociological Forum* 11 (1):97–128.

———. 2004. "Toward a Scientific Theory of Terrorism." *Sociological Theory* 22:1–4.

Deller, Karlheinz. 1987. "Assurbanipal in der Gartenlaube." *Baghdader Mitteilungen* 18:229–38.

Dengchuan Zhouzhi. 1855. (Gazetteer of Dengchuan department), comp. Hou Yunjin.

Dennis, G. 1993. "Religious Services in the Byzantine Army." In *Eulogema. Studies in Honor of Robert Taft. Studia Anselmiana* 110, 107–17. Rome.

———. 1997. "The Byzantines in Battle." In *Byzantium at War (9th–12th c.)*, ed. K. Tsiknakis, 165–78. Athens.

———. 2001."Defenders of the Christian People. Holy War in Byzantium." In *The Crusades from the Perspective of Byzantium and the Muslim World*, ed. A. E. Laiou and R. P. Mottahedeh, 31–39. Washington, D.C.: Dumbarton Oaks.

Détorakis, T., and J. Mossay. 1988. "Un office inédit pour ceux qui sont morts à la guerre, dans le *Cod. Sin. Gr. 734–735.*" *Le Muséon* 101:183–211.

Develin, R. 1978. "Tradition and Development of Triumphal Regulations in Rome." *Klio* 60:429–38.

Dillon, Michael. 1999. *China's Muslim Hui Community*. Surrey: Curzon Press.

Dobash, R. Emerson, and Russell P. Dobash, eds. 1998. *Rethinking Violence Against Women*. SAGE Series on Violence Against Women. Thousand Oaks, CA: Sage.

Dochuk, Darren. 2005. *From Bible Belt to Sunbelt: Plain Folk Religion, Grassroots Politics and the Southernization of Southern California*. Ph.D. dissertation, University of Notre Dame.

Domke, David. 2004. *God Willing? Political Fundamentalism in the White House, the "War on Terror," and the Echoing Press*. London: Pluto Press.

Douglas, Mary. 1966. *Purity and Danger*. Harmondsworth: Pelican Books.

———. 1970. *Natural Symbols*. Harmondsworth: Pelican Books.

———. 2002. *Purity and Danger: An Analysis of the Concepts of Pollution and Taboo*, with a new preface by the author. London: Routledge.

Douglass, Frederick. 1997. *Narrative of the Life of Frederick Douglass, An American Slave, Written by Himself*, ed. William L. Andrews and William S. McFeely. New York: Norton.

Driel, G. von. 1969. *The Cult of Assur*. Assen, The Netherlands: Koninklijke Van Gorcum.

Drijvers, J. W. 2002. "Heraclius and the *restitutio crucis*: Notes on Symbolism and Ideology." In *The Reign of Heraclius (610–641): Crisis and Confrontation*, ed. G. J. Reinink and B. H. Stolte. Groningen Studies in Cultural Change 2. Leuven, Belgium: Peeters, 175–90.

Dumézil, G. 1996. *Archaic Roman Religion*. Trans. P. Drapp. Vols. 1 and 2 (rev.). Baltimore: Johns Hopkins University Press.

Durant, Will. 1957. *The Reformation: A History of European Civilization from Wyclif to Calvin: 1300–1564*. The Story of Civilization Series: Part VI. New York: Simon and Schuster.

Durkheim, Emile. 1915. *The Elementary Forms of the Religious Life*. London: George Allen and Unwin.

Dyer, Charles. 2003. *The Rise of Babylon: Is Iraq at the Center of the Final Drama?* (Updated ed. 2003; 1st ed. 1991.) Chicago: Moody Press.

Dyson, Stephen L. 1971. "Native Revolts in the Roman Empire." *Historia* 20:239–74.

Edwards, Lee. 1999. *The Conservative Revolution: The Movement that Remade America*. New York: Free Press.

Eichler, Margrit. 1981. "Charismatic Prophets and Charismatic Saviors." *Mennonite Quarterly Review* 55 (January): 45–61.

Elshtain, Jean Bethke. 2003. *Just War Against Terror: The Burden of American Power in a Violent World*. New York: Basic Books.

Erasmus, Daniel J. 2003. *The Last Fall of Babylon . . . and the Coming Kingdom*. Longwood, FL: Xulon Press.

Erman, Adolf. 1971. *Life in Ancient Egypt*. Trans. H. M. Tirard. New York: Dover.

Eusebius. 1999. *Vita Constantini* (Eusebius, Life of Constantine). Ed. and trans. Averil Cameron and S. G. Hall. Oxford.

Evans, Michael D. 2003. *Beyond Iraq: The Next Move. Ancient Prophecy and Modern Day Conspiracy Collide*. Lakeland, FL: White Stone Books.

Faqir, Fadia. 2001. "Intrafamily Femicide in Defence of Honour: The Case of Jordan." *Third World Quarterly* 22, 1:65–82.

Fauth, W. 1979. "Der könliche Garten und Jäger im Paradeisos." *Persica* 8:1–5.

Favro, D. 1994. "The Street Triumphant. The Urban Impact of Roman Triumphal Parades." In *Streets: Critical Perspectives on Public Space*, ed. Z. Çelik, D. Favro, R. Ingersoll. Berkeley: University of California, Berkeley Press.

Feldman, Noah. 2005. *Divided by God*. New York: Farrar, Straus, Giroux.

Feldner, Yotam. 2000. "'Honor Murders'—Why the Perps Get off Easy." *Middle East Quarterly* 7 (December 2000): 41–50.

Fenn, Richard K. 2001. *Beyond Idols: The Shape of a Secular Society*. New York: Oxford University Press.

Ferguson, Niall. 2004. *Colossus: The Price of America's Empire*. New York: Penguin Press.

Finnestad, Ragnhild Bjerre. 1985. *Image of the World and Symbol of the Creator: On the Cosmological and Iconological Values of the Temple of Edfu*. Studies in Oriental Religions, 10. Wiesbaden: Harrassowitz.

Fitzgerald, Frances. 1986. *Cities on a Hill*. New York: Simon and Schuster.

Foster, Benjamin R. 1997. "Epic of Creation." In *The Context of Scripture: Canonical Compositions from the Biblical World*, ed. William W. Hallo and K. Lawson Younger, Jr. Vol. 1. Leiden: E. J. Brill, 390–402.

Foucault, Michel. 1977. *Discipline and Punish: The Birth of the Prison*. New York: Pantheon Books.

———. 1995. *Discipline and Punish: The Birth of the Prison*. Trans. Alan Sheridan. New York: Vintage.

Fowler, W. W. 1916. "Iuppiter and the triumphator." *Clas. Rev.* 30:153–57.

Frankfurter, David. 1992. "Lest Egypt's City Be Deserted: Religion and Ideology in the Egyptian Response to the Jewish Revolt (116–117 C.E.)." *Journal of Jewish Studies* 43:203–220.

———. 2004. "On Sacrifice and Residues: Processing the Human Body." In *Religion im kulturellen Diskurs: Festschrift für Hans G. Kippenberg zu seinem 65. Geburtstag*. Ed. B. Luchesi and K. von Stuckrad. Religionsgeschichtliche Versuche und Vorarbeiten, 52. Berlin: Walter de Gruyter, 511–33.

Franklin, Satya Bharti. 1992. *The Promise of Paradise: A Woman's Intimate Story of the Perils of Life with Rajneesh*. New York: Station Hill Press.

Frohnmayer, Attorney General David. 1985. *Opinions of the Attorney General of the State of Oregon July 1, 1983–June 30, 1985*.

Frolow, A. 1953. "La vraie croix et les expéditions d'Héraclius en Perse." *Revue des études byzantines* 11, 88–93.

Frykholm, Amy Johnson. 2004. *Rapture Culture: Left Behind in Evangelical America*. Oxford: Oxford University Press.

Fukuyama, Francis. 1989. "The End of History?" *The National Interest*, summer.

Gafni, Isaiah M. 1997. *Land, Center and Diaspora: Jewish Constructs in Late Antiquity*. Sheffield: Sheffield Academic Press.

Gagé, J. 1933. "*Stavros nikopoios*. La victoire impériale dans l'empire chrétien." *Revue d'histoire et de philosophie religieuses* 13:370–400.

Galán, José M. 1999. "The Egyptian Concept of Frontier." In *Landscapes: Territories, Frontiers, and Horizons in the Ancient Near East: Papers Presented to the XLIV Rencontre Assyriologique Internationale, Venezia, 7–11 July 1997*, ed. L. Milano et al. History of the Ancient Near East Monographs, III/2. Padova: Sargon, 21–28.

Gallup, George, Jr., and D. Michael Lindsay. 1999. *Surveying the Religious Land-scape: Trends in U.S. Beliefs.* Harrisburg, PA: Morehouse Publishing.

Garelli, Paul. 1979. "L'État et la légitimité royale sous l'empire assyrien." In *Power and Propaganda: A Symposium on Ancient Empires,* ed. Mogens Trolle Larsen. Mesopotamia, 7. Copenhagen: Akademisk Forlag, 319–28.

Gautier, P. 1981."La diataxis de Michel Attaliate." *Revue des études byzantines* 39, 4–143.

Geertz, Clifford. 1968. *Islam Observed.* Chicago: University of Chicago Press.

——. 1973. *The Interpretation of Cultures.* New York: Basic Books.

Gignoux, Philippe, and A. Tafazzoli, eds. and trans. 1993. *Anthologie de Zadspram. Édition critique du texte pehlevi.* Paris: Association pour l'avancement des études iraniennes.

Gillette, Maris. 2000. *Between Mecca and Beijing: Modernization and Consumption Among Urban Chinese Muslims.* Palo Alto, CA: Stanford University Press.

Girard, René. 1974. *Violence and the Sacred.* Trans. Patrick Gregory. Baltimore: Johns Hopkins University Press.

——. 1979. "Mimesis and Violence: Perspectives in Cultural Criticism." *Berkshire Review* 14:9–19.

Girling, John. 1981. *Thailand: Society and Politics.* Ithaca, NY: Cornell University Press.

Gladney, Dru C. 1991. *Muslim Chinese: Ethnic Nationalism in the People's Republic.* Cambridge, MA: Council on East Asian Studies, Harvard University Press.

——. 2003. "Islam in China: Accommodation or Separatism?" *The China Quarterly.* June: 145–61.

Glassner, J.-J. 1991. "À propos des jardins mésopotamiens." In *Jardins d'Orient,* ed. R. Gyselen. Res Orientales 3. Leuven: Peters, 9–17.

Goebs, Katja. 2003. *"Niswt n*—Kingship, Cosmos, and Time." In *Egyptology at the Dawn of the Twenty-First Century. Proceedings of the Eighth International Congress of Egyptologists, Cairo, 2000,* ed. Zahi Hawass. Vol. 2. Cairo/New York: American University in Cairo Press, 238–53.

Goertz, Hans-Jürgen. 1980. *Die Täufer: Geschichte und Deutung.* München.

Gokhale, Balkrishna G. 1948. *Buddhism and Aśoka.* Baroda: Padmaja Publications, Indian Historical Research Institute, Studies in Indian History, no. 17.

Goldman, Marion S. 1995. "Continuity in Collapse. Departures from Shiloh." *Journal for the Scientific Study of Religion* 34:342–53.

——. 1999. *Passionate Journeys: Why Successful Women Joined a Cult.* Ann Arbor: University of Michigan Press.

Gombrich, Richard. 1988. *Theravada Buddhism: A Social History from Ancient Benares to Modern Colombo.* London: Routledge.

Gombrich, Richard, and Gananath Obeyesekere. 1988. *Buddhism Transformed: Religious Change in Sri Lanka.* Princeton: Princeton University Press.

Goodblatt, David. 2001. "Judean Nationalism in the Light of the Dead Sea Scrolls." In *Historical Perspectives: From the Hasmoneans to Bar Kokhba in Light of the Dead Sea Scrolls,* ed. David Goodblatt, Avital Pinnick, and Daniel R. Schwartz. Leiden: Brill, 3–27.

Gosling, David L. 1984. "Buddhism for Peace." *Southeast Asian Journal of Social Science* 12:59–70.

Gravers, Mikael. 1993. *Nationalism and Political Paranoia in Burma: An Essay on the Historical Practice of Power*. Richmond, Surrey: Curzon for Nordic Institute of Asian Studies, NIAS Report No. 11.

Grayson, A. K. 1975. *Assyrian and Babylonian Chronicles*. Locust Valley, NY: J. J. Augustin.

Grayson, A. Kirk, ed. 1991. *Assyrian Rulers of the Early First Millennium BC, I (114–859 BC)*. Royal Inscriptions of Mesopotamia, Assyrian Periods, 2. Toronto: University of Toronto Press.

Green, John C. 2003. "Evangelical Protestants and Civic Engagement: An Overview." In *A Public Faith: Evangelicals and Civic Engagement*, ed. Michael Cromartie. Lanham, MD: Rowman & Littlefield.

Green, John C., Mark J. Rozell, and Clyde Wilcox, eds. 2003. *The Christian Right in American Politics: Marching to the Millennium*. Washington, D.C.: Georgetown University Press.

Grieser, D. Jonathan. 1995. "A Tale of Two Convents: Nuns and Anabaptists in Münster, 1533–1535." *Sixteenth Century Journal* 26 (Spring): 31–47.

Groebner, Valentin. 2004. *Defaced: The Visual Culture of Violence in the Late Middle Ages*. Trans. Pamela Selwyn. New York: Zone Books.

Grousset, J. 1934–1936. *Histoire des croisades et du royaume franc de Jérusalem*. 3 vols. Paris.

Gunn, Geoffrey C. 1990. *Rebellion in Laos: Peasant and Politics in a Colonial Backwater*. Boulder: Westview Press.

Guth, James L., Linda Beail, Greg Crow, Beverly Gaddy, Steve Montreal, Brent Nelson, James Penning, and Jeff Walz. 2003. "The Political Activity of Evangelical Clergy in the Election of 2000: A Case Study of Five Denominations." *Journal for the Scientific Study of Religion* 42, no. 4:501–14.

Habinek, T. 2002. "Ovid and Empire." In *The Cambridge Companion to Ovid*, ed. P. Hardie. Cambridge: Cambridge University Press.

Halbertal, Moshe, and Avishai Margalit. 1994. *Idolatry*. Trans. Naomi Goldblum. Cambridge, MA: Harvard University Press.

Haldon, J. 1999. *Warfare, State and Society in the Byzantine World, 565–1204*. London: UCL Press.

Hall, David D. 1989. *Worlds of Wonder, Days of Judgment: Popular Religious Belief in Early New England*. New York: Knopf.

Hall, E. Swan. 1986. *The Pharaoh Smites His Enemies: A Comparative Study*. Münchner ägyptologische Studien, 44. München: Deutscher Kunstverlag.

Hall, Jacquelyn Dowd. 1993. *Revolt Against Chivalry: Jesse Daniel Ames and the Women's Campaign against Lynching*. New York: Columbia University Press.

Hall, John R. 1987. *Gone from the Promised Land*. New Brunswick: Transaction Press.

Hall, John R., Philip Schuyler, and Sylvaine Trinh. 2000. *Apocalypse Observed: Religious Movements and Violence in North America, Europe and Japan*. London: Routledge.

Haller, Max. 1923. "Die Kyros-Lieder Deuterojesajas." In *Eukharisterion: Studien zur Religion und Literatur des Alten und Neuen Testaments. Hermann Gunkel zum 60. Geburtstage*, ed. Hans Schmidt. Göttingen: Vandenhoeck and Ruprecht, 261–77.

Hamerton-Kelly, Robert G. 1992. *Sacred Violence: Paul's Heremeneutic of the Cross*. Minneapolis: Fortress.

Handy, Robert T. 1971. *A Christian America: Protestant Hopes and Historical Realities.* New York: Oxford University Press.

Hardie, P. 2002a. "Ovid and Early Imperial Literature." In *The Cambridge Companion to Ovid*, ed. P. Hardie. Cambridge: Cambridge University Press.

———. 2002b. *Ovid's Poetics of Allusion.* Cambridge: Cambridge University Press.

Hardt, Michael, and Antonio Negri. 2000. *Empire.* Cambridge, MA: Harvard University Press.

Harmatta, J. 1971. "The Literary Patterns of the Babylonian Edict of Cyrus." *Acta Antiqua Academiae Scientiarum Hungaricae* 19: 217–31.

Harris, Ian. 1999. "Buddhism *in Extremis*: The Case of Cambodia." In *Buddhism and Politics in Twentieth-Century Asia*, ed. Ian Harris. London and New York: Continuum, 54–79.

———. 2005. *Cambodian Buddhism.* Honolulu: University of Hawai'i Press.

Harvey, Paul. 2005. *Freedom's Coming: Religious Culture and Shaping of the South from the Civil War through the Civil Rights Era.* Chapel Hill: University of North Carolina Press.

Hauerwas, Stanley. 1983. *The Peaceable Kingdom: A Primer in Christian Ethics.* Notre Dame: University of Notre Dame Press.

He Changling. 1882. *Naian Zouyi* (The memorials of He Changling).

Heinemann, Joseph. 1984. *Prayer in the Period of the Tannaim and Amoraim.* (Heb.) Jerusalem: Magnes Press.

Helgeland, J. 1978. "Roman Army Religion." *Aufstieg und Niedergang der römischen Welt* II.16.1:1470–1505.

Herbert, Patricia. 1982. *The Hsaya San Rebellion (1930–1932) Reappraised.* Melbourne: Monash University, Centre of Southeast Asian Studies, Working Papers, No. 27.

Herr, M. D. 1968. "Religious Persecution and Martyrdom in the Age of Hadrian." (Heb.) *Milhemet qodesh u-martirologiah.* Jerusalem, 79–84.

Hezser, Catherine. 1993–94. "Social Fragmentation, Plurality of Opinion, and Nonobservance of Halakhah: Rabbis and Community in Late Roman Palestine." *Jewish Studies Quarterly* 1:234–51.

Hillerbrand, Hans J., ed. 1988. *Radical Tendencies in the Reformation: Divergent Perspectives.* Volume IX of the Sixteenth Century Essays and Studies Series. Kirksville, MO: Sixteenth Century Journal Publishers, Inc.

Hinton, Alexander Laban. 2005. *Why Did They Kill? Cambodia in the Shadow of Genocide.* Berkeley: University of California Press.

Hitchcock, Mark. 2003. *The Second Coming of Babylon.* Sisters, OR: Multnomah Publishers.

Hofstadter, Richard. 1963. *Anti-Intellectualism in American Life.* New York: Knopf.

Holum, K. 1977. "Pulcheria's Crusade AD 421–22 and the Ideology of Imperial Victory." *Greek, Roman and Byzantine Studies* 18:153–72.

Holum, K., and G. Vikan. 1979. "The Trier Ivory, *adventus* Ceremonial, and the Relics of St. Stephen." *Dumbarton Oaks Papers* 33 (1979):113–33.

Horbury, William. 2003. *Messianism among Jews and Christians: Twelve Biblical and Historical Studies.* London: T. and T. Clark.

Hornung, E. 1956. "Chaotische Bereiche in der geordneten Welt." *Zeitschrift für ägyptische Sprache und Altertumskunde* 81:28–32.

———. 1990. *Conceptions of God in Ancient Egypt: The One and the Many*. Trans. John Baines. Ithaca, NY: Cornell University Press.

Horowitz, Wayne. 1998. *Mesopotamian Cosmic Geography*. Winona Lake, IN: Eisenbrauns.

Hout, Michael, and Claude Fischer. 2002. "Why More Americans Have No Religious Preference: Politics and Generations." *American Sociological Review* 67:165–80.

Houtman, Gustaaf. 1996. "The Biography of Modern Burmese Buddhist Meditation Master U Ba Khin: Life Before the Cradle and Past the Grave." In *Sacred Biography in the Buddhist Traditions of South and Southeast Asia*, ed. Juliane Schober. Honolulu: University of Hawai'i Press, 310–44.

———. 1999. *Mental Culture in Burmese Crisis Politics: Aung San Suu Kyi and the National League for Democracy*. Tokyo: Institute for the Study of Languages and Cultures of Asia and Africa, Monograph Series No. 33.

Howard-Johnston, J. 1994. "The Official History of Heraclius' Persian campaigns." In *The Roman and Byzantine Army in the East*, ed. E. Dabrowa. Kraków, 57–87.

Hrouda, B. 1965. "Die Grundlagen der bildenden Kunst in Assyrien." *Zeitschrift für Assyriologie und Vorderasiatische Archäologie* 57:274–97.

Hughes, Richard T. 2003. *Myths America Lives By*. Urbana: University of Illinois Press.

Hunter, James Davison. 1987. *Evangelicalism: The Coming Generation*. Chicago: University of Chicago Press.

Huntington, Samuel. 1996. *The Class of Civilizations and the Remaking of World Order*. New York: Simon and Schuster.

Hutchison, William R. 1992. *The Modernist Impulse in American Protestantism*. Durham, NC: Duke University Press.

Inglehart, Ronald, and Pippa Norris. 2003. "The True Clash of Civilizations." *Foreign Policy* 135 (March–April): 63–70.

Intrater, Keith. 2003. *From Iraq to Armageddon: The Final Showdown Approaches*. West Jefferson, NC: Armageddon Books.

Ishii, Yoneo. 1975. "A Note on Buddhistic Millenarian Revolts in Northeastern Siam." *Journal of Southeast Asian Studies* 6.2:121–26.

Israeli, Raphael. 1997. "A New Wave of Muslim Revivalism in Mainland China." *Issues and Studies* 33:3 (March).

Jackson, Peter A. 1989. *Buddhism, Legitimation, and Conflict: The Political Functions of Urban Thai Buddhism*. Singapore: Institute of Southeast Asian Studies.

Jacobs, Janet Liebman. 1989. *Divine Disenchantment*. Bloomington: Indiana University Press.

Jacobsen, Thorkild. 1975. "Religious Drama in Ancient Mesopotamia." In *Unity and Diversity: Essays in the History, Literature, and Religion of the Ancient Near East*, ed. H. Goedicke and J. J. M. Roberts. Baltimore, MD: Johns Hopkins University Press, 65–97.

Jaffee, Martin. 1997. *Early Judaism*. Upper Saddle River, NJ: Prentice Hall.

James, William. 1994. *The Varieties of Religious Experience*. New York: Random House, Inc.

Jansen-Winkeln, J. 2000. "Die Fremdherrschaften in Ägypten im 1. Jahrtausend v. Chr." *Orientalia* 69:1–20.

Jenni, Ernst. 1954. "Die Rolle des Kyros bei Deuterojesaja." *Theologische Zeitschrift* 10:241–56.

Jensen, Phillip. 2003. "Apocalypse Again and Again." *Christianity Today* 47, no. 4, May.

Jewett, Robert, and John Shelton Lawrence. 2003. *Captain America and the Crusade against Evil: The Dilemma of Zealous Nationalism.* Grand Rapids, MI: W. B. Eerdmans.

Johnson, Benton. 1992. "On Founders and Followers: Some Factors in the Development of New Religious Movements." *Sociological Analysis* 53(S):1–13.

Jo'raev, M., et al., eds. 2000. *Ozbekistonning yangi tarixi.* Vol. 2. Toshkent: Sharq.

Juergensmeyer, Mark. 2000. *Terror in the Mind of God: The Global Rise of Religious Violence.* Berkeley and Los Angeles: University of California Press.

Kaegi, W. 2003. *Heraclius. Emperor of Byzantium.* Cambridge: Cambridge University Press.

Kalavrezou, I. 1997. "Helping Hands for the Empire: Imperial Ceremonies and the Cult of Relics at the Byzantine Court." In *Byzantine Court Culture from 829 to 1204,* ed. H. Maguire. Washington, D.C.: Dumbarton Oaks, 53–79.

Kamala Tiyavanich. 1997. *Forest Recollections: Wandering Monks in Twentieth-Century Thailand.* Honolulu: University of Hawai'i Press.

Kamensky, Jane. 1997. *Governing the Tongue: The Politics of Speech in Early New England.* New York: Oxford University Press.

Kamp, Marianne. 2006. *The New Woman in Uzbekistan: Islam, Modernity, and Unveiling under Communism.* Seattle: University of Washington Press.

Karryeva, Roziia. 1989. *Ot bespraviia k ravenstvu.* Tashkent: Uzbekistan.

Kazhdan, E., et al., eds. 1991. *Oxford Dictionary of Byzantium.* 3 vols. Oxford and New York: Oxford University Press.

Keillor, Steven J. 1996. *This Rebellious House: American History and the Truth of Christianity.* Downers Grove, IL: InterVarsity Press.

Keller, Shoshana. 2001. *To Moscow, Not Mecca: The Soviet Campaign against Islam in Central Asia, 1917–1941.* Westport, CT: Praeger Publishers.

Kellstedt, Lyman A., and John C. Green. 2003. "The Politics of the Willow Creek Association Pastors." *Journal for the Scientific Study of Religion* 42, 4:547–61.

Keyes, Charles F. 1971. "Buddhism and National Integration in Thailand." *Journal of Asian Studies* 30.3:551–68.

———. 1975. "Buddhism in a Secular City: A View from Chiang Mai." In *Visakha Puja B.E. 2518.* Bangkok: The Buddhist Association of Thailand, Annual Publication, 62–72.

———. 1977. "Millennialism, Theravāda Buddhism, and Thai Society." *Journal of Asian Studies* 36.2:283–302.

———. 1978. "Political Crisis and Militant Buddhism in Contemporary Thailand." In *Religion and Legitimation of Power in Thailand, Burma, and Laos,* ed. Bardwell Smith. Chambersburg, PA: Anima Books, 147–64.

———. 1983a. "Economic Action and Buddhist Morality in a Thai Village." In *Peasant Strategies in Asian Societies: Perspectives on Moral and Rational Economic Approaches,* ed. Charles F. Keyes. *Journal of Asian Studies* 42.3:851–68.

———. 1983b. "The Study of Popular Ideas of Karma." In *Karma: An Anthropological Inquiry,* ed. Charles F. Keyes and E. Valentine Daniel. Berkeley: University of California Press, 1–24.

———. 1990. "Buddhist Practical Morality in a Changing Agrarian World: A Case from Northeastern Thailand." In *Attitudes toward Wealth and Poverty in Theravada Buddhism*, ed. Donald K. Swearer and Russell Sizemore. Columbia, SC: University of South Carolina Press, 170–89.

———. 1991. "Buddhist Detachment and Worldly Gain: The Economic Ethic of Northeastern Thai Villagers." In *Yū müang Thai: ruam botkhwām thāng sangkhom pha pen kiat dāē Sāstrācān Sanē Cāmrik* (Collected Essays in Honor of Professor Saneh Chammarik), ed. Chaiwat Satha-Anand. Special issue of *Ratthasātsān* (Journal of Political Science, Thammasat University) 16.1–2:271–98.

———. 1992. "Buddhist Politics and Their Revolutionary Origin in Thailand." In *Innovations in Religious Traditions: Essays in the Interpretation of Religious Change*, ed. Michael A. Williams, Collett Cox, and Martin S. Jaffee. Berlin and New York: Mouton de Gruyter, 319–50.

———. 1993. "Buddhist Economics and Buddhist Fundamentalism in Burma and Thailand." In *Remaking the World: Fundamentalist Impact*, ed. Martin Marty and Scott Appleby. Chicago: University of Chicago Press, 367–409.

———. 1994. "Communist Revolution and the Buddhist Past in Cambodia." In *Asian Visions of Authority: Religion and the Modern States of East and Southeast Asia*, ed. Charles F. Keyes, Laurel Kendall, and Helen Hardacre. Honolulu: University of Hawai'i Press, 43–73.

———. 1999a. "Moral Authority of the Sangha and Modernity in Thailand: Sexual Scandals, Sectarian Dissent, and Political Resistance." In *Socially Engaged Buddhism for the New Millennium: Essays in Honor of the Ven. Phra Dhammapitaka (Bhikkhu P.A. Payutto) on his 60th Birthday Anniversary*, ed. Sulak Sivaraksa. Bangkok: Sathira-Nagapradipa Foundation and Foundation for Children, 121–47.

———. 1999b. "Buddhism Fragmented: Thai Buddhism and Political Order since the 1970s." Keynote address presented at Seventh International Thai Studies Conference, Amsterdam, July.

———. 2002. "Weber and Anthropology." *Annual Reviews in Anthropology* 31:233–55.

Kierkegaard, Soren. 1983. *Fear and Trembling*. Ed. and trans. Howard V. Hong and Edna H. Hong. Princeton: Princeton University Press.

Kieval, Hillel J. 1994–1995. "Representation and Knowledge in Medieval and Modern Accounts of Jewish Ritual Murder." *Jewish Social Studies: History, Culture, Society, New Series* 1:52–72.

Kilmer, Anne Draffkorn. 1999. "An Ideal Animal Totem/Model for Inanna/Ishtar Problems of Geography and Time." In *Landscapes: Territories, Frontiers, and Horizons in the Ancient Near East: Papers Presented to the XLIV Rencontre Assyriologique Internationale, Venezia, 7–11 July 1997*, ed. L. Milano et al. History of the Ancient Near East Monographs, III/3. Padova: Sargon, 53–61.

Kim Dohong. 2004. *Holy War in China: The Muslim Rebellion and State in Chinese Central Asia, 1864–1877*. Palo Alto, CA: Stanford University Press.

King, Winston L. 1964. *A Thousand Lives Away: Buddhism in Contemporary Burma*. Cambridge, MA: Harvard University Press.

———. 1965. "Sasāra Revalued." In *Studies on Asia, 1965*, ed. Robert Sakai. Lincoln: University of Nebraska Press, 201–209.

Kiribamune, Sirima. 1978. "Buddhism and Royal Prerogative in Medieval Ceylon." In *Religion and the Legitimation of Power in Sri Lanka*, ed. Bardwell L. Smith. Chambersburg, PA: Anima, 107–118.

Kirsch, A. Thomas. 1973. "Modernizing Implications of 19th Century Reforms in the Thai Sangha." *Contributions to Asian Studies* 8:8–23.

Kittel, R. 1898. "Cyrus und Deuterojesaja." *Zeitschrift für die alttestamentliche Wissenschaft* 18:149–62.

Kittivuddho *Bhikkhu* (Kittiwutthō Phikkhu). 1976. *Khā Khômmūnit mai bāp* (Killing Communists is Not Demeritorious). Bangkok: Abhidhamma Foundation of Wat Mahādhātu (Mūnnithi Aphitham, Wat Mahāthāt).

Knoppers, Laura Lunger, ed. 2003. *Puritanism and Its Discontents*. Newark, DE: University of Delaware Press.

Knuth, Rebecca. 2003. *Libricide: The Regime-Sponsored Destruction of Books and Libraries in the Twentieth Century*. Westport, CT: Praeger.

Koch, Klaus. 1972. "Die Stellung des Kyros im Geschichtsbild Deuterojesajas und ihre überlieferungsgeschichtliche Verankerung." *Zeitschrift für die alttestamentliche Wissenschaft* 84:352–56.

Koerner, Joseph Leo. 2005. *The Reformation of the Image*. Chicago: University of Chicago Press.

Kohut, Andrew. 2003. "Different Faith, Different Messages." The Pew Research Center for the People and the Press, March 19.

Kolbaba, T. 1998. "Fighting for Christianity: Holy War in the Byzantine Empire." *Byzantion* 68:194–221.

Kolbe, D. 1981. *Die reliefprogramme religiös-mythologischen Charakters in neuassyrischen Palästen*. Frankfurt am Main: Lang.

Kolia-Dermitzaki, A. 1991. *O vizantinos «ieros polemos»* (Byzantine Holy War). Athens.

Kommunisticheskaia Partiia Uzbekistana v tsifrakh: sbornik statisticheskikh materilov, 1924–1977 gg. 1979. Tashkent: Uzbekistan.

Kornfield, Jack. 1977. *Living Buddhist Masters*. Santa Cruz: Unity Press.

Kosmin, Barry A., and Seymour P. Lachman. 1994. *One Nation under God*. Reprint. Three Rivers, MI: Three Rivers Press.

Kosmin, Barry A., Egon Mayer, and Ariela Keysar. 2001. *American Religious Identification Survey*. New York: The Graduate Center of the City University of New York.

Kraft, Kenneth, ed. 1992. *Inner Peace, World Peace: Essays on Buddhism and Nonviolence*. Albany: State University of New York Press.

Krahn, Cornelius. 1968. *Dutch Anabaptism: Origin, Spread, Life and Thought (1450–1600)*. The Hague: Martinus Nijhoff.

Kratz, Reinhard Gregor. 1991. *Kyros im Deuterojesaja-Buch*. Tübingen: J. C. B. Mohr.

Kresten, O. 2001. "Parerga zur Ikonographie des Josua-Rotulus und der illuminierten byzantinischen Oktateuche. I. Die 'Grabstele' von Jericho." In *Novum Millennium. Studies on Byzantine History and Literature Dedicated to Paul Speck*, ed. C. Sode and S. Takács. Aldershot, 185–212.

Kugel, James. 2003. *The God of Old: Inside the Lost World of the Bible*. New York: Free Press.

Kuhrt, Amelie. 1983. "The Cyrus Cylinder and Achaemenid Imperial Policy." *Journal for the Study of the Old Testament* 25:83–97.

———. 1990. "Nabonidus and the Babylonian Priesthood." In *Pagan Priests: Religion and Power in the Ancient World,* ed. Mary Beard and John North. Ithaca, NY: Cornell University Press, 117–55.

Künzl, E. 1988. *Der römische Triumph: Siegesfeiern im antiken Rom.* Munich.

Laato, Antti. 1992. *The Servant of YHWH and Cyrus: A Reinterpretation of the Exilic Messianic Programme in Isaiah 40–55.* Stockholm: Almqvist and Wiksell.

LaHaye, Tim, and Thomas Ice. 2003. *The End Times Controversy.* Eugene, OR: Harvest House Publishers.

Laiou, A. 1993. "On Just War in Byzantium." In *To Ellênikon. Studies in Honor of Speros Vryonis, Jr.,* ed. J. Langdon et al. New Rochelle, 153–77.

Lakoff, George. 1996. *Moral Politics: How Liberals and Conservatives Think.* 2nd. ed. Chicago: University of Chicago Press.

Lalich, Janja. 2004. *Bounded Choice.* Berkeley: University of California Press.

Lambert, W. G. 1963. "The Great Battle of the Mesopotamian Religious Year: The Conflict in the Ak•tu House." *Iraq* 25:189–90.

———. 2002. "The Background of the Neo-Assyrian Sacred Tree." In *Sex and Gender in the Ancient Near East. Proceedings of the 47th Rencontre Assryiologique Internationale, Helsinki, July 2–6, 2001,* ed. S. Parpola and R. M. Whiting. Helsinki: Neo-Assyrian Texts Corpus Project, 321–35.

Lash, Scott, and Sam Whimster, eds. 1987. *Max Weber, Rationality, and Modernity.* London: Allen and Unwin.

Lawler, Andrew. 2004. "Saving Afghan Culture." *National Geographic* (Dec.): 28–41.

Lawson, Guy. 2003. "George W's Personal Jesus." *Gentlemen's Quarterly* (September).

Layard, Austen Henry. 1853. *Discoveries in the Ruins of Nineveh and Babylon.* London: Murray.

Leader, R. 2000. "The David Plates: Transforming the Secular in Early Byzantium." *Art Bulletin* 82:407–27.

Lecoq, Pierre. 1997. *Les inscriptions de la Perse achéménide.* Paris: Gallimard.

Ledi Sayadaw. 1961. *The Manual of Insight: Vipassanā Dīpanī.* Trans. U Nyāna Mahā-Thera. Kandy, Ceylon: Buddhist Publication Society, The Wheel Publication No. 31/32.

———. 1971. *The Requisites of Enlightment: Bodhipakkhiya Dīpanī.* Trans. Sein Nyo Tun. Kandy, Ceylon: Buddhist Publication Society, The Wheel Publication No. 171/74.

Lentricchia, Frank, and Jody McAuliffe. 2003. *Crimes of Art and Terror.* Chicago: University of Chicago Press.

Leo the Deacon. 1828. *Leonis diaconus Caloensis historiae,* ed. C. B. Hase. Bonn.

Li Bingyuan. 1953. "Yongchangfu Baoshanxian Han-Hui hudou ji Du Wenxiu shixing geming zhi yuanqi" (The Yongchang-Baoshan Han-Hui incident and origins of the rise of Du Wenxiu's uprising). In *Huimin qiyi* (Hui rebellions), ed. Bai Shouyi. Shanghai: Zhongguo shenzhou guogang chubanshu, I, 4–5.

Li Xingyuan. [1865] 1974. *Li Wengong Gong zouyi* (The memorials of Li Xingyuan). Taibei: Wenhai Chubanshe.

Lieberman, Saul. 1975. "Persecution of the Jewish religion" (Heb.). In *Salo Wittmayer Baron Jubilee Volume on the Occasion of his Eightieth Birthday*, 214–34. Jerusalem: American Academy for Jewish Research.

Lieberman, Victor. 1993. "Was the Seventeenth Century a Watershed in Burmese History?" In *Southeast Asia in the Early Modern Era: Trade, Power, and Belief*, ed. Anthony Reid. Ithaca, NY: Cornell University Press, 214–49.

Lifton, Robert Jay. 1999. *Destroying the World to Save It: Aum Shinrikyô, Apocalyptic Violence and the New Global Terrorism*. New York: Metropolitan Books.

Lin Zexu. 1935. *Lin Wenzhong gong zhengshu* (The memorials of Lin Zexu). 2 vols. Shanghai: Shangwu Yinshukuan.

Lincoln, Bruce. 1991. *Death, War, and Sacrifice: Studies in Ideology and Practice*. Chicago: University of Chicago Press.

———. 1994. *Authority: Construction and Corrosion*. Chicago: University of Chicago Press.

———. 2003. *Holy Terrors: Thinking about Religion after September 11*. Chicago: University of Chicago Press.

———. 2004. "The Cyrus Cylinder, the Book of Virtues, and the 'Liberation' of Iraq: On Political Theology and Messianic Pretentions." In *Religionen in Konflikt: Vom Bürgerkrieg über Ökogewalt bis zur Gewalterinnerung im Ritual*, ed. Vasilios Makrides and Jörg Rüpke, 248–64. Münster: Aschendorf.

Lincoln, C. Eric, and Lawrence H. Mamiya. 1993. *The Black Church in the African American Experience*. Durham: Duke University Press.

Linenthal, Edward Tabor. 1993. *Sacred Ground: Americans and their Battlefields*. Urbana: University of Illinois Press.

Lingat, Robert. 1926. "La vie réligieuse du Roi Mongkut." *Journal of the Siam Society* 20.2:129–48.

———. 1958. "La double crise de l'église bouddhique au Siam, 1767–1851." *Journal of World History/Cahiers d'histoire mondiale* 4.2:402–25.

Lipman, Jonathan N. 1997. *Familiar Strangers: A History of Muslims in Northwest China*. Seattle: University of Washington Press.

———. 1999. "Sufism in the Chinese Courts: Islam and Qing Law in the Eighteenth and Nineteenth Century." In *Islamic Mysticism Contested: Thirteen Centuries of Controversies and Polemics*, ed. Frederick de Jong and Bernd Radtke. Leiden: Brill, 253–75.

———. 2004. "White Hats, Oil Cakes and Common Blood." In *Governing China's Multiethnic Frontiers*, ed. Morris Rossabi. Seattle: University of Washington Press.

Liutprand of Cremona. 1910. *Legatio*. Trans. E. F. Henderson. *Select historical documents of the Middle Ages*. London, 440–77.

Liverani, Mario. 1979. "The Ideology of the Assyrian Empire." In *Power and Propaganda: A Symposium on Ancient Empires*, ed. Mogens Trolle Larsen. Mesopotamia, 7. Copenhagen: Akademisk Forlag, 297–317.

Lofland, John. 1977. *Doomsday Cult*. Enlarged ed. New York: Irvington.

Lopez, Donald S., Jr., ed. 1995. *Curators of the Buddha: The Study of Buddhism under Colonialism*. Chicago: University of Chicago Press.

Loveland, Anne C. 1996. *American Evangelicals and the U.S. Military, 1942–1993*. Baton Rouge: Louisiana State University Press.

Loy, David R. 1997. "The Religion of the Market." *Journal of the American Academy of Religion* 65 (Spring): 275–90.

Lugo, Luis. 2003. "Religion and Politics: Contention and Consensus." Pew Forum on Religion and the Public Life, July 24.

Luo Bingsen and Zhang Jing. 1998. "Zongjiao yu Jindu" (Religion and Illicit Drugs). *Yunnan Jingxue* (2), 28.

Luo Ping. 1993. "Yunnan Pingyuanjie Yanda Jishi." *Liaowang Zhoukan* 13:20–24.

Lyngby, H. 1963. "Das Problem der Porta Triumphalis im Lichte der neuesten archäologischen Entdeckungen." *Eranos* 61:161–75.

Ma Guanzheng. 1953. "Dianyuan Shisinian Dahuo Ji" (A record of the fourteen years of tragedy in Yunnan). In *Huimin qiyi* (Hui rebellions), ed. Bai Shouyi. Shanghai: Zhongguo shenzhou guogang chubanshu, I, 291–302.

Ma Shaomei. 1989. *Shadian Huizu shiliao* (Historical sources of the Shadian Hui). Kaiyuan, Yunnan.

Ma Tong. 1986. *Zhongguo Yisilan Jiaopai Menhuan Suyuan*. Yinchuan: Ningxia Renmin Chubanshe.

Ma Weiliang. 1999. *Yunnan Huizu lishi yu wenhua yanjiu* (Research on Yunnan Hui history and culture). Kunming: Yunnan Daxue Chubanshe.

MacArthur, John. 2001. *Terrorism, Jihad, and the Bible: A Response to the Terrorist Attacks*. Nashville: W. Publishing Company.

MacCormack, S. G. 1981. *Art and Ceremony in Late Antiquity*. Berkeley: University of California, Berkeley Press.

Madhloom, T. A. 1970. *The Chronology of Assyrian Art*. London: Athlone Press.

Makin, E. 1921. "The Triumphal Route, with Particular Reference to the Flavian Triumph." *JRS* 11:25–36.

Malalgoda, Kitsiri. 1976. *Buddhism in Sinhalese Society, 1750–1900*. Berkeley and Los Angeles: University of California Press.

Manchester, William. 1992. *A World Lit Only by Fire: The Medieval Mind and the Renaissance Portrait of an Age*. Boston: Little, Brown and Company.

Mango, C. 1985. "Deux études sur Byzance et la Perse sassanide, II: Héraclius, Sahrvaraz et la Vraie Croix." *Travaux et mémoires* 9:105–18.

Manor, James. 1985. *Sri Lanka in Change and Crisis*. New York: St. Martin's Press.

Marks, Richard G. 1994. *The Image of Bar Kokhba in Traditional Jewish Literature: False Messiah and National Hero*. University Park, PA: Pennsylvania State University Press.

Marsden, George M. 1982. *Fundamentalism and American Culture: The Shaping of Twentieth-Century Evangelicalism, 1870–1925*. Oxford: Oxford University Press.

———. 1991. *Understanding Fundamentalism and Evangelicalism*. Grand Rapids, MI: William B. Eerdmans Publishing Company.

———. 2006. "The Sword of the Lord: How 'Otherworldly' Fundamentalism Became a Political Power." *Books and Culture: A Christian Review*. http://www.christianitytoday.com/bc/2006/002/3.10.html (accessed March 16, 2006).

Marston, John, and Elizabeth Guthrie, eds. 2004. *History, Buddhism and New Religious Movements in Cambodia*. Honolulu: University of Hawai'i Press.

Martin, David. 1997. *Does Christianity Cause War?* Oxford: Clarendon Press.

———. 2005. *On Secularization: Towards a Revised General Theory*. England: Ashgate Publishing Limited.

Martin, William. 1999. "The Christian Right and American Foreign Policy." *Foreign Policy* 114:66–80.

Marty, Martin A. 1988. "Fundamentalism as a Social Phenomena." *Bulletin of the American Academy of Arts and Sciences* 42.2:15–29.

Marty, Martin E. 1970. *Righteous Empire: The Protestant Experience in America*. New York: Dial.

Marty, Martin E., and R. Scott Appleby, eds. 1991. *Fundamentalisms Observed*. The Fundamentalism Project, vol. 1. Chicago: University of Chicago Press.

———, eds. 1991–1995. The Fundamentalism Project. 5 vols. Chicago: University of Chicago Press.

———, eds. 1993a. *Fundamentalisms and Society: Reclaiming the Sciences, the Family and Education*. The Fundamentalism Project, vol. 2. Chicago: University of Chicago Press.

———, eds. 1993b. *Fundamentalisms and the State: Remaking Polities, Economies, and Militance*. The Fundamentalism Project, vol. 3. Chicago: University of Chicago Press.

———, eds. 1994. *Accounting for Fundamentalisms*. The Fundamentalism Project, vol. 4. Chicago: University of Chicago Press.

———, eds. 1995. *Fundamentalisms Comprehended*. The Fundamentalism Project, vol. 5. Chicago: University of Chicago Press.

Marty, Martin E., and R. Scott Appleby, with Nancy T. Ammerman, Samuel C. Heilman, James Piscatori, and Robert Eric Frykenberg, eds. 1994. *Accounting for Fundamentalisms: The Dynamic Character of Movements*. Chicago: University of Chicago Press.

Mary Dyer, Quaker: Two Letters of William Dyer of Rhode Island, 1659–60. 1927? Cambridge: Cambridge University Press. Printed for Charles Dyer Norton and Daniel B. Dyer.

Matsumoto, Kotaro. 1998. "Economic Development Among the Hui of Yunnan." *Islamic Area Studies Working Paper Series* 6 (March): 1–16.

Matthews, Bruce, ed. 1993. *Religion, Culture and Political Economy in Burma*. Vancouver, B.C.: University of British Columbia, Institute of Asian Research, The Centre for Southeast Asian Research, Research Monograph, 3.

Maung Maung, U. 1980. *From Sangha to Laity: Nationalist Movements of Burma, 1920–1940*. Columbia, MO: South Asia Books, Australian National University Monographs on South Asia, no. 4.

———. 1991. *Burmese Nationalist Movement, 1940–1949*. Honolulu: University of Hawai'i Press.

Mayo, Lawrence Shaw. 1936. *John Endecott: A Biography*. Cambridge, MA: Harvard University Press.

Mazzoleni, G. 1975. *Il diverso e l'uguale: la concettualizzazione della diversità nei contatti interculturali*. Rome: Bulzoni.

McCarthy, Susan. 2004. "Gods of Wealth, Temples of Prosperity: Party-State Participation in the Minority Cultural Revival." *China: An International Journal* 2 (March): 28–52.

McCormack, Win. 1985. *The Rajneesh Files: 1981–1986*. Portland: New Oregon Publishers.

McCutcheon, Russell T. 1997. *Manufacturing Religion: The Discourse on Sui Generis Religion and the Politics of Nostalgia*. New York: Oxford University Press.

———. 2003. *The Discipline of Religion: Structure, Meaning, Rhetoric.* New York: Routledge.

McGeer, E. 1995. *Sowing the Dragon's Teeth. Byzantine Warfare in the Tenth Century.* Washington, D.C.: Dumbarton Oaks.

———. 2003. "Two Military Orations of Constantine VII." In *Byzantine Authors: Literary Activities and Preoccupations: Texts and Translations Dedicated to the Memory of Nicolas Oikonomides,* ed. J. Nesbitt. The Medieval Mediterranean 46. Leiden: Brill, 111–35.

McGrath, Alister E. 1999. *Reformation Thought: An Introduction.* 3d. ed. Oxford: Blackwell Publishing.

Mehta, Gita. 1979. *Karma Kola: Marketing the Mystic East.* New York: Simon and Schuster.

Melander, Henning. 1919. *President Wilson och Cyrus-profetian.* Huddinge: Författarens eget Forlag.

Melton, J. Gordon. 1992. *Encyclopedic Handbook of Cults in America.* New York: Routledge.

Mendelson, E. Michael. 1975. *Sangha and State in Burma: A Study of Monastic Sectarianism and Leadership,* ed. John Ferguson. Ithaca, NY: Cornell University Press.

Meredith, George. 1988. *Bhagwan: The Most Godless Yet the Most Godly Man.* Poona: Rebel Publishing House.

Mergiali-Sahas, S. 2001. "Byzantine Emperors and Holy Relics." *Jahrbuch der Österreichischen Byzantinistik* 51:41–60.

Merkley, Paul Charles. 1998. *The Politics of Christian Zionism: 1891–1948.* London: Frank Cass.

Mieroop, Marc van de. 2003. "Reading Babylon." *American Journal of Archaeology* 107:257–75.

Miles, Jack. 2002. "Theology and the Clash of Civilizations." *Cross Currents* 51:1 (Winter): 451–59.

Millar, Fergus. 1993. *The Roman Near East 31 BC–AD 337.* Cambridge, MA: Harvard University Press.

Miller, J. F. 2000. "Triumphus in Palatio." *AJP* 121 (3): 409–422.

Miller, Perry. 1956. *Errand into the Wilderness.* New York: Harper and Row.

Miller, T. S., and J. Nesbitt, eds. 1995. *Peace and War in Byzantium. Essays in Honor of George T. Dennis, S. J.* Washington, D.C.: Catholic University of America Press.

Millward, James. 1994. "A Uyghur Muslim in Qianlong's Court." *Journal of Asian Studies* 53:2 (May): 427–58.

Milne, Hugh. 1987. *Bhagwan: The God That Failed.* New York: Saint Martin's Press.

Mojab, Shahrzad. 2002. "'Honor Killing': Culture, Politics and Theory." *MEWS Review* 17 (1/2, Spring/Summer). www.amews.org/review/reviewarticles/mojabfinal.htm (accessed April 5, 2004).

Mommsen, Th. 1887. *Römisches Staatsrecht.* 3rd ed. Leipzig.

Moore, Molly. 2001. "In Turkey, 'Honor Killing' Follows Families to Cities." *Washington Post,* Aug. 8, section A1.

Morell, David, and Chai-anan Samudavanija. 1981. *Political Conflict in Thailand: Reform, Reaction, Revolution.* Cambridge, MA: Oelgeschlager, Gunn and Hain.

Morenz, Siegfried. 1960. *Egyptian Religion*. Trans. Ann E. Keep. Ithaca, NY: Cornell University Press.

Morris, Edmund. 1999. *Dutch: A Memoir of Ronald Reagan*. New York: Modern Library.

Morris, R. 1988. "The Two Faces of Nikephoros Phokas." *Byzantine and Modern Greek Studies* 12:83–115.

———. 1995. *Monks and Laymen in Byzantium, 843–1118*. Cambridge: Cambridge University Press.

Mowinckel, Sigmund. 1956. *He That Cometh: The Messiah Concept in the Old Testament and Later Judaism*. Trans. G. W. Anderson. New York: Abingdon Press.

Murdoch, John B. 1974. "The 1901–1902 'Holy Man's' Rebellion." *Journal of the Siam Society* 62.1:47–66.

Nalivkin, V. P., and M. Nalivkina. 1886. *Ocherk byta zhenshchiny osedlago tuzemnago naseleniia Fergany*. Kazan': Tipografiia Imperatorskago Universiteta.

Nash, E. 1968. *Pictorial Dictionary of Ancient Rome*. Vol. I. Reprint. London: A. Zwemer.

Neusner, Jacob. 1993. "When Did Judaism Become a Messianic Religion?" In *Messianism Through History*, ed. Wim Beuken, Sean Freyne, and Anton Weiler. London: SCM Press.

New, David. 2002. *Holy War: The Rise of Militant Christian, Jewish and Islamic Fundamentalism*. Jefferson, NC: McFarland and Company, Inc.

Ng, On-cho. 2003. "The Epochal Concept of 'Early Modernity' and the Intellectual History of Late Imperial China." *Journal of World History* 14.1:37–61.

Nhat Hanh, Thich. 1993. *Love in Action: Writings on Nonviolent Social Change*. Berkeley, CA: Parallax Press.

Niebuhr, Reinhold. 1952. *The Irony of American History*. New York: Charles Scribner's Sons.

Nikam, N. A., and Richard P. McKeon, trans. 1959. *The Edicts of Aśoka*. Chicago: University of Chicago Press.

Noll, Mark A. 1973. "Luther Defends Melchior Hofmann." *Sixteenth Century Journal* 4 (October): 47–60.

———. 1994. *The Scandal of the Evangelical Mind*. Grand Rapids: W. B. Eerdmans.

———. 2001. *American Evangelical Christianity: An Introduction*. Oxford: Blackwell Publishers.

———. 2002. *America's God: From Jonathan Edwards to Abraham Lincoln*. New York: Oxford University Press.

———. 2006. *The Civil War as a Theological Crisis*. Chapel Hill: The University of North Carolina Press.

Noll, Mark A., Nathan O. Hatch, and George M. Marsden. 1989. *The Search for Christian America*. Colorado Springs: Helmers and Howard.

Noret, Jacques. 1982. *Vitae duae antiquae Sancti Athanasii Athonitae*. Corpus Christianorum, Series Graeca 9. Turnhout, Belgium: Brepols.

Northrop, Douglas. 2000. "Languages of Loyalty: Gender, Politics, and Party Supervision in Uzbekistan, 1927–1941." *Russian Review* 59(2):179–200.

———. 2004. *Veiled Empire: Gender and Power in Stalinist Central Asia*. Ithaca, NY: Cornell University Press.

Norton, John. 1659. *The Heart of N-England Rent at the Blasphemies of the Present Generation. Or a Brief Tractate concerning the Doctrine of the Quakers . . .* Cambridge, MA: Samuel Green.

Novák, Mirko. 2002. "The Artificial Paradise: Programme and Ideology of Royal Gardens." In *Sex and Gender in the Ancient Near East. Proceedings of the 47th Rencontre Assryiologique Internationale, Helsinki, July 2–6, 2001,* ed. S. Parpola and R. M. Whiting. Helsinki: Neo-Assyrian Texts Corpus Project, 443–60.

Obeyesekere, Gananath. 1975. "Sinhalese-Buddhist Identity in Ceylon." In *Ethnic Identity: Cultural Continuities and Change,* ed. George de Vos and Lola Romanucci-Ross. Palo Alto, CA: Mayfield Publishing, 231–58.

———. 1995. "On Buddhist Identity in Sri Lanka." In *Ethnic Identity: Creation, Conflict, and Accommodation,* ed. Lola Romanucci-Ross and George A. DeVos. 3d ed. Walnut Creek, CA: Alta Mira Press, 222–47.

O'Connor, David. 2002. "Context, Function and Program: Understanding Ceremonial Slate Palettes." *Journal of the American Research Center in Egypt* 39:5–25.

Oegema, Gerbern S. 1998. *The Anointed and His People: Messianic Expectations from the Maccabees to Bar Kochba.* Sheffield: Sheffield Academic Press.

Oikonomides, N. 1967. "Cinq actes inédits du patriarche Michel Autôreianos." *Revue des études byzantines* 25:113–45.

———. 1995. "The Concept of 'Holy War' and Two Tenth-Century Byzantine Ivories." In *Peace and War in Byzantium. Essays in Honor of George T. Dennis, S. J.,* ed. T. S. Miller and J. Nesbitt. Washington, D.C. : Catholic University of America Press, 62–86.

Olasky, Marvin. 1992. *The Tragedy of American Compassion.* Lanham, MD: Regnery Gateway.

———. 1996. *Renewing American Compassion,* with a foreword by Newt Gingrich. New York: Free Press.

———. 2000. *Compassionate Conservatism: What It Is, What It Does, and How It Can Transform America,* with a foreword by George W. Bush. New York: Free Press.

Oppenheim, A. L. 1965. "On Royal Gardens in Mesopotamia." *Journal of Near Eastern Studies* 24:328–33.

Oshima, T. 2003. "Some Comments on Prayer to Marduk, no. 1, lines 5/7." *Nouvelles Assyriologiques Brèves et Utilitaires,* 109–11.

Osho (Bhagwan Shree Rajneesh). 1993. *The Everyday Meditator: A Practical Guide.* Boston: Charles E. Tuttle Company.

———. 1996. *Meditation: The First and Last Freedom.* New York: St. Martin's Press.

———. 2001 [1982]. *The Goose Is Out.* Mumbai: Osho International Foundation.

Oswalt, John N. 1998. *The Book of Isaiah, Chapters 40–66.* Grand Rapids, MI: William B. Eerdmans.

Ozment, Steven. 1975. *The Reformation of the Cities: The Appeal of Protestantism to Sixteenth-Century Germany and Switzerland.* New Haven: Yale University Press.

———. 1980. *The Age of Reform 1250–1550: An Intellectual and Religious History of Late Medieval and Reformation Europe.* New Haven: Yale University Press.

Pahl, Jon. 1992. *Paradox Lost: Free Will and Political Liberty in American Culture, 1630–1760.* Baltimore: Johns Hopkins University Press.

————. 2003. *Shopping Malls and Other Sacred Spaces: Putting God in Place*. Grand Rapids, MI: Brazos Press.

Palmer, Susan Jean. 1994. *Moon Sisters, Krishna Mothers, Rajneesh Lovers: Women's Roles in New Religions*. Syracuse: Syracuse University Press.

Pal'vanova, Bibi. 1982. *Emantsipatsiia Musul'manki: opyt raskreposhcheniia zhenshchiny sovetskogo vostoka*. Moskva: Nauka.

Pape, Robert A. 2005. *Dying to Win: The Strategic Logic of Suicide Terrorism*. New York: Random House.

Paranavitana, Senerat. 1932. "The Religious Intercourse between Ceylon and Siam in the Thirteenth and Fifteenth Centuries." *Journal of Royal Asiatic Society of Great Britain and Ireland—Ceylon Branch* 32:190–212.

Parpola, Simo. 1993a. "The Assyrian Tree of Life: Tracing the Origins of Jewish Monotheism and Greek Philosophy." *Journal of Near Eastern Studies* 52:161–208.

————. 1993b. *Letters from Assyrian and Babylonian Scholars*. State Archives of Assyria, X. Helsinki: Helsinki University Press.

————. 1997. *Assyrian Prophecies*. State Archives of Assyria, IX. Helsinki: Helsinki University Press.

Pate, C. Marvin, and J. Daniel Hays. 2003. *Iraq: Babylon of the End-Times?* Grand Rapids, MI: Baker Book House.

Paul, G. M. 1993. "The Presentation of Titus in the Jewish War of Josephus: Two Aspects." *Phoenix* 47:56–66.

Payne, R. 1962. *The Roman Triumph*. New York: Abelard-Schuman.

Perdue, Peter. 2005. *China Marches West: The Qing Conquest of Central Eurasia*. Cambridge, MA: Belknap Press of Harvard University Press.

Pertusi, A. 1948. "Una acolouthia militare inedita del X secolo." *Aevum* 22:145–68.

Pestana, Carla Gardina. 1991. *Quakers and Baptists in Colonial Massachusetts*. New York: Cambridge University Press.

Petersen, Mark A. 1997. *The Price of Redemption: The Spiritual Economy of Puritan New England*. Palo Alto, CA: Stanford University Press.

Petit, L. 1904. "Office inédit en l'honneur de Nicéphore Phocas." *Byzantinische Zeitschrift* 13:398–420.

Phaisan Visalo, Phra. 1990. "The Forest Monastery and Its Relevance to Modern Thai Society." In *Radical Conservatism: Buddhism in the Contemporary World—Articles in Honour of Bhikkhu Buddhadasa's 84th Birthday Anniversary*, comp. Thai Inter-Religious Commission for Development and International Network of Engaged Buddhists. Bangkok: The Sathirakoses-Nagapradipa Foundation, 288–300.

Phillips, J. E. 1974a. "Verbs Compounded with trans- in Livy's Triumph Reports." *CP* 69 (1):54–55.

————. 1974b. "Form and Language in Livy's Triumph Notices. *CP* 69 (4):265–73.

Platner, S. B. 1926. *A Topographical Dictionary of Rome. Completed and Revised by T. Ashby*. Oxford: Oxford University Press. (Cited in text as "Platner-Ashby.")

Polonsky, Janice. 1999. "ki-^dutu-è-a: Where Destiny is Determined." In *Landscapes: Territories, Frontiers, and Horizons in the Ancient Near East: Papers Presented to the XLIV Rencontre Assyriologique Internationale, Venezia, 7–11 July 1997*, ed. L. Milano et al. History of the Ancient Near East Monographs, III/3. Padova: Sargon, 89–103.

Pongrazt-Leisten, P. 2001. "The Other and the Enemy in the Mesopotamian Conception of the World." In *Mythology and Mythologies,* ed. R. M. Whiting. Melammu Symposia II. Helsinki: Neo-Assyrian Texts Corpus Project, 195–231.

Porter, B. N. 1993. "Sacred Trees, Date Palms and the Royal Persona of Ashurnasirpal II." *Journal of Near Eastern Studies* 52:129–39.

———. 1997. "What the Assyrians Thought the Babylonians Thought about the Relative Status of Nabû and Marduk in the Late Assyrian Period." In *Assyria 1995: Proceedings of the 10th Anniversary Symposium of the Neo-Assyrian Texts Corpus Project, Helsinki, September 7–11, 1995,* ed. S. Parpola and R. M. Whiting. Helsinki: Neo-Assyrian Texts Corpus Project, 253–60.

———. 2000. "Winged Genie Fertilizing a Date Tree: Seasonal Time and Eternity in Ancient Assyria." In *Tempus Fugit: Time Flies,* ed. Jan Schall. Kansas City, MO: The Nelson-Atkins Museum of Art, 213–18.

———. 2002. "Beds, Sex, and Politics: The Return of Marduk's Bed to Babylon." In *Sex and Gender in the Ancient Near East. Proceedings of the 47th Rencontre Assryiologique Internationale, Helsinki, July 2–6, 2001,* ed. S. Parpola and R. M. Whiting. Helsinki: Neo-Assyrian Texts Corpus Project, 523–35.

———. 2003. *Trees, Kings, and Politics: Studies in Assyrian Iconography.* Orbis Biblicus et Orientalis, 197. Fribourg/Göttingen: Academic Press/Vandenhoeck and Ruprecht.

Porton, Bezalel. 1968. *Archives from Elephantine.* Berkeley: University of California Press.

Pritchard, James B. 1969. *Ancient Near Eastern Texts Relating to the Old Testament.* 3rd ed. Princeton: Princeton University Press.

Purcell, Sarah J. 2002. *Sealed with Blood: War, Sacrifice, and Memory in Revolutionary America.* Philadelphia: University of Pennsylvania Press.

Qin Heping. 2003. "Miandian Dongbei Biandi Dupin Dui Zhongguo de Weihai" (The northeastern Burma border drug threat towards China). In *Xinan bianjiang minzu yanjiu* (Studies on southwestern border ethnic groups), ed. Fang Tie. Vol. III. Kunming: Yunnan Daxue Chubanshe, 196–216.

Qinding Pingding Huifei Fanglüe. 1896. (Imperially commissioned record of the campaign to pacify the Hui rebels), comp. Yixin.

Rajneesh, Bhagwan Shree. 1983. *An introduction to Bhagwwan Shree Rajneesh and His Religion.* Rajneeshpuram, OR: Ma Anand Sheela, Rajneesh Foundation International.

Rammstedt, Otthein. 1966. *Sekte und soziale Bewegung: Soziologische Analyse der Täufer in Münster (1534/35).* Dortmunder Schriften zur Sozialforschung, XXXIV. Köln and Opladen: Westdeutscher Verlag.

Rath, Richard Cullen. 2003. *How Early America Sounded.* Ithaca, NY: Cornell University Press.

Reade, Julian. 1979. "Ideology and Propaganda in Assyrian Art." In *Power and Propaganda: A Symposium on Ancient Empires,* ed. Mogens Trolle Larsen. Mesopotamia, 7. Copenhagen: Akademisk Forlag, 329–43.

———. 1999. *Assyrian Sculpture.* Cambridge, MA: Harvard University Press.

———. 2005. "Religious Ritual in Assyrian Sculpture." In *Ritual and Politics in Ancient Mesopotamia,* ed. Barbara Nevling Porter. American Oriental Series, 88. New Haven, CT: American Oriental Society, 7–61.

Reardon-Anderson, James. 2005. *Reluctant Pioneers: China's Expansion Northward, 1644–1937*. Palo Alto, CA: Stanford University Press.

Regan, G. 2001. *First Crusader. Byzantium's Holy Wars*. London.

Reinink, G. J., and B. H. Stolte, eds. 2002. *The Reign of Heraclius (610–641): Crisis and Confrontation*. Groningen Studies in Cultural Change 2. Leuven.

Reis, Elizabeth. 1997. *Damned Women: Sinners and Witches in Puritan New England*. Ithaca, NY: Cornell University Press.

Reynolds, Craig J. 1973. The Buddhist Monkhood in Nineteenth Century Thailand. Unpublished Ph.D. thesis, Cornell University.

———. 1976. "Buddhist Cosmography in Thai History, with Special Reference to Nineteenth-Century Culture Change." *Journal of Asian Studies* 35.2:203–220.

Reynolds, Frank. 1972. "The Two Wheels of Dhamma: A Study of Early Buddhism." In *The Two Wheels of Dhamma: Essays on the Theravada Tradition in India and Ceylon*, ed. Bardwell L. Smith. Chambersburg, PA: American Academy of Religion, AAR Studies in Religion, 3, 6–30.

Reynolds, Frank E., and Regina T. Clifford. 1987. "Theravāda." Vol. 14 in *The Encyclopedia of Religion*, ed. Mircea Eliade. New York: Collier Macmillan Publishers, 469–79.

Richardson, J. S. 1975. "The Triumph, the Praetors and the Senate in the Early Second Century B.C." *Journal of Roman Studies* 65:50–63.

Richardson, L., Jr. 1992. *A New Topographical Dictionary of Ancient Rome*. Baltimore: Johns Hopkins University Press.

Richey, Russell E., and Donald G. Jones, eds. 1974. *American Civil Religion*. New York: Harper and Row.

Robbins, Thomas, and Dick Anthony. 1995. "Sects and Violence: Factors Enhancing the Volatility of Marginal Religious Movements." In *Armageddon in Waco*, ed. Stuart Wright. Chicago: University of Chicago Press, 236–59.

Roberts, Michael, ed. 1995. *Exploring Confrontations: Sri Lanka, Politics, History and Culture*. New York: Gordon and Breach Science Publishers.

———. 1997. "For Humanity. For the Sinhalese. Dharmapala as Crusading Bosat." *The Journal of Asian Studies* 56.4:1006–32.

Robins, Gay. 1997. *The Art of Ancient Egypt*. Cambridge, MA: Harvard University Press.

Rocher, Emile. 1879. *La Province Chinoise du Yün-nan*. 2 vols. Paris: Libraire de la Société Asiatique.

Rossabi, Morris. 2004. Introduction. In *Governing China's Multiethnic Frontiers*, ed. Morris Rossabi. Seattle: University of Washington Press.

Round, Philip H. 1999. *By Nature and by Custom Cursed: Transatlantic Civil Discourse and New England Cultural Production, 1620–1660*. Hanover, NH: University Press of New England.

Rubin, Julius. 2002. *The Other Side of Joy*. New York: Oxford University Press.

Runciman, S. 1929. *The Emperor Romanus Lecapenus and His Reign*. Cambridge: Cambridge University Press.

———. 1951. *A History of the Crusades, I. The First Crusade*. Cambridge: Cambridge University Press.

Rüpke, Jörg, and Vasilios Makrides, eds. 2005. *Religion(en) in Konflikt. Vom Bürgerkrieg über Ökogewalt bis zur Gewalterinnerung im Ritual*. Münster: Aschendorf.

Russell, Diana, and Roberta Harmes, eds. 2001. *Femicide in Global Perspective.* New York: Teachers College Press.

Russell, John Malcolm. 1998. "The Program of the Palace of Assurnasirpal II at Nimrud: Issues in the Research and Presentation of Assyrian Art." *American Journal of Archaeology* 102:655–715.

———. 1998. *The Final Sack of Nineveh: The Discovery, Documentation, and Destruction of King Sennacherib's Throne Room at Nineveh.* New Haven/London: Yale University Press.

Ryberg, I. S. 1955. *Rites of the State Religion in Roman Art.* Rome: American Academy in Rome.

Sarkisyanz, E. [Manuel]. 1965. *Buddhist Backgrounds of the Burmese Revolution.* The Hague: Martinus Nijhoff.

Sauer, Eberhard. 2003. *The Archaeology of Religious Hatred in the Roman and Early Medieval World.* Gloucestershire, UK: Tempus.

Schaudig, Hanspeter. 2001. *Die Inschriften Nabonids von Babylon und Kyros' des Großen samt den in ihrem Umfeld entstandenen Tendenzschriften.* Münster: Ugarit-Verlag.

Schluchter, Wolfgang. 1981. *The Rise of Western Rationalism: Max Weber's Developmental History.* Trans. Guenther Roth. Berkeley and Los Angeles: University of California Press.

Schmidt, Leigh Eric. 2000. *Hearing Things: Religion, Illusion, and the American Enlightenment.* Cambridge, MA: Harvard University Press.

Schober, Julianne. 1997. "Buddhist Just Rule and Burmese National Culture: State Patronage of the Chinese Tooth Relic in Myanmar. *History of Religions* 36.3:218–43.

Schopen, Gregory. 1997. *Bones, Stones, and Buddhist Monks: Collected Papers on the Archaeology, Epigraphy, and Texts of Monastic Buddhism in India.* Honolulu: University of Hawai'i Press.

———. 2004. *Buddhist Monks and Business Matters: Still More Papers on Monastic Buddhism in India.* Honolulu: University of Hawai'i Press.

Schreiber, Stefan. 2000. *Gesalbter und Konig: Titel und Konzeptionen der koniglichen Gesalbtenerwartung in fruhjudischen und urchristlichen Schriftgen.* Berlin: Walter de Gruyter.

Schulman, Alan R. 1995. "Military Organization in Pharaonic Egypt." In *Civilizations of the Ancient Near East,* ed. Jack M. Sasson. New York: Scribner, 289–301.

Schwartz, Regina M. 1997. *The Curse of Cain: The Violent Legacy of Monotheism.* Chicago: University of Chicago Press.

Schwartz, Seth. 2002. *Imperialism and Jewish Society 200 B.C.E. to 640 C.E.* Princeton: Princeton University Press.

Scott, Tom. 1979. "The German Peasants' War: A Historiographical Review: Part One." *The Historical Journal* 22, 3:693–720.

Seneviratne, H. L. 1978. "Religion and Legitimacy of Power in the Kandyan Kingdom." In *Religion and the Legitimation of Power in Sri Lanka,* ed. Bardwell L. Smith. Chambersburg, PA: Anima, 177–87.

———. 1999. *The Work of Kings: The New Buddhism in Sri Lanka.* Chicago: University of Chicago Press.

Shamsieva, Saodat. 1963. "Na sluzhbe delu partii." *Probuzhdennye velikim Oktiabrem,* ed. I. Finkel'shtein. Tashkent: Gos. Izdat, 186–93.

Shapiro, Gary. 2003. *Archaeologies of Vision: Foucault and Nietzsche on Seeing and Saying*. Chicago: University of Chicago Press.

Silver, Abba Hillel. [1927] 1978. *A History of Messianic Speculation in Israel: From the First through the Seventeenth Centuries*. Reprint. Gloucester, MA.

Simcox, Carroll E. 1937. "The Role of Cyrus in Deutero-Isaiah." *Journal of the American Oriental Society* 57:158–71.

Sirisena, W. M. 1978. *Sri Lanka and South-East Asia: Political, Religious and Cultural Relations from A.D. c. 1000 to c. 1500*. Leiden: E. J. Brill.

Skidmore, Monique. 1996. "In the Shade of the Bodhi Tree: Dhammayietra and the Re-Awakening of Community in Cambodia." *Crossroads* 10.1:1–32.

Skilbeck, Rod. 1995. "The Shroud over Algeria: Femicide, Islamism and the Hijab." *Journal of Arabic, Islamic and Middle Eastern Studies* 2, 2:43–54.

Skylitzes, John. 1973. *Synopsis historion*. Ed. J. Thurn. CFHB 5. Berlin and New York.

Slotkin, Richard. [1973] 2000. *Regeneration through Violence: The Mythology of the American Frontier, 1600–1860*. 2nd ed. Norman: University of Oklahoma Press.

Smart, Ninian. 1969. *The Religious Experience of Mankind*. New York: Charles Scribner's Sons.

Smit, J. W. 1970. "The Netherlands Revolution." In *Preconditions of Revolution in Early Modern Europe*, eds. Robert Forster and Jack P. Greene. Baltimore: Johns Hopkins University Press.

Smith, Bardwell L. 1972. "The Ideal Social Order as Portrayed in the Chronicles in Ceylon." In *The Two Wheels of Dhamma*, ed. Bardwell L. Smith. Chambersburg, PA: American Academy of Religion, AAR Studies in Religion, 3, 31–57.

Smith, Christian. 1998. *American Evangelicalism: Embattled and Thriving*. Chicago: University of Chicago Press.

———. 2000. *Christian America: What Evangelicals Really Want*. Berkeley and Los Angeles: University of California Press.

———. 2003. *Moral, Believing Animals: Human Personhood and Culture*. Oxford: Oxford University Press.

Smith, Donald Eugene. 1965. *Religion and Politics in Burma*. Princeton: Princeton University Press.

Smith, Jonathan Z. 1978. *Map Is Not Territory*. Chicago and London: University of Chicago Press.

———. 1990. *Drudgery Divine: On the Comparison of Early Christianities and the Religions of Late Antiquity*. Chicago: University of Chicago Press.

Smith, Morton. 1963. "II Isaiah and the Persians." *Journal of the American Oriental Society* 83: 415–21.

Smith-Rosenberg, Carroll. 1985. *Disorderly Conduct: Visions of Gender in Victorian America*. New York: Alfred A. Knopf.

Société des Missions-Étrangères de Paris (Paris society of foreign missions). n.d. Archives of the Société des Missions-Étrangères de Paris. Paris.

Soden, Wolfram von. 1983. "Kyros und Nabonid. Propaganda und Gegenpropaganda." In *Kunst, Kultur und Geschichte der Achamenidenzeit und ihr Fortleben*, ed. Heidemarie Koch and D. N. MacKenzie. Berlin: Dietrich Reimer, 61–68.

Solieva, Zulhumor. 1988. "Saodatli zamonlarda yashaimiz." *Saodat* (Toshkent) 11:20–22.

Solomon, Robert L. 1969. *Saya San and the Burmese Rebellion*. Santa Monica, CA: Rand Corporation, Rand Corporation Papers P-4004.

Somboon Suksamran. 1982. *Buddhism and Politics in Thailand*. Singapore: Institute of Southeast Asian Studies.

Sommerfeld, Walter. 1982. *Der Aufstieg Marduks: Die Stellung Marduks in der babylonischen Religion des zweiten Jahrtausends v. Chr.* AOAT, 213. Kevelaer: Neukirchen-Vluyn.

Sonbol, Amira. 1996. "Adults and Minors in Ottoman Shari`a Courts and Modern Law." In *Women, the Family, and Divorce Laws in Islamic History*, ed. Amira Sonbol. Syracuse, NY: Syracuse University Press.

———. 2003. *Women of Jordan: Islam, Labor and the Law.* Syracuse, NY: Syracuse University Press.

Spain, Alexander S. 1977. "Heraclius, Byzantine Imperial Ideology, and the David Plates." *Speculum* 52:217–37.

Spiro, M. E. 1970. *Buddhism and Society: A Great Tradition and Its Burmese Vicissitudes*. New York: Harper and Row.

Spong, John Shelby. 1991. *Rescuing the Bible from Fundamentalism*. New York: HarperCollins Publishers.

Stacey, Robert C. 1998. "From Ritual Crucifixion to Host Desecration: Jews and the Body of Christ." *Jewish History* 12/1:11–28.

Stanley, Brian. 1990. *The Bible and the Flag: Protestant Missions and British Imperialism in the Nineteenth and Twentieth Centuries*. Leicester, UK: Apollos.

Stark, Rodney. 1996. "Why Religious Movements Succeed or Fail: A Revised General Model." *Journal of Contemporary Religion* 11:133–46.

———. 2001. *One True God: Historical Consequences of Monotheism*. Princeton: Princeton University Press.

Stark, Rodney, and Roger Finke. 2000. *Acts of Faith: Explaining the Human Side of Religion*. Berkeley and Los Angeles: University of California Press.

Stayer, James. 1972. *Anabaptists and the Sword*. Lawrence, KS: Coronado Press.

———. 1988. "Christianity in One City: Anabaptist Münster, 1534–35." In *Radical Tendencies in the Reformation: Divergent Perspectives*, ed. Hans J. Hillerbrand. Volume IX of the Sixteenth Century Essays and Studies Series. Kirksville, MO: Sixteenth Century Journal Publishers, Inc., 117–34.

———. 1991/1992. *The German Peasants' War and the Anabaptist Community of Goods*. Montreal: McGill–Queen's University Press.

Stayer, James, Werner Packull, and Klaus Deppermann. 1975. "From Monogenesis to Polygenesis: The Historical Discussion of Anabaptist Origins." *The Mennonite Quarterly Review* 49:83–121.

Steelwater, Eliza. 2003. *The Hangman's Knot: Lynching, Legal Execution, and America's Struggle with the Death Penalty*. Boulder: Westview Press.

Stone, Michael. 1981. "Reactions to Destruction of the Second Temple." *Journal for the Study of Judaism* 12:195–204.

Strickland, Debra Higgs. 2003. *Saracens, Demons, and Jews: Making Monsters in Medieval Art*. Princeton: Princeton University Press.

Strong, John S. 1984. *The Legend of King Aśoka: A Study and Translation of the Aśokāvadāna*. Princeton: Princeton University Press.

————. 2004. *Relics of the Buddha*. Princeton: Princeton University Press.

Stroup, S. C. 2004. "Rituals of Ink?" In *Rituals in Ink. A Conference on Religion and Literary Production in Ancient Rome*, ed. Barchiesi, Rüpke, and Stephens. Franz Steiner Verlag, 141–47.

Sulak Sivaraksa. 1990. "Building Trust Through Economic and Social Development and Ecological Balance: A Buddhist Perspective." In *Radical Conservatism: Buddhism in the Contemporary World—Articles in Honour of Bhikkhu Buddhadasa's 84th Birthday Anniversary*, comp. Thai Inter-Religious Commission for Development and International Network of Engaged Buddhists. Bangkok: The Sathirakoses-Nagapradipa Foundation, 179–98.

————, ed. 1999. *Socially Engaged Buddhism for the New Millennium: Essays in Honor of the Ven. Phra Dhammapitaka (Bhikkhu P.A. Payutto) on his 60th Birthday Anniversary*. Bangkok: Sathira-Nagapradipa Foundation and Foundation for Children.

Sumedho, Bhikkhu. 1999. "Forest Tradition as a Challenge to the Modern World." In *Socially Engaged Buddhism for the New Millennium: Essays in Honor of the Ven. Phra Dhammapitaka (Bhikkhu P.A. Payutto) on his 60th Birthday Anniversary*, ed. Sulak Sivaraksa. Bangkok: Sathira-Nagapradipa Foundation and Foundation for Children, 470–82.

Sunait Chutintharanond. 1997. "King Bayinnaung as Historical Hero in Thai Perspective." In *Comparative Studies on Literature and History of Thailand and Myanmar*. Bangkok: Chulalongkorn University, 9–16.

Swearer, Donald K. 1973. "Thai Buddhism: Two Responses to Modernity." *Contributions to Asian Studies* 4:78–93.

————. 1991. "Fundamentalist Movements in Theravada Buddhism." In *Fundamentalisms Observed*, ed. Martin E. Marty and R. Scott Appleby. The Fundamentalism Project, vol. 1. Chicago: University of Chicago Press.

————. 1992. "Exemplars of Nonviolence in Theravada Buddhism." In *Inner Peace, World Peace: Essays on Buddhism and Nonviolence*, ed. Kenneth Kraft. Albany: State University of New York Press, 63–76.

————. 1995. *The Buddhist World of Southeast Asia*. Albany: State University of New York Press.

Tadmor, Hayim. 1965. "The Inscriptions of Nabonaid: Historical Arrangement." In *Studies in Honor of Benno Landsberger*. Chicago: University of Chicago Press, 351–63.

————. 1997. "Propaganda, Literature, Historiography: Cracking the Code of the Assyrian Royal Inscriptions." In *Assyria 1995: Proceedings of the 10th Anniversary Symposium of the Neo-Assyrian Texts Corpus Project, Helsinki, September 7–11, 1995*, ed. S. Parpola and R. M. Whiting. Helsinki: Neo-Assyrian Texts Corpus Project, 325–38.

————. 1999. "World Dominion: The Expanding Horizon of the Assyrian Empire." In *Landscapes: Territories, Frontiers, and Horizons in the Ancient Near East: Papers Presented to the XLIV Rencontre Assyriologique Internationale, Venezia, 7–11 July 1997*, ed. L. Milano et al. History of the Ancient Near East Monographs, III/1. Padova: Sargon, 55–62.

Taft, R. 1995. "War and Peace in the Byzantine Divine Liturgy." In *Peace and War in Byzantium. Essays in Honor of George T. Dennis, S. J.*, ed. T. S. Miller and J. Nesbitt. Washington, D.C. : Catholic University of America Press, 17–32.

Tambiah, S. J. 1976. *World Conqueror and World Renouncer: A Study of Buddhism and Polity in Thailand against a Historical Background.* Cambridge: Cambridge University Press.

———. 1984. *The Buddhist Saints of the Forest and the Cult of Amulets.* Cambridge Studies in Social Anthropology, 49. Cambridge: Cambridge University Press.

———. 1986. *Sri Lanka: Fratricide and the Dismantling of Democracy.* Chicago: University of Chicago Press.

———. 1993. "Buddhism, Politics, and Violence in Sri Lanka." In *Fundamentalisms and the State: Remaking Polities, Economies, and Militance,* ed. Martin E. Marty and R. Scott Appleby. The Fundamentalism Project, vol. 3. Chicago: University of Chicago Press, 589–619.

Taves, Ann, ed. 1989. *Religion and Domestic Violence in Early New England: The Memoirs of Abigail Abbot Bailey.* Bloomington: Indiana University Press.

Taylor, J. L. 1991. "Living on the Rim: Ecology and Forest Monks in Northeast Thailand." *Sojourn* 6.1:106–25.

———. 1993. *Forest Monks and the Nation-State: An Anthropological and Historical Study in Northeastern Thailand.* Singapore: Institute of Southeast Asian Studies.

———. 1996. "Thamma-chaat: Activist Monks and Competing Discourses of Nature and Nation in Northeastern Thailand." In *Seeing Forests for Trees: Environment and Environmentalism in Thailand,* ed. Philip Hirsch. Chiang Mai, Thailand: Silkworm Books, 37–52.

Taylor, Robert H. 1986. "Burmese Conceptions of Revolution." In *Context, Meaning, and Power in Southeast Asia,* ed. Mark Hobart and Robert H. Taylor. Ithaca, NY: Cornell University Southeast Asia Program, Studies on Southeast Asia, 79–92.

———. 1988. *The State in Burma.* Honolulu: University of Hawai'i Press.

Teeter, Emily. 1997. *The Presentation of Maat: Ritual and Legitimacy in Ancient Egypt.* Chicago: Oriental Institute of the University of Chicago.

Thai Inter-Religious Commission for Development and International Network of Engaged Buddhists, comp. 1990. *Radical Conservatism: Buddhism in the Contemporary World—Articles in Honour of Bhikkhu Buddhadasa's 84th Birthday Anniversary.* Bangkok: The Sathirakoses-Nagapradipa Foundation.

Theophanes. 1883. *Chronographia.* Ed. C. de Boor. Bonn.

———. 1998. *The Chronicle of Theophanes Confessor. Byzantine and Near Eastern History, AD 284–813 (Chronographia).* Trans. C. Mango and R. Scott. Oxford: Clarendon Press.

Theophylacti Simocattae Historiae. 1887. Ed. C. de Boor. Leipzig.

Thierry, N. 1981. "Le culte de la croix dans l'empire byzantin du VIIe siècle au Xe dans ses rapports avec guerre contre l'infidèle. Nouveaux témoignages archéologiques." *Rivista di studi bizantini e slavi* 1:205–28.

Thongchai Winichakul. 2002. "Remembering/Silencing the Traumatic Past: The Ambivalent Memories of the October 1976 Massacre in Bangkok." In *Cultural Crisis and Social Memory: Modernity and Identity in Thailand and Laos.* Richmond, Surrey, UK: Routledge Curzon, 243–83.

Tibi, Amin. 1991. "Byzantine-Fatimid Relations in the Reign of al-Mu'izz li-Din Allah (r. 953–75 AD) as Reflected in Primary Arabic Sources." *Graeco-Arabica* 4:91–107.

Tolles, Frederick B. 1951. *A Quaker's Curse—Humphrey Norton to John Endecott, 1658.* Reprinted from *The Huntington Library Quarterly* XIV, August. San Marino, CA: The Henry E. Huntington Library and Art Gallery.

Turshen, Meredith. 2002. "Algerian Women in the Liberation Struggle and the Civil War: From Active Participants to Passive Victims?" *Social Research* 69 (3):889–911.

Tylor, Edward Burnett. [1871] 1958. *Religion in Primitive Culture.* New York: Harper and Brothers.

U Kyaw Win. 1997. "King Bayinnaung as Historical Hero in Myanmar Perspective." In *Comparative Studies on Literature and History of Thailand and Myanmar.* Bangkok: Chulalongkorn University, 1–8.

Versnel, H. 1970. *Triumphus. An Inquiry into the Origin, Development and Meaning of the Roman Triumph.* Leiden: Brill.

Viellefond, J. 1935. "Les pratiques religieuses dans l'armée byzantine d'après les traités militaires." *Revue des études anciennes* 37:322–30.

Villard, Pierre. 1999. "Les limites du monde connu à l'époque néo-assyrienne." In *Landscapes: Territories, Frontiers, and Horizons in the Ancient Near East: Papers Presented to the XLIV Rencontre Assyriologique Internationale, Venezia, 7–11 July 1997,* ed. L. Milano et al. History of the Ancient Near East Monographs, III/2. Padova: Sargon, 73–81.

Viscuso, P. 1995. "Christian Participation in Warfare. A Byzantine View." In *Peace and War in Byzantium. Essays in Honor of George T. Dennis, S. J.,* ed. T. S. Miller and J. Nesbitt. Washington, D.C. : Catholic University of America Press, 33–40.

Vogler, Günter. 1988. "The Anabaptist Kingdom of Münster in the Tension Between Anabaptism and Imperial Policy." In *Radical Tendencies in the Reformation: Divergent Perspectives,* ed. Hans J. Hillerbrand. Volume IX of the Sixteenth Century Essays and Studies Series. Kirksville, MO: Sixteenth Century Journal Publishers, Inc., 99–116.

Wade, Geoff. 2004. "The Zheng He Voyages: A Reassessment." ARI Working Paper, No. 31, October. www.nus.ari.edu.sg/pub/wps.htm.

Wagenvoort, H. [1941] 1947. *Imperium. Studiën over het "Mana"-begrip in Zede en Taal der Tomeinen.* Amersterdam. 2nd ed., *Roman Dynamism.* Oxford: Oxford University Press.

Waite, Gary. 1992. "The Dutch Nobility and Anabaptism, 1535–1545." *Sixteenth Century Journal* 23, 3:458–85.

Waite, Gary K. 1988. "David Joris' Thought in the Context of the Early Melchiorite and Münsterite Movements in the Low Countries, 1534–1536." *The Mennonite Quarterly Review* 62 (July): 296–317.

Walker, P. E. 1977. "The 'Crusade' of John Tzimisces in the Light of New Arabic Evidence." *Byzantion* 47:301–27.

Wallace-Hadrill, A. 1990. "Roman Arches and Greek Honors: The Language of Power at Rome." *PCPS* 36:143–81.

Wallis, Roy. 1976. *The Road to Total Freedom.* New York: Columbia University Press.

Wang Dingchen. 1953. "Qing Xiantongjian Yunnan Huibian Jiwen" (Chronicle of the Xianfeng-Tongzhi era Hui uprising in Yunnan). In *Huimin qiyi* (Hui rebellions), ed. Bai Shouyi. Shanghai: Zhongguo shenzhou guogang chubanshu, II, 297–306.

Ward, W. R. 1992. *The Protestant Evangelical Awakening*. Cambridge: Cambridge University Press.

Warren, L. B. 1970. "Roman Triumphs and Etruscan Kings: The Changing Face of the Triumph." *JRS* 60:62–64.

Warren, Rick. 1991. "When Is It Right to Fight." Sermon preached in March 1991; it can be found at http://www.cbn.com/spirituallife/inspirationalteaching/Warren_RighttoFighta.asp.

———. 1995. *The Purpose Driven Church*. Grand Rapids, MI: Zondervan Publishing House.

———. 2002. *The Purpose Driven Life*. Grand Rapids, MI: Zondervan Publishing House.

———. 2004. "Honor God with Your V-O-T-E." Retrieved October 21, 2004, from http://www.saddlebackfamily.com/home/todaystory.asp?id=692.

Waschke, Ernst-Joachim. 2001. *Der Gesalbte: Studien zur alttestamentlichen Theologie*. Berlin: Walter de Gruyter.

Watanabe, Ch. E. 1998. "Symbolism of the Royal Lion Hunt in Assyria." In *Intellectual Life in the Ancient Near East: Papers Presented at the 43rd Rencontre Assyriologique Internationale, Prague, July 1–5, 1996*, ed. Jiri Prosecky. Prague: Academy of Sciences of the Czech Republic, Oriental Institute, 439–50.

Weber, Max. 1958. *The Protestant Ethic and the Spirit of Capitalism*. Trans. Talcott Parsons. New York: Scribners.

Weissert, E. 1997. "Royal Hunt and Royal Triumph in a Prism Fragment of Ashurbanipal." In *Assyria 1995: Proceedings of the 10th Anniversary Symposium of the Neo-Assyrian Texts Corpus Project, Helsinki, September 7–11, 1995*, ed. S. Parpola and R. M. Whiting. Helsinki: Neo-Assyrian Texts Corpus Project, 339–58.

Welbon, Guy Richard. 1968. *The Buddhist Nirvāṇa and Its Western Interpreters*. Chicago: University of Chicago Press.

Wellman, James K., Jr. 2002. "Religion without a Net: Strictness in the Religious Practices of West Coast Urban Liberal Christian Congregations." *Review of Religious Research* 44, 2:184–99.

———. 2004. "The Churching of the Pacific Northwest: The Rise of Sectarian Entrepreneurs." In *Religion and Public Culture in the Pacific Northwest: The "None" Zone*, ed. Patricia O'Connell Killen and Mark Silk. Religion by Region Series. Walnut Creek, CA: AltaMira Press.

———. Forthcoming. *Evangelical vs. Liberal: The Clash of Christian Cultures in the Pacific Northwest*. Oxford: Oxford University Press.

Wellman, James K., Jr., and Kyoko Tokuno. 2004. "Is Religious Violence Inevitable?" *Journal for the Scientific Study of Religion* 43, 3:291–96.

Westenholz, Joan. 2000. "The King, the Emperor, and the Empire: Continuity and Discontinuity of Royal Representation in Text and Image." In *The Heirs of Assyria: Proceedings of the Opening Symposium of the Assyrian and Babylonian Intellectual Heritage Project Held in Tvärminne, Finland, October 8–11, 1998*, ed. Sanno Aro and R. M. Whiting. Melammu Symposia I. Helsinki: Neo-Assyrian Texts Corpus Project, 99–125.

Whitby, Mary. 2002a. "A New Image for a New Age: George of Pisidia on the Emperor Heraclius." In *The Reign of Heraclius (610–641): Crisis and Confrontation*, ed.

G. J. Reinink and B. H. Stolte. Groningen Studies in Cultural Change 2. Leuven: Peeters, 197–225.

———. 2002b. "George of Pisidia's Presentation of the Reign of Heraclius and His Campaigns: Variety and Development." In *The Reign of Heraclius (610–641): Crisis and Confrontation*, ed. G. J. Reinink and B. H. Stolte. Groningen Studies in Cultural Change 2. Leuven: Peeters, 157–73.

Wiggermann, Franz A. M. 1992. *Mesopotamian Protective Spirits: The Ritual Texts.* Cuneiform Monographs, 1. Gronigen: Styx.

———. 2002. "L'iconographie de la magie mésopotamienne." In *La magie en Égypte: à la recherché d'une definition. Actes du colloque organize par le musée du Louvre les 29 et 30 septembre 2000.* Paris: Française-musée du Louvre, 373–96.

Wilcox, Clyde. 2000. *Onward Christian Soldiers? The Religious Right in American Politics.* Boulder: Westview Press.

Wilkinson, J. Gardiner. 1994 (1836). *The Ancient Egyptians: Their Life and Customs.* Vol. 1. London: Senate.

Williams, James W., ed. 2000. *The Girard Reader.* New York: Crossroad.

Williams, Linda. 1989. *Hard Core: Power, Pleasure, and the "Frenzy of the Visible."* Berkeley: University of California Press.

Wilson, Constance M. 1971. State and Society in the Reign of Mongkut, 1851–1868: Thailand on the Eve of Modernization. Unpublished Ph.D. dissertation.

———. 1997. "The Holy Man in the History of Thailand and Laos." *Journal of Southeast Asian Studies* 28.2:345–64.

Winter, I. J. 1983. "The Program of the Throne Room of Assurnasirpal II." In *Essays on Near Eastern Art and Archaeology in Honor of Charles Kyrle Wilkinson*, ed. P. O. Harper and H. Pittman. New York: Metropolitan Museum of Art, 15–31.

———. 1993. "'Seat of Kingship'/ 'A Wonder to Behold': The Palace in the Ancient Near East." *Ars Orientalis* 23:27–55.

———. 1995. "Asetheics in Ancient Mesopotamian Art." In *Civilizations of the Ancient Near East*, ed. Jack M. Sasson. New York: Scribner, 2569–80.

———. 1997. "Art in Empire: The Royal Image and the Visual Dimensions of Assyrian Ideology." In *Assyria 1995: Proceedings of the 10th Anniversary Symposium of the Neo-Assyrian Texts Corpus Project, Helsinki, September 7–11, 1995*, ed. S. Parpola and R. M. Whiting. Helsinki: Neo-Assyrian Texts Corpus Project, 359–81.

———. 2000. "*Le Palais imaginaire*: Scale and Meaning in the Iconography of Neo-Assyrian Cylinder Seals." In *Images and Media: Sources for the Cultural History of the Near East and the Eastern Mediterranean (1st Millennium BCE)*, ed. Christoph Uehlinger. Fribourg: University Press, 51–87.

Wiseman, D. J. 1983. "Mesopotamian Gardens." *Anatolian Studies* 33:135–44.

———. 1984. "Palace and Temple Gardens in the Ancient Near East." In *Monarchies and Socio-Religious Traditions in the Ancient Near East: Papers Read at the 31st International Congress of Human Sciences in Asia and North Africa*, ed. H. I. H. Prince Takahito Micasa. Weisbaden: Harrassowitz, 37–43.

Worrall, Arthur J. 1980. *Quakers in the Colonial Northeast.* Hanover, NH: University Press of New England.

Wright, Mary C. 1957. *The Last Stand of Chinese Conservatism: The T'ung-Chih Restoration, 1862–1874.* Palo Alto, CA: Stanford University Press.

Yang Shouqing and Zhao Jiaodong. 2002. *Jinwan Bao*, March 14. http://www.jwb
.com.cn/gb/content/2002-03/14/content_85580.htm (accessed March 9, 2004).

Yang Zhaozhun. 1994. *Yunnan Huizu Shi* (History of the Muslim Yunnanese). Kunming: Yunnan Minzu Chubanshe.

Yunnan Shadian Shijian Beiwen. n.d. (A memorial plaque of the Yunnan Shadian
Incident). http://www.yich.org/ReadNews.asp?NewsID=912 (accessed March
16, 2005).

Yunnan Tongzhi. 1835. (Yunnan gazetteer). Wang Song and Ruan Yuan.

Zhou Yongming. 1999. *Anti-Drug Crusades in Twentieth-Century China: Nationalism,
History and State Building*. Boulder: Rowman & Littlefield.

Zonaras, John. 1897. *Epitome historiarum*. Ed. M. Pinder and T. Büttner-Wobst. 3
vols. Bonn.

Zoroya, Gregg. 2001. "He Puts Words in Bush's Mouth." *USA Today,* 10 April.

Index

Note: Page numbers in italics indicate illustrations.

Abidhamma, 151
Abu Ghraib, 180
Achaemenian Empire, 213, 221–22
Afghanistan, 145, 183, 216
Africa, North, 51, 86
Alexander the Great (of Macedon), 48, 213
Alexandria, 49
al-Qaeda, 185, 215
Amish, 73
Anabaptism, 9, 63–67, 69–75; Dutch, 65. *See also* Amish; Mennonites
anti-trinitarianism, 65
apocalypticism, 65, 68–70, 72, 103, 173, 177, 200–201, 220
Appleby, Scott, 9, 98
Armageddon, 168, 200
Assyria, 16–18; Assur, god of, 17, 19, 21; Assurbanipal, king of, 18–20, *21*; Assurnasirpal II, king of, *17–18*; Ishtar, goddess of, 21; Marduk, god of, 19; Tiamat, god of, 19
Atta, Muhammad, 188–89
Atwill, David, 3

Austin, Anne, 100–101
Avalo, Hector, 5–9
Aztecs, 99, 107

Babylon, 16, *17*, 18, 213–14, 218; Jewish people in, 48, 50, 52; as symbolic of corruption, 220–21
Bandaranaike, S. W. R. D., 155
baptism, 64, 66–67
Baptists, Southern, 195, 205
Bar Kokhba Revolt, 49–50
Bellingham, 100–101
Berger, Michael, 2
Bhikku, Kittivuddho, 157
Big Muddy Ranch, 166, 169, 175
bin Laden, Osama, 179, 183, 186–88
Black, Joel, 3, 9
body, 15
borders: cosmological, 16, 21; crossing, 17; geographic, 16, 22
Boston, 100
Branch Davidians, 165, 167–68
Brend, William, 102
Bucer, Martin, 65

Buddhas, Bamian, 183–85, 187–90
Buddhism: and fundamentalism, 145, 151, 160; and gods, 5; millennialism, 149, 157; and modernism, 147, 149, 151–52, 159; and monarchy, 147–48; and pacifism, 10, 145, 159; "Protestant," 150–51; Theravadin, 145–49, 152, 153, 160; Tibetan, 168; and violence, 145, 148, 152, 155, 157–59; Zen, 172–73
Buddhist nationalism. *See* nationalism
Burma, 151, 153–54
Bush, George W., 200, 215–18, 220–21
Byzantium, 81–84, 86, 89

caesaropapism, 83
caliphate, 84, 86, 89, 187
Calvin, John, 64, 65
Cambodia, 156
Carrasco, Davíd, 99
Catholicism, Roman, 63–66, 70, 73
chaos as god, 23–24
Christian church, 82
Christianity: in China, 125; evangelical, 65, 195–208; and pacifism, 9, 10, 206; and violence, 196
Chulalongkorn, King, 150
Church Fathers, 82
City of Peace, 32
clergy, 82
Constantine I, 82, 87
Constantine VII, 86
Constitution of the United States: Establishment Clause, 97, 171, 176–77
Copeland, John, 103
Cyrus the Great, 213–15, 218, 220–21

Davidson, Donald, 10n3
Dawkins, Richard, 6
Den, 14
Denck, Hans, 65
Dhammayuti-nikāya, 150
Dharmapāla, Angārika, 151, 154
diaspora: Jewish, 49, 51, 58

Douglas, Mary, 14–15
Dusentscher, Johann, 68
Dyer, Mary, 104–5

ecstatic asceticism, 103
Edict of Toleration, 103
Egypt, 51, 56, 58; ancient, 13–14, 16, 21, 23; priests, 51
emperors, Holy Roman, 64, 74, 76. *See also specific names*
empiricism, 7, 8
Endecott, John, 103–4
End of Days, 54
enemy: demonization of, 16, 211–22; as "other," 16
Enuma Elish, 18, 19
eschatology, 63, 76
execration, 23
execution, 30
extremists, 98

Falun Gong, 125
femicide, 3, 131, 135, 138
First Amendment. *See* Constitution of the United States
Fisher, Mary, 100, 101
Foucault, Michel, 21
Fox, George, 100
Franck, Sebastian, 65
fundamentalism: American, 198; Christian, 168; global, 98; religious, 9, 146, 151, 168
Fundamentals, The, 198

Galilee, 49, 51
Germany, 65. *See also* Münster
Gibson, Mel, 180
Girard, René, 2, 8, 98
Goldman, Marion S., 3
Greeks, Seleucid, 48
Goertz, Jürgen, 65

Hadrian, 51, 54
Hagia Sophia, 82, 87
Hebrew Bible, 47, 218
hegemony, 66
Hellenism, 48

Herakleios, 83, 84, 85
heresy, 65, 70, 100–101, 104
Hoffman, Melchior, 63, 65, 70–72
Holder, Christopher, 103
holy land, 81
"honor killings," 3, 131–32, 137, 139

iconoclasm, 84, 181–85, 188–89
icons, 84, 182–83, 188–89; veneration
    of, 85, 183
imperium, 32, 37–38, 40–41
inquisition, religious, 65
insurrection, 63
Islam, 84, 89; in Afghanistan, 179–88;
    in China, 115, 117, 122, 125; and
    modernization, 135; in Uzbekistan,
    131
Israel, 58, 145, 216, 218, 220; "New," 72

James, William, 8
Jerusalem, 47–49, 50, 57, 84; "New," 63,
    66–67, 69, 72, 84
Jesus, 8–9, 83, 202–4, 206–7; Passion of,
    87
jihad, 89, 186
Jones, Jim, 167
Jonestown. *See* People's Temple
Josephus, 36–38, 50
Judaism: messianic, 47, 51–52, 54; and
    pacifism, 10, 47; rabbinic, 9, 55, 58
Judea, 48–49, 51, 57
Juergensmeyer, Mark, 9, 54, 179
Jupiter Feretrius, 34

Kamp, Marianne, 3
Keyes, Charles, 3
Khmer Rouge, 156–58, 160
Knipperdolling, Bernard, 66–68, 70
Krahn, Cornelius, 66, 72

"Lamb's War," 102
lansquenets, 67
laws against Quakers, 101–3, 105
Leddra, William, 106
Leo VI, 89, 91
Lincoln, Bruce, 3, 7, 14–15, 75, 126
literalism, biblical, 65

Luther, Martin, 64–65, 73
Lutheranism, 63, 65–67, 73, 76

Maccabees, 48, 51, 55
Martin, David, 1
martyrdom, 49, 50, 54, 81, 85, 88,
    90–91, 103, 189
Massachusetts Bay, 100
massacres: Baoshan, 119, 120;
    Kunming, 120–21
Matthijs, Jan, 66–68, 71
McGrath, Alister, 65
Mennonites, 73
Mesopotamia, 13–14, 16, 18–19, 23;
    king of, 17
messianism, 51, 52, 54
Miller, Perry, 100
Mindon, King, 151
modernity, 146–47
Mollenheck, Henry, 68, 70
monarchy: Davidic, 48, 55, 71, 83, 219;
    Jewish, 51
Mongkut, King, 150
Muhammad, Khalid Shaikh, 186, 188
Muhammad, the Prophet, 184;
    caricatures of, 181
Münster, 63–76
mutilation, 13

Nabonidus, 213–14
Narmer, 14
Narmer Palette, *15*
National Buddhist Front, 156
nationalism: Buddhist, 145, 150,
    154–58; Jewish, 48, 56
New Testament, 8–9, 71–72, 82, 203
Nikephoros II Phokas, 88, 89, 90
Noegel, Scott B., 2
Norton, Humphrey, 103–4
Norton, John, 108–10

Old Testament, 67, 71, 82, 181, 203
Omar, Mullah Muhammad, 183–84,
    187
order: cosmologic, 15, 22, 24; domestic,
    63; *ma`at*, 23; religious, 149; social,
    65, 73, 103, 139, 147, 149

Oregon, 165–66, 170, 173–76
Orthodox Church, 81–82
Ottama, U, 151–52
"Other," 37, 100

pacifism, 9, 10, 52, 54–55, 58, 64, 66, 72, 75–76, 177
Pahl, Jon, 2
Palestine, 47, 50, 52, 54, 86, 145, 216
Pape, Robert, 10n4
Passion of the Christ, The, 180
People's Temple, 165, 167–68, 175, 177
pharaoh, 14; as a god, 22–23. *See also* Den; Narmer
pilgrimage, 51
pluralism, 76
poisoning, 171
politics and religion, 1–2, 9, 48, 115–16, 132, 197, 199–200
Pol Pot, 156
polygamy, 68, 71
polytheism, 81
propaganda, 14
prophecy, 63, 68–71, 101
Protestantism, 64, 65. *See also* Anabaptism; Lutheranism; Reformed Protestantism
Puritanism, 97, 100–103, 106–8, 110

Quakers, 98, 100–103, 106–8. *See also* laws against Quakers

Rabbinic tradition, 47–48, 50–57
race, 7
Rahman, Sheikh Omar Abdul, 186
Rajneesh, Bhagwan Shree, 166, 169–75, 177
Rajneeshpuram, 165–67, 170–71, 173–77
rationalism, 146
rebellion: Panthay, 115, 118, 121–22; Yakub Beg, 117. *See also* revolt, Jewish
Reformation, 65; era, 64; Radical, 64
Reformed Protestantism, 64
relics, 84, 85, 87, 91, 154

religion: and belief, 7–8; and boundaries, 5, 7, 9, 136, 141, 202; civil, 197; definitions of, 3–5, 211; and experience, 7–8; and identity, 7, 115, 118, 125, 196, 202; institutionalization of, 4; and mutilation, 13; and persecution, 49; and purity, 97; and rationality, 7–8; and state, 9, 63–75, 81, 97; and survival, 6. *See also* sacrifice
religion and fundamentalism, 9, 146, 151, 168
religion and politics, 1–2, 9, 48, 115–16, 132, 197, 199–200
religion and violence, 4–10, 16, 41, 55, 63–64, 70, 74, 76, 91, 99, 116, 120, 132, 146, 157, 159, 165, 166, 168, 173, 175, 177, 179–81, 183, 186–87, 196, 212
revolt, Jewish, 50; Bar Kokhba, 49–53, 55–56; in Egypt, 49; Maccabeean, 51; of 66–70 CE, 49
Revolution, Cultural, 122–23
ritual: destruction, 23; function of, 15; violence, 18, 71–72, 98; warfare, 15
Rome, 29, 30, 49, 51; mythology, 33
Romulan prototriumph, 33–34, 40
Romulus, 33, 34
Rothmann, Bernard, 66–69, 71–72
Rouse, John, 103

sacrifice, 8–9, 15, 97–100, 103, 107–8, 110; of self, 99
sannyasin, 166–67, 169–77
Sayadaw, Ledi, 151
Scandinavia, 65
scapegoat, 8, 98, 103, 110
Second Coming, 70, 71, 72, 200, 203–8
secularism, 9, 199
separatism, 73, 198
September 11 attacks, 145, 159, 179, 182, 185–86, 196
Servetus, Michael, 65
Sheela, Ma Anand, 170, 171, 173–75, 177
sola scriptura, 65
Speyer, Second Diet of, 64

Sri Lanka, 149, 150–51, 153–55
Sri Lanka Freedom Party (SLFP), 155
Stark, Rodney, 7
St. Basil of Caesarea, 82, 88
Stephenson, Paul, 2
St. Lambert's Church, 63
Strasbourg, 65, 66
Stroup, Sarah, 2
Sufism, 119; and pacifism, 9, 10

Taliban, 184–85, 189–90
Tamil Tigers (Liberation Tigers of
    Tamil Eelam), 155
temples, Jewish: destruction of, 49, 52;
    First, 51, 52; and land, 57; Mount,
    51; Second, 47–51, 56; Third, 54
terror, 69, 70, 71
terrorism, 9, 132, 140, 155, 179, 212;
    and gender, 131–32, 134, 139;
    religious, 181, 184–85; by suicide
    bombing, 10n4, 155
Thailand, 153–54, 157; Communist
    Party of (CPT), 157–58
theocracy, 64, 65, 73
Titus, apotheosis of, 40
Torah, 48, 50–51, 55–57
triumphal arch, 39; of Titus, 39, 40–41
triumphator, 30, 37, 38
triumphus (triumph), 29–31, 38, 41;
    rhetorical, 34, 39, 41; ritual, 33–34,
    37, 39, 41

United Guild, 67
United States, 97, 100, 215
unveiling, 131–41
uprising: Pingyuan, 123–24; Shadian,
    122–24

van Leiden, Jan, 66, 68–70, 72–73
veil. *See* unveiling
violence: anti-Muslim, 115; collective,
    165–66, 168, 172–73, 176–77; and
    drug trade, 124–25; ethnic, 116–17,
    119–20, 123–24; iconoclastic, 182,
    183, 185, 189, 191; individualized,
    168; intragroup, 168; legitimized,
    54, 214; Muslim, 121, 126, 132–33,
    137–38, 179–91, 201–2; political, 134,
    145, 154, 179, 180, 196–97; potential,
    32, 165, 167; ritual, 13, 31, 99, 100,
    181; sacred, 180; and sacred texts,
    50; transformation of, 31, 41, 54–55,
    141; and women, 16, 131–39, 141.
    See also religion and violence
von Kerssenbrock, Hermann, 67
von Waldeck, Prince-Bishop Franz, 63,
    66–67, 74

war: holy, 13–14, 17, 23, 24n1, 81,
    83–84, 89–91, 154, 180; in Iraq,
    195–97, 205, 221; just, 81, 205;
    morality of, 82; religious, 154; as
    ritual, 15, 17; sacred, 84, 86; "on
    terror," 180
Warren, Rick, 205–7
Weber, Max, 146
Winthrop, John, 100–101
World Trade Center, 186–90

Yousef, Ramzi, 186, 188

zealots, 54, 74, 154, 184
Zheng He, Admiral, 116
Zion, 56–57; "New," 68, 71
Zoroastrianism, 84

About the Contributors

David G. Atwill is assistant professor of history at Pennsylvania State University. He specializes in ethnicity, borderlands, and Islam in late imperial China. His book *The Chinese Sultanate: Islam, Ethnicity and the Panthay Rebellion in Southwest China, 1856–1873* addresses the complex interethnic and transnational relations of the Hui Muslims in southwest China during the nineteenth century.

Michael S. Berger is associate professor of religious authority and law in Judaism at Emory University's Department of Religion. He writes and lectures on religious authority, medieval and modern Jewish thought, and contemporary Judaism. He published *Rabbinic Authority* (1998) and brought to publication *The Emergence of Ethical Man* (2004), the manuscripts of the late Jewish thinker, Joseph Soloveitchik.

Joel Black is professor of comparative literature at the University of Georgia. He is the author of *The Aesthetics of Murder: A Study of Romantic Literature and Contemporary Culture* (1991) and *The Reality Effect: Film Culture and the Graphic Imperative* (2002), as well as numerous articles.

Marion S. Goldman is professor of sociology and religious studies at the University of Oregon. Her books on alternative religions include *Passionate Journeys: Why Successful Women Joined a Cult* and an edited volume with Mary Jo Neitz, *Sex, Lies, and Sanctity*. She has published articles on Jesus People, Rajneeshees, and the New Left. Her current research focuses on Esalen Institute.

Marianne Kamp is associate professor of history at the University of Wyoming. A specialist on modern Central Asia, she is the author of the book *The New Woman in Uzbekistan: Islam, Modernity, and Unveiling under Communism* (2006), and recent articles including "Between Women and the State: Mahalla Committees and Social Welfare in Uzbekistan," in *The Transformation of Central Asia;* "Three Lives of Saodat: Communist, Uzbek, Survivor," in *Oral History Review;* and "A Structuralist Argument Concerning the Consolidation of Uzbek Identity," in *Ab Imperio*. Kamp has received grants from NCEEER, the Library of Congress, and IREX. Her current research examines the history of agricultural collectivization in Uzbekistan through oral history.

Charles F. Keyes is professor of anthropology and international studies at the University of Washington. He has carried out extensive research in and about Thailand, Vietnam, Laos, and Cambodia. His most recent work includes *On the Margins of Asia: Perspectives on Asia—Sixty Years of the* Journal of Asian Studies (edited, 2006); *Cultural Crisis and Social Memory: Modernity and Identity in Thailand and Laos* (edited with Shigeharu Tanabe, 2002); "Weber and Anthropology," *Annual Reviews in Anthropology* (2002); and "'The Peoples of Asia': Science and Politics in Ethnic Classification in Thailand, China and Vietnam," *Journal of Asian Studies* (2002). He is the past president of the Association for Asian Studies and a recipient in 2004 of an honorary Ph.D. from Mahasarakham University in Thailand.

Bruce Lincoln is the Caroline E. Haskell Professor of History of Religions at the University of Chicago, with joint appointments in classics, medieval studies, and Middle Eastern studies.

Charles A. McDaniel, Jr., is a visiting assistant professor in the J. M. Dawson Institute of Church-State Studies at Baylor University. His research interests include church and state in the Protestant Reformation, twentieth-century Christian social thought, and, more recently, political movements in contemporary Islamic culture. He has a forthcoming book, *God and Money: The Moral Challenge of Capitalism,* scheduled for publication by Rowman & Littlefield in January 2007.

Scott B. Noegel is professor of Biblical and Ancient Near Eastern studies and chair of the Department of Near Eastern Languages and Civilizations at the University of Washington. He received his Ph.D. in 1995 from Cornell University. Dr. Noegel's publications include nearly sixty articles and six books on a variety of biblical and ancient Near Eastern topics. For more information visit http://faculty.washington.edu/snoegel/.

Jon Pahl is professor of the history of Christianity in North America at The Lutheran Theological Seminary at Philadelphia, and adjunct professor in the Department of Religion at Temple University. He is the author of four books, including *Paradox Lost: Free Will and Political Liberty in American Culture, 1630–1760* and *Shopping Malls and Other Sacred Spaces*. He is at work on a volume tentatively entitled *An Empire of Sacrifice: The Religious Origins of American Violence*.

Paul Stephenson is John W. and Jeanne M. Rowe Professor of Byzantine History at the University of Wisconsin, Madison. At the time he composed the chapter in this volume he also held a position at Dumbarton Oaks. His publications include the monographs *Byzantium's Balkan Frontier* (2000) and *The Legend of Basil the Bulgar-slayer* (2003).

Sarah Culpepper Stroup is an assistant professor of classics at the University of Washington, Seattle. Stroup's research interests lie in the areas of Roman literary and textual culture, Greek and Roman spectacle and performance, and Roman social and cultural history. Published work includes several articles on the topics of Roman rhetoric, display, and textual culture; awards include a Getty Foundation Grant for archaeological work at Tel Dor, Israel.

James K. Wellman, Jr., is assistant professor and chair of the Comparative Religion Program, Jackson School of International Studies at the University of Washington. His monograph *Evangelical vs. Liberals: The Clash of Christian Cultures in the Pacific Northwest* is forthcoming.